Mastering Microsoft Endpoint Manager

Deploy and manage Windows 10, Windows 11, and
Windows 365 on both physical and cloud PCs

Christiaan Brinkhoff

Per Larsen

BIRMINGHAM—MUMBAI

Mastering Microsoft Endpoint Manager

Copyright © 2021 Packt Publishing

Group Product Manager: Rahul Nair
Publishing Product Manager: Preet Ahuja
Senior Editor: Athikho Sapuni Rishana
Content Development Editor: Nihar Kapadia
Technical Editor: Nithik Cheruvakodan
Copy Editor: Safis Editing
Language Support Editor: Safis Editing
Project Coordinator: Shagun Saini
Proofreader: Safis Editing
Indexer: Tejal Daruwale Soni
Production Designer: Shankar Kalbhor

First published: October 2021

Production reference: 2121021

Published by Packt Publishing Ltd.
Livery Place
35 Livery Street
Birmingham
B3 2PB, UK.

ISBN 978-1-80107-899-3

www.packt.com

"If you want to go fast, go alone. If you want to go far, go together."

– African proverb

"With Windows 365, we are making Windows available not just on Windows devices, but any device, harnessing the power of the cloud."

– Satya Nadella

Community is important for everyone: please consider sharing your knowledge to help others! Working together will help everyone get to a much higher level!

– Christiaan Brinkhoff

"The way I measure my life is "Am I better than I was last year?""

– Satya Nadella

"You renew yourself every day. Sometimes you're successful, sometimes you're not, but it's the average that counts."

– Satya Nadella

Foreword

The history behind Microsoft Endpoint Manager

I started at Microsoft as a developer right out of college in the early 90s. My first coding assignment was on **Project Hermes**, building an inventory and application delivery tool for the new operating system that Microsoft was about to release – Windows NT. Project Hermes later became **Systems Management Server (SMS)** 1.0. I stayed on the project and eventually became the product and engineering owner responsible for building and releasing Configuration Manager 2007 and 2012. Right after releasing Configuration Manager 2012, I went to lead the engineering team for Intune/MEM and re-architected Intune to become the industry-leading cloud-based device management service. At the start of 2020, I was asked whether I was interested in leading the product and engineering effort for a new startup project called Cloud PC; I remembered saying *sign me up* because I saw it as the last piece of the puzzle to complete the full circle for device management.

When I joined Microsoft, device management as an industry didn't exist. With the introduction of SMS 1.0 and through Configuration Manager 2012, Microsoft created a new IT function – device management. With Intune/MEM, we expanded device management from Windows devices to all devices and we brought device management to the cloud. **Virtual Desktop Infrastructure (VDI)** has existed for decades, but it has always been costly to set up and run and is difficult to adapt to changing business needs. With Windows 365 Cloud PC, we set out to democratize VDI. We want cloud PCs to be easy to provision and manage, just like how IT manages their physical devices today, and in addition, we wanted to remove much of the complexity and cost associated with VDI.

In the last year and a half, we built a brand-new Azure-based service to enable every MEM admin to provision and manage cloud PCs as easily as they can with their physical Windows PCs, or iOS/Android devices. With the full elasticity of Azure, the predictable pricing, and the ability to instantly purchase, provision, and resize cloud PCs, we are creating many new use cases for running a Windows PC in the cloud that cannot be easily achieved by traditional VDI or physical PCs.

On behalf of the hundreds of engineers and product managers that worked tirelessly in the middle of the COVID pandemic building the Windows 365 service, and to all the IT heroes everywhere managing and securing devices, we want to introduce to you a new category of PC – Cloud PC. This book will help you to adopt Windows 365 quickly and gain new superpowers in device management.

Enjoy your newfound power.

Ken Pan

CVP Windows 365 & MMD at Microsoft

The history behind Cloud PC

I joined Microsoft in 2001 as a Hardware Technical Evangelist and Lead Program Manager for Networking. I worked with hardware partners to improve user experiences and expand the market for consumer networking products. During this time of my career, I created several patents around wireless setup, network discovery, and media streaming technologies. The culmination of this work led to the development and standardization of Wi-Fi Protected Setup and the adoption of a number of Microsoft networking technologies in common industry products. Working with partners to bring new value to customers was ingrained in my DNA and is something I have carried forward in my career.

During the Windows 7 era, I transitioned to media streaming and led the product team implementing video in HTML5, DRM, Media CODECs, and media streaming. My team delivered a number of new end user experiences including **PlayTo** and remote media access to Windows Media Player. From there I moved to the Xbox team to deliver **SmartGlass** for Xbox One.

About 10 years into my career at Microsoft, my interests led me to virtualization, which was a culmination of all the technologies I had worked on, such as home networking, audio and video encoding, DRM, media streaming, and device redirection. At that time, Microsoft's first-party virtualization offering (RDS) had a very limited feature set and scalability. Though the technology was heavily used by the tech community for accessing personal desktops, adoption was relatively small in the enterprise space (this was largely led by Citrix).

The RDS team was ripe with talented engineers who had focused their entire careers working on virtualization and the partner ecosystem was clamoring for opportunities to engage with Microsoft to deliver value-added services. This combination of a large talent pool, ready and willing partners, and continued growth of virtualization use cases created just the right environment to develop a new virtualization platform that could reach a broader audience.

RDMi or Remote Desktop Modern Infrastructure was born from this environment of talent and opportunity. RDMi was a transformational virtualization technology built on the Azure App Service platform to provide a **Platform as a Service (PaaS)** virtualization solution. Not long after we introduced RDMi, through strong customer and partner feedback we pivoted to a centrally managed globally distributed implementation of RDMi we later named Windows Virtual Desktop (now called Azure Virtual Desktop). Windows Virtual Desktop was built with partners in mind – partners that extend the capabilities of the core platform, partners who resale the service as is, and partners that bundle the services with other value-added services to deliver end-to-end solutions for customers.

Azure Virtual Desktop delivered on its promise to create a highly flexible platform that offered virtualization solutions that scaled from the smallest deployment to large multi-national enterprise customers. The partner value-added market has flourished and almost every major virtualization technology company has built solutions that interop with the service. Though Azure Virtual Desktop delivered on its promise to create a flexible platform for partners and customers, there was a large untapped market yet to embrace virtualization. Even PaaS virtualization offerings require a deep understanding of virtualization technologies and management of these types of virtualization environments is quite different from how physical devices are managed.

A new opportunity arose to create a virtualization solution for everyone else, from small businesses with no admin staff to large enterprises looking to increase their security and agility and consolidate their endpoint management. A draft whitepaper I called **1DV** (an acronym to represent the development of a first-party desktop virtualization solution) was developed by me and my team and was circulated across the leadership team. This paper and strong signals from our customers led to the formation of the Windows 365 team in Microsoft. Ken Pan and I were tapped to lead this team – a pairing that has proven to be as genius as the technology we have developed together.

Ken and I shared a vision that to truly develop something different, something that Microsoft and the rest of the industry would view as a new category of virtualization, we need to eliminate the complexities that exist in traditional virtualization solutions and build on the skillsets that customers have in deploying and maintaining physical Windows devices. We started with a set of principles that would guide us through the development of the product and retain our vision for a solution that would resonate with the most virtualization averse customers:

- No understanding of virtualization infrastructure required.
- Scale from very small businesses to the largest enterprise customers.
- Meet customers where they are and support migrations to fully modern environments.

- Create an end user experience that is consistent with physical Windows devices.
- Provide a seamless experience to scale up and out as the needs of our customers evolve.
- Predicate fixed monthly pricing options that enable customers to manage their budgets.
- No global admin required; administration is properly distributed to the right admins in familiar portals.

Right around the time we finalized our principles, the world was hit with a global pandemic that would forever change the way we work. The team was only a few months old when COVID hit, and we had just started building out the new team when the world went into lockdown. Seeing as we were developing a new service that would empower users to be productive anywhere in the world, we took on the challenge of putting together a globally distributed team and developing the service using Teams, SharePoint, Azure DevOps, and other tools to keep the team in sync. 8 months later we started our private preview of the service and 8 months after that we went live.

The world will forever be changed by the effects of COVID. Organizations are creating more opportunities for remote workers, and they are migrating their workloads to the cloud to expand their reach to provide corporate resources to a globally distributed workforce. Windows 365 was cast from this new environment and is just the right product to empower organizations to provide secure and elastic Windows Desktops to their globally distributed workforce.

Scott Manchester

Director of Product Management at Microsoft

Contributors

About the authors

Christiaan Brinkhoff works as a Principal Program Manager and Community Lead for the Windows 365 Engineering team at Microsoft, driving new features such as Windows 11 integration and lots of different new community initiatives while bringing his expertise to help customers imagine new virtualization experiences. Christiaan joined Microsoft in 2018 as part of the FSLogix acquisition.

He has also been rewarded with the Microsoft MVP, Citrix CTP, and VMware vExpert community achievements.

Writing a book demands huge dedication and constant energy, especially when you've relocated to Redmond, USA, and your family's growing. I'd like to thank my wife for always supporting me and allowing me to dedicate so much private time to finalizing this book!

Per Larsen works as a Senior Program Manager for Microsoft Endpoint Manager - Customer Acceleration Team - **Commercial Management Experiences (CMX)** Engineering, where he takes learnings from Microsoft's largest and most strategic customers back into the rest of engineering to drive improvements for the service so that customers have a continuously improving product experience. He also helps deploy and adopt Microsoft Endpoint Manager - Microsoft Intune. Per mainly focuses on the management of Windows and special devices such as HoloLens 2, Surface Hub, and Microsoft Teams Room System.

Per was also an MVP in Enterprise Mobility, from 1st July 2016 to when he joined Microsoft on 1st April 2018.

Writing a book during the pandemic and being at home all the time requires dedication and constant energy. I'd like to thank my kids for always supporting me and allowing me to dedicate so much private time to writing this book!

About the reviewers

Seif Bassem is a senior customer engineer in the global technical team at Microsoft, focusing on Azure apps and infrastructure. He has also worked in FastTrack within Microsoft, helping customers to modernize how they provision, manage, and secure their devices using Microsoft Endpoint Manager.

Prior to joining Microsoft, Seif had 10 years of experience in the IT industry leading a team of engineers who were managing and deploying various Microsoft solutions and projects in the financial services sector.

He is a certified Azure solutions architect, administrator, security engineer, and Microsoft 365 Certified Modern Desktop Administrator. He also participated as a CompTIA subject matter expert for the IT Fundamentals Certifications exam preparation.

Peter Cashen is a UK-based technology consultant working through his own company, Kloud 365 Ltd, who has specialized in end user computing since the late 1990s. He has been involved with Microsoft technologies for over 20 years including SMS, System Center Configuration Manager, Endpoint Manager, and other related tools. Peter's clients are from many sectors, including retail, banking, emergency services, secure government, pharmaceutical, legal, and engineering, and there has also been a stint at Microsoft.

Peter is currently helping clients with large Azure Active Directory-only implementations across the globe to enable them to reduce (or eliminate) their on-premises footprint.

It's hard work and challenging – but I thrive on challenges!

Paul Winstanley is a five-time Enterprise Mobility MVP who has over 25 years of IT experience. He's spent the last decade specializing in endpoint management via Microsoft Endpoint Manager, Configuration Manager, and Intune.

Paul is an independent consultant with his own endpoint management company, SCCM Solutions, which was formed in 2013.

He blogs on his SCCMentor website, sharing his knowledge of Configuration Manager, Intune, Windows 10, and MDM, and is active on Twitter @sccmentor.

Originally from Yorkshire, in the North of England, he's lived in London for the past 25 years with his wife, four children, and brother-in-law.

I'd like to thank Sheila, my wife, all the kids, Joseph, Miles, James, and Beth, and my brother-in-law, Paul, for allowing me to pour time into what I do. Also, thanks to the community for sharing ideas and solutions and communicating in a friendly way, which has helped build up great friendships, fix tricky problems, and generally makes my life easier on a day-to-day basis.

Neil McLoughlin is based out of Manchester in the UK. He has worked in the IT industry for over 20 years, working across many different sectors and roles. He spent around 10 years providing Citrix consultancy for large enterprise customers.

Around 5 years ago, Neil discovered the cloud and DaaS and since then has specialized in cloud-based desktop solutions, mainly Azure Virtual Desktop and Microsoft 365.

Neil is passionate about community work and runs the UK Citrix Azure Virtual Desktop User Group and the WVD Community, which is a worldwide community of people interested in Azure Virtual Desktop.

He is currently employed as the UK field CTO for Nerdio but has previously worked for New Signature, Computacenter, and Cap Gemini as a senior consultant.

I would like to thank my wife for giving me the time needed to spend many evenings and weekends locked away in my office reviewing this book, and also Christiaan Brinkhoff, who has been instrumental in giving a helping hand when needed. Thanks, Christiaan, really appreciate all the help and advice!

Marcel Meurer is responsible for the professional IT services business unit at sepago GmbH in Cologne and is the founder of the development company ITProCloud GmbH. In this role, he leads a team of consultants who provide their expertise in Microsoft and Citrix Technologies for customers and partners. His technical focuses are Microsoft Azure platform services, and he has been a Microsoft Azure MVP since 2016.

He loves working in the community. Besides his blog, he publishes tools that simplify working with Azure Cloud - especially in the context of **Azure Virtual Desktop** (**AVD**). His well-known tools include WVDAdmin and Hydra for AVD.

Marcel Meurer graduated as an engineer in electrical engineering from the University of Applied Science Aachen

Table of Contents

Section 2: Windows 365

3
Introducing Windows 365

4
Deploying Windows 365

Section 3: Mastering Microsoft Endpoint Manager

5

Requirements for Microsoft Endpoint Manager

6

Windows Deployment and Management

7

Manager Windows Autopilot

8

Application Management and Delivery

9
Understanding Policy Management

10
Advanced Policy Management

14
Monitoring and Endpoint Analytics

15

Universal Print

Section 4: Tips and Tricks from the Field

16

Troubleshooting Microsoft Endpoint Manager

17

Troubleshooting Windows 365

18

Community Help

Other Books You May Enjoy

Index

Preface

One of the main reasons for the slow adoption of Modern Workplace solutions designed to simplify the management layer of your environment is the lack of understanding and knowledge of the product. With this book, you'll learn everything you need to know to make the shift to the Modern Workplace, running Windows 10, Windows 11, or Windows 365.

Mastering Microsoft Endpoint Manager explains various concepts in detail to give you the clarity to plan how to use **Microsoft Endpoint Manager** (**MEM**) and eliminate potential migration challenges beforehand. You'll get to grips with using new services such as Windows 365 Cloud PC, Windows Autopilot, profile management, monitoring and analytics, Universal Print, and much more. The book will take you through the latest features and new Microsoft cloud services to help you to get to grips with the fundamentals of MEM and understand which services you can manage. Whether you are talking about physical or cloud endpoints it's all covered.

By the end of the book, you'll be able to set up MEM and use it to run Windows 10, Windows 11, and Windows 365 efficiently.

What you will learn:

- Simplify the deployment of Windows in the cloud with Windows 365 Cloud PC.
- Configure advanced policy management within MEM.
- Discover modern profile management and migration options for physical and cloud PCs.
- Harden security with baseline settings and other security best practices.
- Find troubleshooting tips and tricks for MEM, Windows 365 Cloud PC, and more.
- Discover deployment best practices for physical and cloud-managed endpoints.
- Keep up with the Microsoft community and discover a list of MVPs to follow.

Who this book is for

If you are an IT professional, enterprise mobility administrator, architect, or consultant looking to learn about managing Windows on both physical and cloud endpoints for remote working via MEM, this book is for you.

What this book covers

Chapter 1, Introduction to Microsoft 365, teaches you about keeping your resources secure while leveraging other services within Microsoft 365's broader product suite. Understanding the fundamentals of a product is the most important factor for a successful deployment.

Chapter 2, What Is Unified Endpoint Management?, acknowledges how the basics of modern management are sometimes complicated to understand, and so you will learn about the concept of modern management and zero trust with MEM (Intune), the history, and the architectural concept to get a clear understanding of how all the devices from physical, virtual, and mobile all come together in one management console.

Chapter 3, Introducing Windows 365, teaches you everything to get started with this new Microsoft cloud service that simplifies deployment as well as your cloud PC maintenance with MEM.

Chapter 4, Deploying Windows 365, teaches you everything you need to know about how to deploy Windows 365, what the requirements are, and tips and tricks.

Chapter 5, Requirements for Microsoft Endpoint Manager, provides a clear understanding of the different requirements for MEM, from OS versions and URL firewall allow-listing to the required licenses and privileges.

Chapter 6, Windows Deployment and Management, teaches you about deploying Windows 10 Enterprise with MEM – Intune.

Chapter 7, Manager Windows Autopilot, teaches you how and when to use Autopilot to enroll Windows 10 on your physical endpoint devices. What are the recommended approaches and decisions to make beforehand? You will get to know all of this in this chapter.

Chapter 8, Application Management and Delivery, teaches best practices to deploy and manage your Microsoft 365 and line-of-business applications on your Windows 10 endpoints.

Chapter 9, Understanding Policy Management, teaches you about the different policy types, what modern policy management means, and how it works on Windows 10/11 clients compared to Group Policy.

Chapter 10, Advanced Policy Management, teaches you about the different policy options to customize and secure your Windows 10 Enterprise desktops in your environment.

Chapter 11, Office Policy Management, teaches you about the different policy options to customize and secure your Windows 10 Enterprise desktops in your environment.

Chapter 12, User Profile Management, discusses how profile management is a very important factor to ensure a good user experience. You will learn about the different Windows profile types and differences in services to offer similar experiences on different endpoint devices, for example, physical and cloud endpoints with Enterprise State Roaming and Microsoft Edge.

Chapter 13, Identity and Security Management, teaches you how to configure Azure Active Directory in the most secure way possible for your end users and IT department. You will learn what the different options to enable Azure MFA are, about BitLocker, and how to configure Microsoft Defender for Endpoint with end-to-end security-level integration in MEM – Intune.

Chapter 14, Monitoring and Endpoint Analytics, looks at how, after deploying your desktops, it's important to ensure the performance, logon duration segmentation, and quality level of Windows and applications. You will learn in this chapter how you can achieve this with Endpoint Analytics, Productivity Score, and other monitoring capabilities of MEM.

Chapter 15, Universal Print, looks at Universal Print and how, despite businesses doing more and more things in a digital way, printing on physical paper remains important. Universal Print is a relatively new platform service on Azure that can simplify the whole printing configuration and maintenance process compared to a traditional print server environment.

Chapter 16, Troubleshooting Microsoft Endpoint Manager, teaches the most common causes and fixes of deploying Windows 10 Enterprise and other tips and tricks to unblock deployments to go smoothly. Both writers have over 2 decades of field experience in deploying Windows in many forms that they will share in this section.

Chapter 17, Troubleshooting Windows 365, teaches you about all the different troubleshooting errors of Windows 365 Cloud PC to prepare you to respond proactively to any errors that could occur while deploying cloud PCs in your environment.

Chapter 18, Community Help, shares, as the writers have a strong community background, some of the best community blogs out there; some are written by beginners, while some are by Microsoft MVPs.

To get the most out of this book

In order to get the most out of this book, it's good to have a base-level understanding of MEM, Azure, Microsoft 365 cloud services, and such. This is not required, however, as you'll learn all you need to know in this book!

Download the color images

We also provide a PDF file that has color images of the screenshots and diagrams used in this book. You can download it here: `https://static.packt-cdn.com/downloads/9781801078993_ColorImages.pdf`.

Conventions used

There are a number of text conventions used throughout this book.

`Code in text`: Indicates code words in text, database table names, folder names, filenames, file extensions, pathnames, dummy URLs, user input, and Twitter handles. Here is an example: "Enter `Device type restriction - HR` as the name."

A block of code is set as follows:

```
<?xml version="1.0"?>
<HardwareReport>
    <HardwareInventory>
        <p n="ToolVersion" v="3" />
        <p n="HardwareInventoryVersion" v="131" />
```

When we wish to draw your attention to a particular part of a code block, the relevant lines or items are set in bold:

```
msiexec /i " RemoteDesktop_1.2.1755.0_x64.msi" /qn ALLUSERS=2
MSIINSTALLPERUSER=1
```

Bold: Indicates a new term, an important word, or words that you see onscreen. For instance, words in menus or dialog boxes appear in **bold**. Here is an example: "Go to **Tenant admin | Roles | Administrator Licensing**."

> **Tips or important notes**
> Appear like this.

Get in touch

Feedback from our readers is always welcome.

General feedback: If you have questions about any aspect of this book, email us at `customercare@packtpub.com` and mention the book title in the subject of your message.

Errata: Although we have taken every care to ensure the accuracy of our content, mistakes do happen. If you have found a mistake in this book, we would be grateful if you would report this to us. Please visit `www.packtpub.com/support/errata` and fill in the form.

Piracy: If you come across any illegal copies of our works in any form on the internet, we would be grateful if you would provide us with the location address or website name. Please contact us at `copyright@packt.com` with a link to the material.

If you are interested in becoming an author: If there is a topic that you have expertise in and you are interested in either writing or contributing to a book, please visit `authors.packtpub.com`.

Share Your Thoughts

Once you've read *Mastering Microsoft Endpoint Manager*, we'd love to hear your thoughts! Scan the QR code below to go straight to the Amazon review page for this book and share your feedback.

https://packt.link/r/1801078998

Your review is important to us and the tech community and will help us make sure we're delivering excellent quality content.

Section 1: Understanding the Basics

Learn about all the fundamentals of the different Microsoft 365 services, what the benefits are, and how they are different in comparison to other technologies and services on the market.

This part of the book comprises the following chapters:

- *Chapter 1, Introduction to Microsoft 365*
- *Chapter 2, What Is Unified Endpoint Management?*

1
Introduction to Microsoft 365

Understanding the fundamentals of a product is the most important thing for a successful deployment. Keeping your resources secure while leveraging other services within the Microsoft 365 product suite is what you will learn about in this chapter.

In this chapter, we'll go through the following topics:

- Microsoft 365 services
- Azure Virtual Desktop and Windows 365
- Windows 10 and Windows 11

An introduction to Microsoft 365

Microsoft 365 includes many services that you might use in your day job, whether as an IT professional or a non-technical user. The services help you to become more productive by simplifying tasks that would require a lot of work in on-premises environments. A great example would be the shift we've made from Exchange Server to Exchange Online.

What do the services achieve?

In this introductory section of the book, we will briefly explain the Microsoft 365 core services and features that are relevant to the subject of this book, just to get a good baseline understanding of the differences between the various services. You'll also learn about the purpose and benefits of each service.

Microsoft Endpoint Manager

Microsoft Endpoint Manager (**MEM**) is the consolidation of Microsoft Intune and **Microsoft Endpoint Configuration Manager** (**MECM**). It provides one holistic management experience while adding new functionality and intelligent actions without any complex migration or disruption of productivity.

It provides a number of assets to aid your transition to modern management while also increasing customers' security and helping them move to the cloud. MEM now also includes management capabilities for different endpoints:

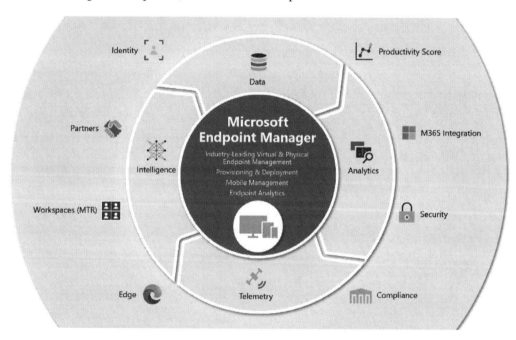

Figure 1.1 – MEM – service portfolio

MEM helps you manage physical and virtual desktops, laptops, tablets, and other mobile devices, including iOS, Android, and macOS devices.

MEM uses **Azure Active Directory** (**Azure AD**) as the primary identity and directory store. It replaces the traditional Active Directory, includes hybrid identity capabilities, and can also integrate with local management infrastructures such as Configuration Manager via Kerberos.

Intune is extremely helpful for devices that are beyond the management scope of Group Policy, such as mobile phones, devices that are not **Active Directory Domain Services** (**AD DS**) domain members, or Windows 10 devices that are joined to Azure AD:

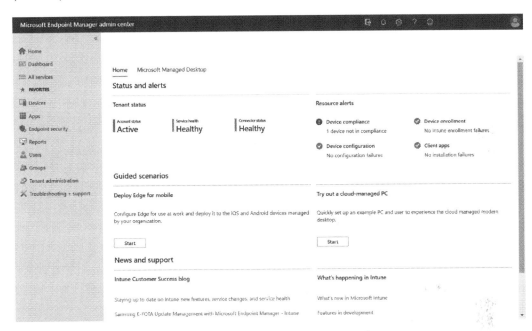

Figure 1.2 – MEM – management console

With MEM, you can achieve the following:

- Let your organization's employees use their personal physical and virtual e ndpoint devices to access organizational data (commonly known as **bring your own device** (**BYOD**)).

- Manage organization-owned phones.

- Control access to Microsoft 365 from unmanaged devices, such as public kiosks and mobile devices.

- Help ensure that devices and apps that do connect to corporate data comply with security policies.

For example, when a user attempts to open one of their **line-of-business (LOB)** apps on their phone or Windows 10 endpoint, Microsoft 365 checks with Azure AD to authenticate the user and verify whether that user can access the data from that app on that device. The granting of access depends on the following:

- Conditional Access policies defined within Azure AD

- Whether the app on that device complies with app configuration and data protection policies (Intune will confirm this for Azure AD)

If the device and app are both compliant with all policies, Azure AD notifies Microsoft 365 that the data can be accessed.

Azure Virtual Desktop

Azure Virtual Desktop, or **AVD** for short, is a Microsoft-managed platform-as-a-service offering on top of the Microsoft Azure cloud. Unlike traditional **virtual desktop infrastructure (VDI)** deployments, all the infrastructure services, such as brokering, web access, load balancing, management, and monitoring, are all set up for you as part of a control plane offering.

Windows 365 Cloud PC

A new way of experiencing Windows, on any device – that's the best way to describe the new Microsoft cloud service **Windows 365 Cloud PC**. Microsoft's vision is to have people use Windows 365 the same way as they would manage a physical endpoint but with the flexibility of the cloud.

Windows 365 is everything you need if you are looking for a simple way of running your Windows desktops in the cloud. You can decrease the costs and complexity of your environment by deploying and managing virtual endpoints in MEM; no additional VDI expertise or resources are needed. More about this will be explained later in this chapter.

AVD and Windows 365 Cloud PC – shared responsibility model 1

As with many cloud services, there is a shared set of security responsibilities. You have control and flexibility, and with that comes responsibility. If you are adopting Windows 365 Cloud PC, it's important to understand that while some components come already secured for your environment, there are other areas where you will need to configure things to fit your organization's security needs:

Responsibility	Traditional VDI	Azure Virtual Desktop	Windows 365
Virtualization Management Plane	Customer/Partner	Microsoft	Microsoft
Identity Platform (Azure AD)	Customer/Partner	Microsoft	Microsoft
Platform Security	Customer/Partner	Microsoft	Microsoft
Networking	Customer/Partner	Microsoft	Microsoft
Data Center	Customer/Partner	Microsoft	Microsoft
Image Management Platform (via MEM)	Customer/Partner	Customer/Partner	Microsoft
Operating System Updates	Customer/Partner	Customer/Partner	Customer/Partner
End User Devices (Physical PC/ Mobile)	Customer/Partner	Customer/Partner	Customer/Partner

Table 1.1 – Shared responsibility model 1

AVD and Windows 365 Cloud PC – shared responsibility model 2

The following table is an extension of the previous one, but it goes a bit deeper in terms of the differences in management experience:

Responsibility	Azure Virtual Desktop	Windows 365
Identity	Azure AD	
End User Devices (Mobile and PCs)	Windows, MacOS, iOS, Android, HTML, Linux SDK	
Image Management and Supported Operating System	Windows Server, Windows 10, Windows 11	Windows 10, Windows 11
Desktops	Personal and Pooled Desktops	Personal Desktops
Deployment	Microsoft Azure and Endpoint Manager	Microsoft Endpoint Manager
Configuration/Management/App Deployment	Microsoft Azure and Endpoint Manager	Microsoft Endpoint Manager
Virtualization Control Plane	Azure Virtual Desktop	
Physical Hosts	Microsoft Azure	
Physical Network		
Physical Data Center		

Table 1.2 – Shared responsibility model 2

Windows 10 Enterprise

Windows 10 Enterprise is one of the primary components of your Microsoft 365 subscription. Windows 10 meets the needs of large and midsize organizations, providing users and organizations with the tools, services, and support to enhance their personal and organizational productivity.

Windows 10 also supports collaboration through Microsoft 365 apps, Microsoft Teams, Microsoft Whiteboard, and OneNote.

Windows 10 helps improve productivity by providing faster, safer ways to get work done across all your users' devices. Users can find apps, settings, documents, and messages by using enterprise search and Cortana, and use Timeline to see a chronological view of their activities and documents. Windows 10 has hardware options ranging from Surface Hub to the new always-connected PCs. These options support users wherever they need or prefer to work. Users can move from one device to another with Continue on PC in Microsoft Edge or take notes directly on a web page with Microsoft Ink. Windows 10 also comes with a robust set of accessibility features, such as a narrator, word prediction, and eye control.

Windows 10 includes tools to help you customize device setup, manage all your devices, and control corporate identities, data, and apps on personal devices without impacting personal data. Maximize security and productivity by staying current with Windows 10. The way to update Windows has changed completely. Major upgrades that previously happened every few years have now changed to updates that happen twice a year. Windows-as-a-Service, the model for Windows 10, provides the flexibility and control needed to manage and distribute updates using your current method or by using Microsoft's infrastructure.

Windows 10 protects, detects, and automatically responds to the most advanced malware and hacking threats, while protecting user identities, devices, and your organization's information. Windows 10 investigates threats as they evolve and automates remediation to make response times faster, thanks to Intelligent Security Graph (which uses security intelligence, machine learning, and behavioral analytics). These security solutions are built in and provide you with full security life cycle management for **endpoint protection (EPP)** and **endpoint detection and response (EDR)**.

It also integrates with other Microsoft 365 services, which cover even the most complex multi-platform environments:

- **Threat protection**: Windows 10 threat protection includes next-generation malware and hacking defense to help protect against threats, including zero-day attacks. It provides a hardened platform that can help prevent encounters, isolate threats, and prevent the execution of malicious apps and content. Windows 10 can detect and respond to the most advanced threats and automatically remediate them.

- **Identity access**: Windows 10 protects user identities against pass-the-hash and pass-the-ticket attacks by helping you move to a world without passwords. **Windows Hello** is a biometric authentication tool that strengthens authentication and helps guard against potential spoofing.

- **Information Protection**: Windows 10 makes it easy to protect data – whether that data is at rest or in use. Windows Information Protection helps protect sensitive information against leaks. When you combine Windows 10 with Azure Information Protection and Microsoft 365, you get a sophisticated solution that meets the highest requirements for data loss prevention with minimal input.

Windows 11 Enterprise

Windows 11 is the next evolutionary phase of Windows; it is the most significant update to the Windows operating system since Windows 10. It offers a lot of innovations focused on enhancing end user productivity in a fresh experience that is flexible and fluid. Windows 11 is designed to support today's hybrid work environment and is intended to be the most secure, reliable, connected, and performant Windows operating system ever.

Windows 11 is built on the same foundation as Windows 10, so the investments you have made in tools for update and device management are carried forward.

Windows 11 is Zero Trust ready and secure by design, with new built-in security technologies that will add protection from the chip to the cloud, while enabling productivity and new experiences. Key security features such as encryption, hardware-based isolation, and malware prevention are turned on by default. Going passwordless has also been made easier by simplifying the steps to deploy Windows Hello for Business.

To address the need for hybrid working in the market right now, location shouldn't matter. Addressing the new *how*, *when*, and *where* we work demands simplicity and security changes in the Windows operating system as well as the delivery of Windows in a simpler way – from the cloud with Windows 365:

Figure 1.3 – Windows 11

You can have a highly secure and consistent experience for users, with all the necessary IT controls, that delivers updates in a non-disruptive way, combined with a new, modern look and feel – that's the best way to describe what Windows 10 offers in a nutshell.

We will explain more about Windows 11 in *Chapter 6, Windows Deployment and Management*.

Productivity Score

The journey to digital transformation is supported by Productivity Score, which provides insights into how your organization uses Microsoft 365 and the technology experiences that support it. Your organization's score reflects the effectiveness of your people's work and technology and can be compared to benchmarks from organizations similar in size to yours.

Productivity Score provides the following:

- Metrics to help you see where you are on your digital transformation journey

- Insights about your data to help you identify opportunities to improve productivity and satisfaction in your organization

- Actions you can take to help your organization use Microsoft 365 products efficiently

The following Productivity Score screenshot shows you the level of insights you get based on scoring metrics in the Microsoft 365 admin portal:

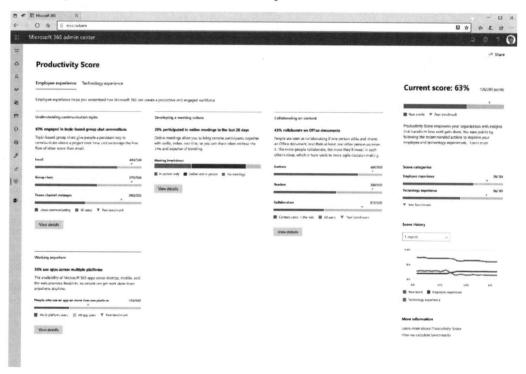

Figure 1.4 – Productivity Score

Your Productivity Score is based on the combined scores of your people and technology experiences categories. Each category is weighted equally, with a total of 100 points. The highest possible Productivity Score is 800.

Endpoint Analytics

Endpoint Analytics is a service that is used to ensure the consistent performance of your MEM deployment and is part of Productivity Score. Everything that is collected comes from measurements of how your business is working. For example, Endpoint Analytics gives you insights into the boot time of your physical device, logon duration, and application startup time.

The insights enable IT admins to reduce support costs by adding capabilities to proactively solve issues in their environment. This can all happen automatically without any involvement of the IT admin:

Figure 1.5 – Endpoint Analytics

Your end-to-end experience can be dramatically improved by Endpoint Analytics and the benefits it brings. Another huge benefit is that all service costs are included; unlike the case with Azure Monitor, there is no need to pay for storage retention!

Desktop Analytics

Desktop Analytics is an important part of the full MEM service; it is cloud-based and integrates with Configuration Manager. The service also provides different levels of insights and intelligence for IT administrators to make proactive decisions about the update readiness of your Windows 10 endpoints. The service combines data from your business with data aggregated from millions of devices connected to Microsoft cloud services.

Here is a list of the different benefits of Desktop Analytics with Configuration Manager:

- Create an inventory of apps running in your organization.
- Assess app compatibility with the latest Windows 10 feature updates.
- Identify compatibility issues and receive mitigation suggestions based on cloud-enabled data insights.
- Create pilot groups that represent the entire application and driver estate across a minimal set of devices.
- Deploy Windows 10 to pilot and production-managed devices.

Here is an example screenshot of how security and feature updates come together in a single, unified experience in Desktop Analytics:

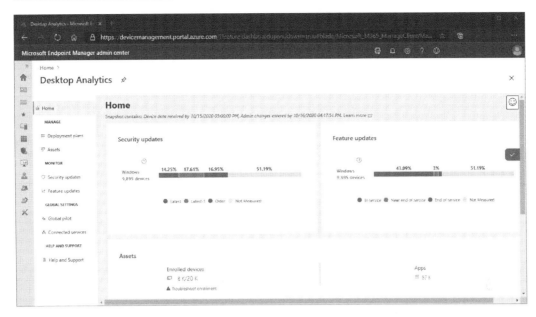

Figure 1.6 – Desktop Analytics – management console

Now that we have talked about all the different enhancements to monitor and analyze your endpoints, we're going to talk about the different Microsoft 365 services that you can use within your physical and cloud-managed desktops.

Microsoft 365 Apps (for Enterprise)

Microsoft 365 Apps for Enterprise includes the Microsoft productivity suite of applications, such as Word, Excel, PowerPoint, Outlook, and Teams, for both Windows and Mac devices. Microsoft 365 Apps isn't a web-based version of Office – instead, it's a full version of Office that your users install and run on their devices. You can use the Office applications that come with Microsoft 365 Apps with the on-premises or online versions of Exchange, SharePoint, or Skype for Business.

You can install Microsoft 365 Apps from a network share or directly from the internet. After it's installed, you don't have to be connected to the internet to use it. However, you'll need to connect at least once every 30 days to ensure that your license is still active.

Microsoft 365 Apps is updated either monthly or semi-annually with new features, security updates, and other quality updates from Microsoft. You can choose which frequency works best for your organization by selecting specific update channels.

Microsoft 365 Apps has a few benefits over Office Professional Plus 2019, such as support for air-gapped devices and device-based activation, and organizations interested in Office 2019 should contact Microsoft for more information.

OneDrive for Business (part of Microsoft 365 Apps)

Microsoft OneDrive is an enterprise file sharing service that allows you to easily store and securely access your files from all your physical, virtual, and mobile devices. You can work together with people from any location, regardless of whether they're inside or outside your organization, while also exploiting comprehensive security capabilities to, for example, only allow data sharing based on several security baseline conditions. All your data in OneDrive is protected through advanced encryption while in transit and at rest in data centers.

OneDrive enhances collaboration capabilities within Microsoft 365 apps by connecting you to your personal and shared files in Microsoft 365. With OneDrive on the web, desktop, or mobile, you can access all your personal files and any files shared with you by other people or teams, including files from Microsoft Teams and SharePoint.

Another great feature is OneDrive cloud backup – also known as OneDrive folder backup (previously Known Folder Move). This service automatically syncs your `Desktop`, `Documents`, and `Pictures` folders on your physical or virtual endpoints to your OneDrive cloud storage. Your files and folders stay protected and are available from any device!

Microsoft Teams

Microsoft Teams is a unified communications collaboration tool that brings different services together to modernize the way you work with colleagues and external businesses. Teams allows you to implement a chat-based workspace as part of your Windows 10 physical and virtual PCs but also as a mobile app on various platforms, which helps you stay up to date both in the office and on the go.

Teams keeps your team in sync by sharing OneDrive and SharePoint documents, insights, and status updates while being able to manage important projects and easily locate people – from anywhere and on any device!

With Microsoft Teams, you can do the following:

- **Communicate through chat, meetings, and calls**: Host audio, video, and web conferences, and chat with anyone inside or outside of your organization.

- **Collaborate with integrated Microsoft 365 apps**: Teams makes teamwork easy by allowing users to co-author and share files with popular Microsoft 365 apps – from Microsoft Word to Microsoft Power BI.

- **Customize your workplace and achieve more**: Using Teams, you can integrate apps from Microsoft and third-party partner services to meet your organization's unique needs.

- **Connect across devices**: Teams and Teams devices work well together for intelligent meeting and calling experiences. Find the right devices for your needs and bring your best ideas to life.

Microsoft Edge

Microsoft Edge has been around for a while as the next modern iteration of Internet Explorer, first released in 2015. After 5 years, a new version of Edge was released, built on top of the open source software project Chromium. This uses the same core engine as the Google Chrome browser.

Microsoft Edge has proven to be very fast. Its alignment with other Microsoft services such as MEM to set policies, as well as the cross-platform support for the app to sync data such as personal history and favorites settings, has been well received. This has resulted in Edge being the default browser for Windows 10 to date.

Microsoft Edge is available on Windows, macOS, iOS, Android, and Linux. You can choose what device you want to use with the same native Edge experience across different platforms.

Universal Print

You might remember the following workflow – or still do it to this day: spin up a Windows Server environment, add the print server role, and start adding your printers and designated drivers to the server. Not very modern or efficient, is it? Universal Print offers the same, and more, features while also eliminating the need for on-premises infrastructure. It enables you to manage printers directly through a centralized portal in Microsoft Azure. Say goodbye to installing (and maintaining) printer drivers on devices and/or golden images. As a bonus, everything works with Azure AD. This means that users can use the same set of credentials they use for other Microsoft services, whether they log on to a physical desktop or a virtual desktop running in the cloud.

Microsoft Defender for Endpoint (formerly MDATP)

Microsoft Defender for Endpoint is the enterprise version of Microsoft Defender which is standard enabled in Windows 10 Enterprise and Windows 11 Enterprise. It's a cloud security platform designed to help enterprise networks prevent, detect, investigate, and respond to advanced threats.

The service is integrated end to end into the MEM console and therefore aligns easily with other compliance and security settings and roles as part of your security baselines.

One of the great features of integrating Defender within MEM is that after your organization onboards a device using the configuration package, you will never have to do it again. All your physical and/or cloud PC will be secured out of the box:

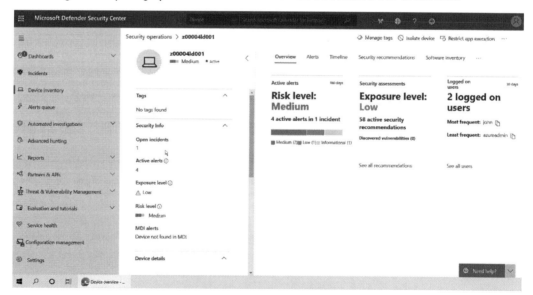

Figure 1.7 – Defender for Endpoint – management console

The Defender for Endpoint configuration process in Intune is very simple and is something we will explain in more detail later in the book.

Exchange Online

Exchange Online is a messaging and collaboration platform for your email, calendar, contact info, and tasks. You can access all of this with Microsoft Outlook, Outlook on the web, or Outlook Mobile. You can access Exchange Online on most devices, including Android, iOS, and Windows 10 devices.

SharePoint Online

SharePoint Online is the cloud evolution of Microsoft SharePoint Server. It helps you create team- or communication-focused sites for efficient collaboration and communication. Internal users with an appropriate Microsoft 365 or SharePoint Online license can use SharePoint Online. They can share files or folders with others inside or outside the organization. Sharing outside the organization can be controlled by site administrators.

With SharePoint Online, users can do the following:

- Build sites, pages, document libraries, and lists.
- Add web parts to customize their pages.
- Share important visuals, news, and updates with a team.
- Search and discover sites, files, people, and news from across their organization.
- Manage their business processes with flows, forms, and lists.
- Sync and store their files in the cloud so anyone can securely work with them.
- Catch up on news on the go with the SharePoint mobile app.

Summary

In this chapter, you learned about all the different Microsoft 365 services you might use in your day job or as part of your journey to using MEM to simplify the management overhead of your environment.

This chapter mainly intended to provide context for the later chapters in the book; we are now switching gears and taking you on the journey of unified endpoint management with MEM.

Questions

1. What are the main benefits of using MEM?

    A. MEM ensures that an organization no longer needs credentials to access and share company data.

    B. MEM prevents remote devices and apps from accessing an organization's resources.

    C. MEM helps keep an organization's cloud and on-premises devices, apps, and data secure.

2. What are the main differences between Windows 365 Cloud PC and AVD?

    A. Windows 365 Cloud PC is designed for simplicity and AVD for flexibility.

    B. Windows 365 Cloud PC has a fixed-price cost model and AVD is consumption-based.

Answers

1. (A)

2. (A)

Further reading

If you want to learn more about MEM after reading this chapter, please use the following free online resources:

- MEM fundamentals: `https://docs.microsoft.com/en-us/learn/paths/endpoint-manager-fundamentals/`

- Introduction to MEM: `https://docs.microsoft.com/en-us/learn/modules/intro-to-endpoint-manager/`

2
What Is Unified Endpoint Management?

The basics of modern management are sometimes complicated to understand. You will learn about the concept of modern management and zero trust with Intune as part of Microsoft Endpoint Manager, along with its history and architectural concepts, to get a clear understanding of how all devices – physical, virtual, and mobile – come together in a single management console.

In this chapter, we'll go through the following topics:

- Paths to modern management
- Microsoft Endpoint Manager and Intune
- Exploring Windows 10 Enterprise in detail
- Bring your own device
- What is zero trust?

Paths to modern management

Having a single management solution for all your endpoints is the main benefit of moving to a unified endpoint management solution like Microsoft Endpoint Manager.

The concept of modern management is not new, but in 2020, with the global COVID-19 pandemic, the majority of companies had most of their workforce working from home. With this new way of working as the primary way, the need for organizations to think differently accelerated.

Since the first Windows 10 release back in 2015, Microsoft has included the **mobile device management** (**MDM**) stack native build in it. Also, since the first release of Windows 10, many companies have explored new management options, with one of these being advancements in cloud technology, while **bring your own device** (**BYOD**) trends have made the move toward modern management more compelling for many organizations, not only for mobile devices running iOS and Android but also for physical and cloud-based Windows PCs.

Modern management is a new approach to managing Windows 10 devices, in the same way as mobile devices are managed by **enterprise mobility management** (**EMM**) solutions. The modern management approach allows your organization to simplify deployment and management, improve security, provide better end user experiences, and lower costs for your Windows devices.

There are three waves to unified endpoint management:

Figure 2.1 – Unified endpoint management phases

With modern management, you can now manage Windows 10 devices of all kinds, from physical and virtual desktop PCs to HoloLens, Microsoft Team Rooms systems, and Surface Hubs, corporate-owned or personal-owned, as well as mobile devices, using a single management platform, Microsoft Endpoint Manager.

Microsoft Endpoint Manager and Intune

What is unified endpoint management and how does this look through the concept of **Microsoft Endpoint Manager**? The following high-level architecture drawing explains how everything within Microsoft Endpoint Manager comes together in one unified endpoint management experience.

There is one console for your physical and cloud PCs via **Windows 365** endpoints and mobile devices. This is the only place where they can be managed in a unified way. Also, the Intune company portal can deploy apps from Configuration Manager, Intune, Windows 365, Azure Virtual Desktop, and Azure Active Directory – one end user experience for all apps!

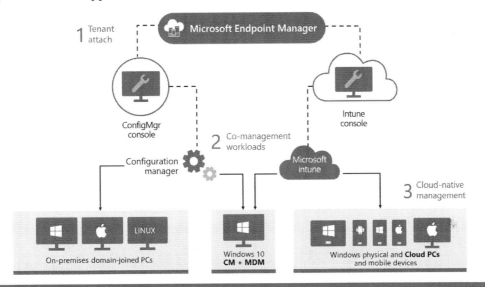

Figure 2.2 – Microsoft Endpoint Manager architecture diagram

The Microsoft Endpoint Manager architecture in the preceding diagram shows the three stages of the cloud management journey using Configuration Manager and Intune in a single, unified endpoint management solution:

1. Tenant attach
2. Co-management workloads
3. Cloud-native management

All new Windows devices should go directly to the cloud with **Azure Active Directory (Azure AD)** with automatic enrollment into Intune. This leverages Windows Autopilot for the best onboarding experience for IT and end users, provided your organization already has a Configuration Manager environment with lots of applications that you are deploying to your on-premises managed devices.

For existing devices, start using tenant-attach capabilities that provide the most flexible path for Configuration Manager customers to start gaining cloud benefits without necessarily enrolling their Windows clients with Intune. Connect the Configuration Manager environment to the cloud and immediately gain access to a host of remote actions and endpoint analytics.

If your organization is ready for the next step, you can start onboarding Windows devices into a co-management state, which means managing Windows clients using both Configuration Manager and Intune. Leverage the best of both worlds by moving one workload to the cloud at a time.

Endpoint Manager admin center portal

The Microsoft Endpoint Manager admin center portal (`https://endpoint.microsoft.com/#home`) is your holistic one-stop admin experience to create policies and manage your devices. It allows IT admins to plug in other key device management services, such as groups, security baselines and settings, Conditional Access, analytics tools, and reporting.

Microsoft Intune is a 100% cloud-based MDM and **mobile application management (MAM)** provider for your apps and devices. Microsoft Intune lets you control features and settings on Android, Android Enterprise, iOS/iPadOS, macOS, and Windows 10 devices. It integrates with other services, including Azure AD, and mobile threat defenders.

Microsoft Intune can create compliance policies and check for the compliance status, which marks the device as compliant or non-compliant. If you have enabled Conditional Access in your Microsoft 365 cloud environment, you can leverage the compliance status from Intune to allow or block access to corporate data.

Intune can also be used for application life cycle management.

Microsoft 365 admin center portal

In the Microsoft 365 admin center portal (`https://admin.microsoft.com`), you can manage and administer all your Microsoft 365 cloud services. The most common task that you perform in this portal is to purchase and assign licenses for your Microsoft services.

Here's a full list of what you can do via the Microsoft 365 admin center:

Menu	What it's for
Home	This is the landing page in the admin center. You'll see where to manage users, billing, service health, and reports.
Users	Create and manage users in your organization, such as employees or students. You can also set their permission level or reset their passwords.
Groups	Create and manage groups in your organization, such as a Microsoft 365 group, distribution group, security group, or shared mailbox. Learn how to create (`https://docs.microsoft.com/en-us/microsoft-365/admin/create-groups/create-groups?view=o365-worldwide`) and manage (`https://docs.microsoft.com/en-us/microsoft-365/admin/create-groups/manage-groups?view=o365-worldwide`) groups.
Resources	Create and manage resources, such as a SharePoint site collection. Learn how to create site collections (`https://docs.microsoft.com/en-us/sharepoint/create-site-collection`).
Billing	View, purchase, or cancel subscriptions for your organization. View past billing statements or view the number of assigned licenses to individual users. Learn how to manage billing (`https://docs.microsoft.com/en-us/microsoft-365/commerce/?view=o365-worldwide`).
Support	View existing service requests or create new ones. Learn more in contact support for business products – admin help (`https://docs.microsoft.com/en-us/microsoft-365/business-video/get-help-support?view=o365-worldwide`).
Settings	Manage global settings for apps, such as email, sites, and the Office suite. Change your password policy and expiration date. Add and update domain names, such as contoso.com. Change your organization profile and release preferences, and choose whether partners can access your admin center.
Setup	Manage existing domains, turn on and manage **multi-factor authentication** (**MFA**), manage admin access, migrate user mailboxes to Office 365, manage feature updates, and help users install their Office apps.

Reports	See at a glance how your organization is using Microsoft 365 with detailed reports on email use, Office activations, and more. Learn how to use the new activity reports (`https://docs.microsoft.com/en-us/microsoft-365/admin/activity-reports/activity-reports?view=o365-worldwide`).
Health	View health at a glance. You can also check out more details and the health history. See *How to check Microsoft 365 service health* (`https://docs.microsoft.com/en-us/microsoft-365/enterprise/view-service-health?view=o365-worldwide`) and *How to check Windows release health* (`https://docs.microsoft.com/en-us/windows/deployment/update/check-release-health`) for more information. Use the message center to keep track of upcoming changes to features and services. We post announcements there with information thathelps you plan for change and understand how it may affect users. Get more details here: **Message center** (`https://docs.microsoft.com/en-us/microsoft-365/admin/manage/message-center?view=o365-worldwide`).
Admin centers	Open separate admin centers for Exchange, Skype for Business, SharePoint, Yammer, and Azure AD. Each admin center includes all available settings for that service. For example, in the Exchange admin center, set up and manage email, calendars, distribution groups, and more. In the SharePoint admin center, create and manage site collections, site settings, and OneDrive for Business. In the Skype for Business admin center, set up instant messaging notifications, dial-in conferencing, and online presence. Learn more about the Exchange admin center in *Exchange Online* (`https://docs.microsoft.com/en-us/exchange/exchange-admin-center`) and *Introduction to SharePoint in Microsoft 365* (`https://docs.microsoft.com/en-us/sharepoint/introduction`). Note: The admin centers available to you depend on your plan and region.

Cloud PC/Windows 365

Windows 365 is everything you need when you are looking for a simplified way of running your Windows desktops in the cloud. It brings decreased costs, while lowering the complexity level of your environment as you deploy and manage virtual endpoints in Microsoft Endpoint Manager; no additional **Virtual Desktop Infrastructure** (**VDI**) expertise or resources are required. More on this will follow later in this chapter.

Azure Active Directory (Azure AD)

Azure AD is the main identity used by Endpoint Manager to manage your devices, users, and groups to perform advanced Conditional Access capabilities, such as MFA and compliance-based filtering. With Azure AD Premium, you can add several additional features to help protect devices, apps, and data, including dynamic groups, autoenrollment, and Conditional Access.

Configuration Manager: Configuration Manager is an on-premises management solution to manage desktops, servers, and laptops that are on your network or internet-based. You can cloud-enable it to integrate with Intune – also known as co-management, Azure AD, Microsoft Defender for Endpoints, and other cloud services. Use Configuration Manager to deploy apps, software updates, and OSes. You can also monitor compliance, query, and act on clients in real time, and much more.

Even Configuration Manager, as an on-premises product, has an update cycle three times a year with a built-in automatic update process tool, so you don't need to find, download, and install updates for your Configuration Manager.

In the new working-from-home situation following COVID-19, you can start leveraging the cloud capability from Endpoint Manager.

Cloud management gateway (CMG)

The **cloud management gateway** (**CMG**) provides a simple way to manage Configuration Manager clients over the internet. You deploy the CMG as a cloud service in Microsoft Azure. Then, without additional on-premises infrastructure, you can manage clients that roam on the internet or are in branch offices across the WAN. You also don't need to expose your on-premises infrastructure to the internet.

Co-management: Co-management combines your existing on-premises Configuration Manager environment with the cloud using Intune and other Microsoft 365 cloud services. You choose whether Configuration Manager or Intune is the management authority for the seven different workload groups.

As part of Endpoint Manager, co-management uses cloud features, including Conditional Access. You keep some tasks on-premises, while running other tasks in the cloud with Intune.

Co-management supports the following workloads:

- Compliance policies
- Windows Update policies
- Resource access policies
- Endpoint protection
- Device configuration
- Office Click-to-Run apps
- Client apps

Compliance policies

Compliance policies define the rules and settings that a device must comply with to be considered compliant by Conditional Access policies. Also, use compliance policies to monitor and remediate compliance issues with devices independently of Conditional Access, beginning with the Configuration Manager assessment rule.

Windows Update policies

Windows Update for Business (WUfB) policies let you configure WUfB policies into a ring concept so you can decide when and how you service Windows 10 and later devices.

You can configure deferral policies for Windows 10 feature updates or quality updates for Windows 10 and later devices managed directly by WUfB.

In Intune, you also have the option to configure Windows 10 feature updates. This policy allows a device to be updated to the Windows version you specify and does not upgrade to a newer Windows feature release on those devices. The Windows feature build you specify in Windows 10 and the later feature updates policy will remain on the device until you choose to change the policy setting. While the feature build remains static, devices will continue to download and install quality and security updates that are available for the feature build.

Resource access policies

Resource access policies configure **virtual private network (VPN)**, Wi-Fi, email, and certificate settings on Windows 10 and later devices.

Endpoint protection

The endpoint protection workload includes the Windows Defender suite of anti-malware protection features:

- **Antivirus**: Antivirus policies help security admins focus on managing the settings for Microsoft Defender Antivirus, Microsoft Defender exclusions, and the Windows Security experience as a policy for Intune-managed devices.

- **Disk encryption**: Endpoint security disk encryption profiles focus on only the settings that are relevant for a device's built-in encryption method, such as BitLocker. This makes it possible for an IT admin to deploy and automatically encrypt end users' Windows devices.

- **Firewall**: Use the endpoint security firewall policy in Intune to configure a device's built-in firewall for devices that run Windows 10. Firewall policies are divided into two, the firewall policy itself and a firewall rule policy.

- **Endpoint detection and response**: When you integrate Microsoft Defender for Endpoint with Intune, use the endpoint security policies for **endpoint detection and response (EDR)** to manage the EDR settings and onboard devices for Microsoft Defender for Endpoint.

- **Attack surface reduction**: When Defender Antivirus is in use on your Windows 10 devices, use Intune endpoint security policies for attack surface reduction to manage those settings for your devices.

  The attack surface reduction policy is divided into different policies:

  A. App and browser isolation

  B. Device control

  C. Attack surface reduction rules

  D. Exploit protection

  E. Web protection for Microsoft Edge Legacy

  F. Application control

- **Account protection**: Account protection policies help you protect the identity and accounts of your users. The account protection policy is focused on settings for Windows Hello and Credential Guard, which is part of Windows identity and access management.

When you switch this workload, the Configuration Manager policies stay on the device until the Intune policies overwrite them. This behavior makes sure that the device still has protection policies during the transition.

The endpoint protection workload is also part of device configuration. The same behavior applies when you switch the device configuration workload. When you switch the device configuration workload, it also includes policies for the Windows Information Protection feature, which isn't included in the endpoint protection workload.

The Microsoft Defender Antivirus settings that are part of the device restrictions profile type for Intune device configuration are not included in the scope of the Endpoint protection slider. To manage Microsoft Defender Antivirus for co-managed devices with the endpoint protection slider enabled, use the new Antivirus policies in **Microsoft Endpoint manager admin center | Endpoint security | Antivirus**. The new policy type has new and improved options available and supports all the same settings available in the device restrictions profile.

The Windows encryption feature includes BitLocker management. We will talk more about BitLocker in *Chapter 10, Advanced Policy Management*, and *Chapter 13, Identity and Security Management*.

Device configuration

The device configuration workload includes settings that you manage for devices in your organization. Switching this workload also moves the resource access and endpoint protection workloads.

You can still deploy settings from Configuration Manager to co-managed devices even though Intune is the device configuration authority. This exception might be used to configure settings that your organization requires but aren't yet available in Intune. Specify this exception on a Configuration Manager configuration baseline. Enable the option to always apply this baseline even for co-managed clients when creating the baseline. You can change it later in the **General** tab of the properties of an existing baseline.

For more information on the Intune feature, refer to the **Create a device** profile in Microsoft Intune.

Office Click-to-Run apps

This workload manages Microsoft 365 apps on co-managed devices. Remember that when moving Microsoft 365 apps that work in Microsoft Intune for existing **System Center Configuration Manager** (**SCCM**)-managed devices, you should not automatically change Microsoft 365 app updates to cloud updates from **Content Delivery Network** (**CDN**). Updates can be managed using administrative templates in Microsoft Intune.

Office updates may take around 24 hours to show up at clients unless the devices are restarted.

Office 365 applications are managed by Intune. This condition in Intune is added by default as a requirement to new Microsoft 365 applications. When you transition this workload, co-managed clients don't meet the requirements of the application, and then they don't install Microsoft 365 deployed via Configuration Manager.

After moving the workload, Microsoft 365 apps assigned from Microsoft Intune show up in the company portal on the device.

Client apps

Use Intune to manage client apps and PowerShell scripts on co-managed Windows 10 devices. After you transition this workload, any available apps deployed from Intune are available in the company portal. Apps that you deploy from Configuration Manager are available in the software center and company portal. The company portal can show both SCCM and Intune available apps as one end user software portal.

Desktop Analytics

Desktop Analytics is a cloud-based service that integrates with Configuration Manager. It provides insight and intelligence for you to make more informed decisions about the update readiness of your Windows clients. The service combines data from your organization with data aggregated from millions of devices connected to the Microsoft cloud. It provides information on security updates, apps, and devices in your organization, and identifies compatibility issues with apps and drivers. Create a pilot for devices most likely to provide the best insights for assets across your organization.

As part of Endpoint Manager, use the cloud-powered insights of Desktop Analytics to keep Windows 10 devices current. Desktop Analytics needs an SCCM client on the devices, and Intune alone is not supported.

Windows Autopilot: Windows Autopilot sets up and pre-configures new devices, getting them ready for use. It is designed to simplify the life cycle of Windows devices, for both IT and end users, from initial deployment through to end of life.

As part of Endpoint Manager, use Autopilot to preconfigure devices and automatically enroll devices in Intune. You can also integrate Autopilot with Configuration Manager and co-management for more complex device configurations (in preview).

It is highly recommended to use Windows Autopilot in Azure AD-only environments to take advantage of the entire suite of Windows Autopilot features, such as Autopilot reset and co-management in Autopilot.

Azure AD: Azure AD is used by Endpoint Manager to identify devices, users, groups, and MFA. Azure AD Premium, which is part of the Microsoft 365 license, has additional features to help protect devices, apps, and data, including dynamic groups, autoenrollment, and Conditional Access. Azure AD Premium is also required for Windows Autopilot as automatic enrollment is a pre-requisite.

Endpoint Manager admin center: The admin center is a one-stop website to create policies and manage your devices. It plugs into other key device management services, including groups, security, Conditional Access, and reporting.

Microsoft Endpoint Manager is an integrated solution for managing all of your devices. Microsoft brings together Configuration Manager and Intune into a single console called the Microsoft Endpoint Manager admin center.

Starting in Configuration Manager version 2002, you can upload your Configuration Manager devices to the cloud service and take action from the **Devices** blade in the admin center:

- **Client details**: This feature gives the IT admin or helpdesk a fast overview of properties and the state of devices.

- **Install applications**: This feature gives the IT admin or helpdesk the option to deploy an application to the end users' devices.

- **Device timeline**: Devices send events once a day to the admin center. Only events collected after the client receives the Enable Endpoint analytics data collection policy are visible in the admin center. Generate test events easily by installing an application or an update from Configuration Manager, or restart the device. Events are kept for 30 days. Use the chart to view events that are collected.

- **Resource Explorer**: From the Microsoft Endpoint Management admin center, you can view the hardware inventory for uploaded Configuration Manager devices by using Resource Explorer.

- **Run scripts**: This option allows additional IT admins or the helpdesk to run PowerShell scripts from the cloud against an individual Configuration Manager-managed device in real time. This provides all the traditional benefits of PowerShell scripts that have already been defined and approved by the Configuration Manager admin in the on-premises environment.

Enabling tenant attach has no end user impact without the IT admin creation policies and deploying them to their devices.

Microsoft Endpoint Manager – from on-premises to the cloud

The unified endpoint management journey is different for each customer. Some customers are using some components of Microsoft Endpoint Manager already, and so the migration is relatively easy:

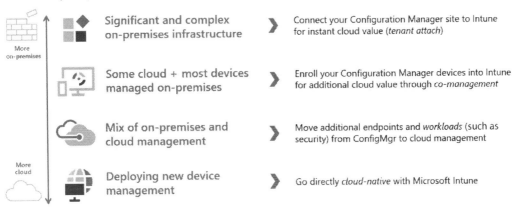

Figure 2.3 – Microsoft Endpoint Manager – on-premises-to-cloud flow

If you are still using complex on-premises infrastructures, the work could be a bit more intense. It's fully dependent on the complexity of your current environment.

Exploring Windows 10 Enterprise in detail

Some Windows features are only available in the Enterprise SKU of Windows, while some MDM capabilities are only available for Enterprise versions.

Windows 10 Enterprise supports the following features and services *exclusively* on top of Windows 10 Pro.

Refer to the following list of additional Enterprise features and services:

- **Intelligent security**:

  - Credential protection

  - Endpoint detection and response

  - **Unified Write Filter (UWF)**

- **Simplified updates**:

  - 30 months of support for September-targeted releases

  - Windows 10 Long-Term Servicing Channel

  - Desktop analytics

- **Flexible management**:

  - Azure Virtual Desktop use rights

  - Microsoft **User Experience Virtualization (UE-V)**

  - Microsoft **Application Virtualization (App-V)**

  - Microsoft FSLogix Profile Container

- **Enhanced productivity**:

  - SMB Direct

  - Persistent memory

- **Support for other Microsoft 365 services**:

  - Azure Virtual Desktop

  - Windows 365

  - Universal Print

First, we will cover how to transform a Windows 10 Pro instance into an Enterprise version in the cloud without reimaging. In the past, when organizations were deploying Windows at scale with an OS deployment tool such as **Microsoft Deployment Toolkit (MDT)** or Microsoft Endpoint Manager Configuration Manager, the IT admin needed to deploy the correct Windows version of Pro or Enterprise.

The most common methods of volume activation require that devices be connected to an organization's network or connected via the VPN to *check in* from time to time with the organization's activation service to maintain their licenses. However, when people work from home and off the corporate or school networks, their devices' ability to receive or maintain activation is limited.

There are several ways to do a Windows activation:

- A key management service
- A multiple activation key
- An Active Directory-based activation
- A Windows 10 subscription activation

Using Windows via a Windows 365 cloud PC

The preceding options to activate Windows 10 Enterprise are built into a Windows 365/cloud PC. If you are going to self-manage and deploy virtual desktops on Azure, this means that Windows 10 Enterprise will be automatically activated via Azure **Key Management Service** (**KMS**).

Azure KMS – cloud PC/Windows 365/AVD

If your Windows desktops are virtual and run on Azure such as with **Azure Virtual Desktop** (**AVD**), you need to connect to the Azure `kms.core.windows.net:1688` KMS server in order to activate your virtual machine. This happens automatically when using images from the Azure image gallery. Make sure that your Azure **virtual network** (**vNET**) can connect to this address, and configure your firewall policies and rules accordingly. You will learn more about this later on in the cloud PC/Windows 365 and requirements chapters.

Windows 11 will be added later this fall to the offering once the OS is made generally available. More on Windows 11 is covered later on in the book.

Key Management Service

KMS activation requires TCP/IP connectivity to, and accessibility from, an organization's private network so that licenses are not accessible to anyone outside of the organization. By default, KMS hosts and clients use DNS to publish and find the KMS key. Default settings can be used, which require little or no administrative action, or KMS hosts and client computers can be manually configured based on network configuration and security requirements.

KMS activations are valid for 180 days (the activation validity interval). KMS client computers must renew their activation by connecting to the KMS host at least once every 180 days. By default, KMS client computers attempt to renew their activation every 7 days. If KMS activation fails, the client computer tries to reach the host every 2 hours. After a client computer's activation is renewed, the activation validity interval begins again.

Multiple activation key

A **multiple activation key** (**MAK**) is used for one-time activation with Microsoft's hosted activation services. Each MAK has a predetermined number of activations allowed. This number is based on volume licensing agreements, and it might not match the organization's exact license count. Each activation that uses an MAK with the Microsoft-hosted activation service counts toward the activation limit.

You can use an MAK for individual computers or with an image that can be duplicated or installed using Microsoft deployment solutions. You can also use an MAK on a computer that was originally configured to use KMS activation, which is useful for moving a computer from the core network to a disconnected environment.

Active Directory-based activation

Active Directory-based activation is like KMS activation but uses Active Directory instead of a separate service. Active Directory-based activation is implemented as a role service that relies on Active Directory Domain Services to store activation objects. Active Directory-based activation requires that the forest schema be updated using adprep. exe on a supported server OS, but after the schema is updated, older domain controllers can still activate clients.

Devices activated via Active Directory maintain their activated state for up to 180 days following the most recent contact with the domain. Devices periodically attempt to reactivate (every 7 days by default) before the end of that period and, again, at the end of the 180 days.

Windows 10 and later Subscription Activation

Starting with Windows 10, version 1703, Windows 10 Pro supports the Subscription Activation feature, enabling users to *step up* from Windows 10 Pro to Windows 10 Enterprise automatically if they are subscribed to Windows 10 Enterprise E3 or E5.

With Windows 10, version 1703, both Windows 10 Enterprise E3 and Windows 10 Enterprise E5 are available as online services via subscription. Deploying Windows 10 Enterprise in your organization can now be accomplished with no keys and no reboots.

For Windows 10, version 1703 or later

Devices with a current Windows 10 Pro license can be seamlessly upgraded to Windows 10 Enterprise. Product key-based Windows 10 Enterprise software licenses can be transitioned to Windows 10 Enterprise subscriptions.

Organizations that have an Enterprise agreement can also benefit from the new service, using traditional Active Directory-joined devices. In this scenario, the Active Directory user that signs in on their device must be synchronized with Azure AD using Azure AD Connect sync.

The Subscription Activation feature eliminates the need to manually deploy Windows 10 Enterprise or Education images on each target device and then later standing up on-premises key management services, such as KMS- or MAK-based activation, entering **Generic Volume License Keys (GVLKs)**, and subsequently rebooting client devices.

Windows as a Service – update release cycle

Windows updates are released every 6 months, somewhere around March and September, via the Semi-Annual Channel release cycle. Every month, quality updates are released, depending on the life cycle policy:

Semi-Annual Channel

Version	Servicing option	Availability date	OS build	Latest revision date	End of service: Home, Pro, Pro Education, Pro for Workstations, and IoT Core	End of service: Enterprise, Education and IoT Enterprise
21H1	Semi-Annual Channel	2021-05-18	19043.1023	2021-05-25	2022-12-13	2022-12-13
20H2	Semi-Annual Channel	2020-10-20	19042.1023	2021-05-25	2022-05-10	2023-05-09
2004	Semi-Annual Channel	2020-05-27	19041.1023	2021-05-25	2021-12-14	2021-12-14
1909	Semi-Annual Channel	2019-11-12	18363.1593	2021-05-20	End of service	2022-05-10

Enterprise and IoT Enterprise LTSB/LTSC editions

Version	Servicing option	Availability date	OS build	Latest revision date	Mainstream support end date	Extended support end date
1809	Long-Term Servicing Channel (LTSC)	2018-11-13	17763.1971	2021-05-20	2024-01-09	2029-01-09
1607	Long-Term Servicing Branch (LTSB)	2016-08-02	14393.4402	2021-05-11	2021-10-12	2026-10-13
1507 (RTM)	Long-Term Servicing Branch (LTSB)	2015-07-29	10240.18932	2021-05-11	End of service	2025-10-14

Figure 2.4 – Windows 10 Enterprise release diagram

Microsoft recommends upgrading to the latest Semi-Annual Channel immediately for early adoption. This will give you the best features and user experience as soon as possible, delivered as part of Windows 10.

WUfB is the new way of manning Windows servicing

WUfB allows IT professionals to utilize the cloud-based Windows Update service to deploy and manage Windows updates. You can use Group Policy or MDM solutions such as Microsoft Intune to configure the WUfB settings that control how and when Windows 10 devices are updated.

WUfB has been available since Windows 10, version 1511, and has been enhanced in Windows 10 releases since. Some of the improvements are designed to provide IT pros with greater control while offering an improved experience for the end user.

Who should use WUfB?

WUfB is intended for devices running Windows 10 Education, Professional, or Enterprise editions managed in organizations. The Windows 10 **Long-Term Servicing Channel** (**LTSC**) is not supported with WUfB:

- All organizations can leverage it to be more efficient in servicing their internet-connected devices.
- Small and medium businesses gain flexibility while continuing to use Windows Update, with more control than previously provided without using System Center Configuration Manager, Microsoft Intune, **Windows Server Update Services** (**WSUS**), or third-party solutions.

Why do I want WUfB?

WUfB can help you to provide the end user with the best Windows update experience and lower the cost of servicing Windows, while giving you much of the flexibility and control available from more complicated and time-consuming solutions:

- Reduce the cost of approving, deploying, and monitoring updates.
- Manage application compatibility within the organization's ecosystem.
- Find the right trade-offs to protect devices, while minimizing disruption to the workforce.
- Manage the infrastructure configurations necessary to support rapid update velocity, including finding the right way to address devices that are rarely connected to the enterprise.

What does WUfB allow me to configure?

When you configure WUfB policy from Microsoft Intune with the configuration setting, WUfB will be enabled. If you have traditionally utilized WSUS for servicing, your clients will connect to both Windows Update in the cloud as well as your WSUS server once you set WUfB settings. If you want to change this behavior, you need to remove your old configuration settings for WSUS on the endpoints.

Through the Windows Update Client settings (through Group Policy, MDM, or the UX), WUfB provides the ability to delay the application of updates. Quality updates and feature updates are treated separately to give you added flexibility.

In addition, you may leverage the "Pause" functionality if you need time to implement remediation to updates after testing them in earlier rings:

- **Feature updates**: Previously referred to as **upgrades**, feature updates contain not only security and quality revisions but also significant feature additions and changes. Feature updates are released semi-annually in the fall and the spring.

- **Quality updates**: Quality updates are traditional OS updates, typically released on the second Tuesday of each month (though they can be released at any time). These include security, critical, and driver updates. WUfB also treats non-Windows updates (such as updates for Microsoft Office or Visual Studio) as quality updates. These non-Windows updates are known as **Microsoft updates**, and you can set devices to receive such updates (or not) along with their Windows updates.

- **Driver updates**: Updates for non-Microsoft drivers that are relevant to your devices. Driver updates are on by default, but you can use WUfB policies to turn them off if you prefer.

- **Microsoft product updates**: Updates for other Microsoft products, such as versions of Office that are installed by using Windows Installer (MSI). Versions of Office that are installed by using Click-to-Run can't be updated by using WUfB. Product updates are off by default. You can turn them on by using WUfB policies.

Windows 10 feature updates policies work in conjunction with your *Windows 10 update ring* policies to prevent a device from receiving a Windows feature version that's later than the value specified in the feature updates policy.

For Windows 10 feature updates policies to be working, Windows 10, version 1709, or later is required. The devices need to be enrolled in Intune MDM and be hybrid AD-joined, Azure AD-joined, or Azure AD-registered. Windows telemetry needs to be turned on, with a minimum setting of Basic. If telemetry is off, Windows can be upgraded to a later version of Windows than defined in the feature updates policy.

When a device receives a Windows 10 feature updates policy, the device updates to the version of Windows specified in the policy. A device that already runs a later version of Windows remains in its current version. By freezing the version, the device's feature set remains stable for the duration of the policy.

A device will not install an update when it has a safeguard hold for that Windows version. When a device evaluates the applicability of an update version, Windows creates the temporary safeguard hold if an unresolved known issue exists. Once the issue is resolved, the hold is removed, and the device can then update.

Unlike using **Pause** with an update ring, which expires after 35 days, the Windows 10 feature updates policy remains in effect. Devices won't install a new Windows version until you modify or remove the Windows 10 feature updates policy. If you edit the policy to specify a newer version, devices can then install the features from that Windows version.

Today, there are more than 3,000 Group Policy settings for Windows 10. Although Microsoft provides extensive guidance on different security features, exploring each one can take a long time. You would have to determine the impact of each setting on your own and then determine the appropriate value for each setting.

WUfB for Windows 10 has a set of policies that you can configure to provide the most secure Windows environments as it is updated, as long as the devices have internet connectivity and still keep the best end user experience by configuring policy settings across a number of areas:

- Configuring deadlines
- Restart behavior
- Accounting for low-activity devices (active hours)
- Delivery optimization
- Power policies

There has always been a tension between the need for being current with software update compliance and the desire to keep the workforce productive. While the security department has a requirement to see a fully updated device fleet within 7 days of a software update, the reality is that deployment of the said update has an associated cost for users, and very few companies can afford to push an update on an entire workforce in the middle of a single working day unless it is a zero-day patch in an emergency.

Given the competing goals of a protected and productive workforce, you may find that you may need to make choices that are less than the best possible selection for maximizing update velocity in favor of an experience more aligned with your business's productivity needs.

Bring your own device

BYOD has different options depending on the Windows SKU. All BYOD scenarios can leverage Windows 365 and Azure Virtual Desktop to get access to either a full desktop or a single application as a remote app.

Windows devices can also be registered with Azure AD to gain access to corporate resources such as email.

Enroll the device in Intune as a personally owned device (BYOD). If an administrator has configured autoenrollment (available with Azure AD Premium subscriptions), the user only has to enter their credentials once. Otherwise, they'll have to enroll separately through MDM-only enrollment and re-enter their credentials.

Microsoft Intune management does not provide the same management capabilities on BYOD; not all Windows editions have the same MDM management setting built in:

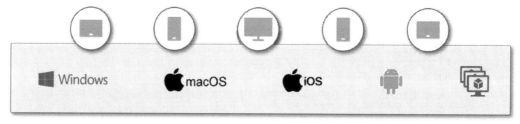

Figure 2.5 – Microsoft Endpoint Manager endpoint support

Windows 10 Enterprise has full management features, whereas both the Home and Pro editions have fewer management capabilities due to Windows limitations. Microsoft provides the option for the IT admin to leverage enrollment restrictions so that you can block personal enrollment into Microsoft Intune.

What is zero trust?

In the past, when organizations created remote access to corporate networks, normally, access was effected with a VPN connection either on a corporate-owned or a personally owned Windows device, only secured by an MFA token.

Today, organizations require a new security model that effectively adapts to the complexity of the modern environment, embraces the mobile workforce, and protects people, devices, applications, and data wherever they are located.

This is the core of zero trust. Instead of believing that everything behind the corporate firewall is safe, the zero trust model assumes a breach and verifies each request as though it originated from an uncontrolled network. Regardless of where the request originates from or what resource it accesses, the zero trust model teaches us to "never trust, always verify."

Verifying identity

The majority of security breaches today involve credential theft, and lapses in cyber hygiene amplify the potential for risk to employees and to organizations at large. That's why one of the primary components of a zero trust system is the ability to verify a user's identity before access is granted to the corporate network.

Start by implementing MFA through the modern experience of Azure Authenticator and Windows Hello for Business on all Windows 10 devices.

Verifying devices

Because unmanaged devices are an easy entry point for bad actors, ensuring that only healthy and trusted devices can access critical applications and data is vital for enterprise security. A fundamental part of our zero trust implementation is to enroll all end user devices in device management systems such as Microsoft Intune.

Enabling compliance policies to check the devices for parameters such as BitLocker encryption, secure boot, and device health verification in this way is essential to managing the policies that govern access to corporate resources.

Microsoft Endpoint Manager is a key piece of this new way of thinking as it makes the device trusted, with a compliance policy to validate whether the devices are compliant.

Conditional Access is the tool built into Azure AD to bring signals together, make decisions, and enforce organizational Conditional Access policies:

- **Signals**: A device or a user sign-in with a specific application or browser.
- **Decision**: What level of access you will be granted based on the policies.
- **Enforcement**: This could be as simple as giving the end user access with an MFA token or denying access:

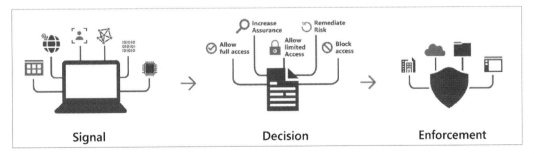

Figure 2.6 – Zero trust verifying devices diagram

Conditional Access policies at their simplest are if-then statements. If a user wants to access a corporate resource, then they must complete an action. For example, if an end user wants to access the corporate Microsoft Teams application then they must come from a compliant device to get access.

IT admins and security admins have two primary goals:

- Empower users to be productive wherever and whenever.
- Protect the organization's data:

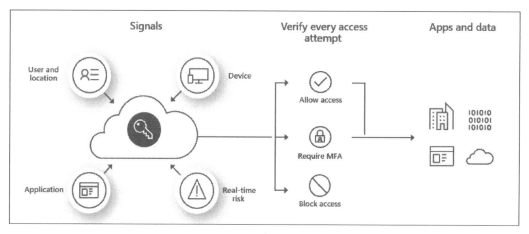

Figure 2.7 – Zero trust verification process flow

By using Conditional Access policies, you can apply the right access controls when needed to keep your organization secure and stay out of your users' way when not needed.

We will be going into more detail on Conditional Access and other security-related improvements in *Chapter 13, Identity and Security Management.*

Summary

In the chapter, we've learned about the fundamentals of unified endpoint management, modern management, and how this relates to Microsoft Endpoint Manager. We also went through the different concepts, services, and products around Windows 10 Enterprise and security-related aspects of zero trust.

In the next chapter, we're going to talk about Windows 365 and explain this service more.

After this section, we'll continue to take a deeper dive, as we are going to talk about the different endpoint scenarios and requirements in terms of what is needed to use Microsoft Endpoint Manager.

Questions

1. How is modern management different from any other management solutions in the market?

    A. Devices are securely managed through one unified management portal experience.

    B. It provides more capabilities for mobile device management.

    C. Other solutions do not support Windows 10 Enterprise.

2. What is the main principle behind zero trust?

    A. Never trust, always verify.

    B. Always trust, never verify.

Answers

1. (A)

2. (A)

Further reading

If you want to learn more about modern management after reading this chapter, please use one of the following free online resources:

*   Modern management and security principles driving our Microsoft Endpoint Manager vision – Microsoft Tech Community: `https://techcommunity.microsoft.com/t5/microsoft-endpoint-manager-blog/modern-management-and-security-principles-driving-our-microsoft/ba-p/946797`

*   Introduction to modern management in Microsoft 365: `https://docs.microsoft.com/en-us/learn/modules/introduction-to-modern-management-in-microsoft-365/`

*   Modern management with Microsoft Endpoint Manager – YouTube: `https://www.youtube.com/watch?v=l03UXEnl0Fg`

Section 2: Windows 365

In this section, you'll learn everything you need to know about the new cloud service Windows 365. As this service has just been released, we decided to dedicate a full chapter to it to get ready to kick the tires.

This part of the book comprises the following chapters:

- *Chapter 3, Introducing Windows 365*
- *Chapter 4, Deploying Windows 365*

3
Introducing Windows 365

In this chapter, you'll learn everything you need to know about Windows 365 from a conceptual perspective.

After reading this chapter, you'll know more about the benefits of using Windows 365 and the different service components. In the next chapter, you'll learn how you can deploy it!

This chapter is very comprehensive – we'll go through the following topics:

- What is Windows 365?
- Microsoft Endpoint Configuration Manager support

What is Windows 365?

Users want technology that is familiar, easy to use, and always available so they can work and create fluidly across devices. Cloud PCs make this possible by combining the power and security of the cloud with the familiarity of a PC. Only Microsoft can bring together a PC and the cloud with a consistent and integrated Windows experience. Windows 365 is the world's first cloud PC. With Windows 365 Cloud PC, Windows evolves from a device-based OS to hybrid personalized computing.

A Cloud PC is your personalized desktop, apps, settings, and content streamed securely from the cloud to your devices. Lowering the complexity level of your environment as you deploy and manage virtual endpoints in Microsoft Endpoint Manager, no additional **Virtual Desktop Infrastructure (VDI)** expertise or resources are needed.

Windows 365 provides you with all the benefits of Windows, without any of the traditional hardware limitations as your desktops are running in the Azure cloud.

You can find all the main principles of the service in the following list:

- Deploy and manage virtual endpoints in Microsoft Endpoint Manager; no additional VDI expertise or resources needed.

- Procure, provision, and deploy in minutes, with optional automated OS updates.

- Access from anywhere to your personalized Windows desktop experience.

- Tailor compute and configurations for an elastic workforce.

- Pick up where you left off on the device of your choice.

- Optimized experiences on Windows endpoints.

- Scale confidently with per-user pricing.

Removing the complexity of traditional VDI deployments

All the building blocks are automated for you, and the service scales with you in the most optimized way possible to use Microsoft 365 apps. It is Microsoft's best expression of Windows and Microsoft 365 and is always secure and up to date.

A Cloud PC can be accessed from anywhere from any device and can scale with a user's changing compute needs, meaning that the user could receive the self-service privileges to release an IT admin from needing to assign a license that provides more compute resources. The same applies to storage upgrades and Cloud PC reboots – more about this later.

Why virtualize Windows in the cloud?

For some of you, this might sound like common sense. However, if you don't know that much about the benefits of using virtualized desktops running on the cloud, here's a quick rundown:

- **Mobility** – Users can access Cloud PC from any device, anywhere.

- **Security** – Business data never leaves the cloud.

- **Scalability** – Adjust to workforce fluctuations.

- **Compatibility** – Old apps can run virtualized.

- **Performance** – Apps remain close to the data.

- **Management** – A single image for many users.

- **Cost** – Utilize the flexibility of the cloud.

Removing complexity while increasing security

Windows 365 removes complexity all around while also adding a higher security level to your endpoints. The service is fully supported by Microsoft Defender for Endpoints and zero-trust principles, with enhancements for Azure AD conditional access rules – securing your virtual desktops has never been easier to configure.

Low costs as a fixed-price model

The other great benefits are the costs involved as this service could decrease the current cost of keeping your VDI environment up and running or any other use case, for example, remote workers connecting via an expensive, unreliable VPN connection. All the services are built using a subscription-based model that aligns with the CapEx needs of most businesses, too.

The following comparison model perfectly shows the differences between traditional Remote Desktop Services (session-based) and VDI, and Azure Virtual Desktop and Windows 365:

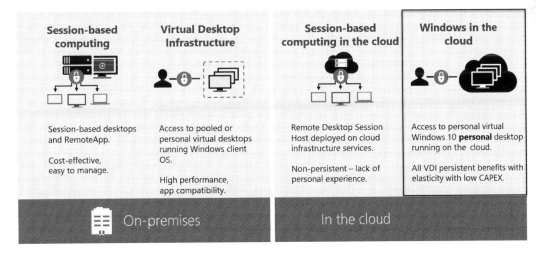

Figure 3.1 – Comparison between an on-premises and in-the-cloud environment

Windows 365 is a fixed-price service with a personal desktop experience completely managed via Microsoft Endpoint Manager.

Comparing Windows 365 Enterprise and Business

Windows 365 is available in two versions, one fully managed and configurable via Microsoft Endpoint Manager (mostly covered in this book), called **Windows 365 Enterprise**, and one that is called **Windows 365 Business**, where you have to provide more services yourself, such as application delivery and management.

Customers can purchase Windows 365 Business directly from the Microsoft 365 admin center portal, set up their account without a domain, and provision and manage their Cloud PCs directly from the Windows 365 home page online.

No other Microsoft licenses are required – you can get started with just a credit card if you want. Windows 365 Business is intended for customers wanting to deploy Cloud PCs for 300 users or fewer across their organization.

Windows 365 Business allows customers to start provisioning a Cloud PC directly after assigning the license to the user from the Microsoft 365 admin center. There is no IT admin interaction needed. The user will be able to access the Cloud PC and become productive in under an hour after the license has been assigned!

In the following table, you can find the list of features available per product to make your decision easier in each scenario:

	Windows 365 Business	Windows 365 Enterprise
Click to provision directly from the product page	•	
"No-domain" set up	•	
Self-serve troubleshooting – reset	•	
"Cloud Save" (minimal Azure storage and potentially **One Drive for Business (ODfB)**)	•	•
Self-serve upgrades		•
Universal Print (UP) integration		•
Partner/programmatic enablement (Graph APIs, **Managed service providers (MSP)** tooling)		•
Custom images		•
Image management (store, replicate, deploy)		•

MEM policy-driven provisioning, management, and guided scenarios		•
EA-based reporting, monitoring		•
Service health, operational health alerts		•
Connection to on-premises (networks, apps, resources) and diagnostics		•
Advanced MEM-based troubleshooting and device management		•

We'd like to give you a bit more information about the Windows 365 Business version of the product. Within Enterprise, there are some prerequisites and Microsoft Endpoint Manager is needed to make the configuration supported for larger organizations.

However, Windows 365 Business only needs a license assigned to the user via the Microsoft 365 admin center to start the provisioning process of the Cloud PC. After assigning a 2vCPU/8 GB/128 GB Cloud PC license, users can directly go to the `windows365.microsoft.com` portal to access their workspace:

Figure 3.2 – Windows 365 Business – provisioning a Cloud PC

This simple procedure is possible due to the support of native Azure AD, which will come with the Enterprise product H2CY22. After the provisioning is done, the user can directly log on to their Cloud PC:

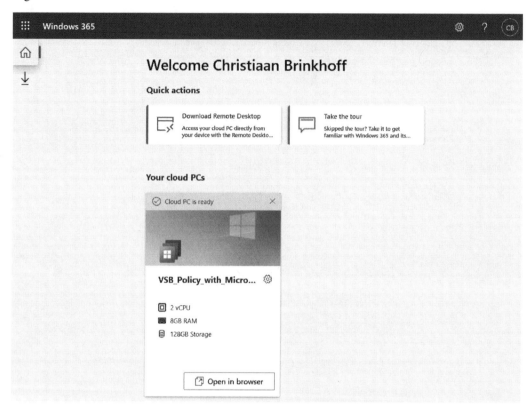

Figure 3.3 – Windows 365 Business Cloud PC ready

We've now explained all the differences between the different products, so you can make the right decision as to whether Business or Enterprise is the better fit. Let's now switch over to Microsoft Endpoint Manager and tell you more about Windows 365 Enterprise.

Microsoft Endpoint Manager

Windows 365 works together with Microsoft Endpoint Manager, hence this book is named *Mastering Microsoft Endpoint Manager*.

From within the **Devices** blade, you will get access to Windows 365 – the Cloud PC service – where you can find the **Overview** dashboard screen showing the status of your environment:

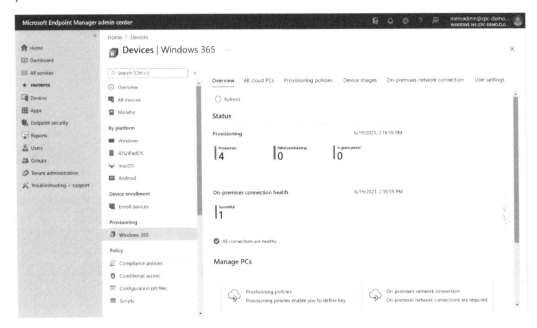

Figure 3.4 – Overview dashboard

When you go to **Devices** in the menu and scroll down to **Provisioning**, you will find the spot to start creating your Cloud PCs:

Device name ↑↓	Provisioning policy ↑↓	Image ↑↓	OPNC ↑↓	PC type ↑↓	Status ↑↓
CPC-Nila-E7R-A9	East US – Finance users	Windows 10 Enterpris...	East US Office location	Windows 365 Enterpri...	✓ Provisioned
CPC-Christia-MP	East US – Finance users	Windows 10 Enterpris...	East US Office location	Windows 365 Enterpri...	✓ Provisioned
CPC-mason-OQ-L6	East US – Finance users	Windows 10 Enterpris...	East US Office location	Windows 365 Enterpri...	✓ Provisioned
CPC-NatasjaL-L5	East US – Finance users	Windows 10 Enterpris...	East US Office location	Windows 365 Enterpri...	✓ Provisioned

Figure 3.5 – Provisioning Cloud PCs

All the prerequisite steps as well as the main steps to provision Cloud PCs are covered later in this chapter.

High-level architecture components and responsibilities

The architecture of Windows 365 is relatively simple to understand and a bit different from **Azure Virtual Desktop** (**AVD**) as some objects now live in a Microsoft-managed environment.

All the blue parts are now managed by Microsoft and the gray elements are the responsibility of the customer/partner. This is different from solutions where you are responsible for most things yourself, meaning more overhead in management and most likely also a higher level of complexity.

Microsoft manages the following services as part of Windows 365:

- Virtualization control plane (information worker (web access) portal, gateway, connection broker, diagnostics, and REST APIs)
- Cloud PCs and Azure compute services (VMs, provisioning, Azure subscriptions, Cloud PC VM provisioning, autoscaling, and so on)

Customers and/or partners manage these components as part of Windows 365:

- Azure Virtual Network (subnets, ExpressRoute, S2S VPN, and so on)
- Microsoft Endpoint Manager (device configuration, settings catalog, PowerShell, and so on)
- Azure Active Directory configuration (hybrid Azure AD, Conditional Access, compliance policies, and so on)
- Active Directory Domain Services configuration (on-premises AD, Azure AD Connect, and so on)
- Physical endpoint clients (Windows, macOS, Linux, Android, iOS, and so on)

Microsoft Endpoint Manager is the **unified management** console on top of all the other services we leverage, such as Azure AD, Defender for Endpoint, Desktop Analytics for monitoring, and Intune to manage your physical and cloud endpoints all at once.

The following diagram shows the high-level architecture of Windows 365 Enterprise with a hybrid Azure AD join as the domain configuration. It outlines the different responsibilities customers and partners have as part of the service as well as what other Microsoft Endpoint Manager components are tightly integrated:

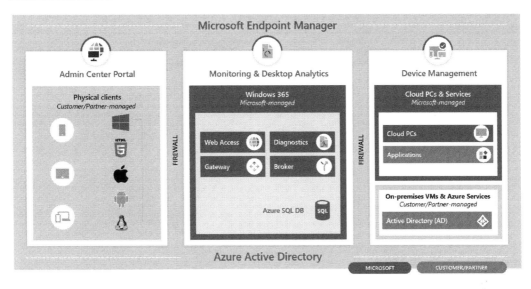

Figure 3.6 – Microsoft Endpoint Manager and Windows 365 architecture

Microsoft Endpoint Configuration Manager support

Configuration Manager is an on-premises management solution to manage desktops, servers, and laptops that are on your network or internet-based. You can cloud-enable it to integrate with Intune, Azure AD, Microsoft Defender ATP, and other cloud services. Use Configuration Manager to deploy apps, software updates, and operating systems. You can also monitor compliance, query and act on clients in real time, and much more.

Co-management and Windows 365

As part of Endpoint Manager, you can continue to use Configuration Manager as you always have. If you're ready to move some tasks to the cloud, consider co-management.

Co-management combines your existing on-premises Configuration Manager investment with the cloud using Intune and other Microsoft 365 cloud services. You choose whether Configuration Manager or Intune is the management authority for the seven different workload groups.

Sizes and performance of fixed-price licenses

The way Windows 365 works is a little bit different from how other virtualization services work. The performance of your Cloud PC is defined per user-assigned license via the Microsoft 365 admin center portal in the same manner as how you assign, for example, Microsoft 365 E3/E5 licenses to users.

There are multiple licenses that reflect different VM sizes. Think about more vCPUs, RAM and OS, and profile storage. Graphically enhanced sizes will be added in the near future.

The following table has all the different Cloud PC licenses that are available today. GPU-enhanced Cloud PC sizes will be added soon, and will most likely already be available when you read this book:

VM/OS disk size	Example scenarios	Recommended apps
1vCPU/2 GB/64 GB	First-line workers, call centers, and education/training/CRM access. Note: This SKU is not supported for Windows 11.	Office light (web-based), Microsoft Edge, OneDrive, lightweight line-of-business apps (for example, a call center application – web apps), Defender support
2vCPU/4 GB/256 GB 2vCPU/4 GB/128 GB 2vCPU/4 GB/64 GB	Mergers and acquisitions, short-term and seasonal, customer services, bring your own PC, and work from home.	Microsoft 365 apps, Microsoft Teams (audio only), Outlook, Excel, PowerPoint, OneDrive, Adobe Reader, Edge, line-of-business apps, Defender support
2vCPU/8 GB/256 GB 2vCPU/8 GB/128 GB	Bring your own PC, work from home, market researchers, government, and consultants.	Microsoft 365 apps, Microsoft Teams, Outlook, Excel, Access, PowerPoint, OneDrive, Adobe Reader, Edge, line-of-business apps, Defender support
4vCPU/16 GB/512 GB 4vCPU/16 GB/256 GB 4vCPU/16 GB/128 GB	Finance, government, consultants, healthcare services, bring your own PC, and work from home.	Microsoft 365 apps, Microsoft Teams, Outlook, Excel, Access, PowerPoint, Power BI, Dynamics 365, OneDrive, Adobe Reader, Edge, line-of-business apps, Defender support

8vCPU/32GB/512GB 8vCPU/32GB/256GB 8vCPU/32GB/128GB	Software developers, engineers, content creators, and design and engineering workstations.	Microsoft 365 apps, Microsoft Teams, Outlook, Access, OneDrive, Adobe Reader, Edge, Power BI, Visual Studio Code, line-of-business apps, Defender support

On-premises connections

An on-premises network connection is needed to connect to your own data center environment. This could be to your own Azure Virtual Network only, but also to your co-location or other private/hybrid cloud environment. Most likely, you are going to install line-of-business applications on top of your Cloud PCs that require a connection to the database or application server that still resides on-premises.

To connect to your on-premises location, you need to have a site-to-site VPN or ExpressRoute (more reliable) to your on-premises network. When you are an enterprise with multiple network locations, you can easily add more by clicking on + **Create connection**, as shown in the screenshot that follows.

The following screenshot is an example of a successful on-premises network connection that is checked and defined as successful by our Watchdog service:

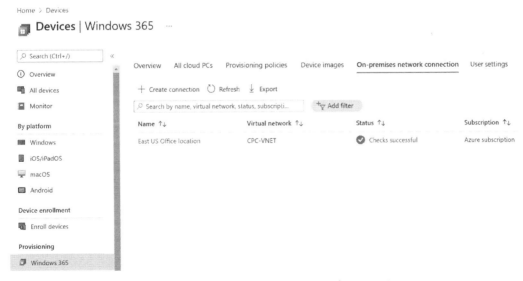

Figure 3.7 – Create an on-premises network connection

More in-depth information about this and how you can configure it can be found later, in *Chapter 4, Deploying Windows 365*.

Provisioning policies

A provisioning policy is what the name suggests – a policy to provision your Cloud PCs. The policy must be configured after you have configured the on-premises connection as this is one of the requirements to move forward.

The provisioning policy includes the baseline configuration of your Cloud PC, such as the image version of Windows 10 Enterprise or Windows 11, the on-premises connection (location), and the Azure AD group that includes the users that should receive this baseline configuration.

Once the provisioning policy is done, it will show up under the **Provisioning policies** menu. You can have multiple policies per either department or location as this would be the most common reason for enterprises to split them into different provisioning policies:

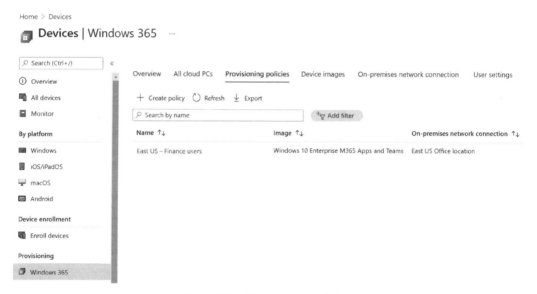

Figure 3.8 – Provisioning policies

Now the information you need to know about provisioning policies has been explained, we will take a deeper dive into the images that are supported as part of the provisioning policy.

Windows 365 – gallery images

As written in the previous section, the image selection option is part of the provisioning policy. There's also the option to select a gallery image running Windows 10 or 11 with pre-baked images per workload type.

For example, the images for our second license size 2vCPU/4 GB/64 GB and higher include Microsoft 365 apps and Teams AV optimizations out of the box, whereas the 1vCPU/2 GB/64 GB Lite image offers an optimized OS experience for that specific workload type to get the best experience possible, as we removed different built-in services from inside the image that you won't need for the type of workloads supported:

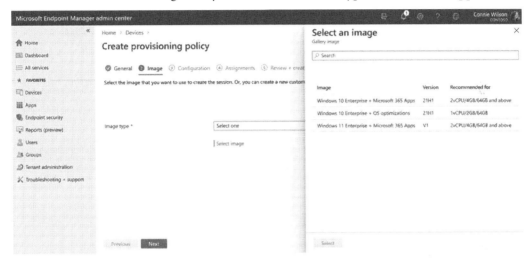

Figure 3.9 – Selecting Windows 365 images

Now, we've explained how you could use the preferred route in selecting images for Windows 365 Cloud PCs. In the next section, we explain how you can use custom images.

Custom images

Some customers prefer to use their own pre-built custom images, also known as **golden images**. This approach is also supported within Windows 365 as an option to select during the provisioning policy configuration wizard.

Supported custom image services are as follows:

- Azure managed image
- Share image gallery

The customer is free to pick whatever solution fits their needs best, as we support both Windows 10 and 11. Some customers prefer the more modern management approach, meaning a baseline image with the latest Windows updates and baseline apps and the rest will be added via Microsoft Intune – app delivery profiles:

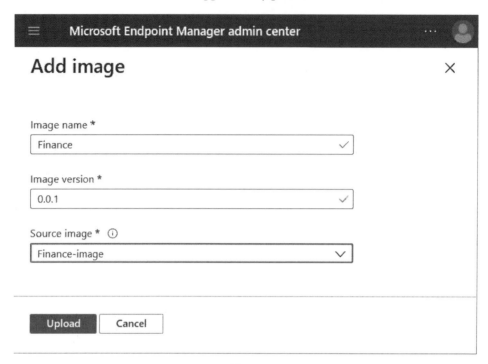

Figure 3.10 – Adding a custom image

Later in the chapter, we are going to explain how you can create your own custom image to use as a baseline in Windows 365 too.

Roles and delegation

Windows 365 offers capabilities to delegate access features and functionalities on top of existing Intune roles within Microsoft Endpoint Manager. For example, you want to give helpdesk employees read-only access to the Windows 365 portal to check whether the Cloud PC is unavailable or not. Other examples include the separation of security-related settings as part of your security policies. Let me explain all the roles in more depth in the following table:

Role	In	Can do
Application manager	Windows 365 Enterprise Cloud PC	Intune Application Managers can manage applications, read device information, and view device configuration profiles.
Cloud PC Administrator	Windows 365 Enterprise Cloud PC	Cloud PC Administrators can take read and write actions in the Cloud PC L2 node in MEM.
Cloud PC Reader	Windows 365 Enterprise Cloud PC	Cloud PC Readers can take read actions in the Cloud PC L2 node in MEM.
Endpoint Security Manager	Windows 365 Enterprise Cloud PC	Intune Endpoint Security Managers can manage security and compliance features such as security baselines, device compliance, Conditional Access, and Microsoft Defender for Endpoint for their Cloud PCs.
Help Desk Operator	Windows 365 Enterprise Cloud PC	Intune Help Desk Operators can perform remote tasks on Cloud PCs and assign applications or policies to the devices.
Intune administrator role	Windows 365 Enterprise Cloud PC	Intune administrator role can assign Intune roles (built-in and custom) to other administrators but cannot assign Cloud PC roles.
Policy and Profile Manager	Windows 365 Enterprise Cloud PC	Intune Policy and Profile Managers can manage compliance policy, configuration profiles, corporate device identifiers, and security baselines for Cloud PCs.
Read Only Operator	Windows 365 Enterprise Cloud PC	Intune Read Only Operators have read-only access to all Intune nodes including the Cloud PC node.
School Administrator	Windows 365 Enterprise Cloud PC	Intune School Administrators can manage Windows 10 devices in Intune for Education.

In the following screenshot, see the list of roles available in the Microsoft Endpoint Manager admin center portal:

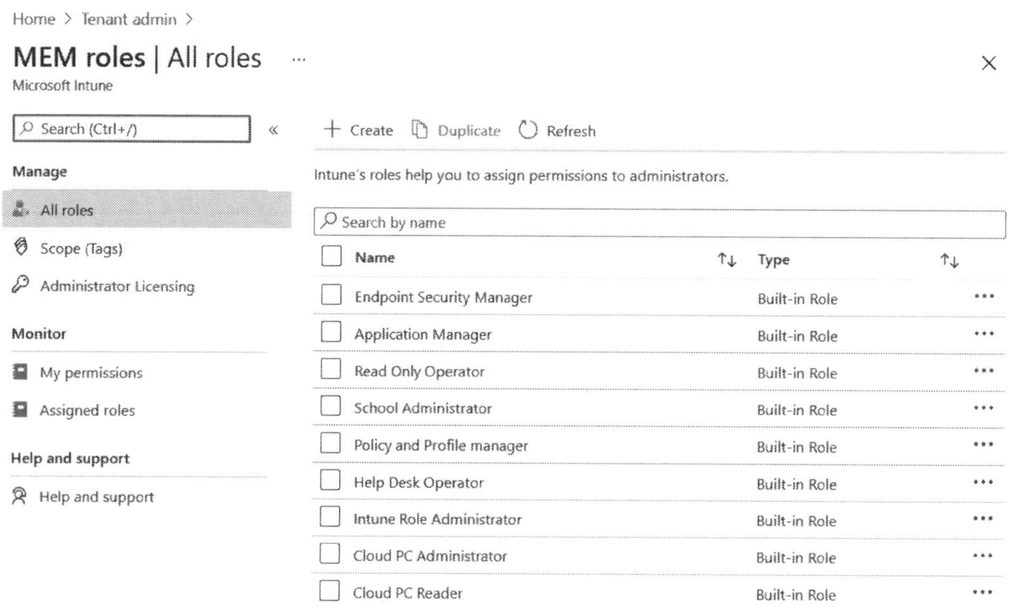

Figure 3.11 – Available Cloud PC roles in Microsoft Endpoint Manager

Assign them directly to your users or Azure AD groups to make them more dynamically available.

The Watchdog service

We shared earlier the vision of Windows 365, making things easier to use as a replacement for complex VDI-related infrastructure. The Watchdog service is the canary in the coal mine and is a great example of taking care of work that you normally must troubleshoot yourself.

After you have finished with the configuration of the on-premises network connection (explained later in this chapter in more detail), the Watchdog service will check your environment for all the prerequisites to use Windows 365, so think about the following items:

- Checking on service URLs

- Network access

- DNS resolving

- Rights to create computer accounts in the right Organization Unit

- Azure AD Connect configuration

- Subnet range – are there enough IP addresses available for your deployment?

- Endpoint connectivity (MEM and AV service URLs)

The other great thing about this feature/service is that it constantly runs in the background. For example, when something changes in your environment, it will try to fix it for you – or send you, as the IT admin, a notification with the resolution of the problem!

In the following screenshot, you can find the result of a successful Watchdog check. You see that it outlines all the requirements for a successful Windows 365 deployment, and more:

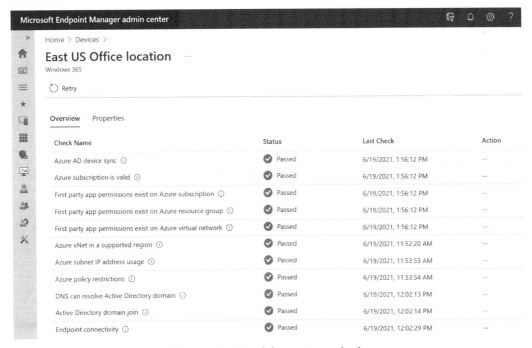

Figure 3.12 – Watchdog service – checks

Optimized Teams on Windows 365

The image gallery – Windows 10 Enterprise images that Microsoft has prepared – includes all the software that is needed to offer an optimized Teams experience as part of your Cloud PC. As an IT admin or user, you only need to install and configure the Microsoft Teams application and then you are ready to use it.

The main benefit of this approach is that you set up Teams audio and video calls directly, peer to peer, from your physical endpoint to the other person, which effectively creates the same experience as you would have on a physical endpoint running Microsoft Teams.

Some of the key benefits of the optimizations are the following:

- High-performance peer-to-peer streaming facilitated by WebRTC – traffic will flow peer-to-peer and be rendered via the endpoint.

- Devices will be redirected as the same hardware device, providing better hardware redirection support.

- On Windows 10 clients, all the benefits of the modern media stack, including hardware video decoding.

Microsoft Edge

Microsoft Edge Chromium has proven to be very fast, and its alignment with other Microsoft services, such as Microsoft Endpoint Manager, to set policies as well as the cross-platform support for the app to sync, for example, personal history and favorites settings, has been greatly received. This resulted in Edge being the default browser in Windows 10 Enterprise to date.

Sleeping tabs

The Edge Engineering team added, not so long ago, sleeping tabs to Edge Chromium as a new native feature of Edge. This feature makes it possible to reduce RAM usage per tab within your browser while you have it in inactive mode. There is also a decrease in CPU utilization while you use this feature.

The feature has been built on top of the core of Chromium's freezing technology. Freezing pauses a tab's script timers to minimize resource usage. A sleeping tab resumes automatically when clicked, which is different than discarded tabs, which require the page to fully be reloaded. This setting is enabled by default and is set to 1 hour.

Startup boost

Startup boost makes your browser start up to 41% faster! When working and browsing online, speed matters. Startup boost maximizes your computer's performance by significantly reducing the time it takes to open the browser after a device reboot or reopening the browser. Initial tests show startup times improve from between 29% and 41% with this feature.

This setting is by default enabled within our marketplace images and works on all Cloud PCs starting with 4 GB RAM upward.

The following screenshot is the **System** settings menu within Microsoft Edge. You can see both **Startup boost** and **Save resources with sleeping tabs** enabled:

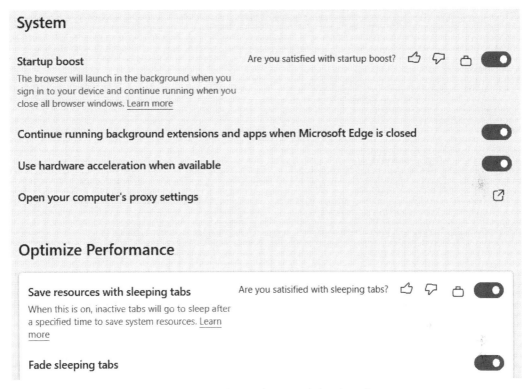

Figure 3.13 – Startup boost and sleeping tabs

Screen capture protection

The screen capture protection feature prevents sensitive information from being captured on the client endpoints. When you enable this feature, remote content will be automatically blocked or hidden in screenshots and screen shares.

It will also be hidden from malicious software that may be continuously capturing your screen's content. We recommend you disable clipboard redirection to prevent the copying of remote content to endpoints while using this feature.

To enable the screen capture protection feature, you only have to run the following command to add the designated registry key to enable the feature in your image:

> **Important Note**
>
> You can push the following setting to your Cloud PCs via PowerShell as
> a scripted action.

```
reg add "HKLM\SOFTWARE\Policies\Microsoft\Windows NT\Terminal
Services" /v fEnableScreenCaptureProtection /t REG_DWORD /d 1
```

With that, we have come to the end of this chapter. Congratulations on successfully making it this far!

Summary

In this chapter, you've learned everything about the fundamentals you need to know regarding the new Windows 365 service. *Are you ready to learn how to kick the tires!?*

In the next chapter, we will learn how to deploy Windows 365.

Questions

1. What service is used to manage, maintain, and operate your Windows 365 cloud desktops?

    A. Microsoft Endpoint Manager

    B. Microsoft Endpoint Configuration Manager

    C. System Center Configuration Manager

2. Is Windows 365 fully integrated and does it work out of the box with other Microsoft 365 cloud services?

    A. Yes

    B. No

Answers

1. (A)
2. (A)

Further reading

If you want to learn more about Windows 365 after reading this section, please go to one of the following chapters of this book:

- *Chapter 4, Deploying Windows 365*
- *Chapter 14, Monitoring and Endpoint Analytics*
- *Chapter 17, Troubleshooting Windows 365*

4
Deploying Windows 365

In this chapter, you'll learn everything you need to know about how to deploy Windows 365, what the requirements are, and the tips and tricks you have to know.

After this chapter, you'll know everything you need to get started with this new Microsoft cloud service, which simplifies deployment as well as cloud PC maintenance with Microsoft Endpoint Manager.

This chapter is very comprehensive and covers the following topics:

- Technical requirements for deploying Windows 365
- Self-service capabilities – IT admin
- Azure AD – MyApps unified (workspace) portal
- Auto-subscribing users in the Remote Desktop client
- Autopilot and cloud PCs – thin client (Kiosk)
- Monitoring and analytics
- Shadow users with Quick Assist
- Windows 11
- Microsoft Managed Desktop

Technical requirements for deploying Windows 365

To use Windows 365, you must meet the following requirements:

- The following are the licenses you will need to use Cloud PC/Windows 365:

  - *Users with Windows Pro endpoints*: W10 E3 + EMS1 E3 or M365 F3/E3/E5/BP

  - *Users with non-Windows Pro endpoints*: Win VDA E3 + EMS1 E3 or M365 F3/E3/F5/BP

- An Azure subscription:

  - Subscription owner (set up network connection)

- **Virtual Network** (**VNet**) in an Azure subscription:

  - Azure VNet must route to a DNS server that can resolve **Active Directory** (**AD**) records either on-premises or on Azure.

- This AD must be in sync with Azure AD to provide **Hybrid Azure AD join** (**HAADJ**). **Azure AD join** (**AADJ**) is currently being worked on.

- Microsoft Intune supported licenses (for example, Microsoft 365 E3):

  - Intune Service Admin or a cloud PC administrator

We will cover some of the subscriptions that are required in more detail.

Azure subscription

Make sure that you have an Azure subscription to configure the Azure VNet; that is, for the on-premises connection within Windows 365. If you already have one set up, you can skip this step.

> **Important Note**
> An Azure subscription will no longer be required as soon as we support Azure AD native. This will happen soon. Windows 365 Business already supports this at the time of writing!

Azure VNet

One of the requirements of using Windows 365 is that you need to have an Azure VNet. This network will be used as a gateway to the internet as part of your cloud PC. If you already have one, this will be an easy task to perform!

Azure VNet – DNS configuration

As part of the HAADJ requirement, you need to have a line-of-sight connection to one of your DNS servers that can talk with your Active Directory domain.

Always make sure to change your DNS to **Custom** and enter the IP address of the DNS service environment that can resolve your AD DS domain:

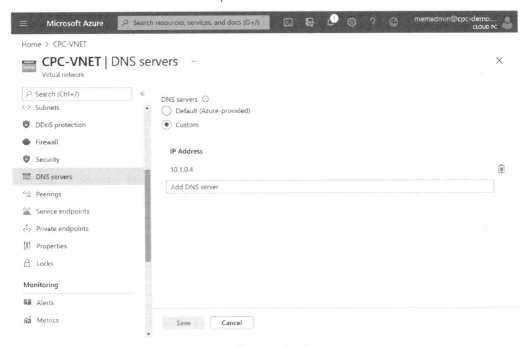

Figure 4.1 – Changing DNS to custom

Azure VNet – required related URLs and ports

To use all Windows 365 services, you must allow traffic to the following service URLs since these services are key to using the service successfully:

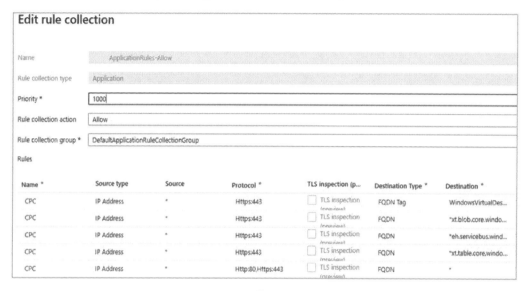

Figure 4.2 – Allowing all URLs

> **Important Note**
> Make sure to allow all the URLs and ports via either Azure Firewall or a third-party firewall. The best way to do this is with tags based on the wildcard and FQDN domain.

Microsoft Endpoint Manager and AVD – service URLs

The following URLs and ports are required to use the Windows 365 services. The service will not function properly when some are not added correctly:

- `https://docs.microsoft.com/en-us/azure/virtual-desktop/safe-url-list`

- `https://docs.microsoft.com/en-us/mem/intune/fundamentals/intune-endpoints:`

  - `cpcsacnrysa1prodprna02.blob.core.windows.net`

  - `cpcsacnrysa1prodprap01.blob.core.windows.net`

  - `cpcsacnrysa1prodprau01.blob.core.windows.net`

- cpcsacnrysa1prodpreu01.blob.core.windows.net
- cpcsacnrysa1prodpreu02.blob.core.windows.net
- cpcsacnrysa1prodprna01.blob.core.windows.net

Now, let's look at the network requirements for the Remote Desktop Protocol.

Remote Desktop Protocol requirements

Windows 365 uses the **Remote Desktop Protocol** (**RDP**), so you should follow the same network bandwidth requirements needed for each scenario in your organization.

Please use the following table as guidance while designing your network infrastructure environment for Windows 365:

Scenario	Default mode	H.264/ AVC 444 mode	Description
Idle	0.3 Kbps	0.3 Kbps	The user has paused their work and there are no active screen updates.
Microsoft Word	100-150 Kbps	200-300 Kbps	The user is actively working with Microsoft Word: typing, pasting graphics, and switching between documents.
Microsoft Excel	150-200 Kbps	400-500 Kbps	The user is actively working with Microsoft Excel: multiple cells with formulas and charts are updated simultaneously.
Microsoft PowerPoint	4-4.5 Mbps	1.6-1.8 Mbps	The user is actively working with Microsoft PowerPoint: typing, pasting, modifying rich graphics, and using slide transition effects.
Web browsing	6-6.5 Mbps	0.9-1 Mbps	The user is actively working with a graphically rich website that contains multiple static and animated images. The user scrolls the pages both horizontally and vertically.
Image gallery	3.3-3.6 Mbps	0.7-0.8 Mbps	The user is actively working with the image gallery application: browsing, zooming, resizing, and rotating images.
A video playback	8.5-9.5 Mbps	2.5-2.8 Mbps	The user is watching a 30 FPS video that consumes half of the screen.
Fullscreen video playback	7.5-8.5 Mbps	2.5-3.1 Mbps	The user is watching a 30 FPS video that's maximized to full screen.

Hybrid Azure AD joined

Before you start configuring Windows 365, you must make sure that your environment is HAADJ-enabled. It's relatively simple to activate. If you aren't already using it, you just have to reopen the **Azure AD Connect** setup and select the **Configure Hybrid Azure AD join** option as part of the **Device options** menu. You can learn more about this in *Chapter 13, Identity and Security Management*, or by going to https://docs.microsoft.com/en-us/azure/active-directory/devices/hybrid-azuread-join-managed-domains.

> **Important Note**
>
> Azure AD native support is coming soon. The self-service version of Windows 365 small business is already supported for Azure AD.

Here, you can find the main Azure AD Connect wizard configuration screen. Here, you need to select **Configure Hybrid Azure AD join** to use Windows 365 Enterprise:

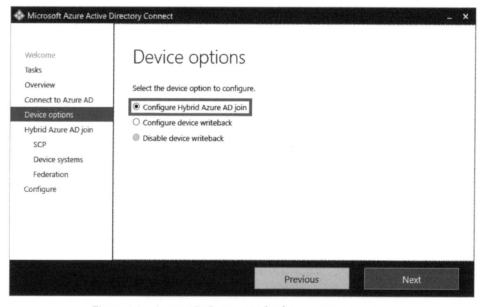

Figure 4.3 – Azure AD Connect Hybrid Azure AD join setup

Once your machines have been created, you will see them listed with a join type of **Hybrid Azure AD joined** in the Azure AD portal:

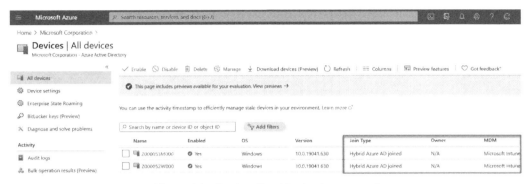

Figure 4.4 – Devices listed in the Azure portal

Purchasing and assigning cloud PC licenses via the Microsoft 365 admin center portal

Make sure that you have either a trial or production license with Microsoft Intune assigned to your tenant before moving on. Perform the following steps:

1. Go to `https://admin.microsoft.com/` and purchase a Windows 365 license per size.

2. Go to **Active users**.

3. Open the required user(s).

4. Assign the Windows 365 cloud PC size license.

The following screenshot shows how I assigned an average knowledge worker Windows 365 cloud PC license to my newborn son, Mason, an avid Windows user already:

Figure 4.5 – Assigning a license

Make sure that the AAD user's location has been set in Azure AD before moving on.

You can also perform this from the Azure portal or automatically via Azure AD group assignment if you're working with more bulk/Enterprise users.

On-premises network connections

On-premises network connections are required so that we can create cloud PCs, join them to a specified domain, and manage them with Microsoft Endpoint Manager.

Before you start, create a connection to an on-premises environment for your line-of-sight connection to AD DS. You should have Network Contributor rights on the VNet to perform these steps.

> **Important Note**
>
> The **Organizational Unit (OU)** section is optional. If you enter the OU location, make sure you enter the **distinguished name (DN)**.

The steps for creating an on-premises network connection are as follows:

1. Click on **On-premises network connection** and then + **Create connection**:

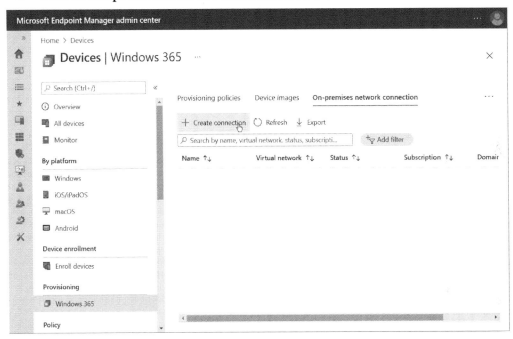

Figure 4.6 – Creating a connection

2. Enter the Azure VNet connection information and suggested subnet where you will create your cloud PCs:

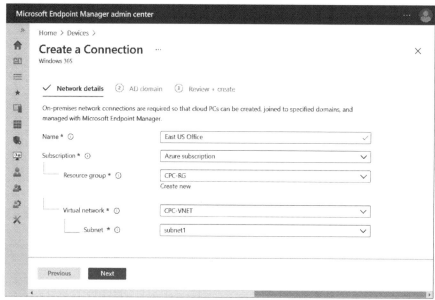

Figure 4.7 – Network details

3. Enter the required AD DS information:

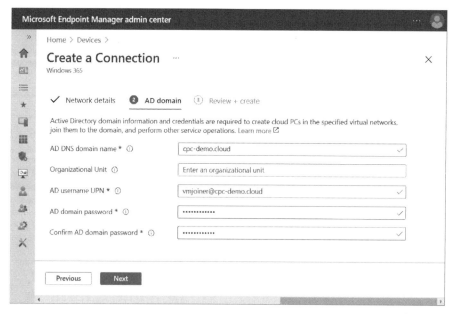

Figure 4.8 – AD domain setup

4. Once all the information has been reviewed and deemed correct, click on **Review + Create**:

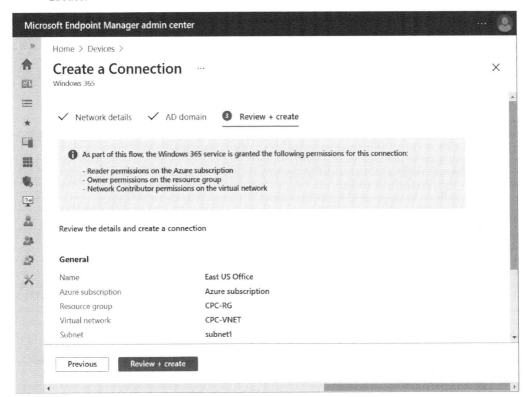

Figure 4.9 – Reviewing all the details

> **Important Note**
> Make sure that the person creating the network connection has reader permissions on the Azure subscription, owner permissions on the resource group, and Network Contributor rights permissions on the VNet.

5.   The next few steps will configure your on-premises network connection. This can take up to 30 minutes to complete. The Watchdog service will do its work on the backend to ensure you are not blocked from implementing a cloud PC:

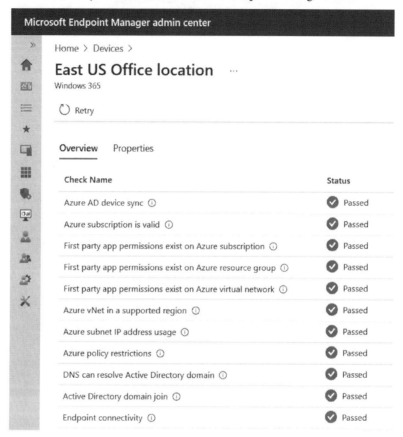

Figure 4.10 – Configuration complete

Now that we have created our on-premises connection, let's provision a cloud PC.

Provisioning a cloud PC

Before we start, make sure that the account you are using has at least the Intune Service Admin role assigned. After provisioning, you can set the rights back to standard MEM RBAC. Perform the following steps:

1. Go to the Admin center portal's **Windows 365** blade to provision policies.

2. Click on + **Create policy**:

Figure 4.11 – Creating a provisioning policy

3. Provide a name for the policy; for example, `East US Office`.

4. Select the on-premises network connection (location) where you wish to place your cloud PCs:

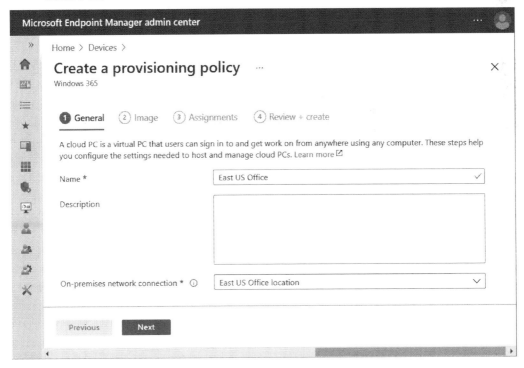

Figure 4.12 – Selecting an on-premises network connection

5. Select your image type, either a gallery or custom image.

6. Click on **Select**.

7. Select your Windows 10 Enterprise image. We recommend that you use the one with Microsoft 365 Apps and Teams pre-installed for the best experience:

Figure 4.13 – Select an image

All your corporate apps will be added once the cloud PC comes online via Microsoft Endpoint Manager.

> **Important Note**
> You can also select a custom image with all your agents and apps pre-installed. The steps to create one will be explained in the next section of this chapter.

8. Select the Azure AD group to apply the provisioning policy.

> **Important Note**
> Every user in that group with a cloud PC license assigned will receive a cloud PC provisioned based on the image and on-premises network connection configuration.

I'm using the **Finance users – AAD** group.

9. Confirm the group's configuration and click **Next**:

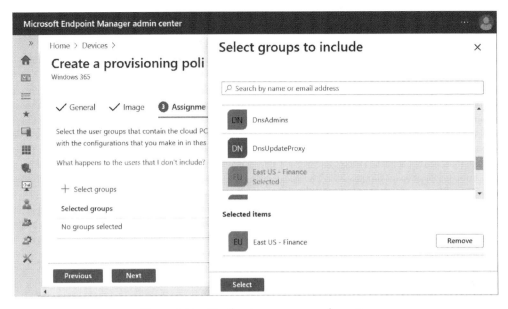

Figure 4.14 – Confirming a group configuration

10. Review your policy settings and click **Create**:

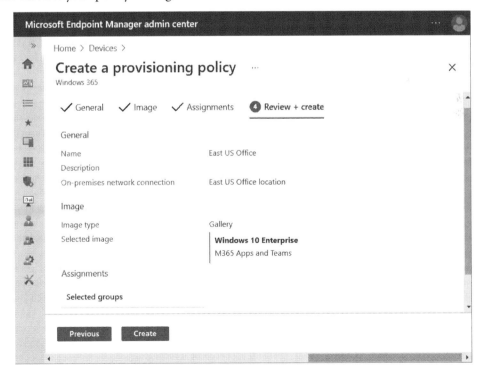

Figure 4.15 – Reviewing the provisioning policy settings

11. If everything has run successfully, you'll see the new provisioning policy in the list:

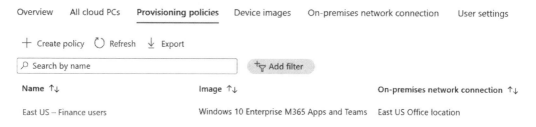

Figure 4.16 – Provisioning policy added successfully

The new cloud PCs will start to provision directly for the AAD group members that you assigned to the provisioning policy. After 20-30 minutes, your cloud PCs will be ready to use and their status will have changed to **Provisioned**.

User settings – self-service

Reducing the burden of work on your IT support department and IT admins is the main goal when using the self-service options within Windows 365. When users have permissions for self-service upgrades (as shown in the following screenshot), they can perform reboots of their Cloud Desktops, as well as upgrading to larger VM sizes for better performance that fits their needs:

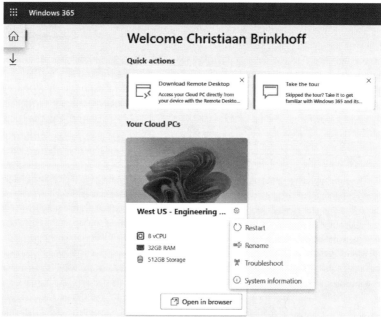

Figure 4.17 – Windows 365 web portal – self-service user settings

Self-service upgrades allow users to upgrade the performance and storage capacities of their cloud PCs without admin approval. This will *NOT* incur any additional costs for your organization. The next section will go over the supported actions for the IT admin.

Self-service capabilities – IT admin

From within Microsoft Endpoint Manager's **Devices** menu, IT admins can reboot cloud PCs remotely. The **Restart** button, which sits next to the **Sync** button to enforce MDM policy settings to the cloud PC, could also be a useful setting to provide.

Reprovisioning the cloud PC

You could also reprovision your cloud PC via the **Reprovisioning** button. Your machine will be reprovisioned, meaning that it will start from scratch in the same way as you started it initially, without any customization needing to be installed on the cloud PC.

You can find the **Reprovision** button under **Devices | Overview | Reprovisioning**:

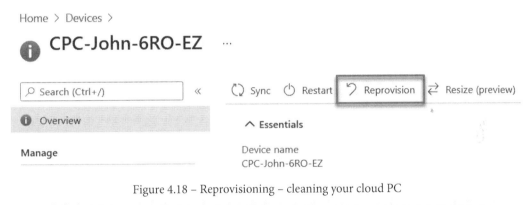

Figure 4.18 – Reprovisioning – cleaning your cloud PC

> **Important Note**
> You need (at least) cloud PC administrator permissions to be able to do this.

IT admins will get the following notification prompt to confirm that reprovisioning works as an extra safety check:

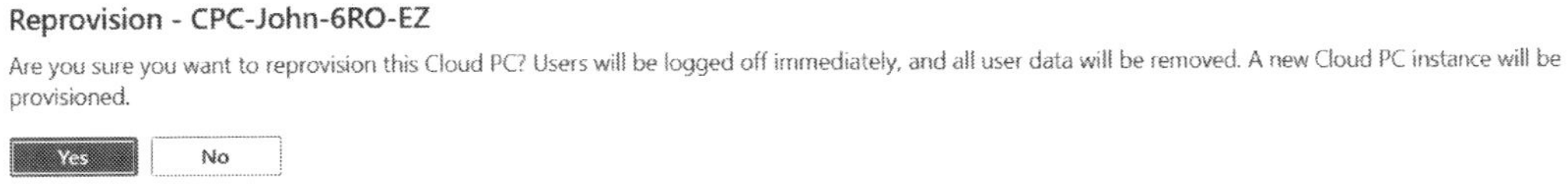

Reprovision - CPC-John-6RO-EZ

Are you sure you want to reprovision this Cloud PC? Users will be logged off immediately, and all user data will be removed. A new Cloud PC instance will be provisioned.

[Yes]   [No]

Figure 4.19 – A prompt for the admin to confirm

Local administrator

Within the Microsoft Endpoint Manager version of cloud PC, users do not have local administrator rights out of the box. When you want all or some of your users to be local administrators, we can build the following feature into Microsoft Endpoint Manager as a configuration profile that makes users local administrators.

Make sure that you only configure the configuration profile for the devices or users that need these rights.

VM SKU upgrades (preview feature)

As an IT admin, you will be able to upgrade the Cloud VM to a bigger size. This means that the user will go, for example, from 1vCPU/2 GB RAM to 2vCPU/4 GB RAM so that more resources are available for their workload.

You can find this feature (in preview) in the **Microsoft Endpoint Manager** portal, under **Devices**, upon clicking the **Resize** button:

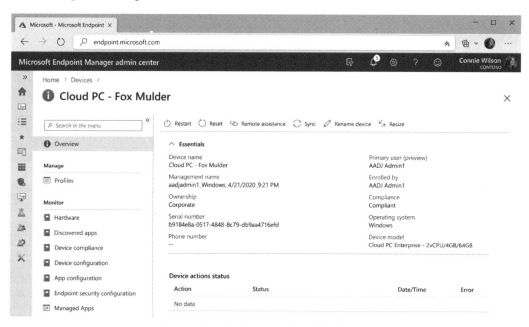

Figure 4.20 – Resizing the cloud PC feature

Image management – creating a custom image (optional)

In traditional VDI environments, rolling out virtual desktops always starts with creating a custom image, also known as a **golden image**. Microsoft understands the need for this, which is why this approach is also supported in Windows 365.

However, the recommendation is to only use the image for baseline applications, agents, OS updates, and language packs. Then, you must add the other configuration items and applications via Microsoft Endpoint Manager and Intune.

> **Important Note**
> This step is optional. Microsoft will also provide marketplace images for both Windows 10 and Windows 11 that you can select during the provisioning policy creation process with Microsoft 365 Apps, Edge, and Teams optimizations pre-installed.

When you wish to build images before you start the cloud PC provisioning process, perform the following steps:

1. Click on + **Add**:

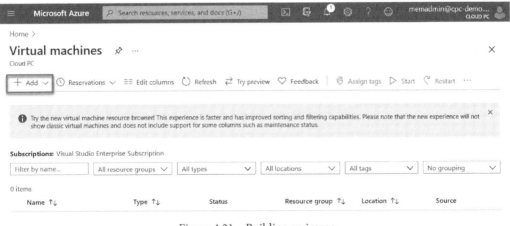

Figure 4.21 – Building an image

2. Create a VM image based on your specifics.

3.   Select **Windows 10 Enterprise or Windows 11 – Gen**, as shown here:

> **Important Note**
>
> Windows 365 supports Windows 10 Enterprise and Windows 11 single-session. Only select Windows 10 Enterprise multi-session when you want to create a custom image for Azure Virtual Desktop.

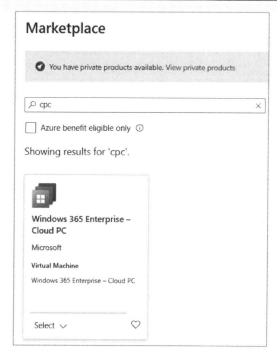

Figure 4.22 – Cloud PC images

4.   Fill in all the other properties and add the custom image to the right Azure VNet (Standard SSD at a minimum) for proper performance.

5.   In the **Advanced** tab, make sure **Gen 2** is selected for **VM generation**; for example, **Windows 10 Enterprise Cloud PC, Version 20H2 + Microsoft 365 Apps - Gen2**:

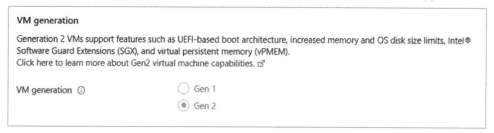

Figure 4.23 – Advanced tab

Important Note

Make sure that your image is created as Gen 2; Microsoft no longer supports adding new Gen 1 images as a part of Windows 365 Enterprise.

6.   Click on **Review + create**:

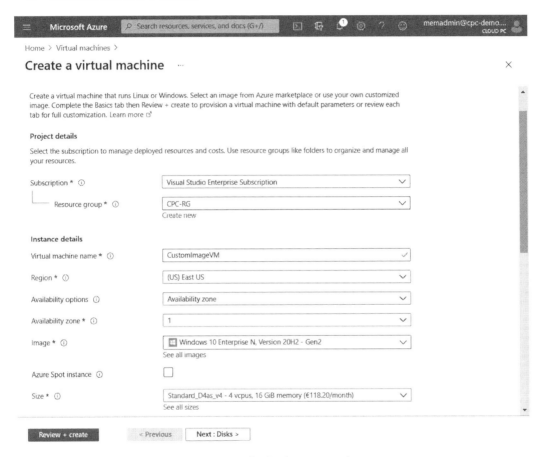

Figure 4.24 – Reviewing your settings

7.   Once the VM has been provisioned, use Azure Bastion or RDP to connect to the custom image virtual machine.

8.   Install your agents and other software on the virtual machine.

> **Important Note**
>
> We recommend that you keep the image as clean as possible and add line-of-business apps via Microsoft Endpoint Manager – Intune to make the image management process simple and modern. Microsoft also provides Microsoft 365 apps within pre-baked marketplace images.

9. Run **sysprep** via the `%WINDIR%\system32\sysprep\sysprep.exe / generalize /shutdown /oobe` command in the VM image.

10. Once you're ready, stop the virtual machine to put it in a stopped (de-allocated) state:

Figure 4.25 – Stopping the VM

11. Click on the **Capture** button to start capturing the image:

Figure 4.26 – Capturing the image

12. Wait for the VM to change its status to **Stopped** (de-allocated).

13. Select **No, capture only a managed image**. Then, click on **Review + create**:

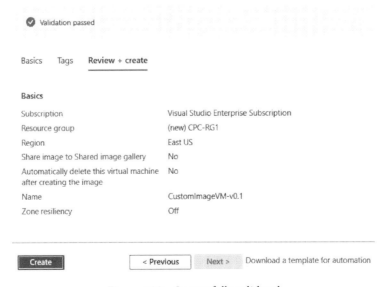

Create an image   ···

Before creating the image. this virtual machine will be deallocated automatically. You can share this image to Shared image gallery. Learn more

Project details

Subscription   Visual Studio Enterprise Subscription   ⌄

⌐⌐⌐⌐⌐⌐⌐⌐⌐ Resource group *   (New) CPC-RG1   ⌄
                                                    Create new

Instance details

Region   (US) East US   ⌄

Share image to Shared image gallery ⓘ   ◯ Yes, share it to a gallery as an image version.
                                            ◉ No, capture only a managed image.

Automatically delete this virtual machine   ☐
after creating the image   ⓘ

Zone resiliency ⓘ   ☐

> ❶ Before creating an image. use "generalize" to prepare the Windows guest OS on the virtual machine. If you create an image
>   from a virtual machine that hasn't been generalized, any virtual machines created from that image won't start. Learn more ↗

Name * ⓘ   CustomImageVM-v0.1   ✓

[Review + create]   [< Previous] [Next : Tags >]

Figure 4.27 – Reviewing your settings

14. Confirm the summary and click on **Create**. The process will now sysprep the image automatically:

Create an image   ···

✅ Validation passed

Basics   Tags   **Review + create**

Basics

Subscription   Visual Studio Enterprise Subscription
Resource group   (new) CPC-RG1
Region   East US
Share image to Shared image gallery   No
Automatically delete this virtual machine   No
after creating the image
Name   CustomImageVM-v0.1
Zone resiliency   Off

[Create]   [< Previous] [Next >]   Download a template for automation

Figure 4.28 – Successfully validated

The image will now be prepared. This process only takes a minute or so.

15. Once the process is ready, you can select a custom image under **Cloud PC – Provisioning policies** as a custom image in Windows 365.

16. Switch back to the Microsoft Endpoint Manager admin center. Go to **Device images** and then click on **+ Add**:

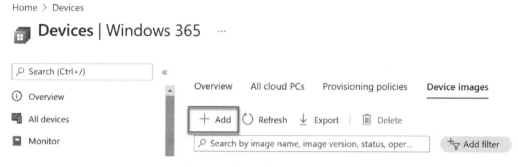

Figure 4.29 – Adding an image

Provide the image's name, version, and the OS build version of Windows 10 Enterprise, as well as the source image.

17. Click on **Upload**:

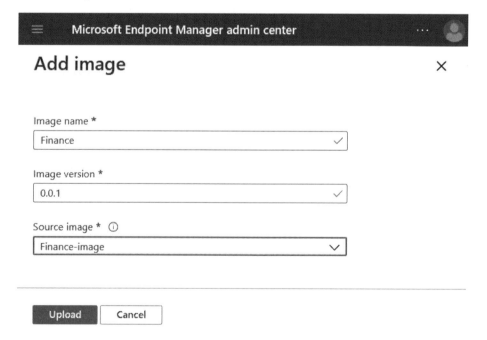

Figure 4.30 – Uploading an image

> **Important Note**
>
> The admin/service account adding the custom image needs contributor or owner role permissions on the storage account's storage blob container.

18. The image upload process will start. Once the process is complete, start creating the provisioning policy, or modify an existing policy.

19. When you update the image, all the new provisioned cloud PCs will receive the new version. Existing cloud PC VMs should initiate a reprovisioning task to get the updates.

> **Important Note**
>
> Be aware of changing existing provisioning policies where users already have their cloud PC VM provisioned. It's not possible to change the image from a marketplace image to a custom image. Your cloud PC will enter a grace period.
>
> You can update your images as much as you want as part of provisioning policies. All the new provisioned cloud PCs will get the latest version, while the existing cloud PCs must be triggered for re-provisioning. You learned how you can initiate this earlier in this chapter.

Supported endpoints

You can access your cloud PCs via Windows 10, Windows 10 IoT Enterprise, and Windows 7 using the available Remote Desktop clients. There are also multiple other clients available for mobile platforms and other operating systems. Linux client support is coming soon, and users can use the web portal on Linux today!

The following table explains the differences between the different endpoints that are supported for Windows 365 at the time of writing:

	Windows Desktop	Store client	Android	iOS/ iPadOS	macOS	Web
Keyboard	X	X	X	X	X	X
Mouse	X	X	X	X*	X	X
Touch	X	X	X	X		X
Serial port	X					
USB	X					
Teams AV Redirection	X					
Multimedia redirection	Coming soon					
Multi-monitor	16 monitors					
Dynamic resolution	X	X			X	X
Screen capture protection	X					
Cameras	X		X	X	X	
Start menu integration	X					
Clipboard	X	X	Text	Text, images	X	Text
Local drive/ storage	X		X	X	X	
Accessibility	X					
Location	X					
Microphones	X	X	Coming soon	X	X	X
Printers	X				X (CUPS only)	PDF print
Scanners	X					
Smart cards	X				X	
Speakers	X	X	X	X	X	X

This makes it easier for you to adjust the device based on the requirements for redirection. We're constantly improving the clients, so there's a likely chance that some features will be supported when you start reading this book.

Supported endpoints – device redirection settings

In terms of needing to support a camera or serial port redirection, this isn't default-enabled as part of the Windows 365 baseline configuration. Out of the box, Windows 365 allows you to redirect local audio, your clipboard, and your microphone.

To allow for more redirection features, you must allocate different configuration sets from within Microsoft Endpoint Manager's Intune configuration profiles. The reason why we left so many settings disabled is due to security. Our service aligns with our zero-trust principles, so we left it disabled by default to let the customers decide what best fits their use case.

By default, end users will have a larger set of features, and admins can choose whether to allow all these redirections or to create policies to block them.

You can enable these settings like so:

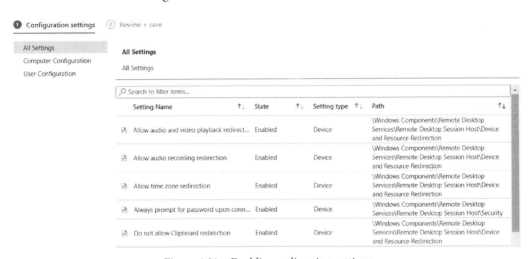

Figure 4.31 – Enabling redirection settings

Information Worker Portal (IWP)

As explained in the *Supported endpoints* section, end users can access their cloud PC from different platforms. The web portal is the most unified method as it only requires an HTML5 supported browser such as Microsoft Edge.

To simplify access, we created the IWP, which you can see in the following screenshot. The portal allows end users to choose between accessing their cloud PC via the browser or the Remote Desktop (MSRDC) client.

If the user has permission to provide self-service upgrades, they will also see the **Restart workspace** option while clicking on the three digits to reboot their cloud PC in case of an emergency, or even due to performance-related issues that require the machine to be rebooted.

To access the IWP portal, users must go to `http://windows365.microsoft.com/` or `https://cloudpc.microsoft.com/` and follow these steps:

1. Log in with your Azure AD credentials, just like you do for other Microsoft cloud services.

2. Upon completing the login process, the IWP portal will be presented to the end user, including all the cloud PC sizes, ready for you to log in.

3. Click on your cloud PC. Open it in your browser, like so:

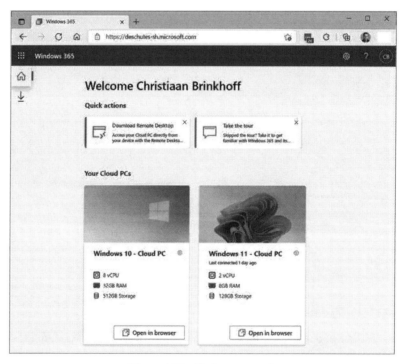

Figure 4.32 – End user portal

You can also restart your cloud PC here.

4. Are you looking for the different endpoint clients we support within Windows 365? Click on the download icon under the home icon in the top-left corner:

Figure 4.33 – Downloading the Remote Desktop client endpoint supported apps

5. Choose your local resources redirection preference.

6. For a couple of months, you have also been able to upload data from your device when you connect via the web portal via the new file transfer upload feature. Enabling this will create a network drive on this computer so that you can transfer files from your local endpoint to your cloud PC:

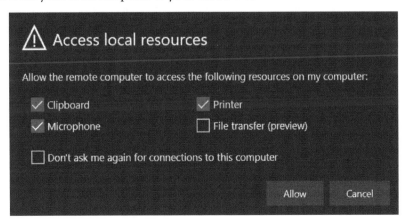

Figure 4.34 – Allowing access to local resources

7. Once your credentials have been verified, you will be logged into your cloud PC – clientless via your browser!

8. You can also run your session full screen in your browser by clicking the button shown in the following screenshot, which can be found in the right-hand corner:

Figure 4.35 – Option to run in full screen

9. Here's a cloud PC session running fullscreen in a browser:

Figure 4.36 – Fullscreen

In the near future, or perhaps by the time you read this book, we will be upgrading our portal experience so that it has a more native look and feel. Here's a sneak peek into that experience:

Figure 4.37 – Future-looking end user logon experience

Now, let's look at Azure AD's MyApps unified workspace portal.

Azure AD – MyApps unified (workspace) portal

You can also access your cloud PC environment via MyApps and consolidate all your other **Software-as-a-Service (SaaS)** applications in one unified portal experience.

You can open the `https://myapps.microsoft.com/` portal on your computer or from the mobile version of the Edge browser on an iOS or Android mobile device.

You can find the end user experience of Azure AD MyApps in the following sections of Windows 365. When you click on the cloud PC app, you will be redirected to the IWP portal using single sign-on:

Figure 4.38 – MyApps portal

Multi-factor authentication and conditional access

We recommend going to *Chapter 13, Identity and Security Management*, later in this book, to learn more about conditional access.

Multi-factor authentication is enabled on your Azure AD tenant by default to ensure that hackers and other intruders stay out of your environment. Enabling this feature on Windows 365 will decrease the possibility of you being hacked by 99.9%. It also incorporates the benefits of simplifying your management layer as the top layer for your operations. Long story short, you should enable this!

It's also fairly easy to do. As per Windows 365, we have a cloud PC app that we can select in the **Conditional access** configuration menu. The steps are as follows:

1. Start the configuration. Go to the **Conditional access** menu in the **Endpoint security** menu within Microsoft Endpoint Manager:

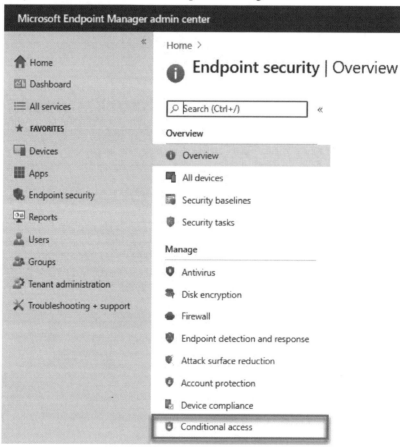

Figure 4.39 – Conditional access

2. Create a new policy and enter a custom name for your Azure MFA policy. Once you've done this, you can go through all the layers in the wizard to activate the correct settings to trigger MFA's secondary authentication:

Figure 4.40 – Entering the name of your policy

3. Select the list of users and/or AAD groups you wish to filter and activate MFA for. I am going to pick cloud PC users.

> **Important Note**
>
> When selecting **All users**, make sure to not lock yourself out! This policy will affect all of your users. We recommend applying a policy to a small set of users first to verify that it behaves as expected.

4. Open the cloud apps or **Actions** menu and select **cloud PC** as the cloud app. Make sure that the cloud app ID for **cloud PC** is `0af06dc6-e4b5-4f28-818e-e78e62d137a5`:

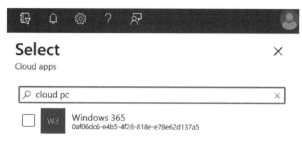

Figure 4.41 – Selecting Windows 365

5. Click on **Conditions** to start the creation process. This will allow you to control the user access layer based on signals from conditions such as risk, device platform, location, client apps, or device state.

6. Select the settings that align best with your security requirements. I'm going to use the device marked as **Compliant** to make sure users with a compliant device can connect to a cloud PC without entering MFA.

> **Important Note**
> All other accounts will be enforced by the MFA prompt.

7. Move to the **Grant** menu. Select the settings that align best with your security requirements.

8. Make sure that you select **Require multi-factor authentication**:

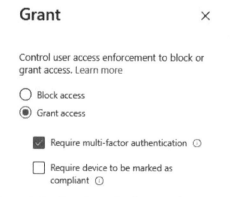

Figure 4.42 – Require multi-factor authentication

9. Go to the **Session** menu. This part is optional; however, the sign-in frequency makes it possible to enforce MFA prompts for as little as 1 hour after your existing token expires.

> **Important Note**
> Especially for **Bring-Your-Own-Device (BYOD)** scenarios, this could be beneficial. Existing sessions on your cloud PC will remain active within the time you configure this setting.

10. The persistent browser feature makes it possible to remain signed in after closing and reopening a browser window.

11. Enable and create the policy by clicking on **ON** and then **Create**.

12. Make sure that the **Enable policy** setting is set to **Off** by default.

13. Confirm that the policy has been added with the **On** state.

Next time you log into your cloud PC, you'll be prompted for MFA!

Security baselines for a cloud PC

Using a virtualized desktop in the Microsoft cloud requires a different security baseline than for physical Windows PCs. Therefore, we created a new baseline optimized for cloud PCs in the profile catalog. Make sure that you select the cloud PC security baseline for the best performance and security settings for your business:

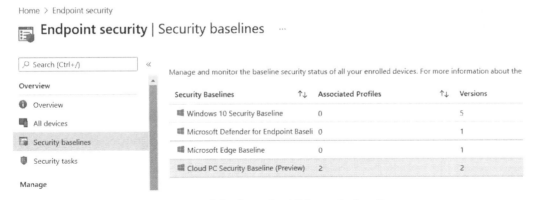

Figure 4.43 – Selecting a cloud PC security baseline

Distributing the Remote Desktop client via Microsoft Endpoint Manager – Intune to your physical endpoints

In this section, you'll learn how to enroll the Remote Desktop client on your physical Windows 10 Enterprise endpoints to use them for Windows 365. The Windows 10 Enterprise – Remote Desktop client gives the richest experience and device redirections available. You can find the full support matrix later in this chapter.

As we explained earlier, in our IWP portal, you have the option to download all the clients manually to your endpoints too; however, as we appreciate that this isn't a scalable option for enterprises, we will also cover enrolling the Remote Desktop – Windows 365 client via Microsoft Endpoint Manager – Intune to your end users' managed devices:

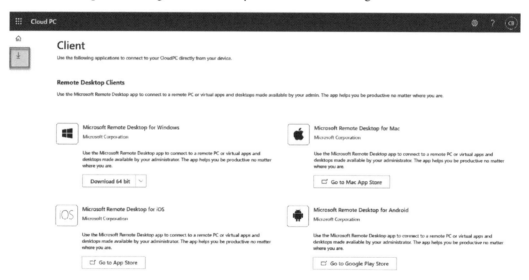

Figure 4.44 – Remote Desktop client

The following steps only work when your physical endpoint has been enrolled in Intune and they have been MDM enrolled. Let's start with the configuration!

1. Download the Microsoft Win32 Content Prep Tool (`https://github.com/Microsoft/Microsoft-Win32-Content-Prep-Tool`).

2. Unzip the tool on the `C:\` drive (you can pick a random folder if you wish):

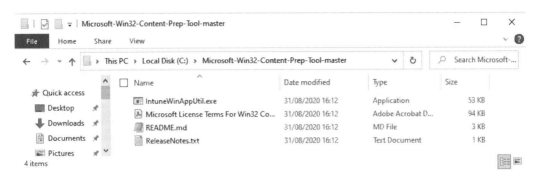

Figure 4.45 – Unzipping the Prep Tool

3. Download the latest Remote Desktop client from `http://aka.ms/wvdclient`.

4. Save the **Microsoft Installer** (**MSI**) in the same folder where the Prep Tool is.

5. Create the Win32 `.Intunewin` package.

6. Open PowerShell and change the directory to the Intune Prep Tool's location; for example, `C:\Microsoft-Win32-Content-Prep-Tool-master`:

```
cd "C:\Microsoft-Win32-Content-Prep-Tool-master"
```

7. Run `\IntuneWinAppUtil.exe` and fill in the following requirements:

    - Specify the source folder as `C:\Microsoft-Win32-Content-Prep-Tool-master`.

    - Specify the setup file as `RemoteDesktop_1.2.1755.0_x64.msi`.

    - Specify the output folder as `C:\Microsoft-Win32-Content-Prep-Tool-master`.

    - **Do you want to specify the catalog folder (Y/N)?** N.

    You can customize the folders as you wish, as shown here:

```
Administrator: Windows PowerShell                                          —  □  ×
Windows PowerShell
Copyright (C) Microsoft Corporation. All rights reserved.

Try the new cross-platform PowerShell https://aka.ms/pscore6

PS C:\WINDOWS\system32> cd\
PS C:\> cd .\Microsoft-Win32-Content-Prep-Tool-master\
PS C:\Microsoft-Win32-Content-Prep-Tool-master> .\IntuneWinAppUtil.exe
Please specify the source folder: C:\Microsoft-Win32-Content-Prep-Tool-master
Please specify the setup file: RemoteDesktop_1.2.1755.0_x64.msi
Please specify the output folder: C:\Microsoft-Win32-Content-Prep-Tool-master
Do you want to specify catalog folder (Y/N)?N
```

Figure 4.46 – Running .\IntuneWinAppUtil.exe

If everything runs correctly, the following creation wizard will start:

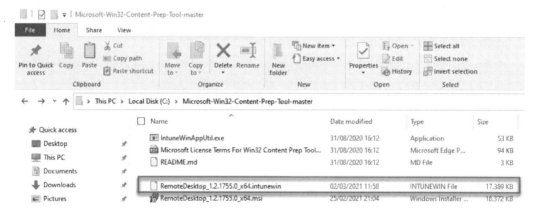

Figure 4.47 – Running successfully

8. If everything runs successfully, you will see the `.intunewim` file listed in the folder. Now, we can switch to Microsoft Endpoint Manager:

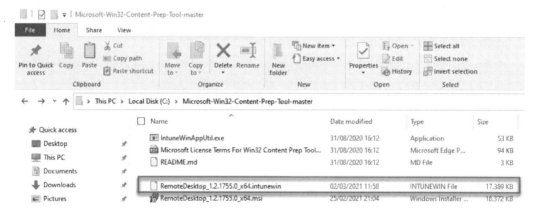

Figure 4.48 – The Intune win32 package has been added

9. Go to `http://endpoint.microsoft.com/` to continue this configuration process in the Microsoft Endpoint Manager admin center.

10. Go to **Apps | Windows apps | Add**:

Figure 4.49 – Adding a new Windows app

11. Select **Windows app (Win32)**.

12. Click on **Select app package file**.

13. Browse and select the `.Intunewim` package file we created earlier, which includes the Remote Desktop client (MSRDC).

14. Click on **OK**:

Figure 4.50 – Selecting a package file

15. On the next screen, you can customize the name of the app.

    Optional: Set **Company Portal** to **Yes** if you wish to make installing the enrollment optional for users:

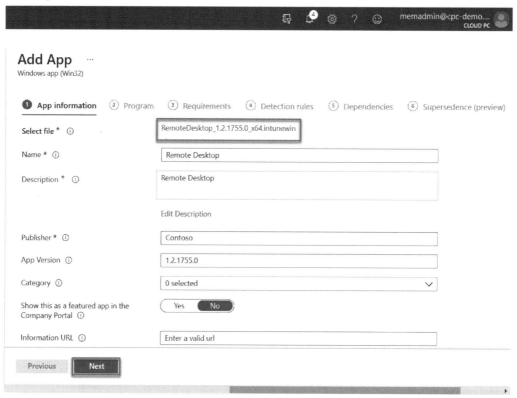

Figure 4.51 – Name of the app

16. Click on **Next**.

17. Use the following settings:

```
msiexec /i " RemoteDesktop_1.2.1755.0_x64.msi" /qn
ALLUSERS=2 MSIINSTALLPERUSER=1
```

The following screenshot shows these settings:

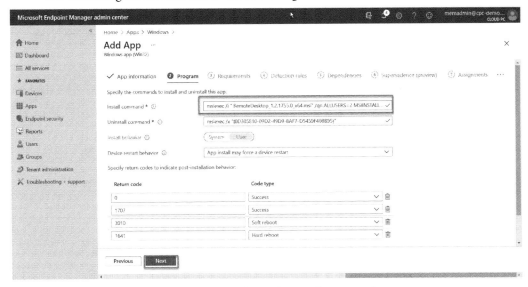

Figure 4.52 – Defining the install command

18. Provide the minimum app requirements:

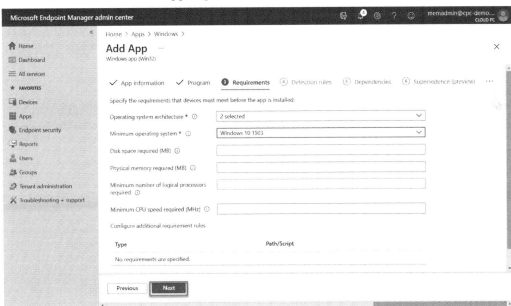

Figure 4.53 – Adding requirements

19. Create a detection rule based on the manual configuration.

20. Select **MSI** to perform the detection based on the MSI product code to see whether the app is already installed on the endpoint.

21. Click on **OK**:

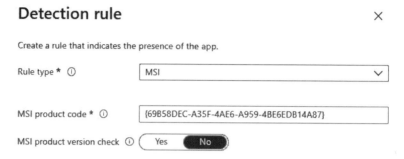

Figure 4.54 – Detection rule

22. We can skip **Dependencies**. Then, click **Next**:

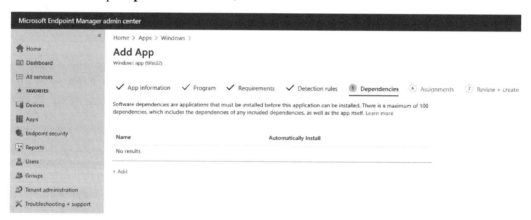

Figure 4.55 – Skipping Dependencies

23. Assign the application to an AAD group, or all devices, to enforce deployment to your physical Windows PCs/endpoints.

> **Important Note**
> The client should not be installed inside your cloud PC VM, but on your physical endpoint. If your physical endpoint is not MEM managed, please update/install the Remote Desktop client manually from here: `http://aka.ms/CPCclient`.

24. Click on **Select** and then **Next**.

25. Edit the assignment if you want to enforce the enrollment or update process.

Optional: There's a new preview feature available, called **Supersedence**, in Microsoft Endpoint Manager. This new feature enables you to update and replace existing Win32 apps with newer versions of the same app. You can learn more by going to `https://docs.microsoft.com/en-us/mem/intune/apps/apps-win32-supersedence`:

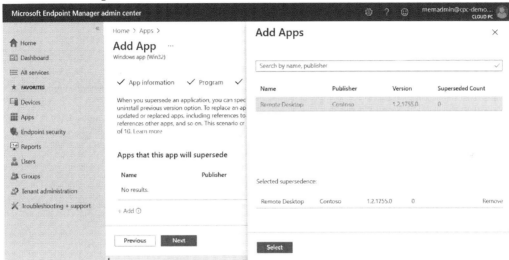

Figure 4.56 – Selecting supersedence

26. Click on **Create** to push the Remote Desktop client to your physical Windows PCs:

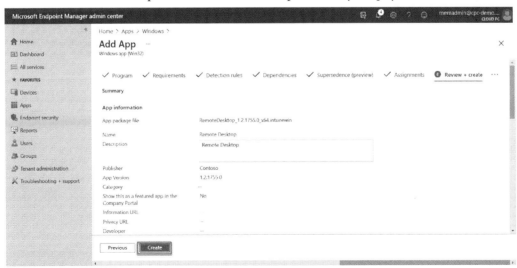

Figure 4.57 – Pushing the Remote Desktop client to your PC

The application will now be pushed to all the endpoints of users who are part of the AAD group filter.

You will see that the Remote Desktop app has been added as a recent app.

The Remote Desktop Windows application has been added to the **Start** menu:

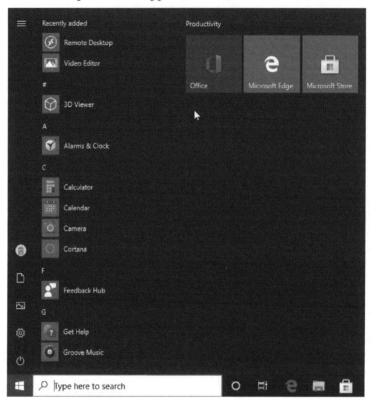

Figure 4.58 – App added to the start menu

27. After registration, you will be able to start your cloud PCs directly from the **Tile** and **Start** menus:

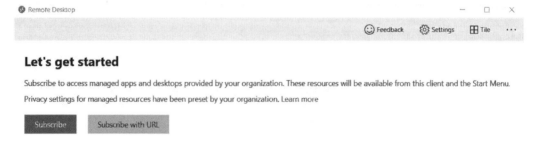

Figure 4.59 – The Let's get started configuration screen

28. Log in with your AAD user account and pass the necessary MFA prompts:

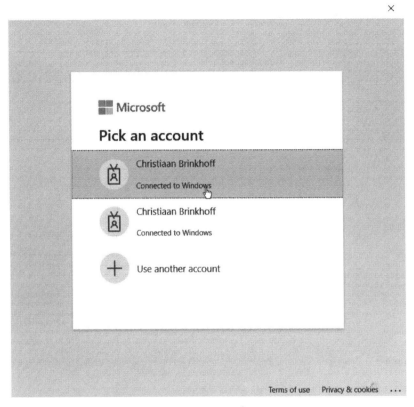

Figure 4.60 – Logging in with your account

You can also pin them directly to the taskbar!

Cloud PCs – device-based filtering

You may encounter scenarios where you already have a configured Microsoft Endpoint Manager tenant to manage your physical endpoints. Existing policies, application delivery rules, or other configuration items could be filtered to **All Devices**. This could cause conflict as there may be cases where the setting should only apply to your physical environment.

All cloud PC devices have a specific model name (contains a cloud PC) and an enrollment profile name (equates to a cloud PC provisioning profile) that can be used to filter them from an all-devices assignment:

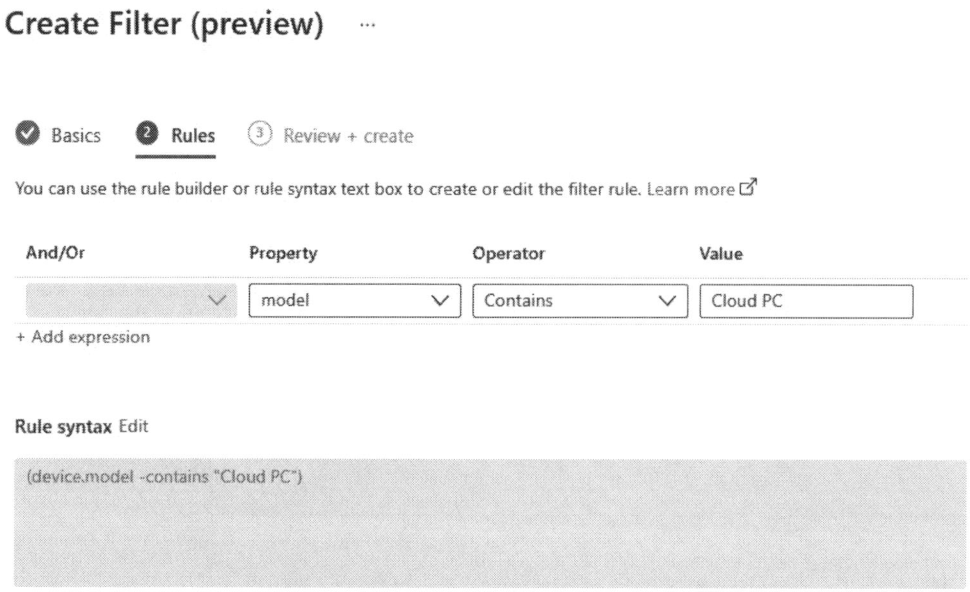

Create Filter (preview)   ...

✓ Basics	② **Rules**	③ Review + create

You can use the rule builder or rule syntax text box to create or edit the filter rule. Learn more ⤢

And/Or	Property	Operator	Value
⌄	model ⌄	Contains ⌄	Cloud PC

\+ Add expression

Rule syntax Edit

```
(device.model -contains "Cloud PC")
```

Figure 4.61 – Creating a device-based filter

Publishing apps and scripted actions

We won't cover application delivery in depth in this chapter as we will do that in *Chapter 8, Application Management and Delivery*. However, I'd like to highlight the following supported formats:

- .MSI
- .exe
- .MSIX
- .AppV
- .AppX

If you want to provide any custom scripted actions and publish them to your cloud PC, that's possible too. You can easily publish the script action as a PowerShell script.

You can find a list of actions/scripts in this GitHub repository https://github.com/CloudManagedDesktops.

Auto-subscribing users in the Remote Desktop client

Note that the following setting only works on Windows 11 as an endpoint and will be backported to Windows 10 soon. There's a chance that when you read this book, the feature will already be available!

Once you have configured the ability to enroll the Remote Desktop client to your Windows 10 endpoints, you have performed the most fundamental step. However, if you stop here, the user who opens the app will be prompted to log in with their Azure AD credentials first before you see your cloud PC(s) to start the session.

This section explains how you can auto-subscribe users to the Remote Desktop (MSRDC/Store) application without the need to enter credentials!

The settings that make this way of logging on possible have to be implemented via **Device | Configuration profiles**, via the **Settings Catalog** feature. The steps are as follows:

1. First, open the **Devices** menu and create a new profile (for Windows 10 and later):

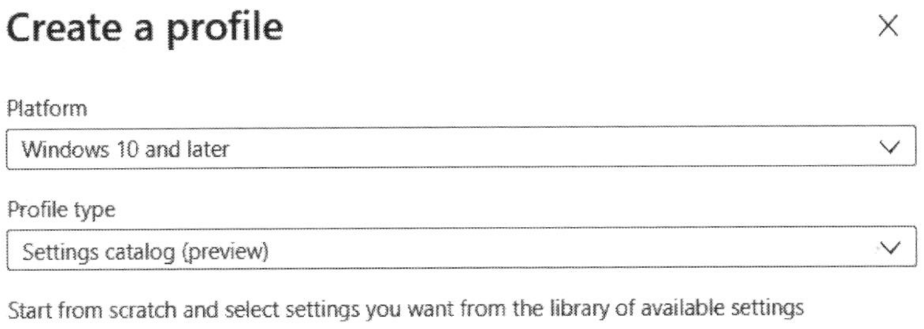

Create a profile   ×

Platform

Windows 10 and later   ⌄

Profile type

Settings catalog (preview)   ⌄

Start from scratch and select settings you want from the library of available settings

Figure 4.62 – Create a profile

2. Make sure that you enter a name for your configuration profile, such as `Auto-subscribe Remote Desktop client`, before you continue:

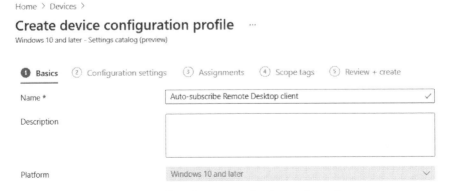

Figure 4.63 – Entering a name for the configuration

3.   Click on + **Add settings** to open the catalog:

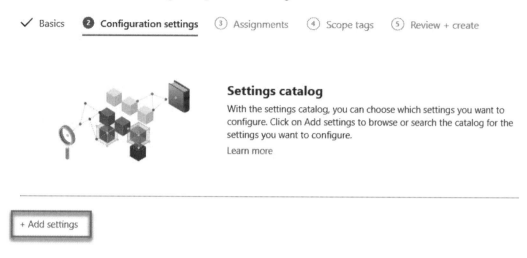

+ Add settings

Figure 4.64 – Opening the settings catalog

4.   Search for Remote Desktop; a list of Remote Desktop-specific settings will appear. Click on **Remote Desktop** and make sure to check the box next to **Auto-subscription (User)**:

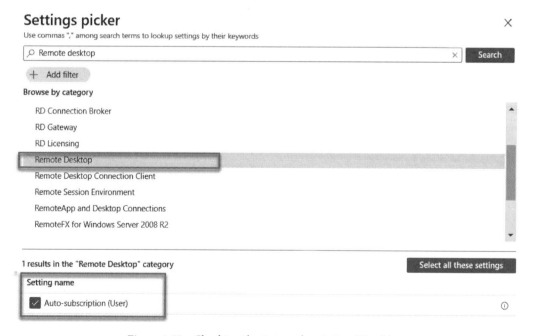

Figure 4.65 – Checking the Auto-subscription (User) box

5. Click on **+Add** and enter the following URL: `https://rdweb.wvd.`
    `microsoft.com/api/arm/feeddiscovery`:

Figure 4.66 – Entering the URL

6. Configure the right assignment settings for your use case, for example, based on
    Azure AD Groups, and conclude the configuration so that you can start enrolling
    these settings to your users/endpoint devices.

7. In the **Devices** menu, you can find the created device configuration profile and the
    status of the enrollment:

Home > Devices >

Auto-subscribe Remote Desktop client   ...
Device configuration profile - Settings Catalog

🗑 Delete

Device status

Succeeded	Error	Conflict	Not applicable
8	0	0	0

View report

Figure 4.67 – Enrollment status

8. After the enrollment, you can click on the Remote Desktop client. You will no longer be asked to log in with your Azure AD credentials, though you may need to do this for MFA via Azure MFA (if it's been enforced):

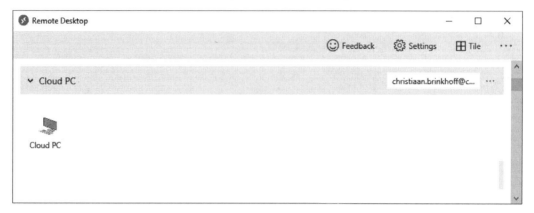

Figure 4.68 – No login required

In the next section, you will learn how to simplify the enrollment process even further.

Autopilot and cloud PCs – lightweight thin client (Kiosk)

The great thing about the combined capabilities of Microsoft Endpoint Manager, Autopilot, and Windows 365 is that you can configure both physical and virtual MEM-managed endpoints.

For example, within Autopilot, you can configure a multi-app Kiosk type of Surface Go, a thin client that only populates the Remote Desktop client. Full configuration and enrollment happens without user interaction and when the client is done, the end user only has to log in with their Azure AD credentials to get access to their cloud PC!

Within the **Device configuration** profile that you attached, for example, to your lightweight thin client, you can configure the auto-launching capability of the Remote Desktop Win32 or Store application to make the experience more awesome:

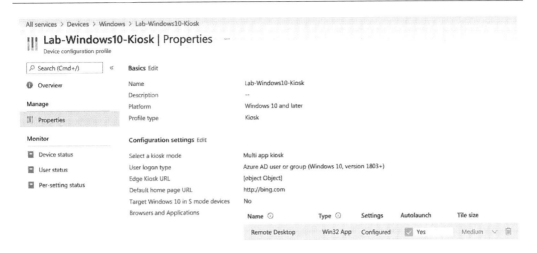

Figure 4.69 – Configuring Kiosk mode profiles

However, that's not all we can do.

When combining this setting with the settings explained in the previous section, *Auto-subscribing users in the Remote Desktop client*, device configuration profile users will automatically log into the Remote Desktop client and directly log into their cloud PCs! That's pretty awesome:

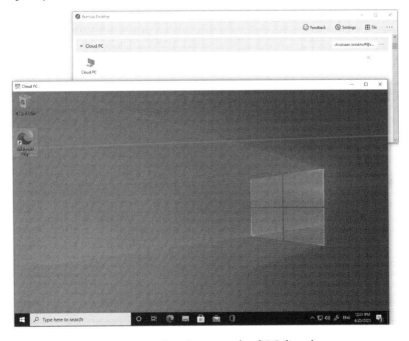

Figure 4.70 – Logging on to cloud PC directly

Now, let's cover monitoring and analytics.

Monitoring and analytics

Ensuring that the performance and quality level of your cloud PC environment is good is just as (or perhaps even more) important as the implementation. Users need to be happy about their cloud PC and it should not impair their productivity.

Windows 365/cloud PC seamlessly integrates with all the monitoring and analytics capabilities that you use today for your physical endpoints. This means that you can easily distinguish between whether the problem is active on the physical endpoint or within the cloud PC session.

You will learn more about monitoring in *Chapter 14, Monitoring and Endpoint Analytics*, where we will take a much deeper dive into the specific metrics of ensuring the performance and quality of your Windows 365/cloud PC environment both proactively and reactively!

Here's a quick preview list of the reports/dashboards that are available at the time of writing:

- Startup performance
- Proactive remediations
- Recommended software
- Application reliability
- Resource performance
- Remoting connection:

Cloud PC sign-in time phases time   ✕

Remoting connection metrics

Review the breakdown of the time it takes employees to connect to their cloud PC desktops. Note that some phases happen rarely, so the average time per cloud PC sign-in is much lower than the average time per phase. Learn more.

Sign-in phase	Avg time per sign-in (sec)	Percent of sign-ins	Avg time per phase (sec)
Remoting sign-in ⓘ	23.76	100	23.76
Core sign-in ⓘ	226.8	400	56.7
Core boot ⓘ	78.17	300	26.06

Figure 4.71 – Sign-in time – logon duration, Endpoint Analytics

> **Important Note**
>
> Endpoint Analytics and monitoring are provided as a free license. There are no consumption-based costs involved, so it's an easy way to calculate your costs next to your Microsoft fixed-pricing licensing model.

Shadow users with Quick Assist

Quick Assist is a new tool (simpler than Remote Assistance – it doesn't require any pre-configuration) you can use to give control of your computer to people you trust over the internet. The other great thing about Quick Assist is that it's free to use as part of your Windows 10 license!

Quick Assist is part of your cloud PC and all other physical Windows 10 operating systems. So, you just have to search for it in your **Start** menu to get started. Pretty simple, right?

Once you've done this, you will have to log in with your Azure AD credentials. If you are the user, you need to enter a 6-digit code. If you are the helpdesk employee or the IT admin, you have to click on **Assist another person**:

Figure 4.72 – Quick assist login

Wait for the session to load.

During the loading process, the helpdesk user will be asked for the type of control they wish to implement:

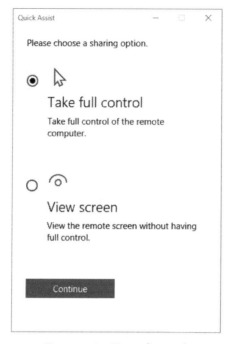

Figure 4.73 – Type of control

The user will receive the prompt afterwards. With you, you are now ready to troubleshoot via Quick Assist.

Windows 11

Windows 365 provided day 1 support for Windows 11 during its **general availability (GA)** on October 5, 2021. Customers can enable the **Trusted Platform Module (TPM)** as part of their cloud PC so that they can use the hardware requirements of Windows 11.

Here, you can see how Windows 11 runs as part of Windows 365 inside the browser. Of course, all the other endpoints, such as Windows and macOS, are supported too:

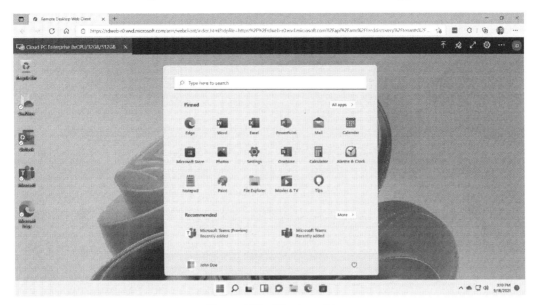

Figure 4.74 – Windows 11

Microsoft Managed Desktop

Microsoft Managed Desktop brings together Microsoft 365 Enterprise, cloud-based device management by Microsoft, and security monitoring, allowing your IT team to focus on core (IT-as-a-Service) business needs.

This service is different from cloud PC/Windows 365, but the service can be used to simplify the management layer of your physical endpoints while you, as a partner or customer, are responsible for your cloud endpoints.

When you are interested in using this service, please contact your Microsoft sales representative. The enablement process starts in the Microsoft Endpoint Manager console, under **Tenant admin**, followed by clicking **Tenant enrollment**:

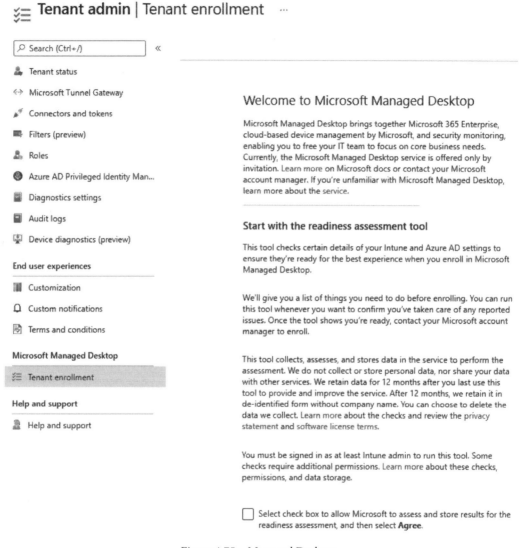

Figure 4.75 – Managed Desktop

With that, we have come to the end of this chapter. Congratulations on completing it!

Summary

In this chapter, you've learned everything you need to know about the new Windows 365 service, from the fundamentals of it to deep-diving into the logistics of configuration. We covered all the steps required to deploy Windows 365 Enterprise, what the prerequisites are, and some other great tips to learn more about different optimizations for your deployment.

In the next chapter, we will take a deeper dive into the different aspects of managing your Windows 365 environment, as well as thinking about monitoring, application distributions for classic Windows applications (Win32) and MSIX, identity and security, and many more aspects.

Questions

1. Can you use Windows 365 in multiple regions across the globe, from the US to Europe, and even to the Middle East, Asia, and New Zealand?

    A. Yes

    B. No

2. What protocol is Windows 365 using as part of connecting to cloud PCs?

    A. Unified Desktop Protocol

    B. Blaster Disaster Protocol

    C. Remote Desktop Protocol

Answers

1. (A)

2. (C)

Further reading

If you want to learn more about Windows 365 after reading this chapter, please go to one of the following other sections in this book:

*   *Chapter 12, User Profile Management*

*   *Chapter 14, Monitoring and Endpoint Analytics*

*   *Chapter 16, Troubleshooting Microsoft Endpoint Manager*

Section 3: Mastering Microsoft Endpoint Manager

The main section explains everything you should know, from A-Z, about the configuration and management process for Microsoft Endpoint Manager as well as other services that you can use to modernize your exiting Windows 10 Enterprise deployment. After reading this section, you will have enough knowledge to start deploying.

This part of the book comprises the following chapters:

- *Chapter 5, Requirements for Microsoft Endpoint Manager*
- *Chapter 6, Windows Deployment and Management*
- *Chapter 7, Manager Windows Autopilot*
- *Chapter 8, Application Management and Delivery*
- *Chapter 9, Understanding Policy Management*
- *Chapter 10, Advanced Policy Management*
- *Chapter 11, Office Policy Management*
- *Chapter 12, User Profile Management*

5
Requirements for Microsoft Endpoint Manager

In this chapter, you will get a clear understanding of the different requirements for **Microsoft Endpoint Manager** (**MEM**), from OS versions and the URL firewall allow-listing to the required licenses and privileges. Before we get started with the technical in-depth content of this book, we will cover the requirements for MEM. Some of the requirements may not have any impact on your environment, and others will have a high impact. For example, network URL firewall requirements are not that important if you are in a zero-trust environment with all Microsoft technologies, but if you for some reason have a firewall, proxy servers, and so on in your environment, then they are highly important.

In this chapter, we'll go through the following topics:

- Endpoint scenarios
- Identity roles and privileges
- Network URL firewall requirements
- Licensing requirements

- Supported OSes

- Windows 11 hardware requirements

- Administrator licensing

Endpoint scenarios

MEM supports different endpoint scenarios that we will cover in depth in this book.

The endpoint scenarios that are supported are as follows:

- Physical desktops

- Cloud PC endpoints

- Mobile devices

Now that we have mentioned the different endpoint scenarios, we're going to explain the different roles available within MEM.

Identity roles and privileges for Microsoft Intune

In order to configure MEM, you first have to make sure that you have the required privileges to do so. The first user created in your Azure **Active Directory** (**AD**) tenant will automatically become the global admin, as a member of the Global Admin role. The Global Admin role has **full Microsoft Intune** rights.

There are also other roles that could help you in delegating access as part of your user-role design. Some of the next steps for Intune require the Global Admin role, so we recommend using this type of account for the initial setup.

Here's a list of the supported roles within MEM.

Compliance Administrator

Users with this role have permission to manage compliance-related features in the Microsoft 365 compliance center, Azure, the Microsoft 365 admin center, and Microsoft Compliance Center.

Users with this role can view all Intune audit data.

Compliance Data Administrator

Users with this role have permission to track data in the Microsoft 365 compliance center, the Microsoft 365 admin center, and Azure.

Users with this role can view all Intune audit data.

Intune Administrator

Users with this role have global permissions within Microsoft Intune.

The Intune Administrator role contains the ability to manage users and devices in order to associate policies, as well as creating and managing all security groups in Azure AD.

> **Important Note**
> Intune Administrator does not have admin rights over Office groups.

Message Center Reader

Users in this role can monitor notifications and advisory health updates in the message center for their organization on Microsoft Intune.

> **Important Note**
> This is important for scoped Intune administrator users.

Security Administrator

Users with this role have permission to manage security-related features in the Microsoft 365 security center, Azure AD authentication, Azure AD Identity Protection, Azure Information Protection, and Microsoft 365 Compliance Center.

Users in this role can view user, device, enrollment, configuration, and application information. However, they cannot make changes to Intune.

Security Operator

Users with this role can manage alerts and have global read-only access to security-related features, including all information in the Microsoft 365 security center, Identity Protection, Azure AD, Privileged Identity Management, and Microsoft 365 Compliance Center.

Users in this role can view user, device, enrollment, configuration, and application information. However, they cannot make changes to Intune.

Security Reader

Users with this role have global read-only access to security-related features, including all information in the Microsoft 365 security center, Azure AD, Privileged Identity Management, Identity Protection, and Microsoft 365 Compliance Center, as well as the ability to read Azure AD sign-in reports and audit logs.

Users in this role can view user, device, enrollment, configuration, and application information. However, they cannot make changes to Intune.

Identity roles and privileges for a Windows 365 cloud PC

In order to use a Windows 365 cloud PC, your Azure AD configuration should be **hybrid Azure AD-joined** (**HAADJ**) to enroll your cloud PCs into Intune.

Azure Subscription Owner

Users with this role have global access to all resources in the Azure subscription. These rights are needed for the initial setup of Windows 365.

This role grants users full access to manage all resources, including the ability to assign roles in Azure RBAC.

Intune Administrator

Users with this role have global permissions within Microsoft Intune.

The Intune Administrator role contains the ability to manage users and devices in order to associate policies, as well as creating and managing all security groups in Azure AD.

> **Important Note**
> Intune Administrator does not have admin rights over Office groups.

Domain Administrator

Users with this role will be able to create computer accounts in your on-premises domain. This is needed to create the computer accounts for cloud PCs in your domain. You can also delegate access via delegation of control directly with the right Organizational Unit on your domain.

Identity roles and privileges for Universal Print

Universal Print introduced two roles, Printer Adminstrator and Technician, to Azure AD. The Printer Administrator is needed to do the initial configuration. A Global Admin account will be sufficient too.

We will talk more about Universal Print later on in the book.

Printer Administrator

Users in this role have full access to manage all aspects of printers in Universal Print.

Printer Technician

Users in this role can register and un-register printers and set the printer status.

Licensing requirements

To use MEM, you have to be entitled to an Intune license. There are also options to obtain a trial license for 30 days to kick the tires and validate the service.

MEM as a service doesn't require an Azure subscription; however, when you use the service together with a cloud PC, you'll need to set up an Azure virtual network and, therefore, you need an Azure subscription. An Azure subscription will not be necessary when Azure AD join is supported with cloud PCs (coming soon).

Here are the types of licenses that provide access to MEM:

- Intune-only license
- Microsoft 365 E3
- Microsoft E5
- **Enterprise Mobility + Security (EMS) E5**

It's likely that your company already owns one of these licenses and therefore already has access to MEM.

Creating a trial account is relatively easy; you just go to `admin.microsoft.com` and click on **Billing**, followed by **Purchase services**. Search for one of the licenses listed previously and purchase the trial (for free). There's no credit card or anything needed for this process:

Figure 5.1 – Microsoft 365 license purchase

Supported OSes

In this section, we'll look at the OSes and web browser versions that support MEM. Let's first look at the OSes:

- Microsoft:

  - Windows 11 (Enterprise **single- and multi-session versions**)

  - Windows 10 (Enterprise **single- and multi-session versions**)

  - Windows 10 Pro, Education

  - Windows 10 Enterprise 2019 LTSC

  - Windows 10 IoT Enterprise (x86, x64)

  - Windows 10 Teams – Surface Hub

  - Windows Holographic for Business

- Supported mobile OSes:

  - Apple:

    - Apple iOS 12.0 and later

    - Apple iPadOS 13.0 and later

    - Mac OS X 10.13 and later

- Google:

  - Android 6.0 and later (including Samsung Knox Standard 2.4 and higher)

Next, we will see what versions of web browsers support MEM.

Required web browser versions

Different administrative tasks require that you use one of the following administrative websites:

- MEM admin portal
- Microsoft 365 admin portal
- Azure portal

The following browsers are supported for these portals:

- Microsoft Edge – Chromium-based (latest version)
- Safari (latest version, Mac only)
- Chrome (latest version)
- Firefox (latest version)

Now that we know about the OS and browser requirements, let's take a look at the hardware requirements for Windows 11.

Windows 11 requirements

Windows 11 is a brand-new Microsoft OS that was announced on 24th June 2021. Windows 11 will be generally available 5th October 2021. The good news is that Windows 11 is completely manageable from MEM, to a similar degree to the CSP/settings that you are familiar with for Windows 10.

However, there are some fundamental changes to the requirements of the hardware for Windows 11 compared to Windows 10 that I'd like to explain:

- **Processor**: 1 **gigahertz** (**GHz**) or faster with two or more cores on a compatible 64-bit processor (`https://aka.ms/CPUlist`) or **system on a chip** (**SoC**).
- **RAM**: 4 **gigabytes** (**GB**) or greater.

- **Storage**: 64 GB* or greater available storage is required to install Windows 11 (additional storage space might be required to download updates and enable specific features).

- **Graphics card**: Compatible with DirectX 12 or later, with a WDDM 2.0 driver.

- **System firmware**: UEFI, Secure Boot-capable.

- **TPM**: **Trusted Platform Module** (`https://docs.microsoft.com/en-us/windows/security/information-protection/tpm/trusted-platform-module-overview`).

- **Display**: High-definition (720p) display, 9" or greater monitor, 8 bits per color channel.

- **Internet connection**: Internet connectivity is necessary to perform updates.

There might be additional requirements over time for updates, and to enable specific features within the operating system.

The requirements are important to follow as you might run into complications once Windows 11 is generally available:

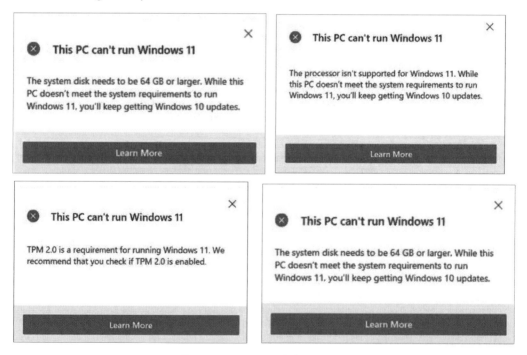

Figure 5.2 – Compatibility errors

You can see screenshots of errors in the Windows 11 installation process in the preceding figure. It detects the hardware requirements before starting the in-place upgrade process.

There are also some other differences between Windows 10 and 11 that you must know before upgrading. You can find them in the following list:

- Start is significantly changed in Windows 11, including the following key deprecations and removals:

  - Live tiles

  - Dynamic previews

  - Named groups and folders of apps

- Pinned apps and sites will not migrate when upgrading from Windows 10.

- New modern icons for Windows.

- Teams is integrated into the OS.

- The Windows Store app has been updated and allows the installation of Win32 applications.

- A new feature with the flexibility of multiple windows and the ability to snap apps side by side.

- Live tiles are no longer available. For glanceable, dynamic content, please check out the new widgets feature.

- Tablet mode is removed and new functionality and capability are included for keyboard attach and detach postures.

- Taskbar functionality has changed, including the following:

  - **People** is no longer present on the taskbar.

  - Some icons may no longer appear in the **system tray** (**systray**), including previous customizations for upgraded devices.

  - Only alignment to the bottom of the screen is allowed.

  - Apps can no longer customize areas of the taskbar.

  - **Timeline** is removed. Some similar functionality is available in Microsoft Edge.

  - **Internet Explorer** is removed. Edge is the recommended replacement and includes IE mode, which may be useful in certain scenarios.

  - **Math Input Panel** is removed.

- **Snipping Tool** continues to be available but the old design and functionality in the Windows 10 version have been replaced with those of the app previously known as Snip & Sketch.

- Center alignment on the desktop.

You can see the new desktop experience and the layout of Windows 11 in the following screenshot:

Figure 5.3 – Windows 11 UI

How do you get Windows 11?

Windows 11 is, until 5th October 2021, only available via the Insiders channels. After that, you will be able to distribute the OS via both physical hardware and the Windows 365 cloud PC service directly or via Azure Marketplace.

Learn more about how to join the Windows insider program in this blog: `https://blogs.windows.com/windows-insider/2021/06/28/announcing-the-first-insider-preview-for-windows-11/`.

Administrator licensing

All Intune administrators need a Microsoft Intune license by default. You can change this in the MEM admin center (`https://endpoint.microsoft.com`) at a later point, so you can give administrators access to MEM without them requiring an Intune license. This option is enabled by default on all tenants created after Intune service release 2006.

To get an administrator license, you need to follow these steps:

1. Go to **Tenant admin | Roles | Administrator Licensing**.

2. Click **Allow access to unlicensed admins**:

Home > Tenant admin > Endpoint Manager roles

Endpoint Manager roles | Administrator Licensing   ...
Microsoft Intune

| Search (Ctrl+/) | « |

Manage

All roles

Scope (Tags)

Administrator Licensing

Allow admins without an Intune license to access Intune. Their scope of access is determined by the Intune roles you've assigned them.
Learn more

Allow access to unlicensed admins

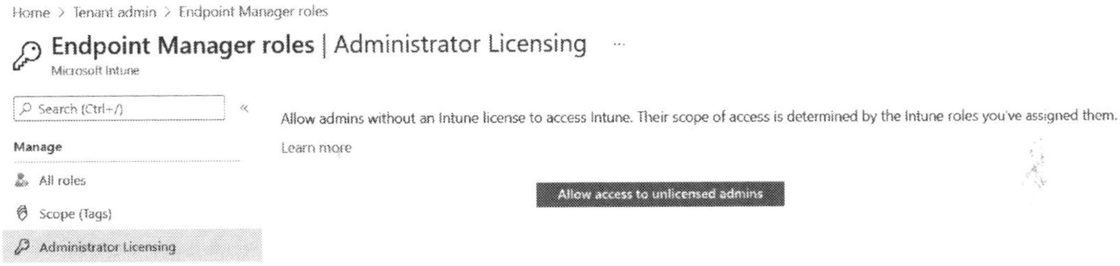

Figure 5.4 – Endpoint Manager admin center – Administrator Licensing

> **Important Note**
> You cannot revert this setting once it is set.

3. In the Microsoft 365 admin center, go to `admin.microsoft.com`. If you are a global admin, you can assign your Intune license:

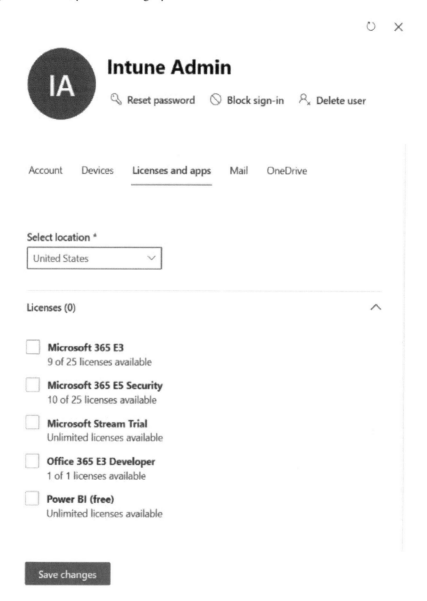

Figure 5.5 – Microsoft 365 admin center – license assignments

The Microsoft Intune license is a part of Microsoft 365 E3, Microsoft 365 F1/F3 for Firstline Workers, EMS E3, as well as standalone Microsoft Intune.

There are many other licenses that give you the right to Microsoft Intune. Always consult your license partner to find out the correct license for your scenario.

A user in your tenant also requires a license to enroll their device into Intune.

A recommendation for assigning your users Intune licenses is to leverage Azure AD group-based licensing.

Azure AD group-based licensing

Microsoft paid cloud services, such as Microsoft 365, EMS, Windows 10, Office 365, Dynamics 365, and other similar products, require licenses. These licenses are assigned to each user who needs access to these services. Administrators use one of the management portals (`admin.microsoft.com` or `aad.portal.azure.com`) and PowerShell cmdlets to manage licenses. Azure AD is the underlying infrastructure that supports identity management for all Microsoft cloud services. Azure AD stores information about license assignment states for users.

Azure AD includes group-based licensing, which means one or more product licenses can be assigned to a group. Azure AD ensures that the licenses are assigned to all members of the group. This includes non-members who then become a member of the group. When they leave the group, those licenses are removed. This licensing management eliminates the need for automating license management via PowerShell to reflect changes in the organization and departmental structure on a per-user basis.

For any groups assigned a license, you must also have a license for each unique member. While you do not have to assign each member of the group a license, you must have at least enough licenses to include all the members. For example, if you have 10,000 unique members who are part of licensed groups in your tenant, you must have at least 10,000 licenses to meet the licensing assignment.

Licenses can be assigned to any security group in Azure AD. Security groups can be synced from on-premises using Azure AD Connect. You can also create security groups directly in Azure AD (also called cloud-only groups), or automatically via the Azure AD dynamic group feature. Office 365 groups cannot be used for group-based licensing.

When a product license is assigned to a group, one or more service plans in the product can be disabled by the administrator. Typically, this assignment is done when the organization is not yet ready to start using a service included in a product. For example, the administrator might assign Microsoft 365 to a department but temporarily disable the Yammer service.

Azure AD automatically manages license modifications that result from group membership changes. Typically, license modifications are effective within minutes of a membership change.

A user can be a member of multiple groups with license policies specified. A user can also have some licenses that were directly assigned, outside of any groups. The resulting user state is a combination of all assigned product and service licenses. The license will be consumed only once if a user is assigned the same license from multiple sources.

In some cases, licenses cannot be assigned to a user. For example, there might not be enough licenses available in the tenant or conflicting services might have been assigned at the same time. Administrators have access to information about users for whom Azure AD could not fully process group licenses. They can then take corrective action based on that information.

Setting the mobile device management authority

As an IT admin, you *must set* a **mobile device management (MDM) authority** before users can enroll devices for management.

Automatic enrollment lets users enroll their Windows 10 and later devices in Intune. Users need to add their work account to their personally owned devices or join corporate-owned devices to Azure AD to enroll. In the background, the device registers and joins Azure AD. Once registered, the device is managed with Microsoft Intune.

All applications and policies assigned to their username or device will start being deployed.

Enabling Windows automatic enrollment

Automatic MDM enrollment means when a Windows device joins Azure AD, the device will automatically be enrolled into Intune with the MDM enrollment flow.

For automatic Windows enrollment, follow these steps:

1. Sign in to the MEM admin center (`https://endpoint.microsoft.com`).

2. Select **Devices | Windows | Windows enrollment** followed by **Automatic Enrollment**:

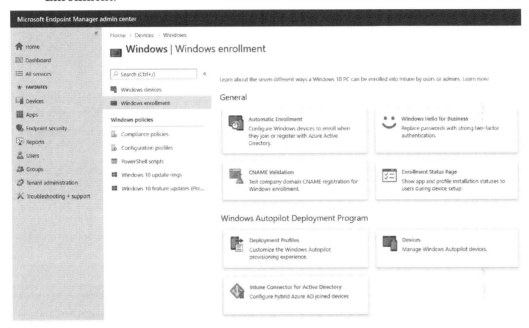

Figure 5.6 – MEM admin center – Windows automatic MDM enrollment

User enrollment can also be scoped to a group of users, if all your users have an Intune license assigned. The best option is to leverage Intune enrollment restriction to configure which Windows devices a user can enroll.

3.   Make sure to select **All** for **MDM user scope**:

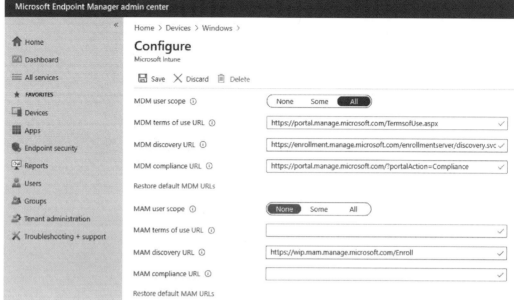

Figure 5.7 – MEM admin center – MDM user scope

Here's what all the options for **MDM user scope** mean:

- **None**: MDM automatic enrollment disabled.

- **Some**: Select the groups that can automatically enroll their Windows devices.

- **All**: All users can automatically enroll their Windows devices.

> **Important Note**
> Automatic MDM enrollment requires an Azure AD premium subscription.

For Windows **bring your own device** (**BYOD**) devices (personal enrollment), the **MAM user scope** takes precedence if both the MAM user scope and the MDM user scope (automatic MDM enrollment) are enabled for all users (or the same groups of users). If you have configured them, the device will not be MDM-enrolled, and **Windows Information Protection** (**WIP**) policies will be applied.

Using Azure Virtual Desktop with Intune

The following steps are not needed within Windows 365, as the enrollment into Intune happens automatically. Also, make sure that you have followed the previous step (setting **MDM user scope** to **All** and **MAM user scope** to **None**) before continuing.

> **Important Note**
> Make sure that the RemoteDesktopServices/AllowUsersToConnectRemotely
> policy isn't disabled.

Keep in mind that the following Windows 10 desktop device remote actions aren't
supported/recommended for Azure Virtual Desktop virtual machines:

- Autopilot reset
- BitLocker key rotation
- Fresh start
- Remote lock
- Reset password
- Wipe

Let's get started with the procedure:

1. Log on to your session host.

2. Open **Local Computer Policy** and click **Administrative Templates | Windows Components | MDM**:

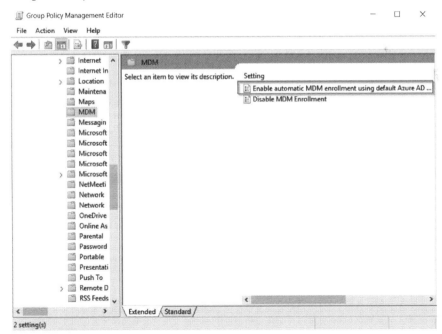

Figure 5.8 – Local group policy – MDM

3. Set the policy to **Enabled**.

4. Set the credential type to **User Credential**:

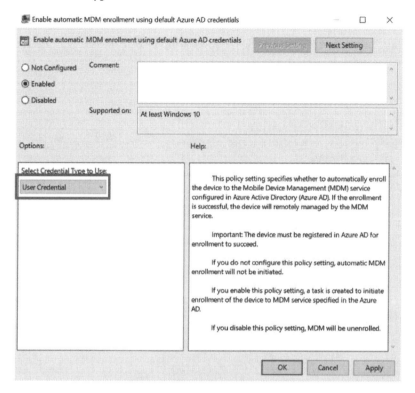

Figure 5.9 – Local group policy – MDM

5. Confirm the MDM enrollment of your session hosts into Azure AD, which should look like the following examples:

Figure 5.10 – Admin center – All devices

As we have just shown you the different options for enrolling Windows devices into Microsoft Intune, we will now show you how you can limit Windows enrollment with Microsoft Intune enrollment restrictions.

Microsoft Intune enrollment restriction for Windows

If you block personally owned Windows devices from enrollment, Intune checks to make sure that each new Windows enrollment request has been authorized as a corporate enrollment. Unauthorized enrollments will be blocked.

> **Important Note**
> Blocking Windows MDM enrollment in the default enrollment restriction will block some scenarios with corporate devices.

Microsoft Intune device restrictions for Windows

In this section, we will see how to create enrollment restrictions for Windows devices:

1. Sign in to the MEM admin center (`endpoint.microsoft.com`).

2. Select **Devices | Enrollment restrictions**:

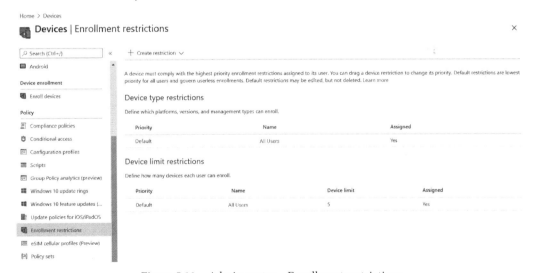

Figure 5.11 – Admin center – Enrollment restrictions

3. Create a device type restriction. Enter `Device type restriction - HR` as the name:

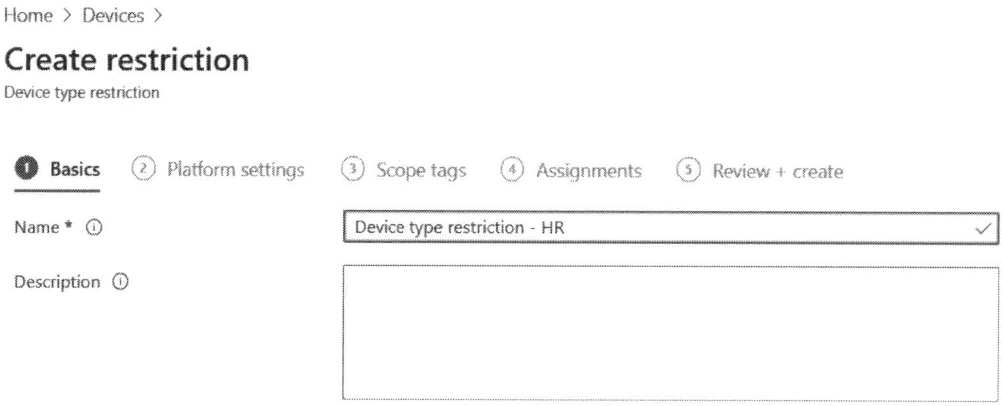

Home > Devices >

Create restriction
Device type restriction

| ● **Basics** | ② Platform settings | ③ Scope tags | ④ Assignments | ⑤ Review + create |

Name * ⓘ

Device type restriction - HR ✓

Description ⓘ

Figure 5.12 – Admin center – Enrollment restrictions

4. Select the block and allow both for MDM and personally owned devices on a specific OS to allow or block device enrollment.

    If you are blocking a specific OS for enrollment, it applies to both corporate and personal device enrollment.

    If you are allowing Windows (MDM) platform enrollment, you can block personal devices; see the following section to understand what *blocking personal Windows devices* means.

    Allow min/max range for the OS version only blocks devices on enrollment and has no effect on devices already enrolled into Microsoft Intune:

Important Note

Windows supports `major.minor.build.rev` for Windows 10 only.

Windows 10 does not provide the rev number during enrollment so, for instance, if you enter `10.0.17134.100` and the device is `10.0.17134.174`, it will be blocked during enrollment.

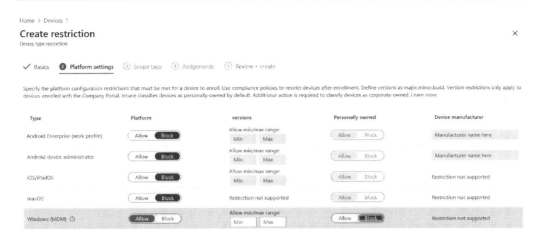

Figure 5.13 – Admin center – Enrollment restrictions – Platform settings

5.   For the **Assignments** step, select **HR Department**.

When you are creating a custom enrollment restriction, you can scope it to apply to specific user groups in your organization, departments, countries, and so on.

Change the assignment settings to filter based on any restrictions you want to provide to avoid groups from enrolling into MDM Intune:

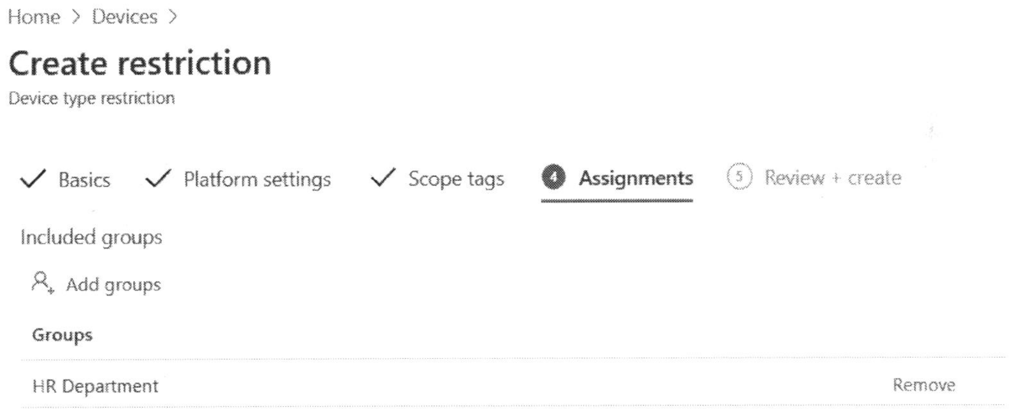

Home > Devices >

Create restriction
Device type restriction

✓ Basics   ✓ Platform settings   ✓ Scope tags   ④ **Assignments**   ⑤ Review + create

Included groups

&+ Add groups

Groups

HR Department   Remove

Figure 5.14 – Admin center – Enrollment restrictions – Assignments

In the next section, let's see how to block personal devices.

Blocking personal Windows devices

If you block personally owned Windows devices from enrollment, Intune checks to make sure that each new Windows enrollment request has been authorized as a corporate enrollment. Unauthorized enrollments will be blocked.

The following methods qualify as being authorized as a Windows corporate enrollment:

- The enrolling user is using a device enrollment manager account.
- The device enrolls through Windows Autopilot.
- The device is registered with Windows Autopilot but isn't an MDM enrollment-only option from Windows Settings.
- The device's IMEI number is listed in **Device enrollment | Corporate device identifiers**.
- The device enrolls through a bulk provisioning package.
- The device enrolls through a **Group Policy Object** (**GPO**), or automatic enrollment from Configuration Manager for co-management.

The following enrollments are marked as corporate by Intune. But since they don't offer the Intune administrator per-device control, they'll be blocked:

- Automatic MDM enrollment with an Azure AD join during Windows setup*
- Automatic MDM enrollment with an Azure AD join from Windows Settings*

The following personal enrollment methods will also be blocked:

- Automatic MDM enrollment with **Add Work Account** from Windows Settings*
- The MDM enrollment-only option from Windows Settings

These won't be blocked if registered with Autopilot.

Microsoft Intune device limit restrictions for Windows

In this section, we will learn how to limit the restrictions for a device. Let's get started:

1. Sign in to the MEM admin center (`endpoint.microsoft.com`).

2. Select **Devices | Enrollment restrictions | Create restriction | Device limit restriction**. Enter `Device type restriction - HR` as the name:

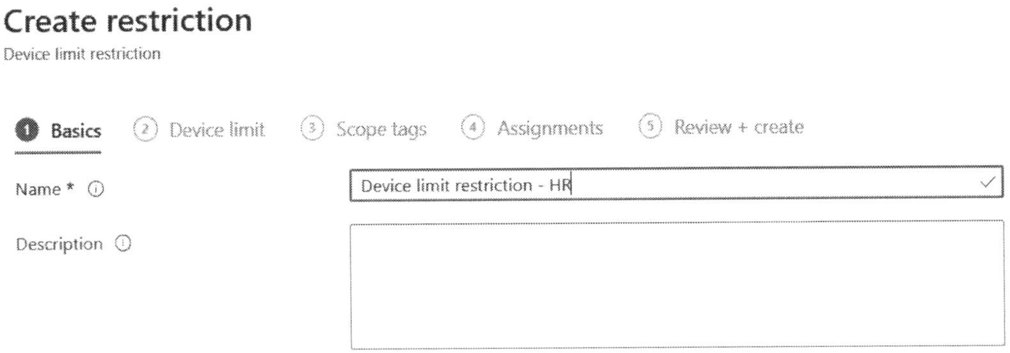

Create restriction
Device limit restriction

① **Basics**   ② Device limit   ③ Scope tags   ④ Assignments   ⑤ Review + create

Name * ⓘ | Device limit restriction - HR   ✓ |

Description ⓘ

Figure 5.15 – MEM admin center – Device limit restriction

3. You can set **Device limit** to a number from 1 to 15. The default in Microsoft Intune is a limit of 5:

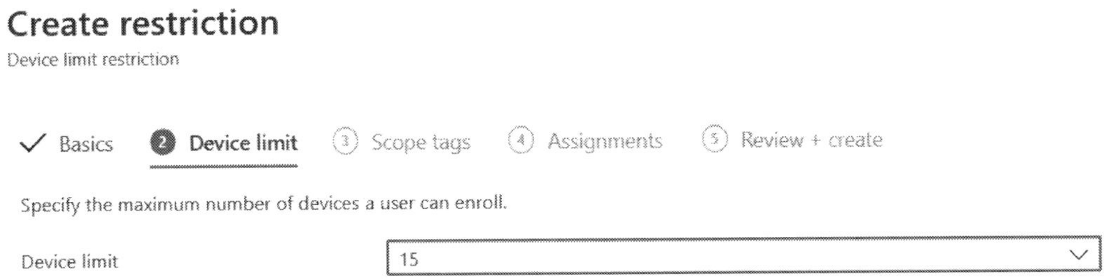

Create restriction
Device limit restriction

✓ Basics   ② **Device limit**   ③ Scope tags   ④ Assignments   ⑤ Review + create

Specify the maximum number of devices a user can enroll.

Device limit | 15   ∨ |

Figure 5.16 – MEM admin center – Device limit restriction

4. For the **Assignments** step, select **HR Department**.

When you are creating a custom enrollment restriction, you can scope it to apply to specific user groups in your organization, departments, countries, and so on:

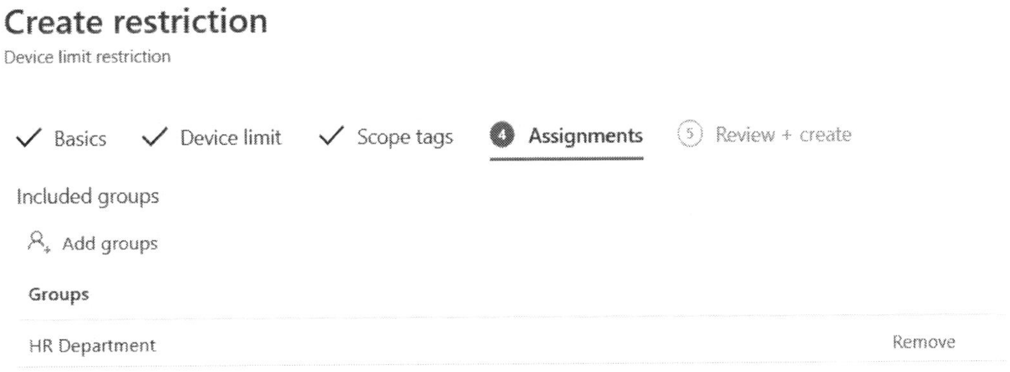

Create restriction
Device limit restriction

✓ Basics   ✓ Device limit   ✓ Scope tags   ④ **Assignments**   ⑤ Review + create

Included groups

 ⚮ Add groups

Groups

HR Department   Remove

Figure 5.17 – MEM admin center – Device limit restriction – Assignments

5.   You always have an overview of default device type restrictions and device limit restrictions that are the default:

A device must comply with the highest priority enrollment restrictions assigned to its user. You can drag a device restriction to change its priority. Default restrictions are lowest priority for all users and govern userless enrollments. Default restrictions may be edited, but not deleted. Learn more

Device type restrictions

Define which platforms, versions, and management types can enroll.

Priority	Name	Assigned	
1	Device type restriction - HR	Yes	...
Default	All Users	Yes	

Device limit restrictions

Define how many devices each user can enroll.

Priority	Name	Device limit	Assigned	
1	Device limit restriction - HR	15	Yes	...
Default	All Users	5	Yes	

Figure 5.18 – MEM admin center – Enrollment restriction – overview

6.   If you have *restricted personal enrollment*, your end users will be met with the **Something went wrong.** screen if the devices are Azure AD-joined and the devices are not in the Windows Autopilot service:

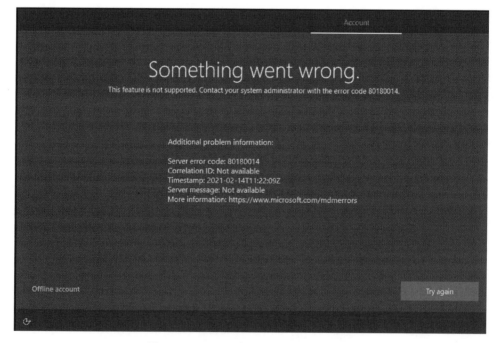

Figure 5.19 – Windows 10 – OOBE error

Now that we have looked at different ways to restrict device enrollment in Microsoft Intune, we will look at the company branding of Microsoft Intune in the next section.

Customizing Intune company portal apps, the company portal website, and the Intune app

You can make your Intune logon screen, company portal, and website custom and add your branding to it. Follow these steps in order to make this possible for your organization:

1. Go to **Tenant administration**. Click on **Customization | Settings | Edit**:

> **Important Note**
> This is the default customization that's applied to all users and devices. It can be edited, but not deleted.

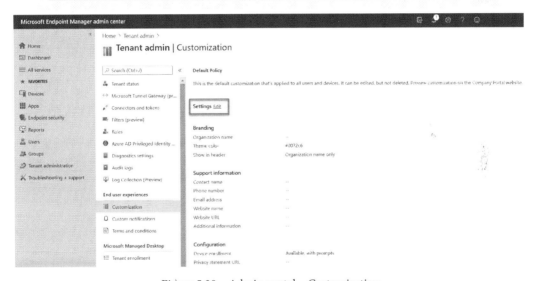

Figure 5.20 – Admin portal – Customization

2. Create branding for your organization's Azure AD sign-in page:

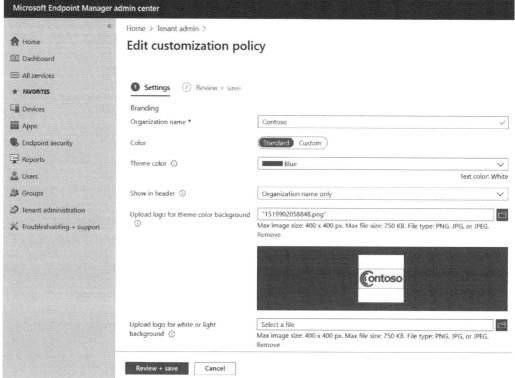

Figure 5.21 – Admin portal – Customization

3. If you set **Color** as **Custom**, you have the option to use hex color codes to match the exact color that your company uses in their digital marketing:

Figure 5.22 – Admin portal – Customization

App Sources is where you choose which additional app sources will be shown in the company portal:

-   Azure AD Enterprise applications

-   Office Online applications

You can use the hide features to prevent or allow users from performing self-service actions on devices in the company portal website and client apps.

The following actions are available:

- Hide the remove button on corporate Windows devices.
- Hide the reset button on corporate Windows devices.
- Hide the remove button on corporate iOS/iPadOS devices.
- Hide the reset button on corporate iOS/iPadOS devices.

You can create a customization policy and assign it to select groups in your organization. When assigned, this type of policy overrides the default policy. If you assign more than one of these policies to a user, the user will get the first policy you created.

You can create a maximum of 10 customization policies in your Microsoft Intune tenant.

The company portal is a self-service app for the end user to get apps from Microsoft Intune, Microsoft Store for Business, Azure AD Enterprise apps, Office Online applications, web link, and Configuration Manager apps (if the device is in a co-management state):

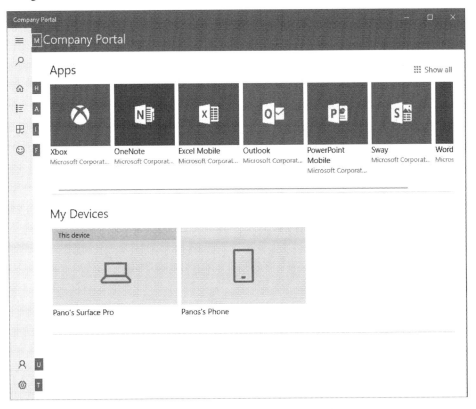

Figure 5.23 – Company portal – example

We have covered the branding part of Microsoft Intune in this section. In the next section, we will cover Microsoft Store for Business integration with Microsoft Intune.

Associating your Microsoft Store for Business account with Intune

Microsoft Store for Business gives you a place to find and purchase apps for your organization, individually or in volume. You can manage volume-purchased apps from the Azure portal by connecting the store to Microsoft Intune. See the following examples:

- You can synchronize the list of apps you have purchased (or that are free) from the store with Intune.

- Apps that are synchronized appear in the MEM admin center; you can assign these apps like any other apps.

- Both online and offline licensed versions of apps are synchronized to Intune. App names will be appended with **Online** or **Offline** in the portal.

- You can track how many licenses are available and how many are being used in the Intune administration console.

- Intune blocks the assignment and installation of apps if there is an insufficient number of licenses available.

- Apps managed by Microsoft Store for Business will automatically revoke licenses when a user leaves the enterprise, or when the administrator removes the user and the user devices.

> **Important Note**
>
> Microsoft Store for Business and Microsoft Store for Education will be retired in the first quarter of 2023. Customers may continue to use the current capabilities for free apps until that time. There will be no support for Microsoft Store for Business and Education on Windows 11. You can still leverage Microsoft Intune to deploy apps from Microsoft Store for Business on Windows 11 both as required and as available in the company portal.

As Microsoft Store for Business is still important to get Store apps to a Windows device, we will still advise you to create the connection with the following guidelines:

1. Sign in to the MEM admin center (`endpoint.microsoft.com`).

2. Select **Tenant administration | Connectors and tokens | Microsoft Store for Business**.

> **Important Note**
>
> First, you'll need to sign up and associate your Microsoft Store for Business account with Intune.

3. Select **Open the business store**:

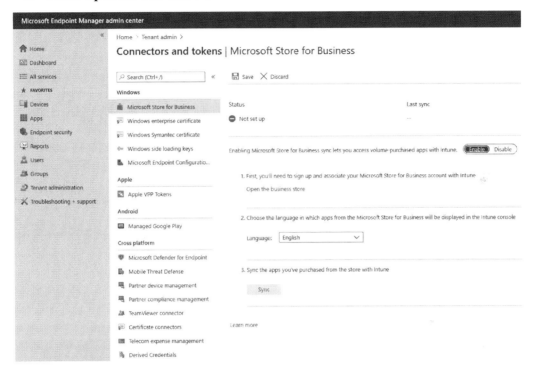

Figure 5.24 – MEM admin center – connecting Microsoft Store for Business

4. You can always *go directly* to Microsoft Store for Business from `http://aka.ms/msfb`.

5. Sign in as a global admin to activate Microsoft Store for Business in your tenant.

6. Click **Manage**:

Figure 5.25 – MEM admin center – Microsoft Store for Business

7. Click **Settings** to start configuring your Microsoft Store for Business.

8. Under **Shopping experience**, change **Show offline apps** to **On**.

    Both online and offline licensed apps that you have purchased from Microsoft Store for Business are synced into Intune. These apps can then be deployed to device groups or user groups.

    Online app installations are managed by the store. Offline apps that are free of charge can also be synced to Intune. These apps are installed by Intune, not by the store:

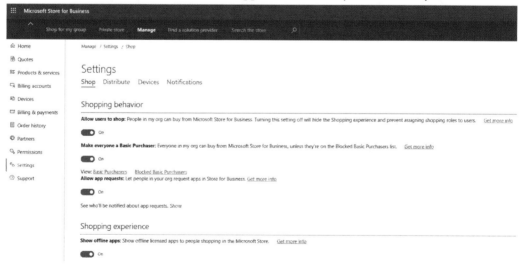

Figure 5.26 – MEM admin center – Microsoft Store for Business

9. Click **Distribute | Activate** (for **Microsoft Intune**):

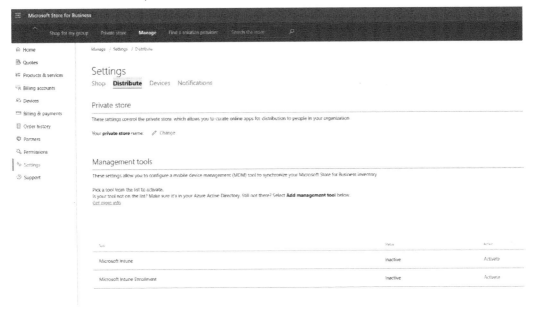

Figure 5.27 – MEM admin center – Microsoft Store for Business

You can configure an MDM tool, in this case, Microsoft Intune, to synchronize your Microsoft Store for Business or Microsoft Store for Education inventory. Microsoft Store management tool services work with MDM tools to manage content.

You could previously only associate one management tool to assign apps with Microsoft Store for Business. You can now associate multiple management tools with the store, for example, Intune and Configuration Manager.

Now that you have associated your Microsoft Store for Business account with your Intune admin credentials, you can manually sync your Microsoft Store for Business apps with Intune by clicking **Sync**.

Microsoft Intune will sync in the background every 24 hours:

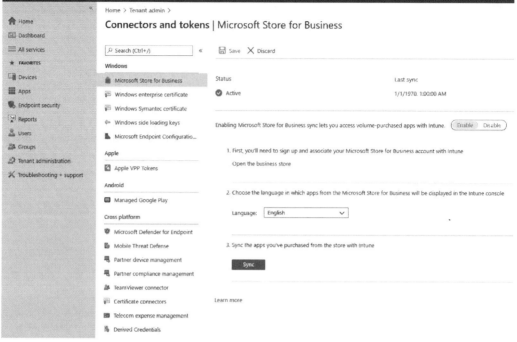

Figure 5.28 – MEM admin center – Microsoft Store for Business

MEM – network URL firewall requirements

The table in this section lists IP addresses and port settings that are required to have full access to, from both your physical endpoint location as well as on Azure. You can find the full list of all the required MEM URLs here: aka.ms/MEMURLs.

> **Important Note**
> Are you using Intune in China? Make sure to open the right level of network access via Intune operated by 21Vianet in China | Microsoft Docs: https://docs.microsoft.com/en-us/mem/intune/fundamentals/china.

Access for managed devices

The following table lists the domains to provide access for managed devices:

Domains
login.microsoftonline.com
*.officeconfig.msocdn.com
config.office.com
graph.windows.net
enterpriseregistration.windows.net
portal.manage.microsoft.com
m.manage.microsoft.com
sts.manage.microsoft.com
portal.fei.msua01.manage.microsoft.com
m.fei.msua01.manage.microsoft.com
portal.fei.amsua0102.manage.microsoft.com
m.fei.amsua0102.manage.microsoft.com
portal.fei.msua02.manage.microsoft.com
m.fei.msua02.manage.microsoft.com
portal.fei.msua04.manage.microsoft.com
m.fei.msua04.manage.microsoft.com
portal.fei.msua05.manage.microsoft.com
m.fei.msua05.manage.microsoft.com
portal.fei.amsua0502.manage.microsoft.com
m.fei.amsua0502.manage.microsoft.com
portal.fei.msua06.manage.microsoft.com
m.fei.msua06.manage.microsoft.com
portal.fei.amsua0602.manage.microsoft.com
m.fei.amsua0602.manage.microsoft.com
fei.amsua0202.manage.microsoft.com
portal.fei.amsua0202.manage.microsoft.com
m.fei.amsua0202.manage.microsoft.com
portal.fei.amsua0402.manage.microsoft.com

Domains
portal.fei.amsua0702.manage.microsoft.com
portal.fei.amsua0801.manage.microsoft.com
portal.fei.msua08.manage.microsoft.com
m.fei.msua07.manage.microsoft.com
m.fei.amsua0702.manage.microsoft.com
m.fei.msua08.manage.microsoft.com
m.fei.amsua0801.manage.microsoft.com
portal.fei.msub01.manage.microsoft.com
m.fei.msub01.manage.microsoft.com
portal.fei.amsub0102.manage.microsoft.com
m.fei.amsub0102.manage.microsoft.com
portal.fei.msub02.manage.microsoft.com
m.fei.msub02.manage.microsoft.com
portal.fei.msub03.manage.microsoft.com
m.fei.msub03.manage.microsoft.com
portal.fei.msub05.manage.microsoft.com
m.fei.msub05.manage.microsoft.com
portal.fei.amsub0202.manage.microsoft.com
m.fei.amsub0202.manage.microsoft.com
portal.fei.amsub0302.manage.microsoft.com
m.fei.amsub0302.manage.microsoft.com
portal.fei.amsub0502.manage.microsoft.com
m.fei.amsub0502.manage.microsoft.com
portal.fei.amsub0601.manage.microsoft.com
m.fei.amsub0601.manage.microsoft.com
m.fei.amsua0402.manage.microsoft.com
portal.fei.msua07.manage.microsoft.com

Domains
portal.fei.msuc01.manage.microsoft.com
m.fei.msuc01.manage.microsoft.com
portal.fei.msuc02.manage.microsoft.com
m.fei.msuc02.manage.microsoft.com
portal.fei.msuc03.manage.microsoft.com
m.fei.msuc03.manage.microsoft.com
portal.fei.msuc05.manage.microsoft.com
m.fei.msuc05.manage.microsoft.com
portal.fei.amsud0101.manage.microsoft.com
m.fei.amsud0101.manage.microsoft.com
fef.msuc03.manage.microsoft.com
Admin.manage.microsoft.com
wip.mam.manage.microsoft.com
mam.manage.microsoft.com
*.manage.microsoft.com

Windows 365 endpoint URLs

Please whitelist traffic to the following URLs when using cloud PC endpoints:

- cpcsacnrysa1prodprna02.blob.core.windows.net
- cpcsacnrysa1prodprap01.blob.core.windows.net
- cpcsacnrysa1prodprau01.blob.core.windows.net
- cpcsacnrysa1prodpreu01.blob.core.windows.net
- cpcsacnrysa1prodpreu02.blob.core.windows.net
- cpcsacnrysa1prodprna01.blob.core.windows.net

Network URL requirements for PowerShell scripts and Win32 apps

To find your tenant location (or **Azure Scale Unit (ASU)**), follow these steps:

1. Sign in to the MEM admin center.

2. Go to **Tenant administration | Tenant details**.

   The location can be found under **Tenant location** as something such as **North America 0501** or **Europe 0202**. Look for the matching number in the following table.

   The rows are differentiated by geographic region, as can be seen in the first two letters in the names (eu = Europe, na = North America, ap = Asia Pacific). Although your organization's actual geographic location might be elsewhere, your tenant location will be one of these three regions:

Azure Scale Unit (ASU)	Storage Name	Content Delivery Network (CDN)
AMSUA0601	naprodimedatapri	naprodimedatapri. azureedge.net
AMSUA0602	naprodimedatasec	
AMSUA0101	naprodimedatahotfix	naprodimedatasec. azureedge.net
AMSUA0102		
AMSUA0201		naprodimedatahotfix. azureedge.net
AMSUA0202		
AMSUA0401		
AMSUA0402		
AMSUA0501		
AMSUA0502		
AMSUA0701		
AMSUA0702		
AMSUA0801		

Azure Scale Unit (ASU)	Storage Name	Content Delivery Network (CDN)
AMSUB0101 AMSUB0102 AMSUB0201 AMSUB0202 AMSUB0301 AMSUB0302 AMSUB0501 AMSUB0502 AMSUB0601	euprodimedatapri euprodimedatasec euprodimedatahotfix	euprodimedatapri. azureedge.net euprodimedatasec. azureedge.net euprodimedatahotfix. azureedge.net
AMSUC0101 AMSUC0201 AMSUC0301 AMSUC0501 AMSUD0101	approdimedatapri approdimedatasec approdimedatahotifx	approdimedatapri. azureedge.net approdimedatasec. azureedge.net approdimedatahotfix. azureedge.net

Windows Push Notification Services – required URLs

Windows Push Notification Services (WNS) enables Microsoft Intune to send toast, tile, badge, and raw updates from the Microsoft Intune cloud service to Windows clients:

- *.notify.windows.com
- *.wns.windows.com
- *.notify.live.net
- login.microsoftonline.com
- login.live.com

Windows 365 and Azure Virtual Desktop – required URLs

The Azure virtual machines you create for Windows 365 and Azure Virtual Desktop must have outbound TCP 443 access to the following URLs via the required Azure virtual network in the customer's Azure subscription. You can find the full list of all the required Azure Virtual Desktop URLs here: `aka.ms/CPCURLs`.

More information about the requirements for Windows 365 can be found in the previous chapter.

You can find a list of all the URLs per service purpose in the following table:

Address	Outbound TCP Port	Purpose
`*.wvd.microsoft.com`	443	Service traffic
`gcs.prod.monitoring.core.windows.net`	443	Agent traffic
`production.diagnostics.monitoring.core.windows.net`	443	Agent traffic
`*xt.blob.core.windows.net`	443	Agent traffic
`*eh.servicebus.windows.net`	443	Agent traffic
`*xt.table.core.windows.net`	443	Agent traffic
`catalogartifact.azureedge.net`	443	Azure Marketplace
`kms.core.windows.net`	1688	Windows activation
`mrsglobalsteus2prod.blob.core.windows.net`	443	Agent and SXS stack updates
`wvdportalstorageblob.blob.core.windows.net`	443	Azure portal support
`169.254.169.254`	80	Azure Instance Metadata service endpoint (`https://docs.microsoft.com/en-us/azure/virtual-machines/windows/instance-metadata-service`)
`168.63.129.16`	80	Session host health monitoring (`https://docs.microsoft.com/en-us/azure/virtual-network/security-overview`)

Universal Print – required URLs

A Windows endpoint that is being used with Universal Print needs to have an internet connection, with access to the following internet (TCP/IP – 443) endpoints:

- `*.print.microsoft.com`
- `*.microsoftonline.com`
- `*.azure.com`
- `*.msftauth.net`
- `go.microsoft.com`
- `aka.ms`

Delivery Optimization

For peer-to-peer traffic, Delivery Optimization uses `7680` for TCP/IP or `3544` for NAT traversal (optionally Teredo). For client-service communication, it uses HTTP or HTTPS over port `80/443`.

Delivery Optimization will help with band-wide consumption on Windows endpoints:

- `*.do.dsp.mp.microsoft.com`
- `*.dl.delivery.mp.microsoft.com`
- `*.emdl.ws.microsoft.com`

Summary

In this chapter, you've learned about the different supported endpoint scenarios within MEM and what the requirements are to use the service.

In the next chapter, we're going to take a deeper dive into how to deploy Windows 10 Enterprise to your endpoints. We're also going to talk about Autopilot and how this deployment service can deliver out-of-the-box configurations for your physical endpoints!

Questions

1. What is the most important set of privileges to have in order to configure MEM?

    A. Global Admin

    B. Azure Owner

    C. Intune Administrator

2. What is the menu option called in MEM to change the branding and logos as part of your organization?

    A. Tenant admin

    B. Customization

    C. Tenant administration

3. What should be the required Azure AD configuration to use Windows 365 and Azure Virtual Desktop?

    A. Azure AD

    B. Azure AD Domain Services

    C. Azure AD hybrid-joined

Answers

1. (C)
2. (B)
3. (C)

Further reading

If you want to learn more about MEM requirements after reading this chapter, please use the following free online resources:

-   Network endpoints for Microsoft Intune | Microsoft Docs: `https://docs.microsoft.com/en-us/mem/intune/fundamentals/intune-endpoints`

-   OSes and browsers supported by Microsoft Intune | Microsoft Docs: `https://docs.microsoft.com/en-us/mem/intune/fundamentals/supported-devices-browsers`

-   Intune operated by 21Vianet in China | Microsoft Docs: `https://docs.microsoft.com/en-us/mem/intune/fundamentals/china`

-   Network requirements and bandwidth details for Microsoft Intune | Microsoft Docs: `https://docs.microsoft.com/en-us/mem/intune/fundamentals/network-bandwidth-use`

6
Windows Deployment and Management

In this chapter, you will get a clear understanding of deploying and updating Windows 10 Enterprise with Microsoft Endpoint Manager's Intune for different cloud PC and physical PC Microsoft Endpoint Manager-managed endpoint scenarios. You'll learn about the different deployment methodologies and other features that you can use to provide Windows updates and management at the enterprise level.

In this chapter, we'll go through the following topics:

- Deploying existing Windows devices into Microsoft Endpoint Manager

- What about on-premises devices?

  - Co-management

  - Tenant attach

- Microsoft Surface and other **Original Equipment Manufacturer (OEM)** devices

- Windows Update for Business

- Windows 10 and Windows 11 update rings

Deploying existing Windows devices into Microsoft Endpoint Manager

This scenario applies to physical Windows endpoints only.

In enterprise companies today, the normal approach is to leverage OS deployment either from Microsoft Endpoint Manager Configuration Manager or Microsoft Deployment Toolkit.

Microsoft Deployment Toolkit is simpler as it only requires access to a share, where the Windows 10 OS driver application is stored.

Both Configuration Manager and Deployment Toolkit often require the device to be on-premises to join the corporate **Active Directory** (**AD**) and have access to the **Preboot eXecution Environment** (**PXE**) server to even getting started with OS deployment.

Over the last few decades, enterprise companies have started to delete all the work that the OEM put into making a device run in the most optimal way with Windows 10, drivers, and the combination of the settings that are needed on a brand-new device to perform in the best way possible. This was done by leveraging a *wipe and load* imaging concept, and only what the company approved to be installed on the devices would be installed. Normally, this would be an older version of Windows, older versions of drivers, and Microsoft Enterprise apps.

If only it were possible to do this in a simpler way and from anywhere. With the outbreak of Covid-19 and almost everybody working from home, luckily, modern technology has allowed us to disconnect from physical locations and move to working from anywhere. This also includes provisioning a brand-new device to an end user's home address without the end user needing to go to the office location and get the new device. This is possible today with modern provisioning, called **Windows Autopilot**. We will cover Windows Autopilot at a high level in this chapter, and in more depth and with real-life examples in the next chapter.

Windows Autopilot is a group of different components of technology that come together into one service to configure new devices out of the box to get them ready for production usage. The cool thing about Autopilot is that you can also use it to reset, repurpose, and recover devices from scratch if you want to start over again. This is all done to release the IT department from doing all this work themselves; there's no infrastructure to manage as Autopilot runs as a cloud service within Microsoft Endpoint Manager, so it's simple and easy to get productive faster!

Enrolling devices – Windows enrollment

In this section, we will learn about several different ways a Windows 10 PC can be enrolled into Intune by users or admins, which you can find under **Devices | Enroll devices | Windows enrollment** inside the admin center portal.

> **Important Note**
>
> Windows 365 Cloud PCs are automatically enrolled into Microsoft Endpoint Manager's Intune.

Automatic enrollment

This section covers configuring Windows devices to enroll when they join or register with **Azure Active Directory** (**AAD**). We covered this in the previous chapter, *Chapter 5*, *Requirements for Microsoft Endpoint Manager*, so please go back to that chapter to learn more.

You see the Windows enrollment dashboard here, which is your starting point for configuring most elements in the section:

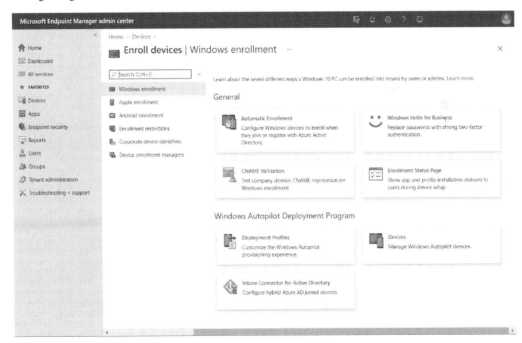

Figure 6.1 – Windows enrollment

Testing company domain CNAME registration for Windows enrollment

Configuring a CNAME in your DNS saves your users from having to enter the address of the **Mobile Device Management** (**MDM**) server when enrolling their Windows devices.

After configuring the CNAME resource records in your DNS, enter the corresponding domain to confirm that it has been configured correctly.

Changes to DNS records might take up to 72 hours to propagate. You can find the configuration option that makes this possible in the following screenshot:

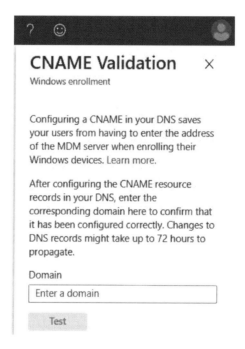

Figure 6.2 – CNAME validation setup

Let's now switch over to the **Enrollment Status Page** screen to learn more about the results and status of your enrollment into Microsoft Endpoint Manager.

Enrollment Status Page

The **Enrollment Status Page** screen displays the provisioning progress after a new device is enrolled, as well as when new users sign in to the device. This enables IT administrators to optionally prevent (block) access to the device until it has been fully provisioned, while at the same time giving users information about the tasks remaining in the provisioning process.

The default enrollment status page applies to all users and all devices, but you can create multiple enrollment status page profiles with different configurations that are needed for your scenario.

These profiles are specified in priority order; the highest priority that is applicable will be used. Each enrollment status page profile can be targeted to groups containing devices or users. When determining which profile to use, the following criteria will be followed:

- The highest-priority profile targeted to the device will be used first.

- If there are no profiles targeted to the device, the highest-priority profile targeted to the current user will be used. (This only applies in scenarios where there is a user. In white-glove and self-deploying scenarios, only device targeting can be used.)

- If there are no profiles targeted to specific groups, then the default enrollment status page profile will be used.

The enrollment status page is not just applicable to Windows Autopilot devices but to all devices that are enrolled into Microsoft Intune that have it assigned either to users or devices.

We will cover Windows Autopilot in depth, including how to set it up and configure the enrollment status page for different scenarios, in the next chapter.

In the following screenshot, you can see how to capture devices on the **Enrollment Status Page** screen:

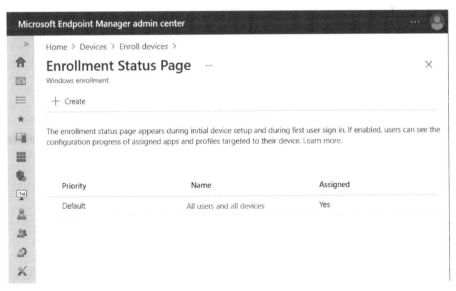

Figure 6.3 – Enrollment Status Page screen

Windows Autopilot

In this section, you will learn a bit more about Autopilot. We will spend a lot of time on Autopilot in *Chapter 7*, *Manager Windows Autopilot*, later on in the book.

Windows Autopilot works with so-called deployment profiles that let you customize the out-of-the-box experience for your devices. This makes it easier for customers to create their own set of configuration items out of the box without any user interaction. We'll explain more about this in the next chapter.

Windows Autopilot simplifies the Windows device life cycle, for both IT and end users, from initial deployment to end of life. Using cloud-based services, Windows Autopilot does the following:

- Reduces the time IT spends on deploying and managing devices

- Reduces the infrastructure required to onboard and maintain devices

- Has the option to use break-fix and Autopilot Reset for end users or IT admins

More about the Autopilot enrollment flow can be learned from the following diagram, based on the profiles explained earlier in this section:

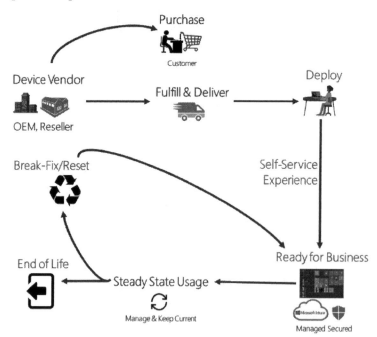

Figure 6.4 – Autopilot process

Once you have deployed Windows Autopilot, it is important that your organization keeps up to date with the latest Windows releases. Many companies refer to this as *being evergreen*. To help your organization stay current, you should look into Windows Update for Business.

What about existing infrastructures?

We talked about the broader unified endpoint management concept of Microsoft Endpoint Manager in the first two chapters, explaining that you could manage and maintain all your devices from one single unified dashboard console.

We do recognize that not all customers are moving directly to Microsoft Endpoint Manager in an AAD-managed manner. Therefore, co-managing existing on-premises Windows 10 devices and hybrid AAD-joined devices is supported too within Microsoft Endpoint Manager. This would create the same unified endpoint management experience for your hybrid configuration.

Co-management and tenant attach

Co-management is not a new feature, as it has been around for a while. Co-management makes it possible to move workloads from Configuration Manager (formerly **System Center Configuration Manager** (**SCCM**)) to Microsoft Endpoint Manager's Intune. It tells the Windows 10 clients that are managed by Configuration Manager who the management authority is for different workloads and also allows you to see and manage them from the Microsoft Endpoint Manager console. To make it simple, a co-managed device is managed by both Configuration Manager and Microsoft Endpoint Manager at the same time.

Tenant attach is a bit different and limited in terms of management capabilities as tenant attach makes it possible to only add your Configuration Manager environment to Microsoft Endpoint Manager, meaning you can leverage the capabilities available in Microsoft Endpoint Manager. Tenant attach allows you to perform actions on your Configuration Manager-managed clients using the MEM portal, such as installing apps, running scripts, and so on.

For example, with co-management, your existing Windows 10 Enterprise endpoints manager through Configuration Manager mainly listens to Configuration Manager for app deployment and security policies, while it looks at Intune for compliance policies and device configuration policies. This helps businesses to combine the benefits of both Configuration Manager and Microsoft Endpoint Manager without making an impactful cutover directly to Microsoft Endpoint Manager.

> **Important Note**
>
> To use co-management, you have to be using Configuration Manager version 2002 (at least).

In order to enable co-management within Configuration Manager, you must go through the **Co-management Configuration Wizard** screen to enable device upload.

Make sure to click **Sign in** and log on with a global administrator account.

The supported client OS versions for co-management are the following:

- Windows 10
- Windows 8.1

Make sure to select both of these options:

- **Upload to Microsoft Endpoint Manager admin center**
- **Enable automatic client enrollment for co-management**

> **Important Note**
>
> If you only want to enable tenant attach and decide to only see your Configuration Manager environment, you simply have to unselect the **Enable automatic client enrollment for co-management** option.

The **Upload to Microsoft Endpoint Manager admin center** option enables tenant attach:

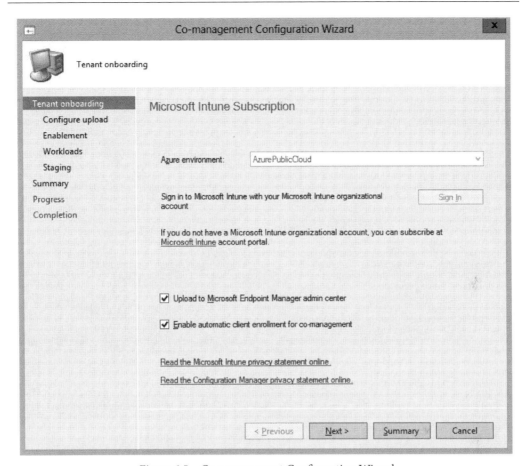

Figure 6.5 – Co-management Configuration Wizard

Enable this first setting, which adds all your devices automatically to Microsoft Endpoint Manager as co-managed devices.

Or, create collections to only add certain devices to the Microsoft Endpoint Manager **Devices** menu instead, as you can see is the second option in the following screenshot:

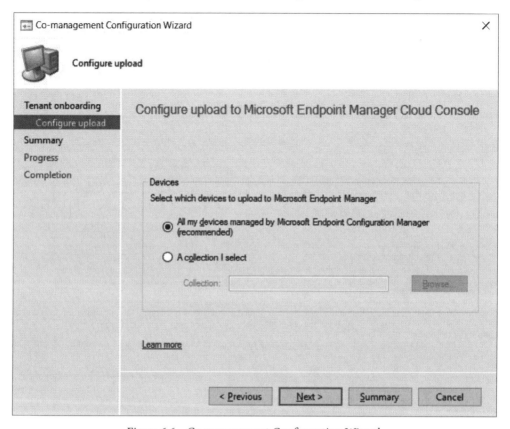

Figure 6.6 – Co-management Configuration Wizard

After the setup, the following completion confirmation should pop up on the screen to confirm that everything went as expected:

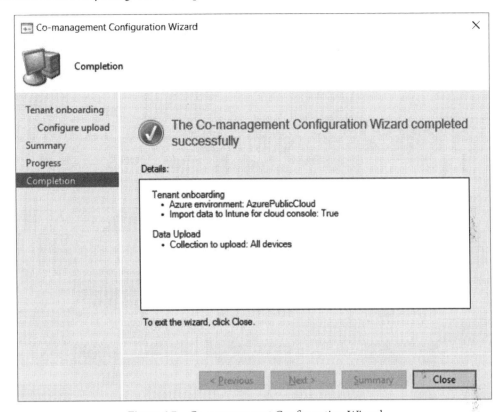

Figure 6.7 – Co-management Configuration Wizard

Devices are now added.

Also, make sure to select the **Enable Endpoint Analytics for devices uploaded to Microsoft Endpoint Manager** option when you want to actively monitor your devices in Endpoint analytics next to your Microsoft Endpoint Manager-managed devices.

In the following screenshot, you can see how to upload device information from your Configuration Manager environment into Endpoint analytics. You will learn more about Endpoint analytics in *Chapter 14, Monitoring and Endpoint Analytics*:

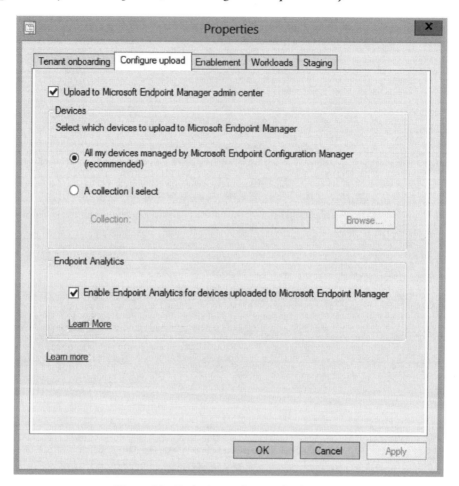

Figure 6.8 – Endpoint analytics upload setting

We'll talk about the benefits of Endpoint analytics later on in the book in more depth if you want to learn more about what the added value in the context of monitoring is.

After the wizard, in the Configuration Manager console, you'll see the connection to your Microsoft Endpoint Manager tenant under **Cloud Services | Co-management**, as in the following screenshot:

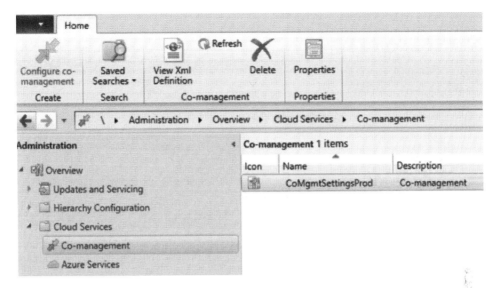

Figure 6.9 – Co-management overview in Configuration Manager

If you do everything correctly, your devices will also show up in the Microsoft Endpoint Manager admin center console, under **All devices**:

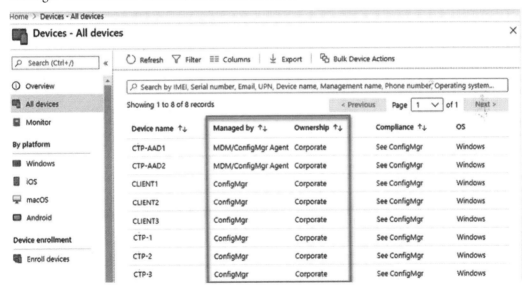

Figure 6.10 – Device status in Microsoft Endpoint Manager

When to use what solution

It might be a bit confusing to understand when to use what management scenario for your organization, so here's a quick table that clarifies this best:

Identity	Management	Provisioning
Active Directory only	Configuration Manager + tenant attach	OS deployment
Hybrid AAD-joined	Microsoft Endpoint Manager's Intune *or* tenant attach + co-management	Microsoft Endpoint Manager and other OS deployments (Configuration Manager/**Microsoft Deployment Toolkit (MDT)**) Windows 365 Cloud PC Enterprise
AAD only	Co-management *or* Microsoft Endpoint Manager's Intune	Windows Autopilot Windows 365 Cloud PC Business

This will help you to make the best decision that aligns with your current and perhaps future scenarios. The good thing is that Microsoft Endpoint Manager supports them all from a unified manageability perspective while you work on your journey toward full modern management in the Microsoft cloud!

Devices that are co-managed, or devices that are enrolled in Intune, may be joined directly to AAD, or they may be hybrid AAD-joined but they must have a cloud identity.

Windows Update for Business

In the first chapter, we covered an overview of Windows Update for Business. In this chapter, we will cover how to get it configured.

When you have devices that use Windows Update for Business to manage and control the update workflow, there are several policies that are of interest. To maximize the update velocity while remaining mindful of user productivity impact, Microsoft suggests a specific set of policies with recommended values. In this section, we will walk through these policies and how to configure them.

Windows Update for Business policies, in this section, apply to Microsoft Intune or co-managed devices with the **Windows Update policies** workload set to Microsoft Intune.

Types of updates managed by Windows Update for Business

Windows Update for Business is designed to provide IT admins with the capability to manage policies for several types of updates to Windows 10 devices:

- **Feature updates**: Previously referred to as **upgrades**, feature updates contain significant feature additions and changes along with security and quality revisions. Feature updates are released semi-annually in the fall (H1) and the spring (H2).

- **Quality updates**: Quality updates are traditional OS updates, typically released on the second Tuesday of each month, though they can be released at any time of the month. These include driver, security, and critical updates.

- **Driver updates**: Updates for non-Microsoft drivers that are relevant to your devices. Driver updates are on by default, but you can use Windows Update for Business policies to turn them off if you prefer.

- **Microsoft product updates**: Windows Update for Business also treats non-Windows updates (such as updates for Microsoft Office, .NET, or Visual Studio) as quality updates. These non-Windows updates are known as **Microsoft updates** and you can set devices to receive such updates (or not) along with their Windows updates.

But first, how do Windows updates work? There are four phases to the Windows update process:

1. **Scan**: A device checks the Microsoft update server or your **Windows Server Update Services** (**WSUS**) endpoint at random intervals to see whether any updates have been added since the last time updates were searched, and then evaluates whether the update is appropriate by checking the guidelines (for example, group policies) that have been set up by the administrator. This process is invisible to the user.

2. **Download**: Once the device determines that an update is available, it begins downloading the update. The download process is not visible to the user. The download happens in multiple sequential phases with feature updates.

3. **Install**: After the update is downloaded, depending on the device's Windows Update settings, the update is installed on the system.

4. **Commit and restart**: Once installed, the device usually (but not always) must be restarted in order to complete the installation and begin using the update. Before that phase, a device runs the previous version of the software.

At each stage of the process, there are opportunities to increase the velocity via policies and settings, and our recommendations follow.

Enforcing compliance deadlines for updates

Deploying feature or quality updates for many organizations is only part of the equation for managing their device ecosystem. The next important part is the ability to enforce update compliance. Windows Update for Business provides controls to manage deadlines for when devices should migrate to newer versions.

How to handle conflicting or legacy policies

We sometimes find that administrators set devices to get both Group Policy settings and MDM settings from an MDM server such as Microsoft Intune. Depending on how they are ultimately set up, policy conflicts are handled differently:

- **Windows updates**: Group Policy settings take precedence over MDM.

- **Microsoft Intune**: If you set different values for the same policy on two different groups, you will receive an alert and neither policy will be set until the conflict is resolved.

It is crucial that you disable conflicting policies for devices in your organization to update as expected. For example, if a device is not reacting to your MDM policy changes, check to see whether a similar policy is set via Group Policy with a differing value.

If you find that the velocity is not as high as you expect or some devices are slower than others, it may be time to clear all policies and settings and specify only the recommended update policies outlined in this document.

How to set up and configure Windows Update for Business

Microsoft Intune provides two policy types to manage Windows Update for Business:

- **Windows 10 update ring**: This policy is a collection of settings that configures when Windows 10 updates get installed. Windows 10 update ring policies have been supported since Windows 10 version 1607, so it is not something completely new.

- **Windows 10 feature updates**: This policy updates devices to the Windows version you specify, and then freezes the feature set version on those devices. This version freeze remains in place until you choose to update them to a later Windows version. While the feature version remains static, devices can continue to install quality and security updates that are available for their feature version. Windows 10 feature update policies are supported for devices that run Windows 10 version 1709 or later.

The steps to set up and configure Windows Update for Business are as follows:

1. Sign in to the Microsoft Endpoint Manager admin center (`https://endpoint.microsoft.com`).

2. Select **Devices | Windows | Windows 10 update rings | Create profile**:

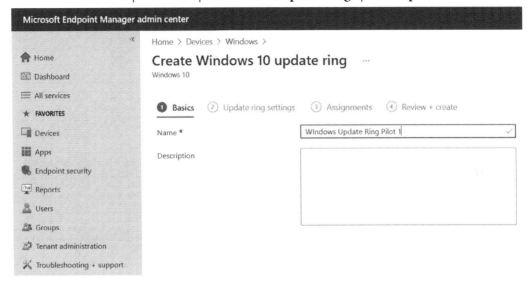

Figure 6.11 – Create Windows 10 update ring

3. In the **Update settings** section, fill in the **Servicing channel**, interval quality, and feature updates settings:

Update settings

Servicing channel ⓘ	Semi-Annual Channel ⌄
Microsoft product updates * ⓘ	Allow Block
Windows drivers * ⓘ	Allow Block
Quality update deferral period (days) * ⓘ	0
Feature update deferral period (days) * ⓘ	0
Set feature update uninstall period (2 - 60 days) * ⓘ	10

Figure 6.12 – Create Windows 10 update ring

For **Servicing channel**, **Semi-Annual Channel** is the default and the channel that is in production, whereas if you select **Windows Insider** for **Servicing channel**, Microsoft Intune automatically configures the Windows Update settings so that the Windows Insider build will work. More about Windows Insider for Business in a later section.

Here's a breakdown of the different configuration settings for update ring:

- **Semi-Annual Channel**
- **Semi-Annual Channel (targeted) for 1809 and below**
- **Windows Insider – Fast**
- **Windows Insider – Slow**
- **Release Windows Insider**

An IT administrator can defer the installation of both feature and quality updates from deploying to devices within a bounded range of time from when those updates are first made available on the Windows Update service.

This deferral can be used to allow time to validate deployments as and when they are pushed to devices.

Deferrals work by allowing you to specify the number of days after an update is released before it is offered to a device. In this way, you can create a ring deployment with different deferral days for the following:

- Pilot group
- Production ring 1
- Production ring 2
- Broad deployment

The update release rings are visualized in the following diagram to help you understand the order better:

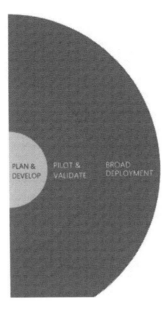

Figure 6.13 – Windows update release rings

When moving to servicing-based Windows updates, you need controlled ways of rolling out updates to representative groups of devices. Deployment rings in Windows 10 are similar to the deployment groups most organizations have been using in the past with other deployment tools; deployment rings are simply a method to separate groups of machines into a controlled deployment timeline.

You can create as many deployment rings as you need and assign them to device groups. You assign policies for Windows 10 update rings and Windows 10 feature updates to groups of devices.

You can set a feature update deferral period of 365 days; the device will not install a feature update that has been released for less than 365 days. This is not a great option if you want to be 100% in control of the feature updates that are being installed on your corporate devices or if you want to skip feature updates and only apply them once a year to your corporate devices.

In the following table, you can find the settings you can configure with the deferral period time per category:

Category	Maximum deferral period	Suggested configurations
Feature updates	365 days	7
Quality updates	30 days	7
Non-deferrable	None	N/A

For **Microsoft product updates**, the default selection is **Allow**. The two available options are as follows:

- **Allow**: Select **Allow** to scan for app updates from Microsoft Update.
- **Block**: Select **Block** to prevent scanning for app updates.

> **Tip**
>
> The recommended value is **Allow** so that you keep all Microsoft products that are installed on the device updates, such as C++, .NET, and so on.

For **Windows drivers**, the default selection is **Allow**. The two options available are as follows:

- **Allow**: Select **Allow** to include Windows Update drivers during updates.
- **Block**: Select **Block** to prevent scanning for drivers.

> **Tip**
>
> The recommended value is **Allow** so that you keep all your drivers updated directly from Windows Update, both for security-related fixes in drivers and firmware as well as stability – be aware that this is an on/off switch for enabling or disabling all or nothing driver updates from Windows Update.

Set feature update uninstall period (days) (2 - 60 days) allows you to set the number of days you can remotely uninstall a feature update from a device.

From within your update ring policy in Microsoft Intune, you can choose to uninstall a Windows feature or quality update on devices.

See the following screenshot for how you can update a ring policy in the Microsoft Endpoint Manager admin center console:

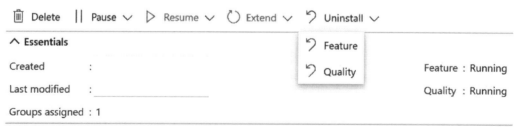

Figure 6.14 – Update ring policy

4. In the **User experience settings** section, you can create the user experience behavior around applying updates:

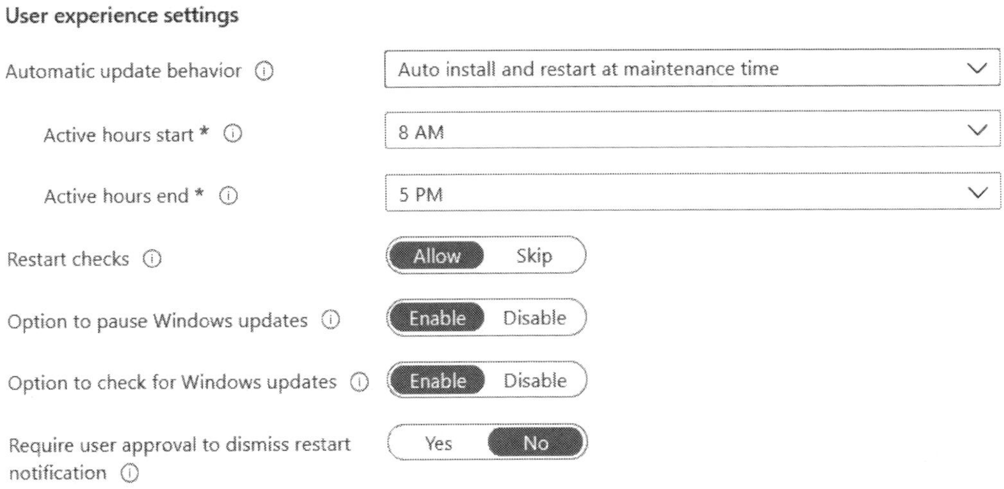

User experience settings

Automatic update behavior ⓘ	Auto install and restart at maintenance time ⌄
Active hours start * ⓘ	8 AM ⌄
Active hours end * ⓘ	5 PM ⌄
Restart checks ⓘ	**Allow** Skip
Option to pause Windows updates ⓘ	**Enable** Disable
Option to check for Windows updates ⓘ	**Enable** Disable
Require user approval to dismiss restart notification ⓘ	Yes **No**

Figure 6.15 – Update ring policy Active hours

The following screenshot shows the default settings for a Windows Update for Business policy in Intune, which also specifies Windows' active hours from 8 A.M. to 5 P.M. unless you change it in the policy:

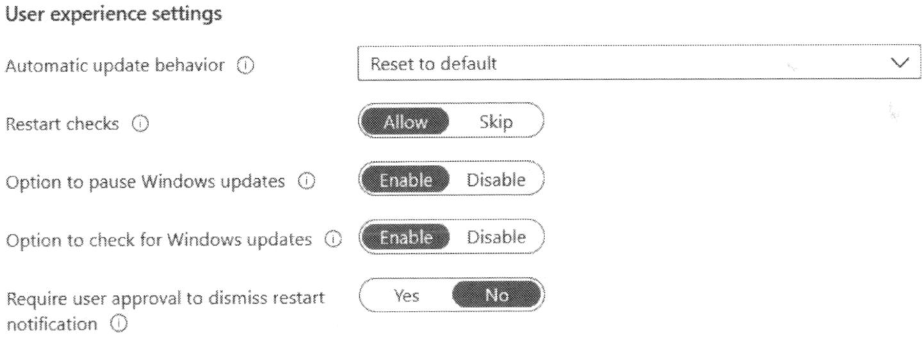

User experience settings

Automatic update behavior ⓘ	Reset to default ⌄
Restart checks ⓘ	**Allow** Skip
Option to pause Windows updates ⓘ	**Enable** Disable
Option to check for Windows updates ⓘ	**Enable** Disable
Require user approval to dismiss restart notification ⓘ	Yes **No**

Figure 6.16 – Update ring policy Reset to default

By using **Reset to default** instead, which is the Microsoft-recommended setting, your end users can set active hours themselves and leverage intelligent active hours if the end user does not configure active hours. This is more important than ever when employees are working different hours than they used to before working from home was the new normal:

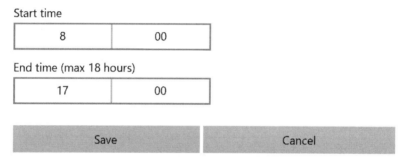

Active hours

Set active hours to let us know when you typically use this device. We won't automatically restart it during active hours, and we won't restart without checking if you're using it.

Start time

| 8 | 00 |

End time (max 18 hours)

| 17 | 00 |

| Save | Cancel |

Figure 6.17 – Active hours client side

Restart checks can be set to skip all checks before restarting. This includes the battery level being at 40%, the user presence, the display needed, presentation mode, fullscreen mode, phone call state, game mode, and so on.

Option to pause Windows updates gives the end user the option to pause an update with Windows Update for up to 7 days.

If you discover a problem while deploying a feature or quality update, it can be paused by the IT administrator for 35 days from a specified start date to prevent other devices from installing it until the issue is mitigated. If you pause a feature update, quality updates are still offered to devices to ensure they stay secure. The pause period for both feature and quality updates is calculated from the start date that you set.

From within your update ring policy in Microsoft Intune, you can choose to pause Windows feature or quality updates on devices:

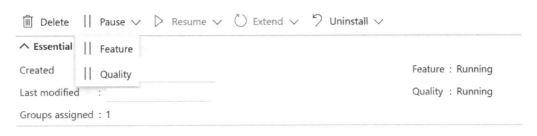

Figure 6.18 – Update ring policy

Option to check for Windows updates is a setting in Windows Update that, when enabled, lets device users check the update service for updates.

For **Require user approval to dismiss restart notification**, specify the method by which the auto-restart required notification is dismissed. For the best end user experience, set this to **Yes**, but when your end users are in control, it can slow down the update compliance for your devices. It is recommended to leave it as the default: **No**. You can find the settings in the following screenshot:

Remind user prior to required auto-restart with dismissible reminder (hours) ⓘ	Number of hours, 2, 4, 8, 12, or 24 ✓
Remind user prior to required auto-restart with permanent reminder (minutes) ⓘ	Number of minutes, 15, 30, or 60 ✓
Change notification update level ⓘ	Use the default Windows Update notifications ∨

Figure 6.19 – Update ring policy

For **Remind user prior to required auto-restart with dismissible reminder (hours)**, specify the period for auto-restart warning reminder notifications. Allowed values are **2**, **4**, **8**, **12**, or **24**. The default value is 4 hours. The recommendation is to leave it blank.

For **Remind user prior to required auto-restart with permanent reminder (minutes)**, specify the period for auto-restart imminent warning notifications. Allowed values are **15**, **30**, or **60**. The default value is **15**. The recommendation is to leave it blank.

Change notification update level specifies what Windows Update notifications users see. The recommendation is to set it to **Use the default Windows Update notifications**, so that the end user gets as many notifications as possible and has the option to take action on this accordingly.

If you have a kiosk device, an ATM, or another device with no user on it, it is recommended to set it to **Turn off all notifications, including restart warnings**, as there are no end users to respond to the notifications on those devices. You can find the settings in the following screenshot:

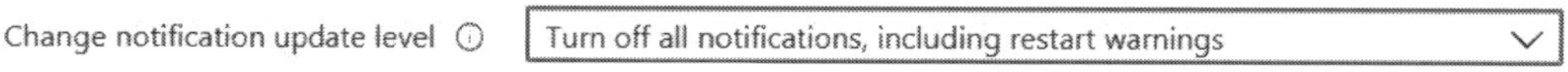

Change notification update level ⓘ | Turn off all notifications, including restart warnings | ⌄

Figure 6.20 – Update ring policy notification level

Use deadline settings allows you to leverage deadline settings. The recommend setting is **Allow**. Leveraging the **Allow** setting gives you, as an IT administrator, the option to set deadlines for both feature and quality updates.

For **Deadline for feature updates**, the number of days allowed is 2 to 30. It is recommended to set it to **7**, so a Windows feature update will have a deadline of 7 days before it is forced to do the installation and reboot.

For **Deadline for quality updates**, the number of days allowed is 2 to 30. It is recommended to set it to **5**, so a Windows quality update will have a deadline of 5 days before it is forced to do the installation and reboot. This will not prevent the end user from installing the quality updates before the deadline has reached the end.

For **Grace period**, the number of days allowed is 0 to 7. It is recommended to set it to **2** days, so if an end user comes back from vacation, they will have 2 days to get the updates installed and restart their device.

For **Auto reboot before deadline**, the recommended setting is **Yes**. This specifies whether the device should auto-reboot before the deadline. **Yes** will ensure that the reboot happens with as little end user interaction as possible. **No** will ensure that the end user is always present on the devices for a reboot.

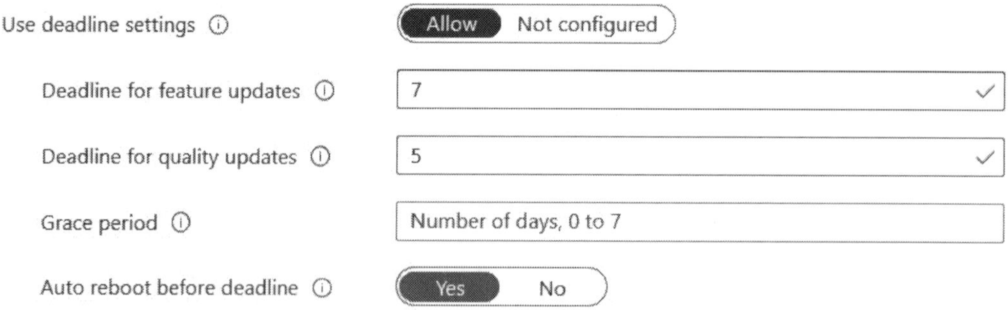

Use deadline settings ⓘ   (Allow   Not configured)

Deadline for feature updates ⓘ | 7 | ✓

Deadline for quality updates ⓘ | 5 | ✓

Grace period ⓘ | Number of days, 0 to 7 |

Auto reboot before deadline ⓘ   (Yes   No)

Figure 6.21 – Update ring policy Use deadline settings

When you specify different deadlines for automatic Windows updates and OS restart, the end user notifications will look like this:

- The user receives a toast notification, a few days after which the user receives this dialog:

Figure 6.22 – Toast notification

- The user receives this notification 15 minutes before the restart, if the user scheduled a restart or if an auto-restart is scheduled:

Figure 6.23 – Restart notification

If the restart is still pending after the deadline passes, the following notifications are shown:

- 12 hours before the deadline passes, the user receives this notification:

Figure 6.24 – Notification before deadline passes

- The user is forced to restart to keep their devices in compliance once the deadline has passed and receives this notification:

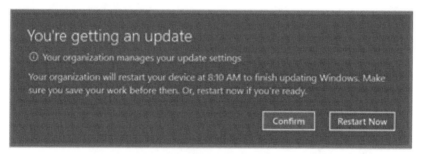

Figure 6.25 – Notification after deadline passes

For the best experience with Windows Update, follow these guidelines:

- Use devices for at least 6 hours per month, including at least 2 hours of continuous use.

- Keep devices regularly charged. Plugging in devices overnight enables them to automatically update outside of active hours.

- Make sure that devices have at least 10 GB of free space (enable a Storage Sense policy).

- Give devices unobstructed access to the Windows Update service.

The next section will explain everything you need to know about preventing applying updates to devices that include known issues. Let's take a look.

Safeguard holds

Safeguard holds prevent a Windows 10 device with a known issue from being offered a new feature update. Microsoft renews the offer once a fix is found and verified. Microsoft uses safeguard holds to ensure customers have a successful experience as their device moves to a new version of Windows 10.

The time a specific Windows 10 device or hardware model has safeguard holds varies depending on the time required to investigate and fix an issue. During this time, Microsoft works diligently to procure, develop, and validate a fix and then offer it to affected devices. Microsoft monitors quality and compatibility data to confirm that a fix is complete before releasing the safeguard hold. Once Microsoft removes the safeguard hold, Windows Update will automatically resume offering the Windows feature that was on the safeguard hold. A safeguard hold is not the same as an IT administrator leveraged pause in a Windows Update for Business deployment ring.

The aim of safeguards is to protect the device and user from a failed or poor upgrade experience.

When using Windows Update for Business and a device has a safeguard hold, the end user will see this message in the Windows Update part of the local settings app on the Windows 10 device:

Figure 6.26 – Feature update

As there is a reason for safeguard holds, it is not recommended to manually attempt to upgrade Windows until the issue that is causing the safeguard hold is resolved.

Windows 10 feature updates

Windows 10 feature updates policies work in conjunction with your Windows 10 update ring policies from Microsoft Intune, to prevent a device from receiving a Windows feature version that is later than the value specified in the feature updates policy.

A feature update in the Windows update ring policy should be configured to **0**, which you can do in the following setting in Microsoft Endpoint Manager:

Figure 6.27 – Update ring policy setting

Feature updates for the update ring must be running. They must not be paused.

The device updates to the version of Windows specified in the policy. However, it remains at its current version if the device is already running a later version of Windows. By freezing the version, the device's feature set remains stable for the duration of the policy.

Microsoft Intune Windows 10 feature updates require the following prerequisites:

- Be enrolled in Intune MDM and be hybrid AD-joined, AAD-joined, or AAD-registered.

- Have Telemetry turned on, with a minimum setting of **Basic**.

We are now going to configure the Windows 10 feature update profile settings in Microsoft Endpoint Manager:

1. Sign in to the Microsoft Endpoint Manager admin center (`https://endpoint.microsoft.com`).

2. Select **Devices** | **Windows** | **Windows 10 Feature Updates** | **Create profile**:

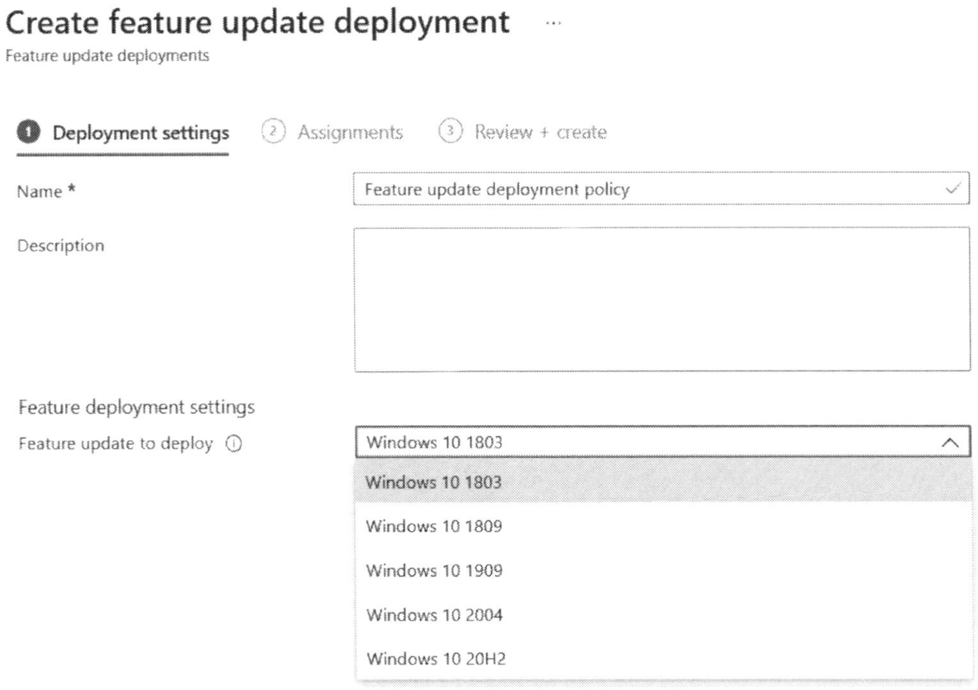

Create feature update deployment …

Feature update deployments

① Deployment settings   ② Assignments   ③ Review + create

Name *   Feature update deployment policy

Description

Feature deployment settings

Feature update to deploy ⓘ   Windows 10 1803   ⌃

                                        Windows 10 1803

                                        Windows 10 1809

                                        Windows 10 1909

                                        Windows 10 2004

                                        Windows 10 20H2

Figure 6.28 – Create feature update deployment

You can select feature updates to be deployed as follows:

- **Windows 10 1803**

- **Windows 10 1809**

- **Windows 10 1909**

- **Windows 10 2004**

- **Windows 10 20H2**

By setting this policy, the specified Windows feature is not downloaded and installed from Microsoft Intune but it tells the devices to send the information on what feature update the devices should be on when Windows Update sync is performed at the next scheduled time after receiving the policy from Microsoft Intune.

Opting out of safeguard holds

Opting out of Windows Update safeguard holds is available on Windows Update for Business devices running Windows 10 version 1809 and above and installed with the October 2020 security update.

Safeguard holds prevent a device with a known compatibility issue from being offered a new OS version. The offering will proceed once a fix is issued and is verified on a held device.

The safeguard holds protection is provided by default to all devices trying to update to a new Windows 10 feature update version via Windows Update.

IT admins can, if necessary, opt devices out of safeguard protections using group policy settings or via the **Disable safeguards for Feature Updates** MDM settings.

The MDM policy can be configured as a custom policy from Microsoft Intune. More details on how to create a custom policy in Microsoft Intune will be covered in *Chapter 10, Advanced Policy Management*. When you are creating the custom policy in Microsoft Intune, you need to fill out every mandatory field like in this example:

Figure 6.29 – OMA-URI Settings

More details are as follows:

- **Name**: `DisableWUfBSafeguards`
- **Description**: `This policy will disable safeguards`
- **OMA-URI**: `./Vendor/MSFT/Policy/Config/Update/DisableWUfBSafeguards`
- **Data type**: **Integer**
- **Value**: **1**

The supported values for this option are as follows:

- **0** (default): Safeguards are enabled, and devices may be blocked for upgrades until the safeguard is cleared.

- **1**: Safeguards are not enabled, and upgrades will be deployed without blocking on safeguards.

Opting out of the safeguards can put devices at risk of known performance issues. The recommendation is only opting out in an IT-controlled environment for validation purposes.

The **Disable safeguards policy** option will revert to **Not Configured** on a device after moving to a new Windows 10 version, even if previously enabled. This ensures the admin is consciously disabling Microsoft's default protection from known issues for each new feature update.

Disabling safeguards does not guarantee your device will be able to successfully update. The update may still fail on the device and will likely result in a bad experience post upgrade as you are bypassing the protection given by Microsoft pertaining to known issues.

In the next section, you'll learn about options to deploy Windows updates faster.

Expediting a Windows patch

Expediting quality patching is done to deploy updates faster than normal across your device estate. If an important quality update is released and has an important security fix, you can leverage the expedite policy.

By creating an expedite policy, the expectation is to get more than 90% of devices with an expedited policy assigned, updated, and restarted within 2 days. That also means that when using this type of policy, it can have a negative impact on your end users' productivity as it has a way more aggressive reboot behavior. Two to three times more devices are updated successfully in the first week of deployment compared to devices configured with Windows Update for Business ring policy settings.

One benefit of expediting an update is that you won't need to modify the existing quality update settings of your Windows 10 update rings. An expedited profile will temporarily override any Windows Update for Business settings and use the necessary settings from the expedited policy instead; this is to ensure the expedited update is installed as quickly as possible on the targeted devices. The settings from your Windows Update for Business policy will be automatically restored to the correct state after the expedited update successfully installs.

Support for expediting an update policy is available on Windows 10 devices that are still receiving updates through Windows Update and have not reached the end of service. Devices need to be hybrid AAD-joined or AAD-joined for the policy to work.

Expedited updates use **Windows Push Notification Services** (**WNS**) and push notification channels to deliver the message to devices that there's an expedited update to install. This is done to speed up installation. This process enables devices to start the download and install from Windows Update as an expedited update as soon as possible, without having to wait for the device to go through the normal scheduled check-in process for talking to the Windows Update backend service.

To configure a quality update profile, do the following:

1. Sign in to the Microsoft Endpoint Manager admin center (`https://endpoint.microsoft.com`).

2. Select **Devices** | **Windows** | **Windows 10 Quality Updates** | **Create profile**:

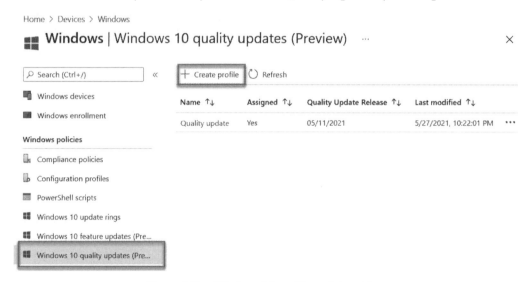

Figure 6.30 – Windows 10 quality update settings

You can select quality updates to be deployed. You can always select the three latest patches released for Windows 10:

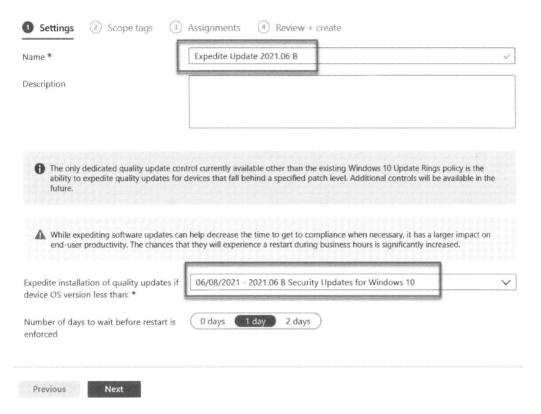

Figure 6.31 – Windows 10 quality update profile

Important Note

Use 2 days for the best end user experience. If the update is very important, select 0 days, but be aware that the devices this policy is assigned to will force a reboot after the patch is downloaded and installed.

You can see how the notifications keep getting more and more aggressive as the deadline approaches:

1. You will start by getting the message **restart in x days** depending on the number of days set in the policy:

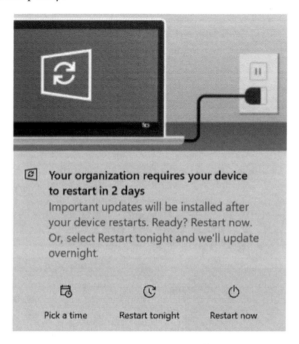

Figure 6.32 – Restart in x days

2. Then, it will get more aggressive and show this message on the end user's screen 2 days before the restart, where the end user has the option to pick a time:

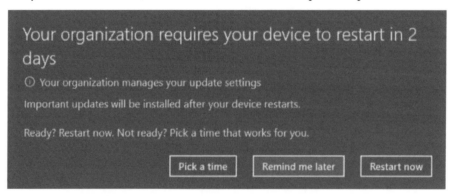

Figure 6.33 – Notification to pick a time for restart

3. Then, it will get even more aggressive and show this message on the end user's screen 2 hours before the restart. The end user has the option to confirm and wait or restart now:

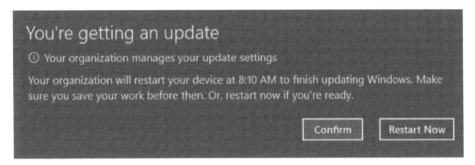

Figure 6.34 – Notification 2 hours before restart

4. 15 minutes before the restart deadline, the end user only has the option to restart:

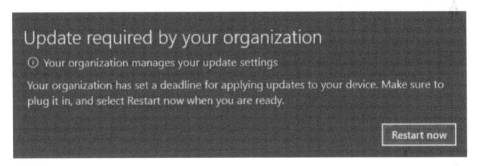

Figure 6.35 – Forced restart

Windows 11 update

Windows 11 was released on October 5 as **General Availability** (**GA**) and can now be used as part of your production workloads. Microsoft Endpoint Manager supports Windows 11 from day one from a configuration management perspective.

For example, you can push the Windows 11 update to your physical or cloud PCs as update ring. Make sure to select the right Windows 11 service channel.

You can read more about this in this official Microsoft blog article: `https://techcommunity.microsoft.com/t5/windows-it-pro-blog/commercial-previews-for-windows-11-and-windows-10-version-21h2/ba-p/2676467`.

You can click **Download** and **install** in the following screen to start the update:

Figure 6.36 – Windows 11 update

The Windows Insider Program for Business

Register for the Windows Insider Program for Business. The benefit of enrolling your corporate tenant for the Windows Insider Program for Business is that you as an IT admin can manage installations of Windows 10 and Windows 11 Insider preview builds across multiple devices in your organization using Microsoft Intune.

Register with either your AAD work account, which we recommend for the best experience, or your personal Microsoft account. If you use your organization's account, you'll be able to give Microsoft feedback on behalf of your organization to help shape Windows to meet your business's specific needs. You must register with your AAD account to manage Windows 10/11 Insider preview builds centrally across your organization (`https://insider.windows.com/en-us/for-business`):

Figure 6.37 – Windows Insider Program

You need to register with your global admin account for Windows Insider for Business:

Register for the Windows Insider Program

To register your organization's domain with the Windows Insider Program ("Program"), read the Program Agreement and Privacy Statement, then accept the terms of the program.

> Program Agreement

☑ I accept the terms of this agreement. (Required)

Register now

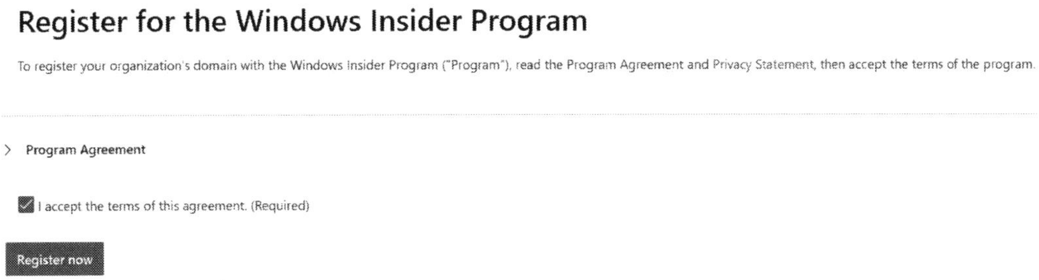

Figure 6.38 – Windows Insider Program

You need to read the program agreement and click **I accept the terms of this agreement. (Required)**:

Register your domain

To register a domain, you must have registered for the program with your work account in Azure Active Directory (AAD), and you must be assigned a Global Administrator role on that AAD domain.

You've already registered your domain

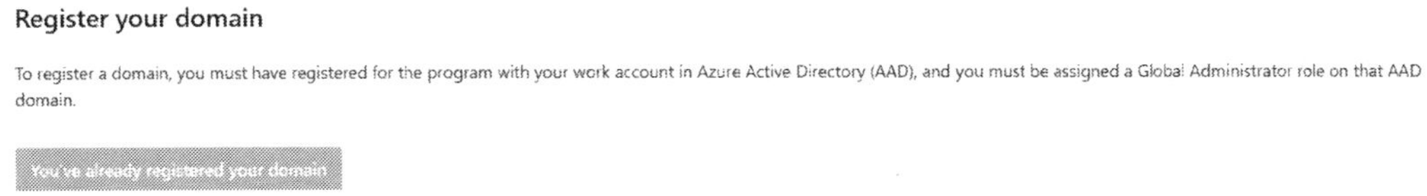

Figure 6.39 – Windows Insider Program registration

Now your domain is registered to leverage Windows Insider for Business.

You can now create a Windows Update for Business ring deployment with Windows Insider rings and assign it to a group of test devices:

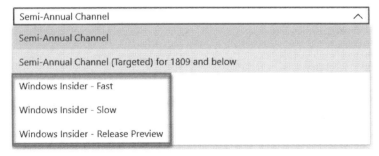

Figure 6.40 – Windows Insider deployment ring

Your end user can now send feedback in the Feedback Hub with their AAD account and other members of your organization can see this feedback.

Select the **Feedback** section from the side menu.

Under the **Filter** dropdown, select **My organization**. This will show all the feedback from users in your organization who are also signed in to the Feedback Hub using their registered AAD accounts:

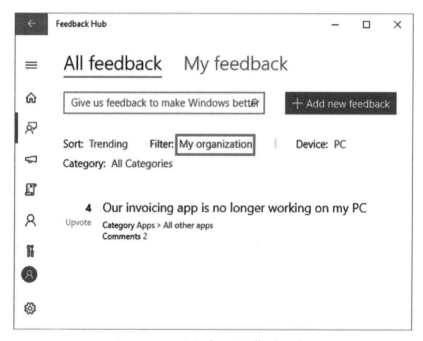

Figure 6.41 – Windows Feedback Hub

Updating Microsoft 365 apps

When you are starting to leverage Windows Update for Business either on a cloud-managed device or a co-managed device, you should also be looking at how you are managing updating Microsoft 365 apps.

There are two options:

- **Servicing profile for Microsoft 365 apps**: You can see an overview of the devices in the **Servicing Profile** section of the Microsoft 365 apps admin center (`config.office.com`), including details on the next build rollout, projected waves, and information on any device failures and issues.

From there, you can click on **Devices**, **Actions**, **Issues**, and **Settings** to get more information on devices managed by the servicing profile:

Figure 6.42 – Microsoft 365 apps servicing policy

- **Administrative templates to configure policies**: Administrative templates are the way that you are used to configuring policy settings in your on-premises environment with group policies.

  The recommendation is to look at the new servicing capabilities provided by the Office 365 Apps admin center. We will cover this in depth in *Chapter 8*, *Application Management and Delivery*, later in this book.

This has brought us to the end of the chapter.

Summary

In the chapter, you've learned about all the subjects you need to know in order to start deploying and updating Windows with Microsoft Endpoint Manager and Windows Update for Business for different endpoint scenarios.

We went through the different options on how to update Windows and what policy settings you should apply. If you are used to leveraging SCCM for deploying Windows Update, you probably already have some kind of ring deployment when you are deploying Windows Updates in your business. With Windows Update for Business, you can start taking the same approach as Windows Update for Business has ring-based deployments as well.

If you are not already running Windows Insider for Business, we explained why it is a good idea to start, and now you are ready to configure Windows Insider for Business in your organization. In the next chapter, we're going to take a deeper dive into the world of Windows Autopilot.

Questions

1. What is Windows Update for Business?

    A. A way to update Microsoft apps

    B. A way to update Microsoft Edge

    C. A way to update Windows

2. What is the maximum number of days for **Set feature update uninstall period**?

    A. 30

    B. 60

    C. 90

3. What is Windows Insider for Business?

    A. A way to get pre-releases of Windows

    B. Windows Information Protection

    C. Microsoft 365 apps pre-release

Answers

1. (C)
2. (B)
3. (A)

Further reading

If you want to learn more about the Microsoft Endpoint Manager requirements after reading this chapter, please use one of the free online resources listed here:

- Learn about using Windows Update for Business – Azure, Microsoft Docs: `https://docs.microsoft.com/en-us/mem/intune/protect/windows-update-for-business-configure`

- Understanding hybrid Azure AD join and co-management: `https://techcommunity.microsoft.com/t5/microsoft-endpoint-manager-blog/understanding-hybrid-azure-ad-join-and-co-management/ba-p/2221201`

7
Manager Windows Autopilot

In this chapter, you will learn about Windows Autopilot, how it works, and why it could be beneficial for your organization to simplify the delivery process of your physical endpoints.

Windows Autopilot is a collection of technologies used to preconfigure brand-new devices and get them into a state where the end user can be productive.

Windows Autopilot is designed to easily onboard a brand-new device from anywhere. Previously, enterprises relied on **Operation System Deployment (OSD)**, but during the global Covid pandemic, where many employees were working from home, more and more enterprises were looking for alternatives to get new devices to their end users even when working from home. Windows Autopilot is a perfect fit for this scenario, where an **Original Equipment Manufacturer (OEM)** or reseller can send the device directly to the end user, who can then unbox the new device, get it up and running, and start working without any need to go into the office.

In this chapter, we'll go through the following topics:

- Windows Autopilot overview
- Uploading the hardware ID to Windows Autopilot
- Windows Autopilot for existing devices
- Windows updates during the **Out-of-Box Experience** (**OOBE**)
- **Enrollment Status Page (ESP)**
- Autopilot reporting and diagnostics
- Cloud configuration scenario
- Edge kiosk self-deployment scenario
- Wiping and resetting your devices
- Fresh start

Technical requirements

Windows Autopilot has some prerequisites:

- **Azure Active Directory** (**AAD**) automatic enrollment needs to be configured.
- The user needs an Intune license.
- The device needs to be registered in the Windows Autopilot service.
- AAD branding.

Windows Autopilot overview

Windows Autopilot is a provisioning method for modern devices. It is not an OSD in the traditional manner. Windows Autopilot requires a cloud identity and cloud device identity, which can be either a *hybrid AAD join* or an *AAD join*. In this book, we will only cover Windows Autopilot with AAD-joined devices as this is the most modern way of device provisioning.

Windows Autopilot overview

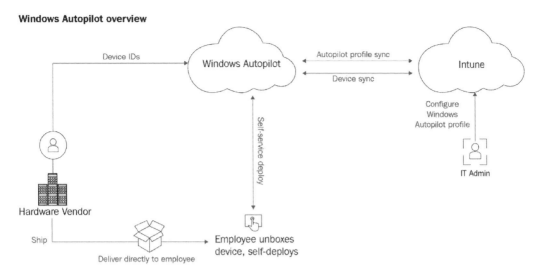

Figure 7.1 – Autopilot process

You get started with Autopilot by getting your devices uploaded to the Autopilot service, creating and assigning an Autopilot profile, and then creating and assigning an ESP profile (this step is optional, but recommended).

After your device is shipped, the user simply has to enter their credentials before automatic enrollment starts. It is as simple as that:

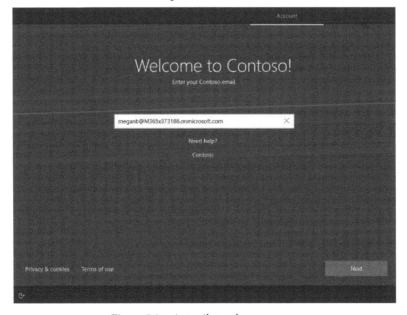

Figure 7.2 – Autopilot welcome screen

After entering the correct credentials, enrollment starts, and all your configuration items, policies, certificates, and applications are applied to your physical endpoint device.

As soon as this phase is completed, the user can see the desktop:

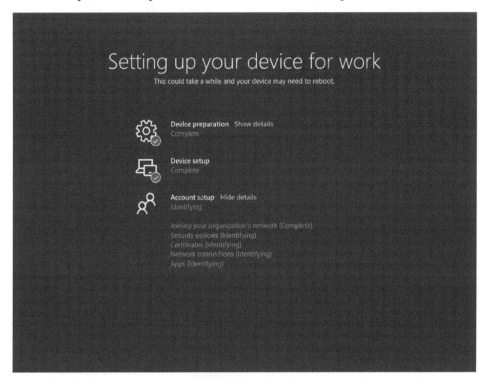

Figure 7.3 – Autopilot setup device

If you use Enterprise State Roaming, you will see your desktop in a familiar way, as most pieces of your profile will come from the cloud down to the device.

By the way, Windows 11 works with Autopilot too, and the experience is completely modernized, as you can see in the following screenshot:

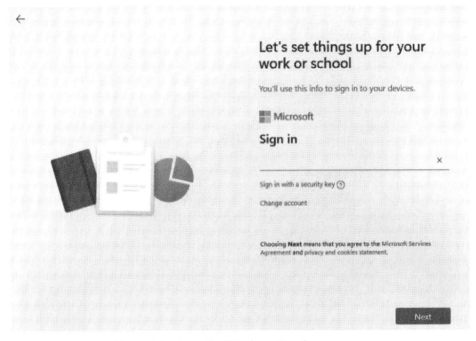

Figure 7.4 – Autopilot Windows 11 welcome screen

Once you proceed and enter the AAD credentials of your user who has the Autopilot and other Microsoft Endpoint Manager profile configurations assigned to their account, the device enrollment setup process starts to kick in, as in the following example as part of Windows 11:

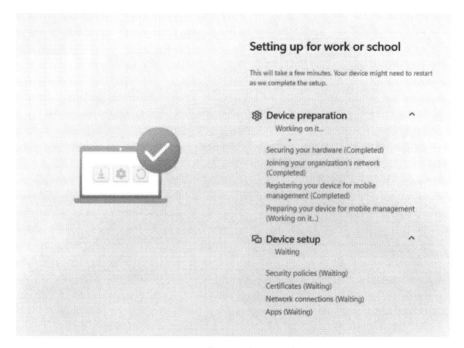

Figure 7.5 – Autopilot Windows 11 device setup

In the next section, we're going to explain how you can add your devices to Windows Autopilot with the hardware ID as a unique indicator.

Uploading the hardware ID to Windows Autopilot

The Windows Autopilot hardware hash is a 4K string retrieved from a running Windows 10 OS on the device by running Get-WindowsAutoPilotInfo.ps1:

```
New-Item -Type Directory -Path "C:\Temp\Autopilot"
Set-Location -Path "C:\Temp\Autopilot"
Set-ExecutionPolicy -Scope Process -ExecutionPolicy
Unrestricted
Install-Script -Name Get-WindowsAutoPilotInfo
Get-WindowsAutoPilotInfo.ps1 -OutputFile AutoPilotHWID.csv
```

Windows Autopilot device registration can be done within your organization manually, for testing, or for devices your organization already owns.

It is used to collect the hardware identity of devices (hardware hashes) and upload this information in a **Comma-Separated Values** (**CSV**) file to the Windows Autopilot service from the Microsoft Endpoint Manager admin center, and also to capture the hardware hash for manual registration, which requires booting the device into Windows 10. Therefore, this process is intended primarily for testing and evaluation scenarios.

The recommended way to get your brand-new devices into the Windows Autopilot service is to have your OEM or a Microsoft **Cloud Solution Provider** (**CSP**) partner upload the information.

For *Microsoft Surface* or *HoloLens* devices, you can open a support case with Microsoft Devices Autopilot Support: `https://prod.support.services.microsoft.com/supportrequestform/0d8bf192-cab7-6d39-143d-5a17840b9f5f`. You only need to provide the following information:

- AAD tenant ID
- AAD domain name
- Proof of ownership
- Device serial numbers

This process can also be used to deregister Autopilot from your tenant.

You can have a CSP partner upload your devices into Windows Autopilot with very little information compared to when you do it in Microsoft Intune yourself:

- `ProductKey` only
- `SerialNumber` + `OemManufacturerName` + `ModelName`

Let's describe each of these fields:

- `ProductKey`: This is the Windows product ID, that is, the PKID, a 13-digit number that corresponds to the Windows product key that was inserted into the firmware of the device at the time of manufacture (using OAv3).
- `SerialNumber`: This is the unique value assigned by the OEM to each device manufactured.
- `OemManufacturerName`: This is the value specified by the OEM in the **System Management Basic Input/Output System** (**SMBIOS**) firmware of the device, for example, *Microsoft Corporation* or *LENOVO* (more on that later).

- ModelName: This is the value specified by the OEM in the SMBIOS firmware of the device for the particular model, for example, *Surface Pro 7*.

To register Windows Autopilot devices manually, the process is as follows.

You can have up to 500 rows in the CSV file. The header and line format are shown next, which include the device serial number, the Windows product ID, the hardware hash, the group tag, and the assigned user:

```
<serialNumber>,<ProductID>,<hardwareHash>,
<optionalGroupTag>,<optionalAssignedUser>
```

> **Important Note**
>
> Import Windows Autopilot devices from a CSV file. When assigning users in the CSV file, make sure that you are assigning the correct **User Principal Name (UPN)** as there is no validation of UPNs during the import process. This means that if an incorrect UPN is in the CSV file, a user will not be assigned to the Windows Autopilot device object.

Assigning a user to a specific Autopilot device does not work if you are using **Active Directory Federation Services (ADFS)**.

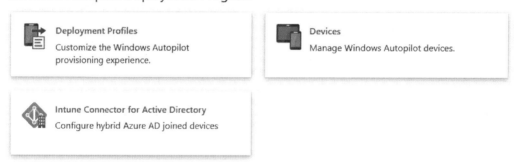

Figure 7.6 – Windows Autopilot Deployment Program

Go to the Microsoft Endpoint Manager admin center, `https://endpoint.microsoft.com/`, and choose **Devices** | **Windows** | **Windows enrollment** | **Devices**.

Choose **Import**:

Home > Windows >

Windows Autopilot devices ...
Windows enrollment

◯ Sync ▽ Filter | ↑ Import ↓ Export | ♈ Assign user ◯ Refresh 🗑 Delete

∧ **Essentials**

Last sync request : 04/10/21, 12:48 AM   Last successful sync : 04/10/21

Windows Autopilot lets you customize the out-of-box experience (OOBE) for your users.

🔎 Search by serial number

	Serial number	Manufacturer	Model	Group Tag
☐				
☐				
☐				

Figure 7.7 – Windows Autopilot devices

Browse for your `autopilot.csv` file and then choose **Import**.

You will get the following message in the portal: **Import in progress. Elapsed time: 0 min**. This process can take up to 15 minutes.

Figure 7.8 – Add Windows Autopilot devices

Select a device. Choose **Assign user**.

Browse for your user and choose the user you want to assign to the device:

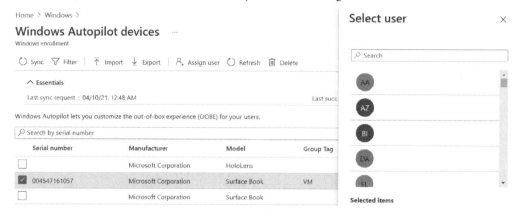

Figure 7.9 – Assign user

When you are selecting a device in the **Windows Autopilot devices** blade, you will get some more information and some attributes that can be changed as an IT admin:

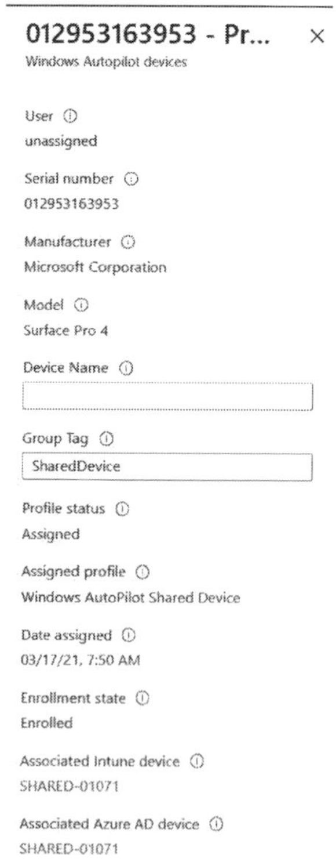

012953163953 - Pr...   ×
Windows Autopilot devices

User ⓘ
unassigned

Serial number ⓘ
012953163953

Manufacturer ⓘ
Microsoft Corporation

Model ⓘ
Surface Pro 4

Device Name ⓘ
[   ]

Group Tag ⓘ
[SharedDevice   ]

Profile status ⓘ
Assigned

Assigned profile ⓘ
Windows AutoPilot Shared Device

Date assigned ⓘ
03/17/21, 7:50 AM

Enrollment state ⓘ
Enrolled

Associated Intune device ⓘ
SHARED-01071

Associated Azure AD device ⓘ
SHARED-01071

Figure 7.10 – Windows Autopilot device

In the following table, you can see the different types of settings and values that can be present in a Windows Autopilot object:

Setting	Value
User	UPN.
User Friendly Name	Can be changed and it will be shown during OOBE provisioning.
Serial number	Serial number.
Manufacturer	Example: "Microsoft Corporation."
Model	Example: "Surface Book 2."
Device Name	Can be configured and the device will get this name as part of the onboarding process (will cause a reboot while the device name is being set during OOBE).
Group Tag	Blank unless it is set in the autopilot upload file. Can be changed and will affect a dynamic AAD group.
Profile status	Assigned or not assigned.
Assigned profile	Name of the profile assigned to the device.
Date assigned	Timestamp of when the profile was assigned to the device.
Enrollment state	Specifies whether the device has enrolled in Microsoft Intune. Enrolled or Not enrolled.
Associated Intune device	N/A means that there's no associated device. N/A is the state until the device has gone through the Autopilot process for the first time, or the Intune object has been deleted.
Associated Azure AD device	N/A means that there's no associated device AAD object.
Last contacted	Timestamp of when the device was last contacted. Doesn't mean that the device has never been in contact with Microsoft Intune.
Purchase order	Purchase order ID is sent from the OEM when they are uploading devices on behalf of your organization.

Newer Windows 10 versions have a 4K hardware hash that is used in the Windows Autopilot service. Examples include where a new hardware hash is needed if the TPM or motherboard is replaced. Some ways that a device is known in the Windows Autopilot service are based on the SMBIOS UUID, **Media Access Control** (**MAC**), or the disk serial number – the reason for this is that there is no unique identifier for a Windows device. If we look at what information is contained in the Autopilot hardware hash, then we also get an idea of why we need a new hardware hash following a motherboard replacement.

The minimum requirements for unique values in the SMBIOS are as follows:

- `ProductKeyID`
- `SmbiosSystemManufacturer`
- `SmbiosSystemProductName`
- `SmbiosSystemSerialNumber`
- `SmbiosSkuNumber`
- `SmbiosSystemFamily`
- `MacAddress`
- `SmbiosUuid`
- `DiskSerialNumber`
- `TPM EkPub`

Where is Windows Autopilot device information stored?

Windows Autopilot data is stored in the **United States** (**US**), and not in the region where your AAD tenant is located. It is not customer data that is stored, but business data, which enables Microsoft to provide the Windows Autopilot service.

First, you need to download the Windows **Assessment and Deployment Kit** (**ADK**) from `https://docs.microsoft.com/en-us/windows-hardware/get-started/adk-install`:

> **Important Note**
> You need to use at least ADK version 1703.

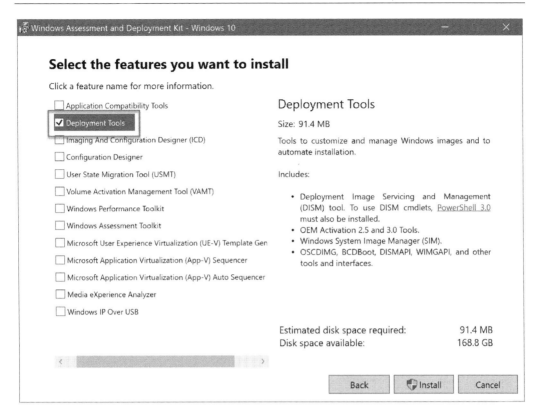

Figure 7.11 – Windows ADK

Following the installation of Microsoft ADK, you can find the tool you need here:

```
C:\Program Files (x86)\Windows Kits\10\Assessment and
Deployment Kit\Deployment Tools\amd64\Licensing\OA30\oa3tool.
exe
```

Say you run the following command:

```
oa3tool.exe /DecodeHwHash=HardwareHash
```

Then, you'll get the result of what is stored in the hardware hash:

```
OEM Activation Tool 3.0
(c) Copyright 2019 Microsoft Corp.
Version: 10.0.19041.1
```

The decoded hardware hash is as follows:

```xml
<?xml version="1.0"?>
<HardwareReport>
    <HardwareInventory>
        <p n="ToolVersion" v="3" />
        <p n="HardwareInventoryVersion" v="131" />
        <p n="ToolBuild" v="10.0.17134.1" />
        <p n="OSType" v="FullOS" />
        <p n="OsCpuArchitecture" v="x64" />
        <p n="OsBuild" v="10.0.17134.1" />
        <p n="OsSystemTime" v="2018-05-18T12:51:13Z" />
        <p n="OsLocalTime" v="2018-05-19T18:51:13+30:00" />
        <p n="ProcessorModel" v="        Intel(R) Xeon(R) CPU
E3-1220L V2 @ 2.30GHz" />
        <p n="ProcessorPackages" v="1" />
        <p n="ProcessorThreads" v="2" />
        <p n="ProcessorCores" v="2" />
        <p n="ProcessorHyperThreading" v="false" />
        <p n="SmbiosRamArrayCount" v="1" />
        <p n="SmbiosRamSlots" v="1" />
        <p n="SmbiosRamErrorCorrection" v="None" />
        <p n="SmbiosRamMaximumCapacity" v="2048" />
        <p n="TotalPhysicalRAM" v="2" />
        <p n="SmbiosFirmwareVendor" v="Microsoft
Corporation" />
        <p n="SmbiosSystemManufacturer" v="Microsoft
Corporation" />
        <p n="SmbiosSystemProductName" v="Virtual Machine"
/>
        <p n="SmbiosSystemSerialNumber" v="2378-0002-7885-
9434-1355-6165-71" />
        <p n="SmbiosUuid" v="192a7ab2-4b1d-4433-9026-
3b54c6e8353c" />
        <p n="SmbiosSkuNumber" v="None" />
        <p n="SmbiosSystemFamily" v="Virtual Machine" />
        <p n="SmbiosSystemVersion" v="Hyper-V UEFI Release
v1.0" />
```

```
            <p n="SmbiosBoardManufacturer" v="Microsoft
Corporation" />
            <p n="SmbiosBoardProduct" v="Virtual Machine" />
            <p n="SmbiosBoardVersion" v="Hyper-V UEFI Release
v1.0" />
            <p n="ChassisType" v="0x03" />
            <p n="Disk1.DiskCapacity" v="80" />
            <p n="Disk1.DiskType" v="HDD" />
            <p n="Disk1.StorageBusType" v="SAS" />
            <p n="Disk1.IncursSeekPenalty" v="255" />
            <p n="Disk1.TrimEnabled" v="1" />
            <p n="Disk1.DiskSerialNumber" v="|Virtual Disk
|Msft      " />
            <p n="InternalDiskCount" v="1" />
            <p n="TotalDiskCapacity" v="80" />
            <p n="OpticalDiskDriveType" v="true" />
            <p n="PhysicalMedium" v="Unspecified" />
            <p n="MacAddress" v="00:15:5D:00:0A:49" />
            <p n="DisplayResolutionHorizontal" v="1024" />
            <p n="DisplayResolutionVertical" v="768" />
            <p n="DisplaySizePhysicalH" v="0" />
            <p n="DisplaySizePhysicalY " v="0" />
            <p n="DigitizerSupportID" v="(null)" />
            <p n="PowerPlatformRole" v="Desktop" />
            <p n="Status" v="0x00000000" />
            <p n="OfflineDeviceIdType" v="UEFI_VARIABLE_
RANDOMSEED" />
            <p n="OfflineDeviceId"
v="deabBSuZ84Ttjnd+ipi2q9gwdtwBUrOYwUmzOEOnbYo=" />
            <p n="DiskSSNKernel" v="|Virtual Disk      |Msft      "
/>
      </HardwareInventory>
</HardwareReport>
```

The OEM activation tool 3.0 successfully completed its required processes.

Windows Autopilot for existing devices

If you do not want to collect and upload the devices into Autopilot, some other options are available to you.

For devices already in Intune, which can be AAD-joined devices or co-managed devices, you can leverage **Convert all targeted devices to Autopilot** in the Autopilot profile:

Figure 7.12 – Convert all targeted devices to Autopilot

Select **Yes** to register all targeted devices to Autopilot if they are not already registered. The next time registered devices go through the Windows OOBE, they will go through the assigned Autopilot scenario.

Please note that certain Autopilot scenarios require specific minimum builds of Windows. Please make sure that your device has the required minimum build to go through the scenario.

Removing this profile won't remove affected devices from Autopilot. To remove a device from Autopilot, use the **Windows Autopilot devices** view.

You can also leverage Windows Autopilot for existing devices by doing traditional OS deployment from **System Center Configuration Manager (SCCM)** or the **Microsoft Deployment Toolkit (MDT)**.

All that you need to do is to put the Autopilot profile in `%windir%\provisioning\AutoPilot\AutopilotConfigurationFile.json`.

When you have created an Autopilot profile in Microsoft Intune, you can export it by leveraging the `WindowsAutopilotIntune` PowerShell module:

```
Install-Module WindowsAutopilotIntune -Force
Install-Module Microsoft.Graph.Intune -Force
Connect-MSGraph
Get-Autopilotprofile
```

You will get a list of all Autopilot profiles in your tenant. The following is an example. We will leverage the ID to get it and convert it to the JSON content required:

```
@odata.type                      : #microsoft.graph.
azureADWindowsAutopilotDeploymentProfile
id                               : 264c05b0-683c-4537-87ff-
```

```
1ff5151d5b98
displayName                     : Intune Book
description                     :
language                        : os-default
createdDateTime                 : 4/10/2021 9:59:13 AM
lastModifiedDateTime            : 4/10/2021 9:59:13 AM
enrollmentStatusScreenSettings  :
extractHardwareHash             : True
deviceNameTemplate              : OSD-%RAND:5%
deviceType                      : windowsPc
enableWhiteGlove                : True
roleScopeTagIds                 : {0}
outOfBoxExperienceSettings      : @{hidePrivacySettings=True;
hideEULA=True; userType=standard; deviceUsageType=singleUser;

skipKeyboardSelectionPage=True; hideEscapeLink=True}
```

When you are calling the command with the unique Autopilot profile ID, you can convert it to the JSON file you need on the Windows device during the image process:

```
Get-Autopilotprofile -id 264c05b0-683c-4537-87ff-1ff5151d5b98 |
ConvertTo-AutopilotconfigurationJSON
{
    "CloudAssignedDomainJoinMethod":  0,
    "CloudAssignedDeviceName":  "OSD-%RAND:5%",
    "CloudAssignedAutopilotUpdateTimeout":  1800000,
    "CloudAssignedForcedEnrollment":  1,
    "Version":  2049,
    "CloudAssignedTenantId":    "c56dd45b-1da6-4bd0-a53b-
1466782d6ee5",
    "CloudAssignedAutopilotUpdateDisabled":  1,
    "ZtdCorrelationId":    "264c05b0-683c-4537-87ff-
1ff5151d5b98",
    "Comment_File":    "Profile Intune Book",
    "CloudAssignedAadServerData":
"{\"ZeroTouchConfig\":{\"CloudAssignedTenantUpn\":\"\",
\"ForcedEnrollment\":1,\"CloudAssignedTenant
Domain\":\"osddeployment.dk\"}}",
```

```
    "CloudAssignedOobeConfig":  1310,

    "CloudAssignedTenantDomain":  "osddeployment.dk",

    "CloudAssignedLanguage":  "os-default"

}
```

Then, you can copy the content of the Autopilot profile to Notepad and save it as `AutopilotConfigurationFile.json`.

Windows devices can be grouped by a correlator ID when enrolling using Autopilot for existing devices through Configuration Manager. The correlator ID is a parameter of the Autopilot configuration file. The `enrollmentProfileName` AAD device attribute is set to equal `OfflineAutopilotprofile-<correlator ID>` automatically. So, arbitrary AAD dynamic groups can be created based on the correlator ID by using the `enrollmentProfileName` attribute.

To create a Windows Autopilot profile, perform the following steps:

1. In the Microsoft Endpoint Manager admin center, `https://endpoint.microsoft.com/`, choose **Devices** | **Windows** | **Windows enrollment** | **Deployment profiles**.

2. Then, choose **Create profile** | **Windows PC**.

3. In the **Enter a Name for the Profile** field, enter `Autopilot Default profile`.

4. Set **Convert all targeted devices to Autopilot** to **No**.

   Select **Yes** to register all targeted devices to Autopilot if they are not already registered. The next time registered devices go through the Windows OOBE, they will go through the assigned Autopilot scenario.

5. Leave every other setting as its default unless you have a reason to change it.

In the OOBE step, configure the following values and then click **Next**:

Setting	Value
Deployment mode	User-Driven.
Join to Azure AD as	Azure AD joined.
Microsoft Software License Terms	Hide.
Privacy settings	Hide.
Hide change account options	Hide.
User account type	Standard.
Allow White Glove OOBE	No.

Setting	Value
Language (Region)	Operating system default.
Automatically configure keyboard	Yes.
Apply device name template	You can choose to apply a device name template. Use a name prefix that can help you identify your devices with this configuration, for example: `OSD-%RAND:x%`

> **Important Note**
>
> **Language (Region)** requires an Ethernet connection doing OOBE to have any effect; otherwise, this OOBE wizard will be shown to the end user. The OS default will only have an effect if the OS is a single OS, so this OOBE wizard page will not be shown if the OS is both `en-US` and `nl-NL` as an example.
>
> **Automatically configure keyboard** requires an Ethernet connection with doing OOBE to have any effect; otherwise, this OOBE wizard will be shown to the end user.

If an `unattend.xml` file is present on the device during the OOBE phase, Windows Autopilot will most probably fail, so if you are performing the imaging of existing devices, just ensure that the files are not present in `%WINDIR%\Panther\Unattend unattend.xml` and `%WINDIR%\Panther\unattend.xml`.

Windows updates during the Out-of-Box Experience (OOBE)

The IT admin cannot opt out of these critical updates as part of the Windows Autopilot provisioning as they are required for the device to operate properly.

Critical driver updates and critical Windows **Zero-Day Patch** (**ZDP**) updates will begin downloading automatically during the OOBE after the user has connected to a network. Thereafter, Autopilot functional and critical updates are automatically downloaded and installed as well.

Feature updates and quality updates will not be updated during this phase of the OOBE.

Windows will alert the user that the device is checking for, and applying, the updates:

Alright, you're connected. Now, we'll check for any updates...

Figure 7.13 – Windows checks for updates during the OOBE

> **Important Note**
>
> If you are using a custom image without any driver integrated, Windows can download drivers as part of this process, and reboots can occur and break the Windows Autopilot experience. The recommendation for Windows Autopilot is to leverage an OEM image for brand-new devices, a custom image with the correct drivers for existing devices, and also when you are testing Windows Autopilot for existing devices, to give the best and the closest experience to a brand-new device.

Auto-assigning Windows Autopilot profiles in Intune

There are two ways to assign an Autopilot profile to a device from Microsoft Intune – static or dynamic AAD groups. Static groups do not give you the automation that you want in an enterprise, so in this section, we will walk you through the automatic profile assignment.

ZTDID is the unique identifier for a device in the Windows Autopilot service. The ZTDID and Group Tag are both attributes on the AAD device object. The Group Tag is a value that you can put in the CSV when you are uploading the device into Windows Autopilot, and this value is something that you can choose. With a Group Tag that you create, you can leverage the Group Tag to group Autopilot devices for a specific purpose, such as an information worker, shared device, Microsoft Teams Rooms system, kiosk device, or something else. A Group Tag can be changed in the Autopilot object at a later point in time if you want the device object to be in a different AD dynamic device group. Remember to click **Sync** in the **Autopilot device** blade; otherwise, you need to wait for the change until the sync has been run in the background.

You will have the standard information – **Device Serial Number**, **Windows Product ID**, **Hardware Hash** – so you just have to create a custom column named `OrderID` with the value you want to use to create your Autopilot dynamic group for profile assignment, for example, `EdgeKIOSK`.

After importing the Autopilot information into Microsoft Intune, you can use Microsoft Graph Explorer to see the device with the information you just created. You need to look for the AAD device object as the Microsoft Intune device object is first created when Windows executes **Mobile Device Management** (**MDM**) enrollment in Microsoft Intune.

Go to Graph Explorer: `https://developer.microsoft.com/en-us/graph/graph-explorer`:

Figure 7.14 – Graph Explorer

Signing in to Graph Explorer

Enter `https://graph.microsoft.com/v1.0/devices` to get all the devices – then you can find the device you just created and see that it has the ZTDID, with a unique value, and the Group Tag is shown as `OrderID in Graph`. You can also run the graph call with the ID at the end and only get the value for a single device: `https://graph.microsoft.com/v1.0/devices/[id]`. The data is stored in a multi-value attribute called `physicalIds`:

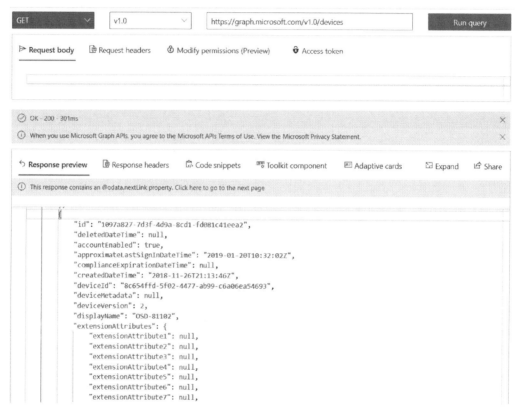

Figure 7.15 – Graph Explorer devices

Then, you can find `physicalIds` as an attribute on the device object in the graph, to verify that there is a ZTDID on the `AzureAD` device object – ZTDID means it is an Autopilot object. You can also see `OrderID` (`OrderID` is the same as Group Tag in the Microsoft Endpoint Manager admin center):

```
"physicalIds": [
    "[HWID]:h:6755414090630361",
    "[ZTDID]:ab1e4d57-66e5-4143-bb43-753be871075f"
```

```
    "[OrderId]:EdgeKIOSK",
    "[USER-HWID]:44cd8da3-8f37-49e0-aa01-
93c7179969d1:6755414090630361",
    "[GID]:g:6825777827713522",
    "[USER-GID]:44cd8da3-8f37-49e0-aa01-
93c7179969d1:6825777827713522",
    ],
```

Now we have all the information we need to create two dynamic AAD groups, one for all Autopilot devices and one for `EdgeKIOSK`.

We will create three dynamic groups so we can distinguish between the different Windows Autopilot scenarios. We are naming the groups `All AutoPilot Devices`, `All AutoPilot EdgeKIOSK`, and `All AutoPilot JSON`.

In the Microsoft Endpoint Manager admin center, `https://endpoint.microsoft.com/`, choose **Groups**.

Choose **New Group**.

Enter the following in the **Group name** field: `All Autopilot Devices`.

Choose **Dynamic Device** for **Membership type**:

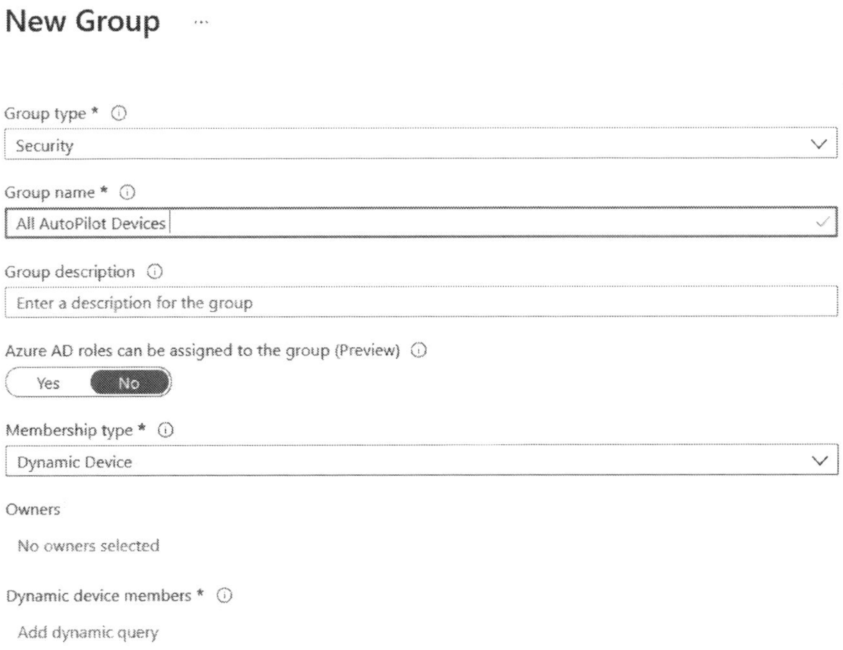

New Group ⋯

Group type * ⓘ
```
Security                                                    ∨
```

Group name * ⓘ
```
All AutoPilot Devices                                       ∨
```

Group description ⓘ
```
Enter a description for the group
```

Azure AD roles can be assigned to the group (Preview) ⓘ
```
Yes    [ No ]
```

Membership type * ⓘ
```
Dynamic Device                                              ∨
```

Owners
  No owners selected

Dynamic device members * ⓘ
  Add dynamic query

Figure 7.16 – New AAD device group

The first group, **All AutoPilot Devices**, has a dynamic group membership rule such as this:

```
(device.devicePhysicalIDs -any _ -contains "[ZTDId]") -and -not
(device.devicePhysicalIDs -any _ -eq "[OrderID]: EdgeKIOSK")
```

This rule will find all devices with the ZTDID and exclude all devices where the value of `OrderID` is EdgeKIOSK:

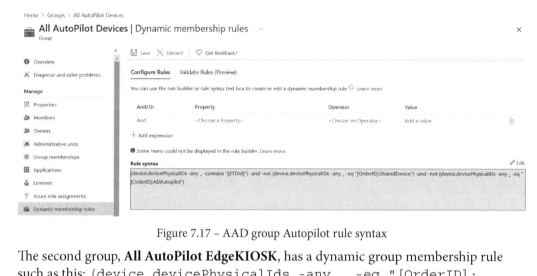

Figure 7.17 – AAD group Autopilot rule syntax

The second group, **All AutoPilot EdgeKIOSK**, has a dynamic group membership rule such as this: `(device.devicePhysicalIds -any _ -eq "[OrderID]: EdgeKIOSK")`.

This rule will find all devices where the value of `OrderID` is equal to `EdgeKIOSK`.

You can also just create the AAD dynamic groups with PowerShell:

```
Install-Module AzureAD

$AzureAdCred = Get-Credential

Connect-AzureAD -Credential $AzureAdCred

# Create a dynamic group called "All AutoPilot Devices"

New-AzureADMSGroup -Description "All AutoPilot Devices"
-DisplayName "All AutoPilot Devices" -MailEnabled $false
-SecurityEnabled $true -MailNickname "Win" -GroupTypes
"DynamicMembership" -MembershipRule "(device.devicePhysicalIDs
-any _ -contains "[ZTDId]") -and -not (device.
devicePhysicalIDs -any _ -eq "[OrderID]:SharedDevice")"
-MembershipRuleProcessingState "On"

# Create a dynamic group called "All AutoPilot EdgeKIOSK"
```

```
New-AzureADMSGroup -Description "All AutoPilot EdgeKIOSK"
-DisplayName "All AutoPilot EdgeKIOSK" -MailEnabled
$false -SecurityEnabled $true -MailNickname "Win"
-GroupTypes "DynamicMembership" -MembershipRule "(device.
devicePhysicalIds -any _ -eq "[OrderID]:EdgeKIOSK")"
-MembershipRuleProcessingState "On"
```

```
# Create a dynamic group called "All AutoPilot JSON"
```

```
New-AzureADMSGroup -Description "All AutoPilot JSON"
-DisplayName "All AutoPilot JSON" -MailEnabled $false
-SecurityEnabled $true -MailNickname "Win" -GroupTypes
"DynamicMembership" -MembershipRule "(device.
enrollmentProfileName -eq "OfflineAutopilotprofile-264c05b0-
683c-4537-87ff-1ff5151d5b98")" -MembershipRuleProcessingState
"On"
```

Now you have imported the hardware information into Windows Autopilot and created all the groups you need to process by configuring the enrollment status page.

Enrollment Status Page (ESP)

Many think that ESP and Windows Autopilot are one and the same. That is not necessarily the whole truth as ESP is a core Windows function and can be set as a Windows CSP.

ESP can be used as part of any Windows Autopilot provisioning scenario. It can also be used separately from Windows Autopilot as part of the default OOBE for AAD join, as well as for any new users signing in to the device for the first time.

Basically, what that means is that any Windows 10 devices that join AAD in the OOBE phase will have the ESP shown to the end user, irrespective of whether it is a Windows Autopilot device, as long as there is an ESP assigned to the user or device.

You can create multiple ESP profiles with different configurations that specify the following:

- Showing the installation progress
- Blocking access until the provisioning process is complete
- Time limits
- Allowed troubleshooting operations

We will show you how to do this in this section and, in a later section, with a Windows Autopilot kiosk scenario.

ESP implementation Windows CSP

ESP uses the `EnrollmentStatusTracking` **Configuration Service Provider (CSP)** and the `FirstSyncStatus` CSP to track the installation of different apps:

- The `EnrollmentStatusTracking` CSP: `/Vendor/MSFT/EnrollmentStatusTracking`.

- The `EnrollmentStatusTracking` CSP: Windows Client Management | Microsoft Docs (`https://docs.microsoft.com/en-us/windows/client-management/mdm/enrollmentstatustracking-csp`).

- The `EnrollmentStatusTracking` CSP is supported in Windows 10 version 1903 and later.

- The `EnrollmentStatusTracking` CSP is used to track the installation of the Microsoft Intune Management extension and Microsoft Intune Win32 apps that are target devices and/or users that are blocked by the ESP.

- The `FirstSyncStatus` CSP: `./Vendor/MSFT/DMClient/Provider/ProviderID/FirstSyncStatus`.

- The DMClient CSP – Windows Client Management | Microsoft Docs (`https://docs.microsoft.com/en-us/windows/client-management/mdm/dmclient-csp`).

- The `FirstSyncStatus` CSP is supported in Windows 10 version 1709 and later.

- The `FirstSyncStatus` CSP is responsible for delivering the ESP CSP payload from Microsoft Intune to the Windows 10 client. The payload includes ESP settings such as the timeout period and applications that are required to be installed. It also delivers the expected MSI (line-of-business) applications, Microsoft Store for Business apps, Wi-Fi profiles, and SCEP certificate profiles, as well as policies for Microsoft Edge, assigned access, and Kiosk Browser.

We will look at the steps to create an ESP as follows:

1. Create the first ESP by starting the Microsoft Endpoint Manager admin center, `https://endpoint.microsoft.com/`, and choose **Devices | Windows | Windows enrollment | Enrollment Status Page**.

2. Choose a profile under **Settings**.

3. Choose **Yes** for **Show app and profile installation progress**.

4. Choose **Yes** for **Block device use until all apps and profiles are installed**.

5. Choose **Selected** for **Block device use until these required apps are installed if they're assigned to the user/device**.

6. Choose **Select apps**, and then select **Select | Save** for the apps.

In the **Settings** step, configure the following values and then click **Next**:

Setting	Value
Show app and profile configuration process	Yes
Show an error when installation takes longer than the specified number of minutes	60
Show custom message when time limit error occurs	Yes (you may modify the default message)
Allow users to collect logs about installation errors	Yes
Only show page to devices provisioned by out-of-box experience (OOBE)	Yes
Block device user until all apps and profiles are installed	Yes
Allow users to reset the device if an installation error occurs	Yes
Allow users to use the device if an installation error occurs	No
Block device user until these required apps are installed if they are assigned to the user/device	All or select up to 100 apps

Now that we have seen how to create an enrollment page, let's move on and learn about Autopilot reporting and diagnostics.

Autopilot reporting and diagnostics

Run cmd.exe as an administrator, and then you can run MdmDiagnosticsTool to get logs from the local device:

```
c:\windows\system32\MdmDiagnosticsTool.exe -area Autopilot -cab
C:\temp\MdmDiagnostics.cab
```

You will then get the MdmDiagnostics.cab file, where you can extract the content to a folder to get access to the content:

```
AgentExecutor-20210331-083241.log
```
```
AgentExecutor.log
```
```
ClientHealth.log
```
```
DeviceHash_DESKTOP-86N39H3.csv
```
```
DiagnosticLogCSP_Collector_Autopilot.etl
```

```
DiagnosticLogCSP_Collector_DeviceEnrollment.etl
```

```
DiagnosticLogCSP_Collector_
DeviceProvisioning_2021_1_31_20_4_38.etl
```

```
DiagnosticLogCSP_Collector_
DeviceProvisioning_2021_2_11_4_18_29.etl
```

```
DiagnosticLogCSP_Collector_
DeviceProvisioning_2021_2_24_19_11_54.etl
```

```
DiagnosticLogCSP_Collector_
DeviceProvisioning_2021_3_13_3_31_33.etl
```

```
IntuneManagementExtension-20210228-125401.log
```

```
IntuneManagementExtension-20210319-102847.log
```

```
IntuneManagementExtension.log
```

```
LicensingDiag.cab
```

```
LicensingDiag_Output.txt
```

```
MdmDiagLogMetadata.json
```

```
MdmDiagReport_RegistryDump.reg
```

```
MdmLogCollectorFootPrint.txt
```

```
microsoft-windows-aad-operational.evtx
```

```
microsoft-windows-appxdeploymentserver-operational.evtx
```

```
microsoft-windows-assignedaccess-admin.evtx
```

```
microsoft-windows-assignedaccess-operational.evtx
```

```
microsoft-windows-assignedaccessbroker-admin.evtx
```

```
microsoft-windows-assignedaccessbroker-operational.evtx
```

```
microsoft-windows-crypto-ncrypt-operational.evtx
```

```
microsoft-windows-devicemanagement-enterprise-diagnostics-
provider-admin.evtx
```

```
microsoft-windows-devicemanagement-enterprise-diagnostics-
provider-debug.evtx
```

```
microsoft-windows-devicemanagement-enterprise-diagnostics-
provider-operational.evtx
```

```
microsoft-windows-moderndeployment-diagnostics-provider-
autopilot.evtx
```

```
microsoft-windows-moderndeployment-diagnostics-provider-
managementservice.evtx
```

```
microsoft-windows-provisioning-diagnostics-provider-admin.evtx
```

```
microsoft-windows-provisioning-diagnostics-provider-autopilot.
evtx
```

```
microsoft-windows-provisioning-diagnostics-provider-
```

```
managementservice.evtx
```

```
microsoft-windows-shell-core-operational.evtx
```

```
microsoft-windows-user device registration-admin.evtx
```

```
Sensor-20210105-105450.log
```

```
Sensor-20210207-191747.log
```

```
Sensor.log
```

```
setupact.log
```

```
TpmHliInfo_Output.txt
```

```
_IntuneManagementExtension.log
```

The most important information you are getting from the MDM diagnostics tools is as follows:

```
Registry Dump
```

```
MdmDiagReport_RegistryDump.reg captures the
```

```
HKEY_LOCAL_MACHINE
```

```
HKEY_ CURRENT_USER
```

```
Registry values associated with autopilot device provisioning
are written to HKEY_LOCAL_MACHINE\SOFTWARE\Microsoft\
Provisioning\Diagnostics\AutoPilot
```

```
HKEY_CURRENT_USER\software\microsoft\
enterprisemodernappmanagement and HKEY_LOCAL_MACHINE\software\
microsoft\enterprisemodernappmanagement
```

In the case of reporting inside the Microsoft Endpoint Manager admin center, the process is as follows.

In the Microsoft Endpoint Manager admin center, `https://endpoint.microsoft.com/`, choose **Devices | Monitor | Autopilot deployments (preview)**.

You can see your Windows Autopilot deployments from the last 30 days:

Data is retained for the last 30 days

Enrollment date	Enrollment meth...	Serial number	Device name	User	Autopilot profile	Enrollment status...	Deployment total...
03/11/21, 9:46 PM	User-driven AAD	034092382057	PCL-SB2-13	admin@osddeployme...	Windows AutoPilot D...	Success	56 mins 22 secs
03/11/21, 7:41 PM	User-driven AAD	034092382057	DESKTOP-8KC9FUT	jane@osddeployment...	Windows AutoPilot D...	Success	0 secs
03/23/21, 9:02 PM	User-driven AAD	K2PDCG001536089	OSD-359S0	frederik@famlarsen.se	Windows AutoPilot D...	Success	9 mins 29 secs
03/11/21, 10:46 AM	User-driven AAD	034092382057	PCL-SB2-13	jane@osddeployment...	Windows AutoPilot D...	Success	18 mins 16 secs
03/21/21, 11:05 AM	User-driven AAD	034092382057	PCL-SB2-13	jane@osddeployment...	Windows AutoPilot D...	Success	27 mins 4 secs

Figure 7.18 – Autopilot report

You can see the following attributes:

- **Enrollment date**
- **Enrollment method**
- **Serial number**
- **Device name**
- **User**
- **Autopilot profile**
- **Enrollment status page deployment state**
- **Deployment total time**

Company Portal

Company Portal is a self-service tool for end users so that they can install apps that the IT admin has made available for end users.

For Windows 10 Autopilot-provisioned devices, it is recommended that you associate your Microsoft Store for Business account with Intune. The Company Portal app will be installed in the device context when assigned to the Autopilot group and will be installed on the device before the user logs in. You can choose to install the Company Portal (offline) app using the steps shown next:

1. In the Microsoft Endpoint Manager admin center, `https://endpoint.microsoft.com/`, choose **Apps** | **Windows**.

2. From the list of Windows apps, select **Company Portal** (Offline).

3. Assign Company Portal as a required app to your selected Autopilot device group.

4. As this is an offline app, be sure to change **License type** to **Device licensing**.

Configuring automatic BitLocker encryption for Autopilot devices

With Windows Autopilot, BitLocker encryption settings can be configured to be applied before automatic encryption starts. This configuration ensures that the default encryption algorithm is not applied automatically. Other BitLocker policies can also be applied before automatic BitLocker encryption begins.

BitLocker automatic device encryption uses BitLocker drive encryption technology to automatically encrypt internal drives after the user completes the OOBE on *Modern Standby* or **Hardware Security Testability Specification** (**HSTI**)-*compliant hardware*.

In the case of Modern Standby requirements or HSTI validation, this requirement is met by one of the following:

- Modern Standby requirements are implemented. These include requirements for **Unified Extensible Firmware Interface** (**UEFI**) Secure Boot and protection from unauthorized **Direct Memory Access** (**DMA**).

- Starting with *Windows 10 version 1703*, this requirement can be met through an HSTI test.

- The Platform Secure Boot self-test (or additional self-tests as configured in the registry) must be reported by the HSTI as implemented and passed.

- Excluding Thunderbolt, the HSTI must not report any non-allowed DMA buses.

- If Thunderbolt is present, the HSTI must report that Thunderbolt is configured securely (the security level must be SL1 – *User Authorization* or higher).

Windows 10 (Modern Standby) expands the *Windows 8.1 Connected Standby power model*. Connected Standby, and consequently Modern Standby, enable an instant on/instant off user experience, like smartphone power models. Just like a phone, the S0 low-power idle model enables the system to stay connected to the network while in a low-power mode.

By leveraging the `powercfg/a` command, you can see whether your device supports Modern Standby (`S0 Low Power Idle`):

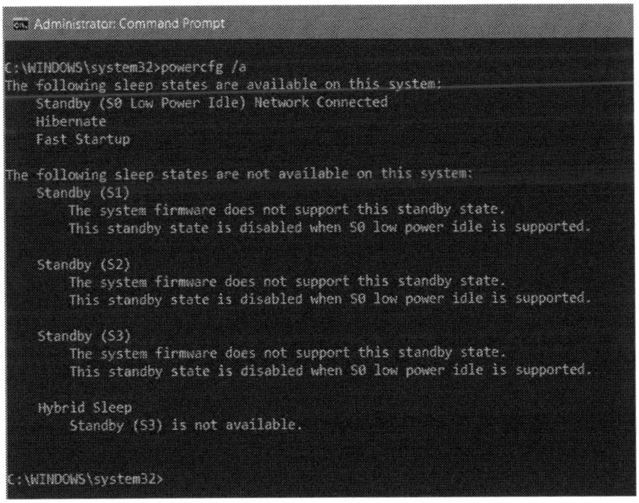

Figure 7.19 – powercfg

> **Important Note**
>
> BitLocker automatic device encryption starts during the OOBE experience. However, BitLocker drive protection is enabled only after users sign in with an AAD account. Until then, protection is suspended, and data is not protected.

The BitLocker encryption algorithm is used when BitLocker is first enabled. The algorithm sets the strength for full volume encryption. Available encryption algorithms are AES-CBC 128-bit, AES-CBC 256-bit, XTS-AES 128-bit, and XTS-AES 256-bit encryption. BitLocker will use the default encryption method of XTS-AES 128-bit or the encryption method specified by any setup script.

To make sure the BitLocker encryption algorithm you want is set before automatic encryption occurs for Autopilot devices, make sure the following requirements are fulfilled:

- The device contains a **Trusted Platform Module (TPM)**, either TPM 1.2 or TPM 2.0.

- UEFI Secure Boot is enabled.

- Platform Secure Boot is enabled.

- DMA protection is enabled.

- Configure the **Encryption method** settings in the Windows 10 Endpoint Protection profile to the encryption algorithm you want.

- Assign the policy to your Autopilot device group. The encryption policy must be assigned to devices in the group, not users.

- Enable the Autopilot ESP for these devices. If the ESP is not enabled, the policy won't apply before encryption starts.

> **Important Note**
>
> When you enable `EncryptionMethodByDriveType`, you must specify values for all three drives (OS, fixed data, and removable data); otherwise, it will fail (`500` return status). For example, if you only set the encryption method for the OS and removable drives, you will get a `500` return status.

Create the BitLocker policy in Intune for automatic BitLocker encryption as follows:

1. In the Microsoft Endpoint Manager admin center, `https://endpoint.microsoft.com/`, choose **Devices** | **Windows** | **Configuration profiles**.

2. Choose **Create Profile**.

3. Select **Platform | Windows 10 and later**.

4. Select **Profile type | Templates | Template name | Endpoint Protection**.

5. Select **Name | Autopilot Bitlocker | Next**.

6. Expand **Windows Encryption**.

7. Select **Windows Settings | Encrypt devices | Require**:

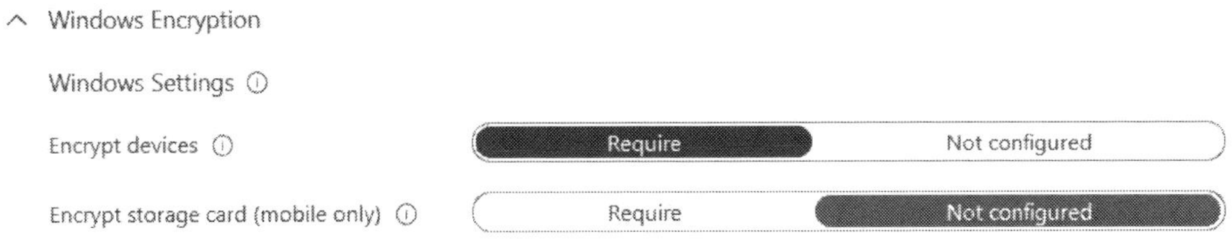

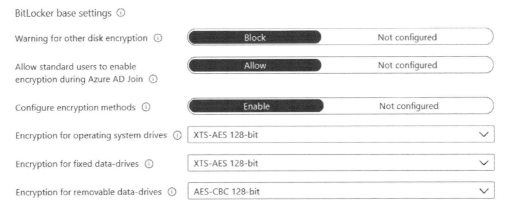

Figure 7.20 – Windows Encryption

The BitLocker base settings should be as follows:

1. Select **BitLocker base settings | Warning for other disk encryption | Block**.

    Selecting **Block** will disable the BitLocker configuration prompt and the warning prompt for other disk encryptions. Block is needed to automatically BitLocker encrypt a device.

2. Select **Allow standard users to enable encryption during Azure AD Join | Allow**.

    This setting, when set to **Allow**, enables the end user to automatically encrypt the device when they are not a local admin.

3. For **Configure encryption methods**, select what your organization requires. The Windows default is **XTS-AES 128-bit**, which is also the recommended value in the Windows security baseline:

Figure 7.21 – BitLocker base settings

The BitLocker OS drive settings are as follows:

1. Select **Additional authentication at startup | Require**:

Figure 7.22 – BitLocker OS drive settings

2. Select **OS drive recovery | Enable**.

3. Select **Save BitLocker recovery information to Azure Active Directory | Enable**.

4. Enable the BitLocker recovery information to be stored in AAD on the device object, so end users can retrieve it themselves on devices where they are the primary user. The AAD admin with the right privileges can always retrieve the BitLocker recovery key.

5. Select **Store recovery information in Azure Active Directory before enabling BitLocker | Requir**. This will prevent users from enabling BitLocker unless the computer successfully backs up the BitLocker recovery information to AAD. Selecting **Require** will ensure that the recovery keys are successfully stored in AAD before enabling encryption:

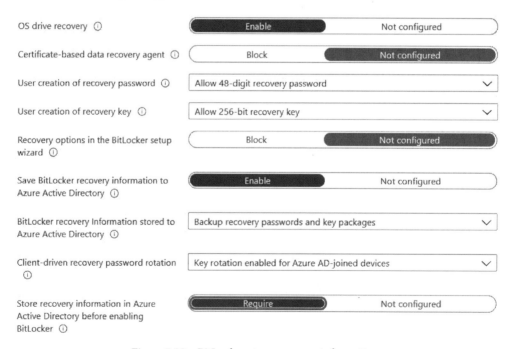

Figure 7.23 – BitLocker store recovery information

> **Important Note**
>
> If testing Autopilot and BitLocker encryption on Hyper-V or any other virtual platform, we recommend you have 2–4 GB of memory assigned and 2–4 virtual CPUs.

6. For automatic BitLocker encryption to work, you need to enable **Trusted Platform Module** for the virtual device:

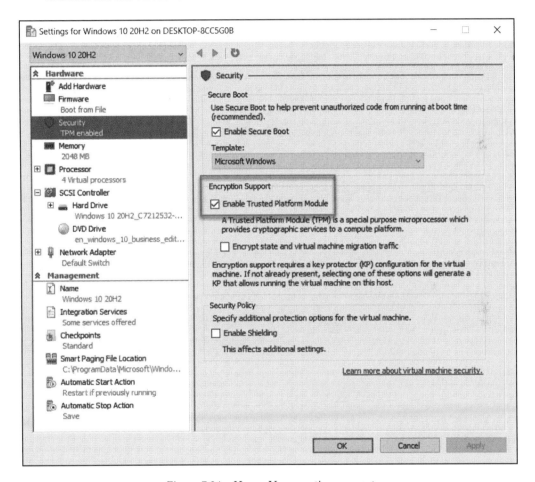

Figure 7.24 – Hyper-V encryption support

When testing on a virtual device such as Hyper-V, you might experience different behavior than if you are testing on a physical device.

To start testing Autopilot in an easy way, there is already a guided scenario called cloud configuration in Microsoft Intune. This will be covered in the next section.

Cloud configuration scenario

You can leverage deploying Windows 10 in a cloud configuration. In the Microsoft Endpoint Manager admin center, `https://endpoint.microsoft.com/`, choose **Troubleshooting + support | Guided scenarios (preview)**.

Optimize your Windows 10 devices for the cloud with a simple, secure, standardized configuration fit for your needs:

1. Select **Start** in the **Deploy Windows 10 in cloud configuration** guided scenario.
2. In the introduction, select **Next**.

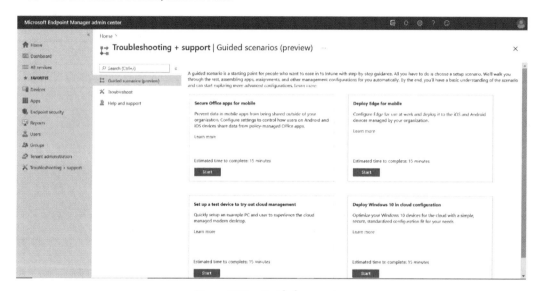

Figure 7.25 – Guided scenarios

Introduction

Windows 10 in a cloud configuration helps to standardize and simplify device management for users with focused workflow needs. You can use a cloud configuration to configure new devices or to repurpose and extend the life of existing hardware. It works on any Windows 10 Pro, Windows 10 Enterprise, or Windows 10 Education device. Let's now learn more and evaluate the cloud configuration.

The following guided workflow makes it easy to deploy the recommended apps and device configurations found in the cloud configuration overview and setup guide.

Who is this configuration useful for?

Windows 10 cloud configuration is designed for device users with simplified needs, such as productivity and browsing. Ideal candidates are the following groups of users in your organization:

- Those who use a focused set of apps curated by IT for their workflow needs, such as email, Microsoft Teams, a browser, and essential productivity and line-of-business apps. Apps can be delivered directly to the device or through virtualization.

- Those who have no dependency on an on-premises infrastructure to be successful in their role.

- Those who use devices that do not require complex setting configurations or custom agents.

- As an admin, you get to enjoy the benefits of a standardized device configuration applied across the organization, simplifying management, troubleshooting, and device replacements.

- End users enjoy a familiar Windows 10 experience optimized for the cloud with just the apps and settings they need.

What you will need to continue

Make sure you have enabled automatic enrollment. You can manage automatic enrollment settings under **Devices | Windows | Windows enrollment | Automatic enrollment**.

Basic

This is the step where you are configuring Windows Autopilot:

1. For **Apply device name template**, select **Yes**.
2. Enter a name for the Autopilot naming template, such as `Win-%RAND:5%`.

3.   Enter a resource prefix name, such as `CloudConfig`:

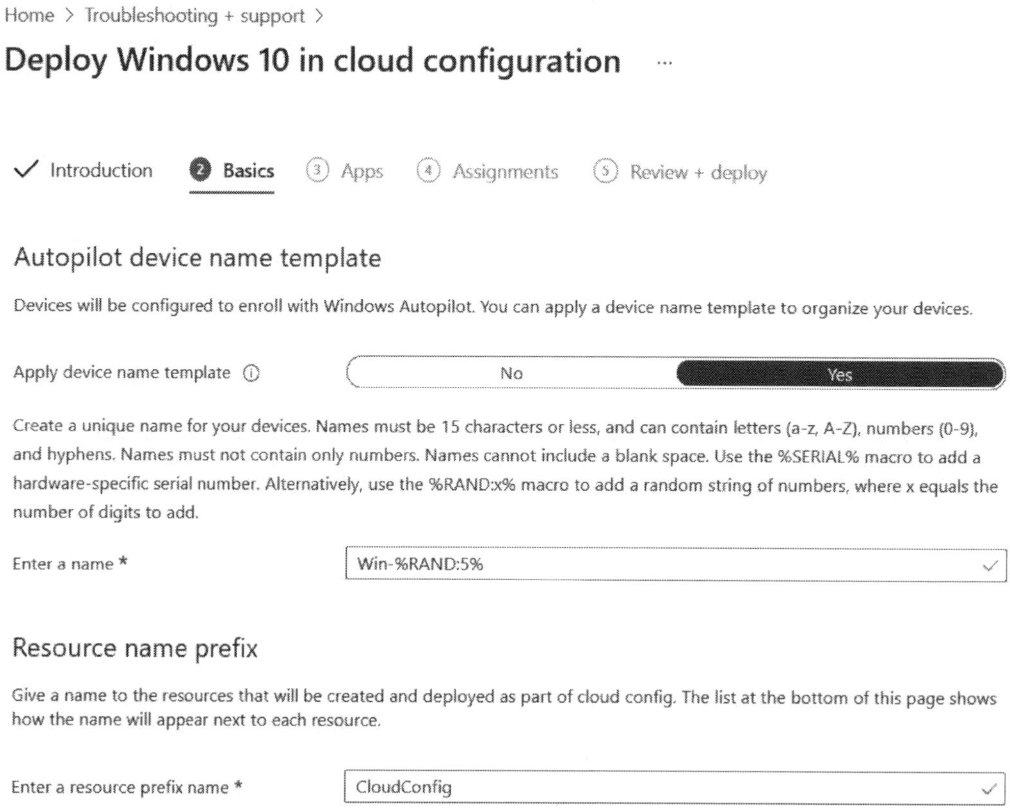

Home > Troubleshooting + support >

Deploy Windows 10 in cloud configuration   ...

✓ Introduction   ❷ **Basics**   ③ Apps   ④ Assignments   ⑤ Review + deploy

Autopilot device name template

Devices will be configured to enroll with Windows Autopilot. You can apply a device name template to organize your devices.

Apply device name template ⓘ   [No   **Yes**]

Create a unique name for your devices. Names must be 15 characters or less, and can contain letters (a-z, A-Z), numbers (0-9), and hyphens. Names must not contain only numbers. Names cannot include a blank space. Use the %SERIAL% macro to add a hardware-specific serial number. Alternatively, use the %RAND:x% macro to add a random string of numbers, where x equals the number of digits to add.

Enter a name *   [Win-%RAND:5%   ✓]

Resource name prefix

Give a name to the resources that will be created and deployed as part of cloud config. The list at the bottom of this page shows how the name will appear next to each resource.

Enter a resource prefix name *   [CloudConfig   ✓]

Figure 7.26 – Cloud configuration basics

Resources to be created

All these profiles will have the prefix selected:

- CloudConfig M365 (Teams)
- CloudConfig Microsoft Edge
- CloudConfig security baseline
- CloudConfig Autopilot profile
- CloudConfig ESP
- CloudConfig OneDrive Known Folder Move settings
- CloudConfig Microsoft Edge app settings

- CloudConfig compliance policy
- CloudConfig built-in app removal script
- CloudConfig update ring

Apps

This is the section where you choose the apps you want to deploy as part of the cloud configuration scenario.

Go to **Select additional M365 apps (optional)** | **Outlook** and add other apps if they need to be installed on the device:

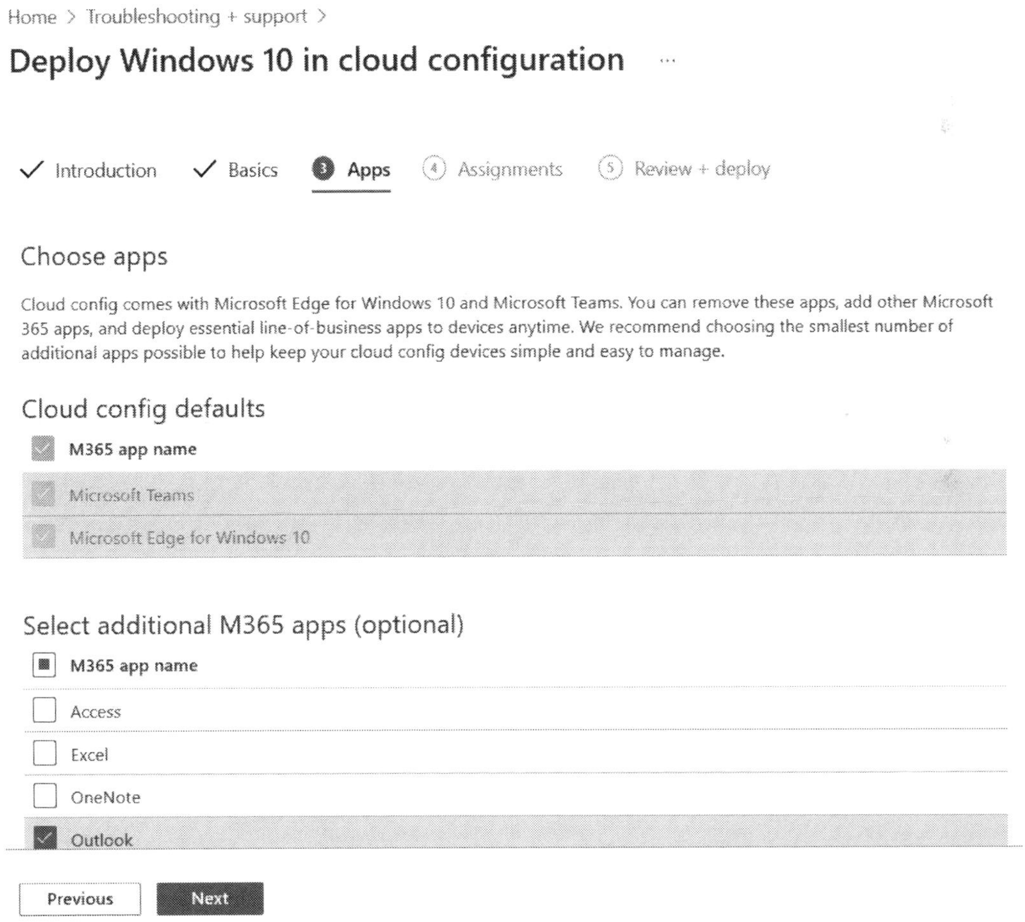

Home > Troubleshooting + support >

Deploy Windows 10 in cloud configuration   ...

✓ Introduction   ✓ Basics   **③ Apps**   ④ Assignments   ⑤ Review + deploy

Choose apps

Cloud config comes with Microsoft Edge for Windows 10 and Microsoft Teams. You can remove these apps, add other Microsoft 365 apps, and deploy essential line-of-business apps to devices anytime. We recommend choosing the smallest number of additional apps possible to help keep your cloud config devices simple and easy to manage.

Cloud config defaults

☑	M365 app name
☑	Microsoft Teams
☑	Microsoft Edge for Windows 10

Select additional M365 apps (optional)

■	M365 app name
☐	Access
☐	Excel
☐	OneNote
☑	Outlook

Previous   Next

Figure 7.27 – Cloud configuration apps

Assignments

Select **Create a new group** and for **Group name**, choose CloudConfig.

This will create an empty group so you can put devices in that group and test the deployment as necessary:

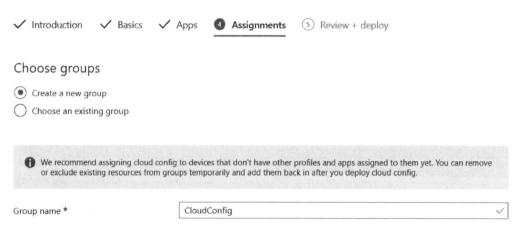

Figure 7.28 – Cloud configuration assignments

Deploying

Review your settings in the summary and select **Deploy**:

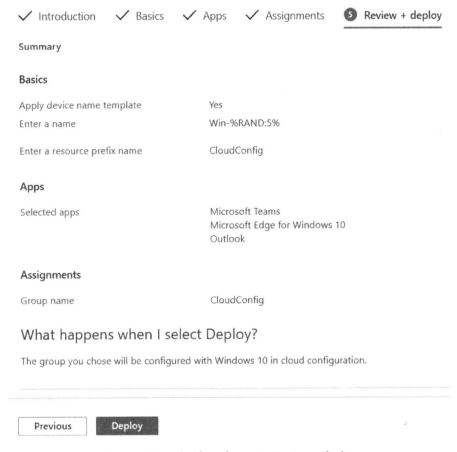

Home > Troubleshooting + support >

Deploy Windows 10 in cloud configuration   ...

✓ Introduction   ✓ Basics   ✓ Apps   ✓ Assignments   ⑤ **Review + deploy**

Summary

Basics

Apply device name template	Yes
Enter a name	Win-%RAND:5%
Enter a resource prefix name	CloudConfig

Apps

Selected apps	Microsoft Teams Microsoft Edge for Windows 10 Outlook

Assignments

Group name	CloudConfig

What happens when I select Deploy?

The group you chose will be configured with Windows 10 in cloud configuration.

Previous   Deploy

Figure 7.29 – Cloud configuration Review + deploy

4. All the profiles will now be created:

Home > Troubleshooting + support >

Deploy Windows 10 in cloud configuration   ...

✓ Deployment succeeded.

Deployment details

Resource	Resource Type	More	Resource	Assignment
CloudConfig	AAD Security Group	Docs ↗	✓ Created	--
CloudConfig M365 (Teams)	M365 App Suite	Docs ↗	✓ Created	✓ Assigned
CloudConfig Microsoft Edge	App	Docs ↗	✓ Created	✓ Assigned
CloudConfig security baseline	Windows 10 security baseline	Docs ↗	✓ Created	✓ Assigned
CloudConfig Autopilot profile	Autopilot profile	Docs ↗	✓ Created	✓ Assigned
CloudConfig ESP 20210419_0:04:18	Enrollment Status Page	Docs ↗	✓ Created	✓ Assigned
CloudConfig OneDrive Known Folder Move	Administrative template	Docs ↗	✓ Created	✓ Assigned
CloudConfig Microsoft Edge app settings	Administrative template	Docs ↗	✓ Created	✓ Assigned
CloudConfig compliance policy	Compliance policy	Docs ↗	✓ Created	✓ Assigned
CloudConfig built-in app removal script	Script	Docs ↗	✓ Created	✓ Assigned
CloudConfig update ring 20210419_0:04:18	Windows 10 update ring	Docs ↗	✓ Created	✓ Assigned

Figure 7.30 – Cloud configuration deployment succeeded

Here is what can you do next:

- Add devices to the group you configured.

- Add your preregistered Autopilot devices or other existing devices to the group you configured. For existing devices, we recommend removing other profiles and apps and resetting them, so they start fresh with just the cloud configuration applied.

- Deploy essential line-of-business apps and configurations.

We recommend keeping additional essential configurations to a minimum, including the number of line-of-business apps you deploy on top of the cloud configuration. This helps keep device management and troubleshooting simpler.

Deploying essentials that users might need to access work or school resources

Be sure to configure the certificates, VPN profiles, Wi-Fi profiles, and desktop/app virtualization clients that enable access to your organization's resources.

Monitoring your cloud configuration devices

Use Microsoft Endpoint Manager to monitor the deployment status and device health of your cloud configuration devices. For information on how to monitor each of the components, refer to the cloud configuration overview and setup guide.

This is an easy way to start testing Windows Autopilot and cloud-configured devices. In the next section, we will cover how to deploy devices running in kiosk mode and that are being provisioned by Windows Autopilot.

Edge kiosk self-deployment scenario

From Windows 10 20H2, Microsoft Edge, based on Chromium, is built into the OS delivered. This scenario will cover how to configure Microsoft Edge in kiosk mode for a single app with Microsoft Endpoint Manager:

1. Upload Autopilot devices with a group tag such as `EdgeKIOSK`.
2. Create a specific ESP for the Edge kiosk.
3. Create a Windows Autopilot profile.
4. Create some profiles that can benefit the kiosk scenario.
5. Create a kiosk profile.

Creating a specific ESP for the Edge kiosk

A kiosk device can be userless, and by using Windows Autopilot self-deploying mode, no user has to sign in when onboarding the device into AAD or Microsoft Intune, so we will create an ESP and assign it to the Autopilot group for this specific scenario.

Create an ESP with the settings you prefer:

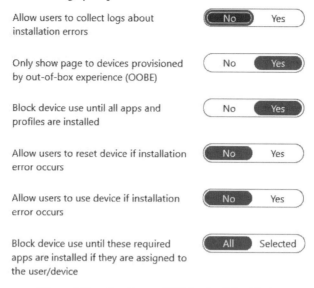

Allow users to collect logs about installation errors — No | Yes

Only show page to devices provisioned by out-of-box experience (OOBE) — No | Yes

Block device use until all apps and profiles are installed — No | Yes

Allow users to reset device if installation error occurs — No | Yes

Allow users to use device if installation error occurs — No | Yes

Block device use until these required apps are installed if they are assigned to the user/device — All | Selected

Figure 7.31 – Creating an ESP for the Edge kiosk

Assign it to the AAD **All Autopilot KIOSK** dynamic group, which will disregard the default ESP profile as is it assigned to a device group.

Creating a Windows Autopilot profile

Create a new Autopilot profile specific to this scenario:

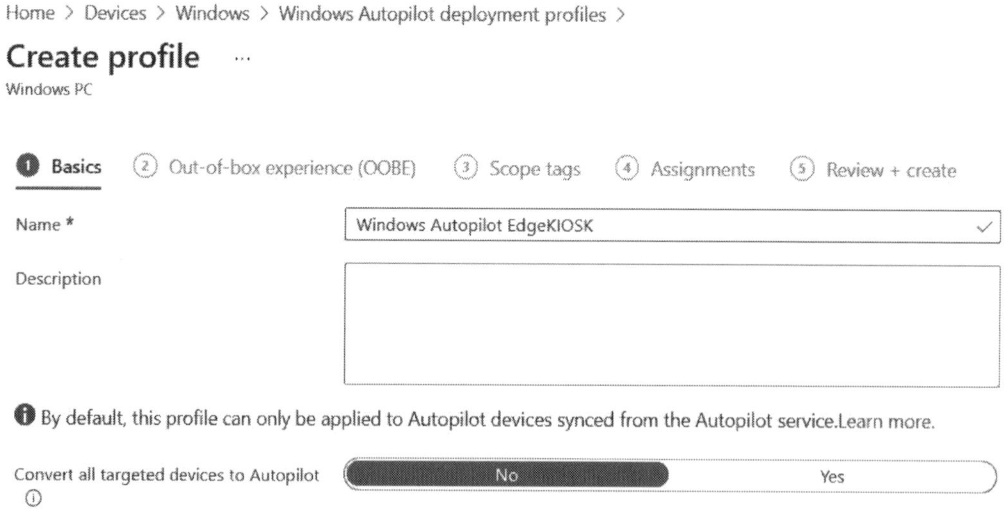

Home > Devices > Windows > Windows Autopilot deployment profiles >

Create profile   ...
Windows PC

(1) **Basics**   (2) Out-of-box experience (OOBE)   (3) Scope tags   (4) Assignments   (5) Review + create

Name *   Windows Autopilot EdgeKIOSK   ✓

Description

By default, this profile can only be applied to Autopilot devices synced from the Autopilot service. Learn more.

Convert all targeted devices to Autopilot   No | Yes

Figure 7.32 – Windows Autopilot profile for the Edge kiosk

Set **Deployment mode** to **Self-Deploying (preview)** to onboard the device as a userless device:

Home > Devices > Windows > Windows Autopilot deployment profiles >

Create profile   ···
Windows PC

| ✓ Basics | ❷ Out-of-box experience (OOBE) | ③ Scope tags | ④ Assignments | ⑤ Review + create |

Configure the out-of-box experience for your Autopilot devices

Deployment mode * ⓘ	Self-Deploying (preview) ⌄
Join to Azure AD as ⓘ	Azure AD joined ⌄
Microsoft Software License Terms ⓘ	Show / Hide

ⓘ Important information about hiding license terms

Privacy settings ⓘ	Show / Hide

ⓘ The default value for diagnostic data collection has changed for devices running Windows 10, version 1903 and later. Learn more

Hide change account options ⓘ	Show / Hide
User account type ⓘ	Administrator / Standard
Language (Region) ⓘ	Operating system default ⌄
Automatically configure keyboard ⓘ	No / **Yes**
Apply device name template ⓘ	**No** / Yes

Figure 7.33 – Windows Autopilot profile OOBE

Self-Deploying (preview)

Self-deploying mode does not presently associate a user with the device (since no user ID or password is specified as part of the process).

Self-deploying mode uses a device's TPM 2.0 hardware to authenticate the device in an organization's AAD tenant. Therefore, devices without TPM 2.0 can't be used with this mode. Devices must also support TPM device attestation. This Windows Autopilot scenario will require a device with a physical TPM, so a virtual device will not work.

To achieve a 100% zero-touch onboarding experience, an Ethernet connection is required; otherwise, the device will prompt you for a region and keyboard layout.

Creating a custom Windows 10 profile to disable user ESP

This is to ensure that the user portion of the ESP will not show up on the Edge kiosk as it is a userless device:

- **Name**: `Disable User ESP`
- **Description**: `Disable User ESP for Edge KIOSK`
- **OMA-URI**: `./Vendor/MSFT/DMClient/Provider/ProviderID/FirstSyncStatus/SkipUserStatusPage`
- **Data type**: `Boolean`
- **Value**: `True`

Creating a custom Windows 10 profile to disable FirstLogonAnimation

This policy setting allows you to control whether users see the first sign-in animation when signing in to the computer for the first time. This applies to both the first user of the computer who completes the initial setup and users who are added to the computer later. It also controls whether Microsoft account users are offered the opt-in prompt for services during their first sign-in.

If you do not configure this policy setting, the user who completes the initial Windows setup will see the animation during their first sign-in. If the first user had already completed the initial setup and this policy setting is not configured, new users signing in to this computer do not see the first logon animation.

In this Edge kiosk scenario, we just want a fast and easy onboarding experience:

- **Name**: `Disable FirstLogonAnimation`
- **Description**: `Disable FirstLogonAnimation for Edge KIOSK`
- **OMA-URI**: `./Device/Vendor/MSFT/Policy/Config/WindowsLogon/EnableFirstLogonAnimation`
- **Data type**: `Integer`
- **Value**: `0`

Creating a settings catalog Windows 10 profile to reboot the device

As shown in this example, you can configure the policy to have the device reboot every night at 3 A.M:

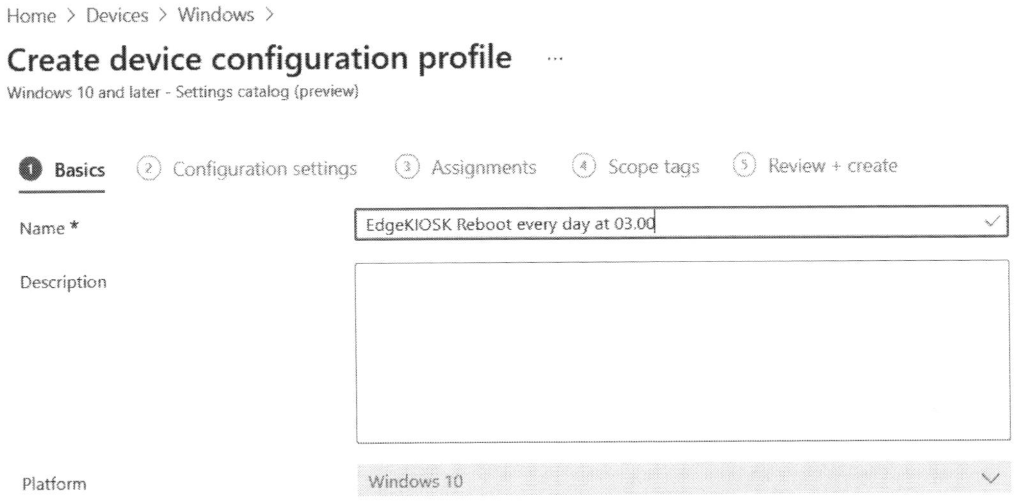

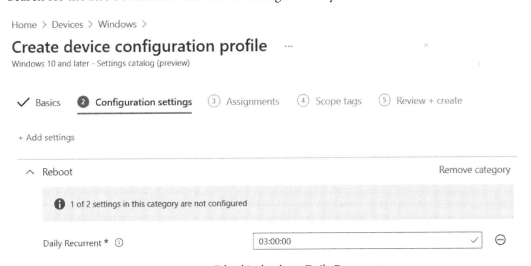

Figure 7.34 – Edge kiosk reboot settings catalog

Search for the **Reboot** section and add it. Configure **Daily Recurrent** to 03 : 00 : 00:

Home > Devices > Windows >

Create device configuration profile   ...
Windows 10 and later - Settings catalog (preview)

✓ Basics   ② **Configuration settings**   ③ Assignments   ④ Scope tags   ⑤ Review + create

+ Add settings

∧ Reboot   Remove category

ⓘ 1 of 2 settings in this category are not configured

Daily Recurrent * ⓘ   03:00:00   ✓   ⊖

Figure 7.35 – Edge kiosk reboot Daily Recurrent

Creating a Windows 10 template kiosk profile

Configure Windows 10 to be in single-app kiosk mode. We are using the built-in profile type template with the template name **Kiosk** in Microsoft Intune. This profile type will guide you through the necessary configuration steps. If you require more advanced settings in the kiosk profile, you need to create a custom kiosk policy with the kiosk profile in XML format:

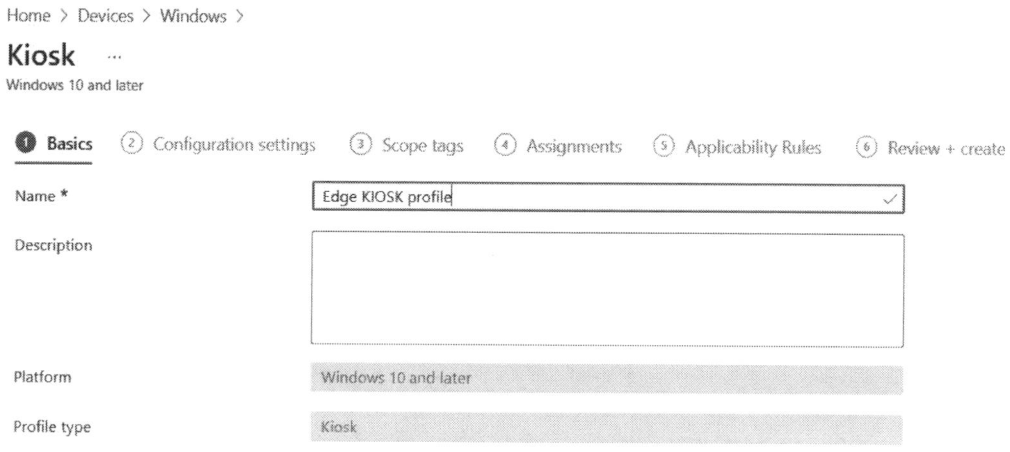

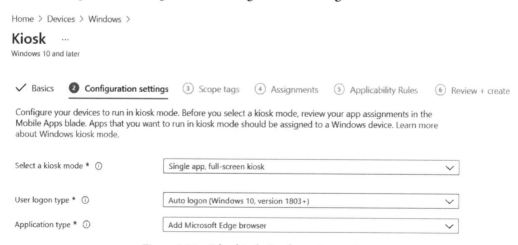

Figure 7.36 – Edge kiosk profile

The following are the settings on the **Configuration settings** tab:

Home > Devices > Windows >

Kiosk   ...
Windows 10 and later

✓ Basics   ② **Configuration settings**   ③ Scope tags   ④ Assignments   ⑤ Applicability Rules   ⑥ Review + create

Configure your devices to run in kiosk mode. Before you select a kiosk mode, review your app assignments in the Mobile Apps blade. Apps that you want to run in kiosk mode should be assigned to a Windows device. Learn more about Windows kiosk mode.

Select a kiosk mode * ⓘ | Single app, full-screen kiosk   ⌄ |

User logon type * ⓘ | Auto logon (Windows 10, version 1803+)   ⌄ |

Application type * ⓘ | Add Microsoft Edge browser   ⌄ |

Figure 7.37 – Edge kiosk Configuration settings

Additional Edge settings need to be configured in a Windows 10 template Administrative Templates profile:

This kiosk profile requires Microsoft Edge version 87 and later with Windows 10 version 1909 and later. Learn more about Microsoft Edge kiosk mode.

Edge Kiosk URL * ⓘ | https://bing.com   ✓ |

Microsoft Edge kiosk mode type ⓘ | Public Browsing (InPrivate)   ⌄ |

Refresh browser after idle time ⓘ | 5 |

Figure 7.38 – Edge kiosk settings

Kiosk mode supported features

In this table, you can see what settings are available for different Microsoft Edge versions:

Feature	Digital/ Interactive Signage	Public Browsing	Available with Microsoft Edge Version (and Higher)
InPrivate Navigation	Y	Y	89
Reset on inactivity	Y	Y	89
Read-only address bar (policy)	N	Y	89
Delete downloads on exit (policy)	Y	Y	89
F11 blocked (enter/exit fullscreen)	Y	Y	89
F12 blocked (launch Developer Tools)	Y	Y	89
Multi-tab support	N	Y	89
Allow URL support (policy)	Y	Y	89
Block URL support (policy)	Y	Y	89
Show home button (policy)	N	Y	89
Manage favorites (policy)	N	Y	89
Enable printer (policy)	Y	Y	89
Configure the new tab page URL (policy)	N	Y	
End session button*	N	Y	89
All internal Microsoft Edge URLs are blocked, except for edge://downloads and edge://print	N	Y	89
Ctrl + N blocked (open a new window) *	Y	Y	89
Ctrl + T blocked (open new tab)	Y	N	89
Settings and more (...) will display only the required options	Y	Y	89
Restrict the launch of other applications from the browser	Y	Y	90/91
UI print settings lockdown	Y	Y	90/91

It is recommended to configure other profiles, such as Windows Defender, Windows Update for Business, and other policies that may be relevant to your kiosk scenario.

This scenario is also possible with kiosk mode for multiple apps; it just requires a different configuration in the kiosk profile in Microsoft Endpoint Manager.

Autopilot Reset

Windows Autopilot Reset is only for AAD-joined devices.

Windows Autopilot Reset takes the device back to a business-ready state, allowing the same user or a new user to sign in and get productive quickly and simply. The first user who signs in to the device following the Windows Autopilot reset becomes the new primary user and owner of the device.

Here is what makes Windows Autopilot Reset so special:

- It removes personal files, apps, and settings.
- It maintains the device's identity connection to AAD, so it keeps the same AAD object.
- It maintains the device's management connection to Intune, so it keeps the same Microsoft Intune Windows object.

When using Windows Autopilot Reset, the process automatically keeps the following information from the device:

- It keeps the region, language, and keyboard that are configured on the device.
- It keeps the Wi-Fi connection details.
- It provisions packages previously applied to the device.
- A provisioning package is present on a USB drive when the reset process is started.
- It retains AAD device membership and Microsoft Intune enrollment information.

Windows Autopilot Reset will block the user from accessing the desktop until this information is restored, including reapplying any provisioning packages until the Microsoft Intune sync is completed.

Perform the following steps in the Microsoft Endpoint Manager admin center, `https://endpoint.microsoft.com/`:

1. Choose **Devices | Windows | Configuration Profiles**.
2. Choose **Create Profile**.

3. Choose **Platform Windows 10 and Later** and **Profile Type Templates**.

4. Choose **Device restrictions | Create**.

5. Enter `Enable Autopilot Reset` as the name.

6. Choose **General | Autopilot Reset | Allow**:

Figure 7.39 – Autopilot Reset

7. Allow users with administrative rights to delete all user data and settings using *Ctrl + Win + R* at the device lock screen so that the device can be automatically reconfigured and re-enrolled into management.

8. Assign the profile to your Autopilot device group.

9. You, as an IT admin, can also initiate Autopilot Reset directly from a device in Microsoft Intune:

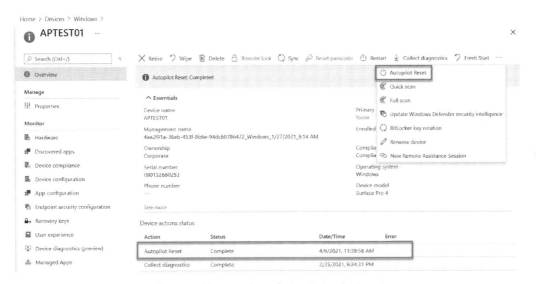

Figure 7.40 – Windows device Autopilot Reset

10. In the **Device actions status** section, you will see the Autopilot Reset status for whether it has completed or failed.

11. Other reset scenarios from within Microsoft Intune include those not relying on the device to be a Windows Autopilot device.

> **Important Note**
>
> If **Windows Defender Application Control (WDAC)** is configured with the reputation of the app determined by Microsoft's Intelligent Security Graph, Autopilot Reset might fail.

Windows Autopilot Reset has a great use case for a device reset if the same user needs to reuse the devices again, where other options are available in other scenarios. In the next section, we will cover wiping and resetting.

Wiping and resetting your devices

A factory reset returns the device to its default settings. This removes all personal and company data and settings from this device. You can choose whether to keep the device enrolled and the user account associated with this device. You cannot revert this action. Are you sure you want to reset this device? Here are the options available to you:

- **Wipe device, but keep enrollment state and associated user account**.

- **Wipe device, and continue to wipe even if device loses power. If you select this option, please be aware that it might prevent some Windows 10 devices from starting up again.**.

  This option makes sure that the wipe action can't be circumvented by turning off the device. This option will keep trying to reset the device until successful. In some configurations, this action may leave the device unable to reboot.

  This issue may be caused when the installation of Windows has major corruption that is preventing the OS from reinstalling. In such a case, the process fails and leaves the system in the Windows Recovery Environment:

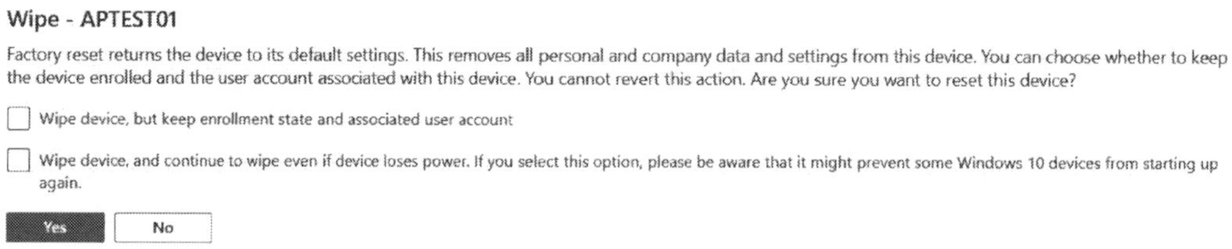

Wipe - APTEST01

Factory reset returns the device to its default settings. This removes all personal and company data and settings from this device. You can choose whether to keep the device enrolled and the user account associated with this device. You cannot revert this action. Are you sure you want to reset this device?

☐ Wipe device, but keep enrollment state and associated user account

☐ Wipe device, and continue to wipe even if device loses power. If you select this option, please be aware that it might prevent some Windows 10 devices from starting up again.

[Yes]   [No]

Figure 7.41 – Windows device wipe

- **Wipe device, but keep enrollment state and associated user account**:

Retained during a wipe	Not retained
User accounts associated with the device	User files
Machine state (domain join, AAD-joined)	User-installed apps (store and Win32 apps)
MDM enrollment	Non-default device settings
OEM-installed apps (store and Win32 apps)	
User profile	
User data outside of the user profile	
User auto logon	

Fresh start

Cleaning the device will remove all preloaded Win32 apps. You can choose whether to retain user data on the device and whether you are sure you want to clean the device:

Figure 7.42 – Windows device Fresh Start

You can also set the following options:

- Keep the device AAD joined.

- A device is enrolled in MDM again when an AAD-enabled user signs in to the device.

- Keep the contents of the device user's Home folder, and remove any apps and settings.

> **Important Note**
>
> If you do not retain user data, the device will be restored to the default OOBE completed state, retaining the built-in administrator account. That account is disabled by default on Windows Autopilot devices and you can find yourself in a situation where you are not able to sign in to the device.
>
> BYOD devices will be unenrolled from AAD and MDM. AAD-joined devices will be enrolled in MDM again when an AAD-enabled user signs in to the device.

Windows Recovery Environment

In many reset scenarios, your devices need to have Windows Recovery Environment enabled. You can check this as follows:

- With `Reagentc/info` in Command Prompt in an administrator context

- With the Windows Recovery Environment and a system reset configuration:

```
Windows RE status:              Enabled
Windows RE location:                \\?\GLOBALROOT\device\
harddisk0\partition4\Recovery\WindowsRE
     Boot Configuration Data (BCD) identifier: 0d1ee6b6-
134c-11eb-abb4-f32d64eb2b10
     Recovery image location:
     Recovery image index:       0
     Custom image location:
     Custom image index:         0
REAGENTC.EXE: Operation Successful.
```

If the status is `Disabled`, you will need to troubleshoot why the Windows Recovery Environment is disabled.

Summary

In the chapter, you've learned about Windows Autopilot and the difference between user-driven and self-deploying modes, how it works, and why it could be beneficial for your organization to simplify the delivery process of your physical endpoints.

We covered what is included in Windows Autopilot device IDs and how to create AAD groups based on different attributes to automate different end user scenarios.

We explained what ESP is, how to configure it, and how to disable the user part of ESP in special scenarios.

In the next chapter, we're going to explain to you everything in relation to application delivery and management via Microsoft Endpoint Manager.

Questions

1. What is the name of the policy that disables the Windows first logon animation process?

    A. `FirstLogonAnimationExperience`

    B. `FirstExperience`

    C. `FirstLogonAnimation`

    D. `WindowsLogonAnimation`

2. What is the default BitLocker encryption method on Windows 10?

    A. AES-CBC 128-bit

    B. XTS-AES 128-bit

    C. AES-CBC 258-bit

    D. XTS-AES 258-bit

Answers

1. (C)

2. (B)

Further reading

If you want to learn more about Windows Autopilot after reading this chapter, please use the following free online resources, and join the Autopilot Microsoft Tech Community!

*   Windows Autopilot | Microsoft Tech Community: `https://techcommunity.microsoft.com/t5/windows-management/windows-autopilot/m-p/90052`

*   Windows Autopilot documentation | Microsoft Docs: `https://docs.microsoft.com/en-us/mem/autopilot/`

*   Windows AutoPilot: An introduction | Microsoft Tech Community: `https://techcommunity.microsoft.com/t5/windows-deployment/windows-autopilot-an-introduction/td-p/87291`

8
Application Management and Delivery

In this chapter, you will learn how to deploy and manage your Microsoft 365 and **line-of-business (LOB)** applications to your Windows 10 endpoints, a very important element in every Windows 10 Enterprise deployment. Applications are what make end users productive, but applications can also be tools that help either the end user or the IT admin.

In this chapter, we will cover the following topics:

- Application delivery via Microsoft Endpoint Manager
- Different application types you can deploy
- Community tool – Win32App Migration Tool
- Deploying Microsoft 365 apps
- Microsoft 365 Apps admin center
- Deploying Microsoft Teams
- OneDrive
- What is MSIX?

Application delivery via Microsoft Endpoint Manager

We've been explaining the benefits of using a modern unified endpoint management solution from the same management experience. Of course, the same benefits apply for delivering applications to your endpoints, whether they're running Windows 10 Enterprise on a virtual cloud or physical endpoints via Microsoft Endpoint Manager.

Another important layer is security. Normally, installing apps would require installation rights, for example, local administrator permissions on your Windows 10 Enterprise endpoint. Delivering your app via Microsoft Endpoint Manager allows you to assign and install apps – in a modular fashion – without the need to make the user a local administrator.

Adding applications modularly (separately) from the image would also drastically simplify your image maintenance process. For example, within a legacy virtual desktop infrastructure, you would have created a so-called master image. This is not required with Microsoft Endpoint Manager – Intune as all applications can be managed separately from the OS image layer. After you enroll your Windows 10 Enterprise images, all your assigned applications are added automatically based on user, group, or device filtering. Sounds pretty cool, right?

To start delivering apps, you must go to the **Apps** menu in Microsoft Endpoint Manager. You begin your journey of configuring and assigning the application to your users or devices. It's easy, and different application formats are supported, explanations for which you will find in this chapter of the book.

Different application types you can deploy

Delivering applications to your end users, whether they are working primarily on a physical or virtual cloud desktop, is a very important factor for enterprises.

Most enterprises have been doing this for years with SMS, ConfigMgr, and **Microsoft Endpoint Configuration Manager** (**MECM**) (to their on-premises infrastructure). Within Microsoft Endpoint Manager – Intune, the process is easier as the backend infrastructure is pre-built to start deploying apps almost immediately!

So, what format of apps are supported as delivery types for each OS? Let's give you a complete rundown so that you can decide what is the best approach for your business.

When you create a new app in Microsoft Intune, you start by selecting an app type that is appropriate for the app you want to deliver to your devices:

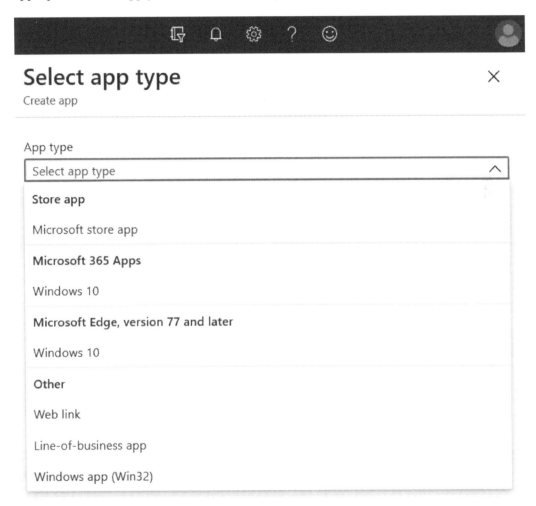

Figure 8.1 – Select app type

Supported Windows 10 app delivery types are covered in more detail in the following sub-sections.

LOB applications

Within Intune, you can deploy different formats in different methods. The supported formats are modern apps, such as **Universal Windows Platform** (**UWP**) apps and **Windows App Packages** (**AppX**), as well as more classic formats such as Win32 apps, including simple **Microsoft Installer** (**MSI**) package files.

.MSI – via the LOB app

MSI format installers are supported by both the LOB and the Windows app (Win32) options within Intune, with the latter more enhanced for app dependencies.

MSIX – via the LOB app

MSIX is Microsoft's new Windows app package format that provides a modern packaging experience to all Windows apps. The MSIX package format preserves the functionality of existing app packages and/or install files in addition to enabling new, modern packaging and deployment features to Win32, WPF, and Windows Forms apps. We'll go more deeply into MSIX later on in the book.

MSIX combines the best features of MSI, .appx, and App-V.

AppX – via the LOB app

The AppX application distribution file format was first introduced with Microsoft Windows 8. Also known as modern (UWP) apps, files with an AppX extension added are directly ready for distribution and installation.

Within the Windows Store as part of Windows 10 Enterprise, apps are automatically distributed in the AppX – UWP format.

AppX is very beneficial for distributing applications supported for multiple devices, including PCs, tablets, and smartphones that run on Windows.

> **Important Note**
>
> When you use Autopilot, we recommend that you do not mix LOB apps with the Windows 32 app (Win32) as a delivery option – you can find more information about this in *Chapter 7, Manager Windows Autopilot*.

To configure a simple LOB app, while in the Microsoft Endpoint Manager console, you must go to **Apps** in the menu to start the configuration:

Line-of-business app
To add a custom or in-house app, upload the app's installation file. Make sure the file extension matches the app's intended platform. Intune supports the following line-of-business app platforms and extensions:
• Android (APK)
• iOS (IPA)
• macOS (.IntuneMac)
• Windows (.msi, .appx, .appxbundle, .msix, and .msixbundle)
Learn more

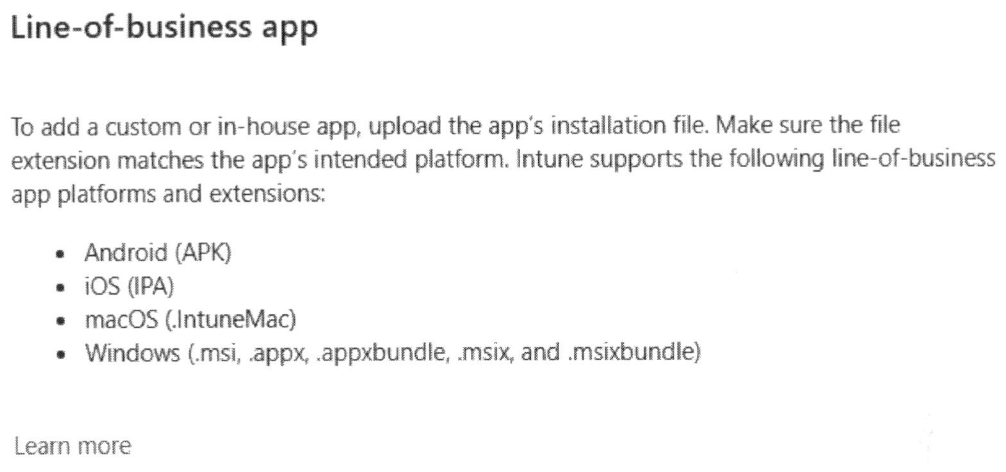

Figure 8.2 – LOB app

You start the configuration via the + **Add** button:

Home > Apps
Apps | All apps
Search (Ctrl+/)
Overview
All apps
Monitor
By platform
Windows
+ Add
Refresh
Filter
Export
Columns
Search by name or publisher
Name
Type
Status
Assigned

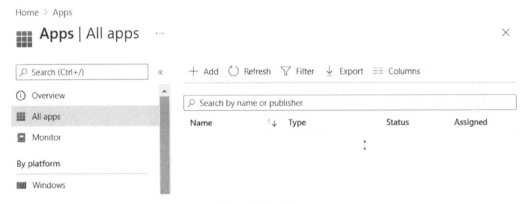

Figure 8.3 – All apps

The following menu shows all the supported app types, as mentioned previously. To start with the configuration for the most simple way to deploy an MSI file, you select **Line-of-business app**.

To deploy MSI files and other Win32 application formats in a more advanced manner, we recommend you use the Windows app (Win32) option – explained in the next section:

> **Important Note**
> Win32 supports delivery optimization and setting dependencies, where LOB does not support these.

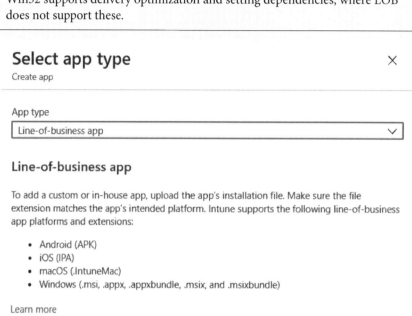

Figure 8.4 – App type – Line-of-business app

Search for the `.msi` file (`.exe` isn't supported – please use the Win32 app type for this instead):

Figure 8.5 – App package file

Give the LOB application the correct app name, description, and publisher.

There are other optional values that you could select:

- App installation context (user or device)
- App version ignorance
- Command-line arguments (parameters for the installation)
- Category to define the type of application
- List the application in the company portal (or not)

As you can see, limited capabilities are available here.

When you need more, please use the Win32 app approach:

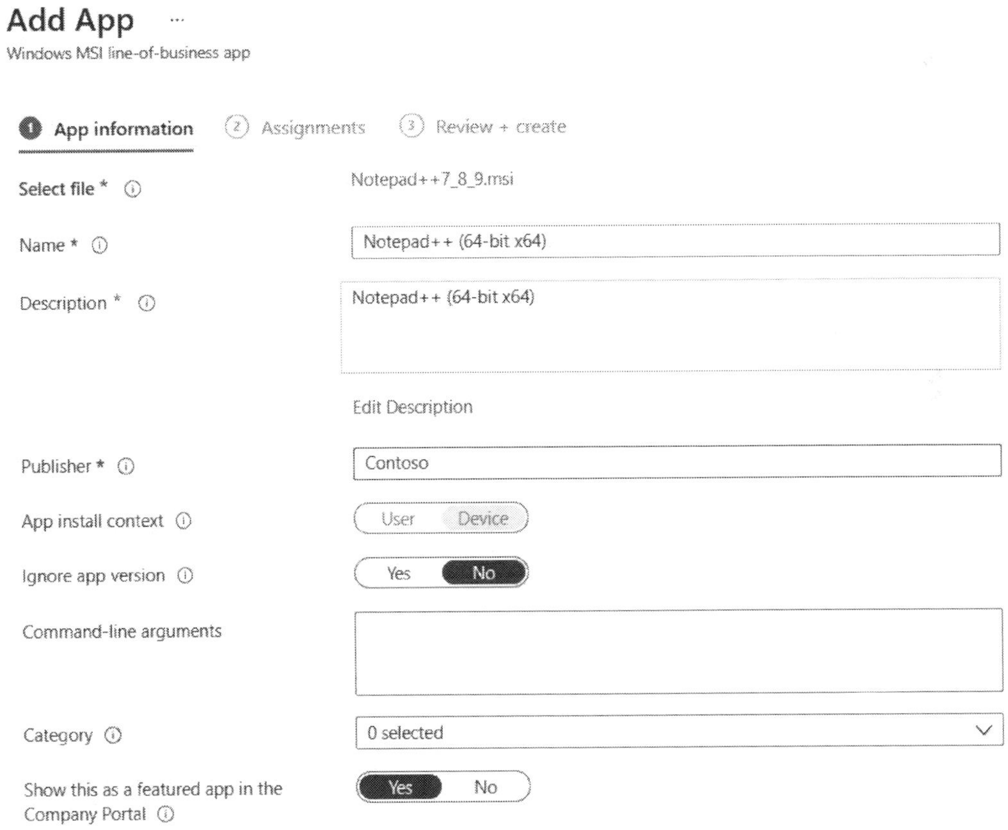

Add App   ···
Windows MSI line-of-business app

① App information	② Assignments	③ Review + create

Select file * ⓘ   Notepad++7_8_9.msi

Name * ⓘ   Notepad++ (64-bit x64)

Description * ⓘ   Notepad++ (64-bit x64)

                           Edit Description

Publisher * ⓘ   Contoso

App install context ⓘ   User   Device

Ignore app version ⓘ   Yes   No

Command-line arguments

Category ⓘ   0 selected   ⌄

Show this as a featured app in the   Yes   No
Company Portal ⓘ

Figure 8.6 – Add App – Windows MSI app information

Create the right AAD user, AAD group, or device-based filtering for your Windows MSI LOB app.

Start the deployment of the application after you have verified the configuration summary:

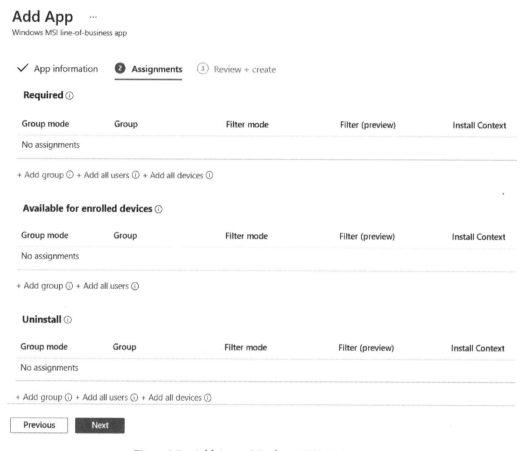

Figure 8.7 – Add App – Windows MSI Assignments

Enrollment starts directly for the designated users and devices after you see the following prompt in the top right-hand corner of the admin center.

Following a successful installation, Notepad++ pops up in the Start menu as a new recently added application:

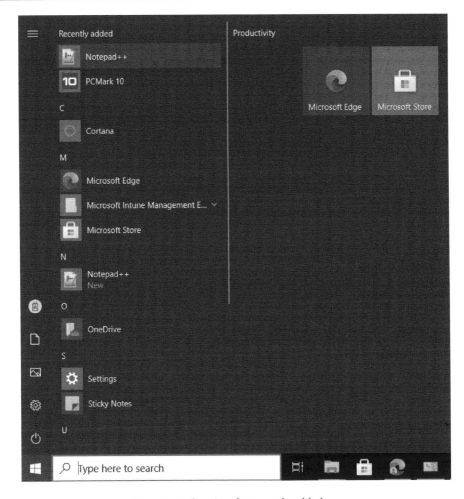

Figure 8.8 – Starting the recently added app

Then, the end user can start using the app or pin it to the Start menu.

.IntuneWin – via the Windows app (Win32)

The IntuneWin format is a way to preprocess Windows Classic (Win32) apps. The tool converts application installation files to the .intunewin format.

After you use this tool on the app installer folder, you'll be able to create an app enrollment configuration that allows enhanced deployment capabilities such as, for example, OS version dependencies and uninstallation methods when you need to remove applications remotely.

> **Important Note**
>
> Intune will install the Intune Management extension on the device
> if a PowerShell script or a Win32 app is targeted at the user or device.

When you select the most common application format, which is Win32, you must go through the following process. You have to encapsulate the `.exe` or `.msi` file in an IntuneWin file that we need as part of the app configuration set.

Here are the high-level steps of the process flow to understand the process:

1. Select your Win32 application installation file (`.exe` or `.msi`) and create the IntuneWin file as a package.

2. Start the app configuration in Microsoft Endpoint Manager – Intune.

3. Configure the necessary application info, such as the publisher and names.

4. Configure the application details to install the application, such as silent installation and uninstallation parameters.

5. Configure any requirements you have for the application, such as dependencies or the need for a PowerShell script to run before the installation starts.

6. Enable supersedence mode to update the older version of the application (more on this later). This feature is in preview.

7. Configure return code for logging purposes.

To start the configuration and delivery of a Windows 32 application (Win32), you must select the app type as follows:

Figure 8.9 – Select app type

Add a custom or in-house Win32-based app. Upload the app's installation file in `.intunewin` format. The following example demonstrates the packaging process for the most famous app used in demos – Notepad++.

The capabilities to filter out and create dependencies are much greater than with the previous LOB approach. The capabilities we use in this section apply to any Win32 application you have. Let's begin:

1. Firstly, download the Microsoft Win32 Content Prep Tool: `https://github.com/Microsoft/Microsoft-Win32-Content-Prep-Tool`.

2. Unzip the tool, for example, on the `C:\` drive (you could pick a random folder as well).

3. Save your application `.exe` or `.msi` file in, for example, the same folder as the Prep Tool (selected previously). It could also be saved somewhere else, of course. *I'm using Notepad++ for this example because it's free:*

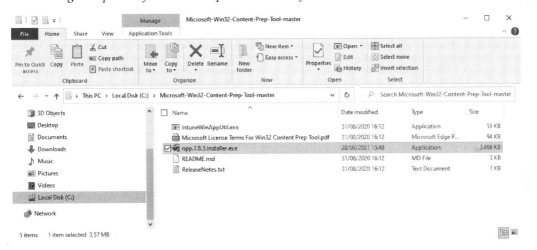

Figure 8.10 – Browse for your app

4. Now we start creating the `Win32` `.Intunewin` package.

5. Open PowerShell and change the directory to the Intune Prep Tool location, for example, `C:\Microsoft-Win32-Content-Prep-Tool-master`:

```
cd "C:\Microsoft-Win32-Content-Prep-Tool-master"
```

This command gives the following output:

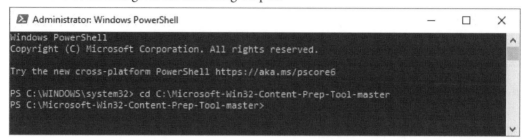

Figure 8.11 – Win32 Content Prep Tool master

6. Run `.\IntuneWinAppUtil.exe` and fill in the following requirements:

    • **Please specify the source folder**: `C:\Microsoft-Win32-Content-Prep-Tool-master`

    • **Please specify the setup file**: `npp.7.8.5.Installer.exe`

    • **Please specify the output folder**: `C:\Microsoft-Win32-Content-Prep-Tool-master`

    • **Do you want to specify catalog folder (Y/N)?** N

```
PS C:\Microsoft-Win32-Content-Prep-Tool-master> .\IntuneWinAppUtil.exe
Please specify the source folder: C:\Microsoft-Win32-Content-Prep-Tool-master
Please specify the setup file: npp.7.8.5.Installer.exe
Please specify the output folder: C:\Microsoft-Win32-Content-Prep-Tool-master
Do you want to specify catalog folder (Y/N)?N
```

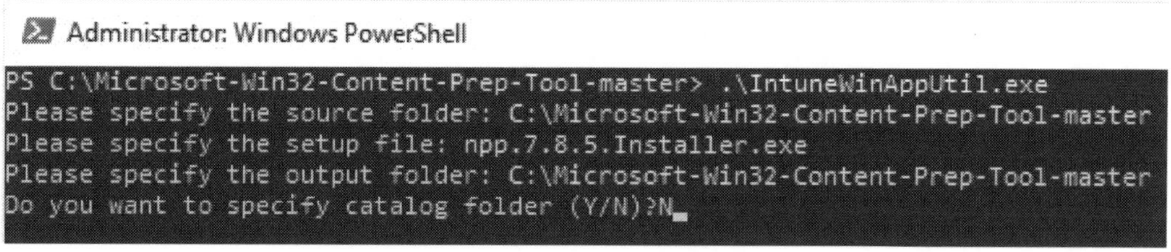

Figure 8.12 – IntuneWinAppUtil

> **Important Note**
> You can customize the folders as you like. This is just an example.

7. If everything ran successfully, you will see the `.intunewim` file listed in the folder. We can now switch to Microsoft Endpoint Manager:

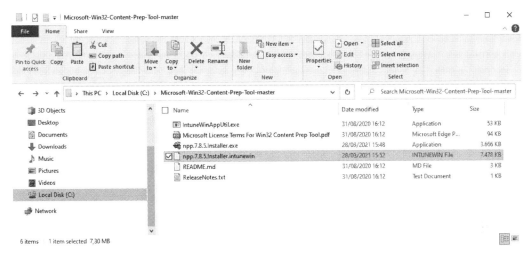

Figure 8.13 – Intunewim

8. Go to `http://endpoint.microsoft.com/` to continue in the Microsoft Endpoint Manager admin center. Go to the **Apps** field:

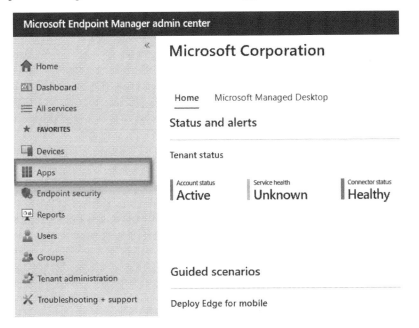

Figure 8.14 – Apps

9. Click on **Windows**:

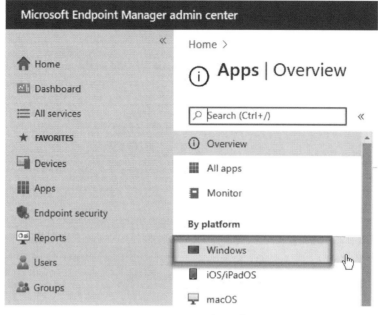

Figure 8.15 – Apps | Windows

10. Click on **Add**:

Figure 8.16 – Adding an app

11. Select **Windows apps (Win32)**. Click on **Select app package file**:

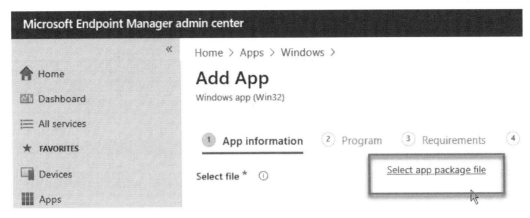

Figure 8.17 – Select app package file

12. Browse and select the .intunewin package file created earlier. Click on **OK**:

App package file   ×

App package file * ⓘ

"npp.7.8.5.Installer.intunewin"

Name: npp.7.8.5.Installer.exe
Platform: Windows
Size: 7.3 MiB
MAM Enabled: No

OK

Figure 8.18 – App package file

13. On the next screen, you can customize the name of the app.

   Optional: Set **Show this as a featured app in the Company Portal** to **Yes** if you prefer to make enrollment optional as regards user installation:

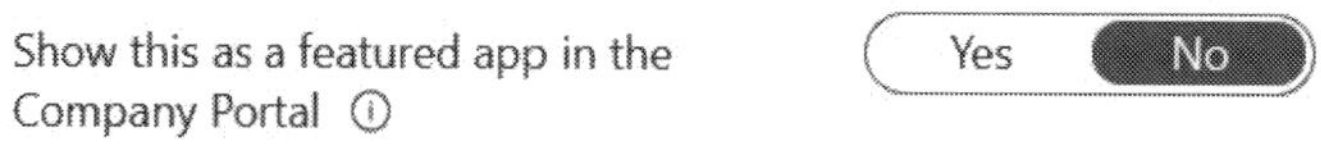

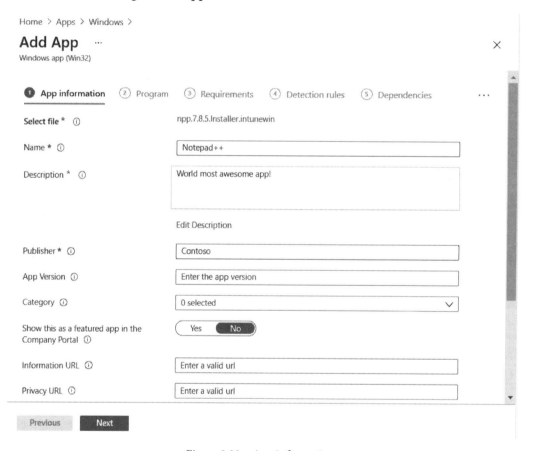

Figure 8.19 – Showing as a featured app

14. Enter the settings in the **App information** tab as follows:

Figure 8.20 – App information

15. Make sure to enter the app version manually to use features such as supersedence better, as this allows you to detect previous versions more easily when the application vendor doesn't include the version in the installation file:

App Version ⓘ

| 7.8.5 |

Figure 8.21 – App Version

16. Enter in the application-specific parameters to provide the silent installation of your application: `npp.7.9.Installer.exe/S`.

    Pick the installation behavior of your application. If it's a system install application, select **System** (the most used for all users), and **User** if the app should be installed as a user (inside the user profile):

Install behavior ⓘ   (System) User

Figure 8.22 – Install behavior

17. If your app required a reboot, please update the **Device restart behavior** section to whatever best fits your use case:

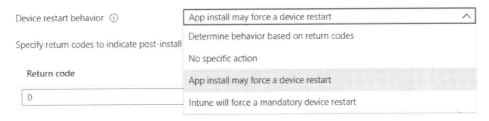

Device restart behavior ⓘ

App install may force a device restart ⌃

Specify return codes to indicate post-install

Determine behavior based on return codes

No specific action

Return code

App install may force a device restart

0

Intune will force a mandatory device restart

Figure 8.23 – Device restart behavior

18. Provide the minimum app requirements, for example, the OS version.

    Use the return codes to address the issue of whether the app has been installed successfully. This allows you to detect any failures in other Microsoft Endpoint Manager services, such as Endpoint Analytics, so as to perform auto-remediation actions:

Return code	Code type	
0	Success ⌄	🗑
1707	Success ⌄	🗑
3010	Soft reboot ⌄	🗑
1641	Hard reboot ⌄	🗑
1618	Retry ⌄	🗑

Figure 8.24 – Return codes

19. Once all the settings are done, click on **Next** to define the requirements of the application:

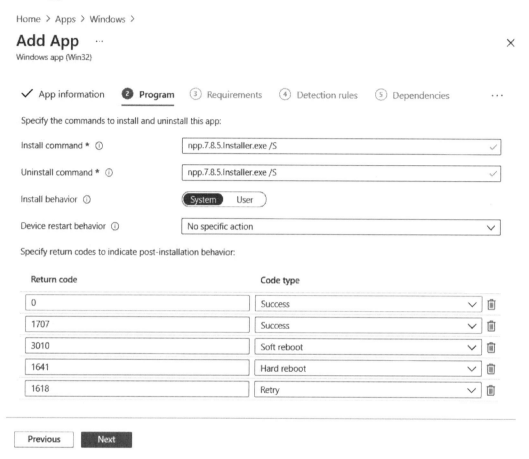

Figure 8.25 – Add App | Program

20. Specify the requirements that devices must meet before the app is installed. The following requirements are supported, as you can see:

- **Disk space required (MB)**

- **Physical memory required (MB)**

- **Minimum number of logical processors required**

- **Minimum CPU speed required (MHz)**

- **Configure additional requirement rules**

Home > Apps > Windows >

Add App   ···

Windows app (Win32)

✓ App information   ✓ Program   ❸ Requirements   ④ Detection rules   ⑤ Dependencies   ···

Specify the requirements that devices must meet before the app is installed:

Operating system architecture * ⓘ	2 selected ⌄
Minimum operating system * ⓘ	Windows 10 1903 ⌄
Disk space required (MB) ⓘ	
Physical memory required (MB) ⓘ	
Minimum number of logical processors required ⓘ	
Minimum CPU speed required (MHz) ⓘ	

Configure additional requirement rules

Type	Path/Script
No requirements are specified.	

+ Add

Previous   **Next**

Figure 8.26 – App requirements

21. As explained at the start, you could also add scripted actions to the installation of your application as a requirement. For example, you can run a PowerShell script first:

Add a Requirement rule   ✕

Create a requirement.

Requirement type * ⓘ
Select one   ⌃
File
Registry
Script

Figure 8.27 – Add a Requirement rule script

22. You must add the information of the script and the requirements when you want to use this feature/run this script prior to the installation process:

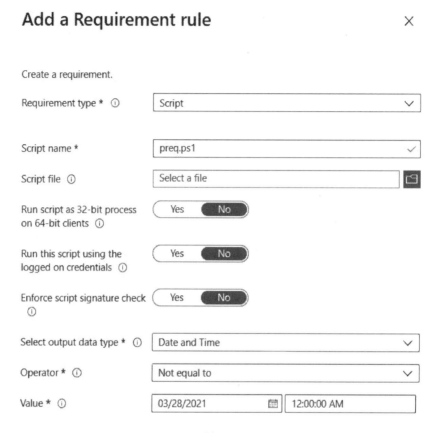

Figure 8.28 – Add a Requirement rule

23. Create the detection rule to check whether the application has been installed as it indicates the presence of the app in the location you define:

Detection rule   ×

Create a rule that indicates the presence of the app.

Rule type * ⓘ

| File | ⌄ |

Path * ⓘ

| C:\Program Files\Notepad++\ | ✓ |

File or folder * ⓘ

| notepad++.exe | ✓ |

Detection method * ⓘ

| File or folder exists | ⌄ |

Associated with a 32-bit app on 64-bit clients ⓘ

   Yes   No

Figure 8.29 – Detection rule

24. Software dependencies are applications that must be installed before this application can be installed.

When there are dependencies on other applications before the installation should run, you could add those as a dependency. The installation or upgrade of your application will not run when the application isn't detected.

You can have up to a maximum of 100 dependencies configured:

Add dependency   ×

Search by name, publisher

Name	Publisher	Dependency Count
Remote Desktop	Contoso	0

Figure 8.30 – Add dependency

When adding dependencies to a Win32 app, you can browse between your already created Win32 apps or Microsoft Edge apps that are built in.

Supersedence mode

There is a new preview feature available called Supersedence in Microsoft Endpoint Manager. This new feature enables you to update and replace existing Win32 apps with newer versions of the same app. This will enable you to do comprehensive versioning.

When you supersede an application, you can specify which app will be updated or replaced. To update an app, disable the **Uninstall previous version** option. To replace the application version, you must enable the **Uninstall previous version** option. There is a maximum of 10 updated or replaced apps, including references to other apps:

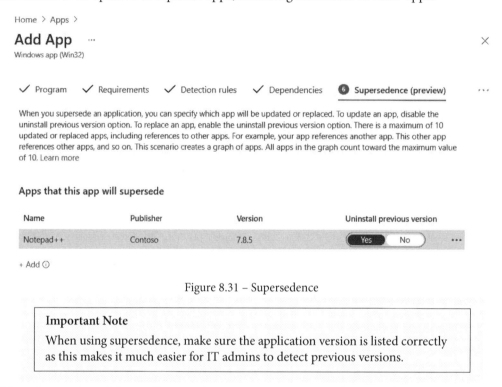

Figure 8.31 – Supersedence

> **Important Note**
> When using supersedence, make sure the application version is listed correctly as this makes it much easier for IT admins to detect previous versions.

Select the version of the application that you want to supersede/upgrade:

Figure 8.32 – Add Apps supersedence

Assign the application to an (AAD) group or all devices, to enforce deployment to your physical Windows PCs/endpoints:

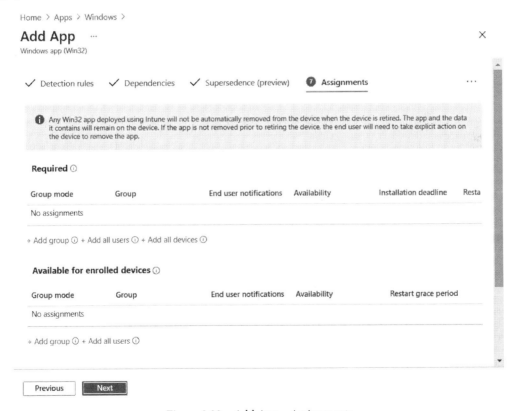

Figure 8.33 – Add App – Assignments

Edit the assignment if you want to enforce the enrollment or update process.

Other great options are the option to schedule the update process based on different time zones and sequences that you can define:

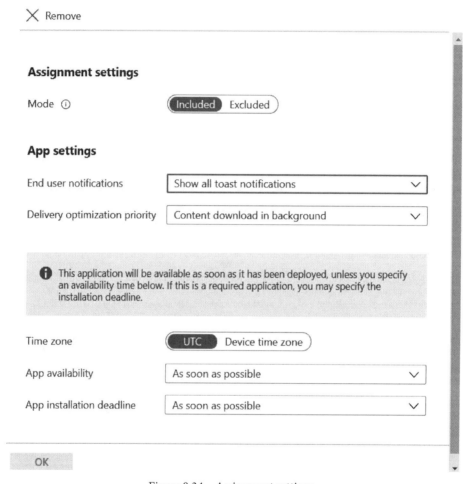

Figure 8.34 – Assignment settings

Confirm that your app configuration is set. If everything aligns, you can start the deployment by clicking on **Create**. *Always double-check your settings*:

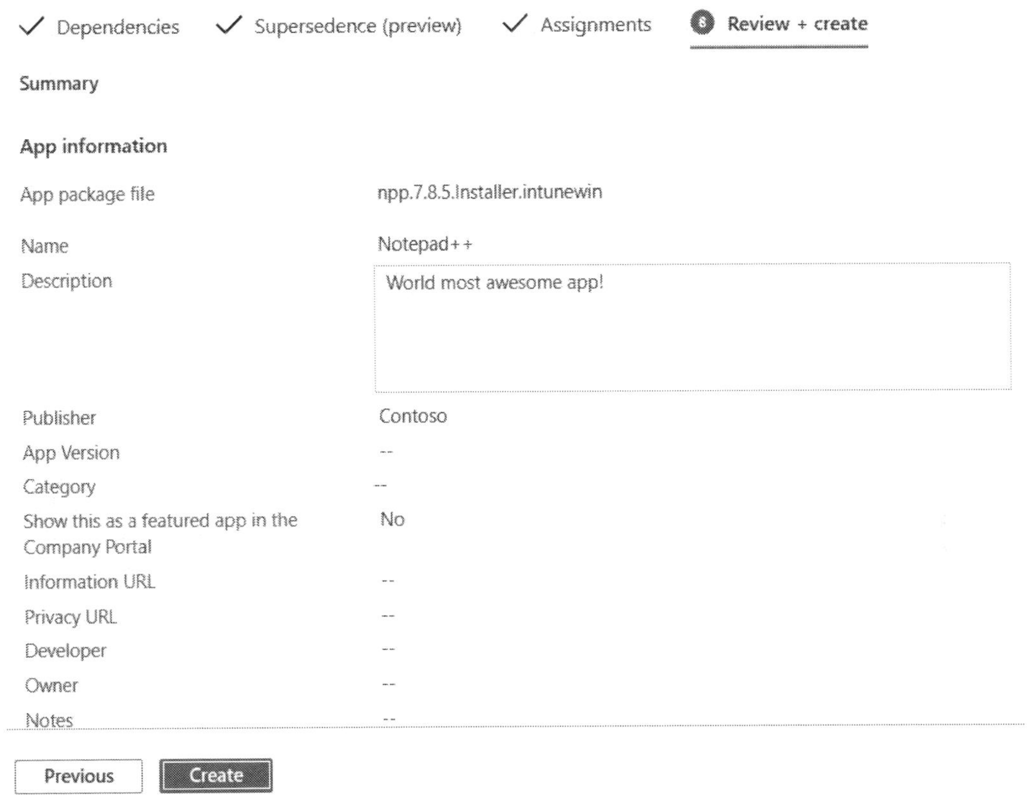

✓ Dependencies   ✓ Supersedence (preview)   ✓ Assignments   ⑧ **Review + create**

Summary

App information

App package file   npp.7.8.5.Installer.intunewin

Name   Notepad++

Description   World most awesome app!

Publisher   Contoso

App Version   --

Category   --

Show this as a featured app in the   No
Company Portal

Information URL   --

Privacy URL   --

Developer   --

Owner   --

Notes   --

[Previous]   [**Create**]

Figure 8.35 – Review + create

The application will now be pushed to all the endpoints of users who are part of the AAD group filter:

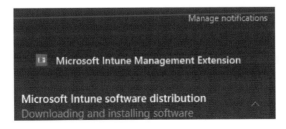

Figure 8.36 – Microsoft Intune Management Extension toast notification

You can repeat the same steps for all your applications in your environment or choose to use MSIX for application virtualization first to simplify your application distribution process.

The application will show up as a recently added application in the user's Start menu.

Community tool – Win32App Migration Tool

The tool is community-driven and was created by Ben – a Microsoft MVP – and is designed to migrate your existing SCCM/MECM Configuration Manager application to a deployment type that is supported within Microsoft Endpoint Manager – Intune as an application delivery package.

The tool does everything automatically, so instead of manually checking application and deployment types, the tool does it in a bulk manner for you and, by way of output, it creates the .intunewin file for you.

You can download the tool for free here. As mentioned previously, it is community-driven, meaning it's not officially supported by Microsoft support: https://github. com/byteben/Win32App-Migration-Tool.

This is great work by ByteBen – an Enterprise Mobility MVP. The tool runs in PowerShell with verbose logging onscreen:

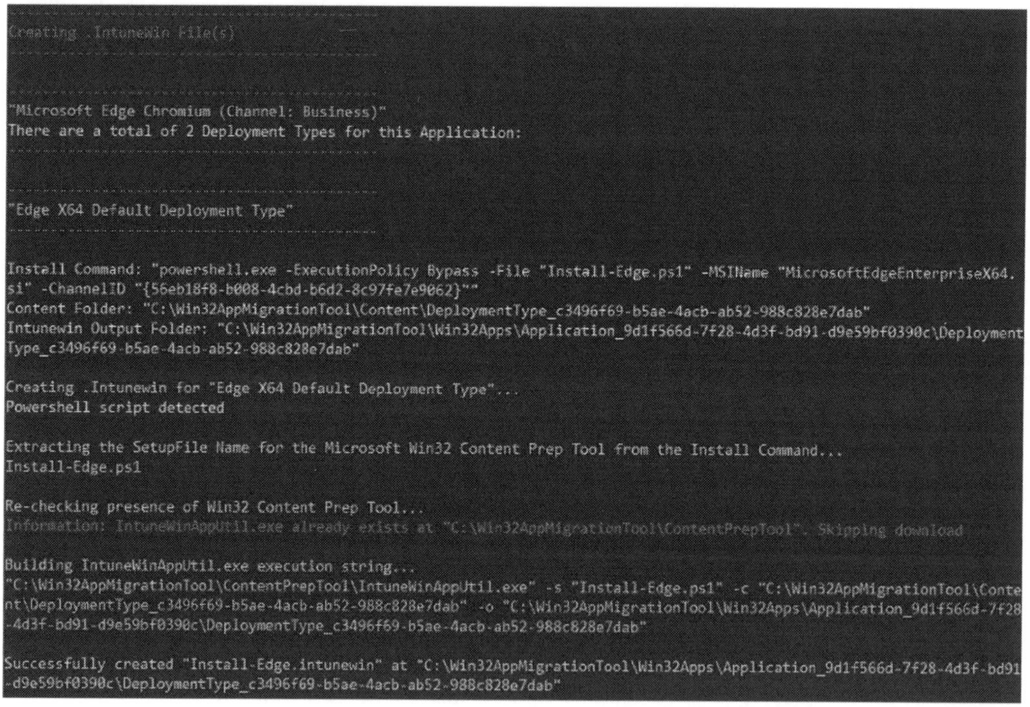

Figure 8.37 – Win32 App Migration Tool

This concludes the section about Win32 apps in Microsoft Intune. In the next section, we will cover Microsoft 365 apps in depth.

Deploying Microsoft 365 apps

Office Click-to-Run is the new way of deploying Microsoft 365 Apps – Office to your endpoints. The installation takes place in the following five different stages, as the following example describes, and involves active downloading from the internet. Therefore, the installation elements are very small.

Microsoft 365 apps are not like other apps in Microsoft Intune, as it is a policy that is deployed to the managed devices. The policy is similar to other CSPs deployed through the MDM channel to the device:

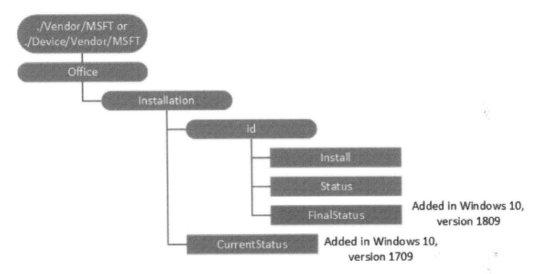

Figure 8.38 – Office CSP

As it is a policy and not a Win32 app, that is also the reason why you cannot use it as a dependency in a Win32 app. The CSP writes to the reg key Computer\HKEY_LOCAL_MACHINE\SOFTWARE\Microsoft\OfficeCSP, where it created a default key with the value http://go.microsoft.com/fwlink/?LinkID=829801, at which point the setup.exe file downloads the file to the local device together with the XML file stored in the same registry location with a GUID.

The combination of setup.exe/configure [the name of the Microsoft 365 Apps XML file] will then start downloading all the binaries from Office CDN (the default option in the Microsoft Intune UI and configuration XML).

Once installation is complete, the FinalStatus reg key will be updated as follows:

- When status = 0: 70 (succeeded)
- When status != 0: 60 (failed)

Microsoft Endpoint Manager app delivery supports the direct enrollment of Microsoft 365 apps from within the app profile configuration menu.

It's just a drop-down menu that allows you to include or exclude Microsoft 365 apps from installation (without the need for an ODT – XML file):

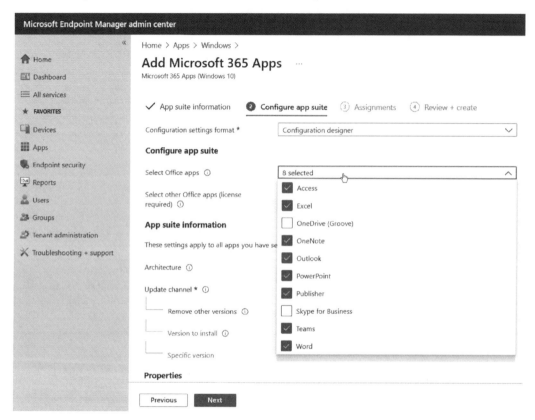

Figure 8.39 – Add Microsoft 365 Apps

When you have selected the Office apps you want in this deployment, you can continue in the Microsoft 365 Apps wizard.

Update channels

Select whether to use the 32- or 64-bit version of your chosen Microsoft 365 apps and select the update channel that best aligns with your business requirements:

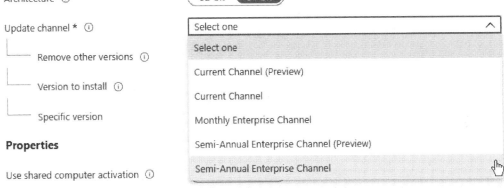

Figure 8.40 – App suite information

Other great settings that are directly supported from within the console are the following list of features:

Figure 8.41 – Properties

Shared computer activation lets you deploy Microsoft 365 apps to computers that are used by multiple users. Normally, users can only install and activate Microsoft 365 apps on a limited number of devices, such as five PCs. Using Microsoft 365 apps with shared computer activation doesn't count against that limit.

Office Customization Tool

The Microsoft 365 App type enrollment flow also supports custom configuration XML files. The Office Customization Tool is normally used in on-premises environments to deploy Office in large organizations.

You could incorporate that configuration set inside your app type configuration and Intune will take over the specific exclusion and other configuration settings:

Add Microsoft 365 Apps ···

Microsoft 365 Apps (Windows 10)

✓ App suite information   ② **Configure app suite**   ③ Assignments   ④ Review + create

Configuration settings format *   Enter XML data   ⌄

Configuration file

Use the Office Customization tool to create the configuration files that are used to deploy Office in large organizations. Learn more

```
<Configuration>
 <Add OfficeClientEdition="32" Channel="Current">
  <Product ID="O365ProPlusRetail">
   <Language ID="en-us" />
  </Product>
 </Add>
 <AppSettings>
  <User Key="software\microsoft\office\16.0\excel\security"
      Name="vbawarnings"
      Value="3"
      Type="REG_DWORD"
      App="excel16"
      Id="L_VBAWarningsPolicy" />
 </AppSettings>
</Configuration>
```

Validate XML

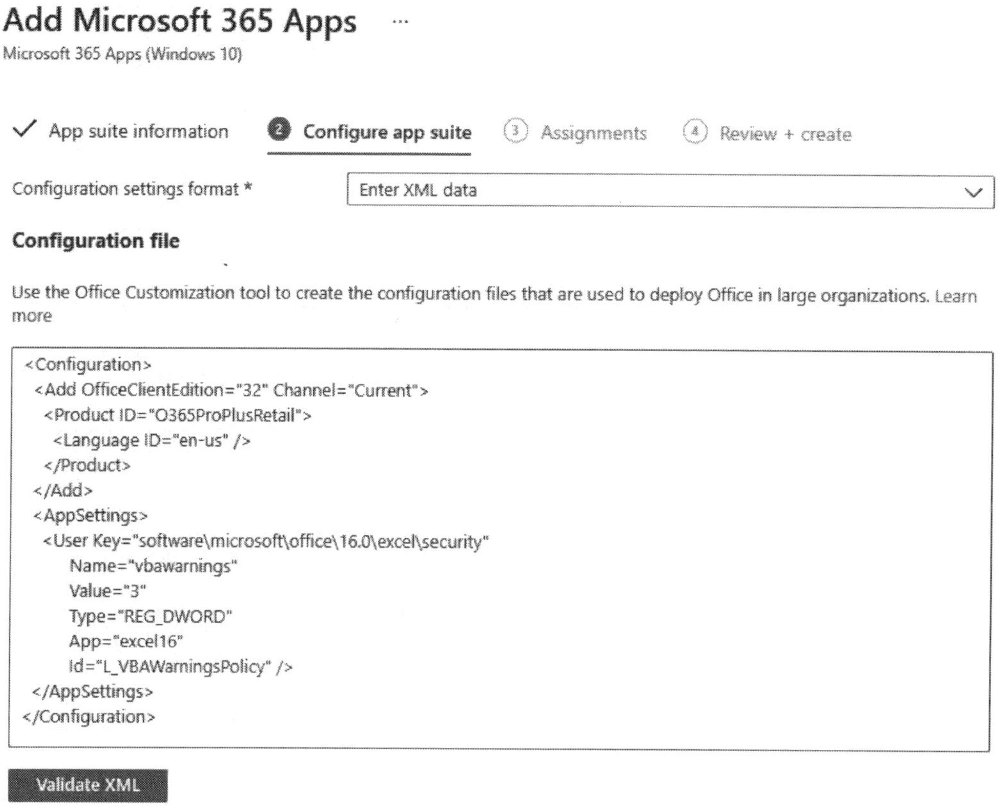

Figure 8.42 – Configuration file

Choose the Office language versions that you want to install. Office automatically installs versions for any languages that have been installed in Windows. Use these settings if you want to install additional languages:

Languages   ✕

Choose the Office language versions that you want to install. Office automatically installs in any languages that have been installed in Windows. Use these settings if you want to install additional languages.

Language	Locale	Type
☐ Arabic	ar-sa	Core
☐ Bulgarian	bg-bg	Core
☐ Chinese Simplified	zh-cn	Core
☐ Chinese Traditional	zh-tw	Core

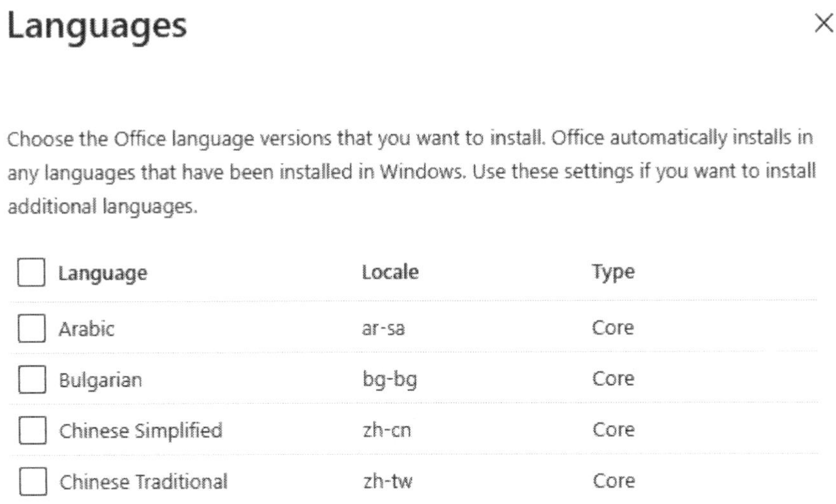

Figure 8.43 – Languages

You need to have the Office language setting the same as in the Microsoft 365 app that you are deploying to your users as the Office CSP only supports one assignment per device.

Microsoft 365 Apps admin center

In *Chapter 6, Windows Deployment and Management*, we already talked a bit about updating Microsoft 365 apps in general. We're now going to talk in a little more detail about the following option inside the `config.office.com` admin center portal, which brings you to the following page:

> **Important Note**
>
> The Microsoft 365 admin center should be used in extension to the previous section regarding the delivery of Microsoft 365 apps.

Figure 8.44 – Microsoft 365 Apps admin center

After logging on with your (Intune) administrator credentials, you must go to **Servicing** to start creating custom profiles for Microsoft 365 apps.

In that menu, if this is the first time you are logging in to this configuration portal, you'll be asked to enable the service as it's still in preview mode. Make sure to click on the **Enable preview features** button:

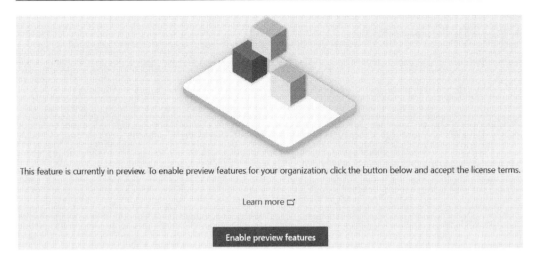

Figure 8.45 – Enable preview features

Accept the terms to continue to the service to start provisioning and maintaining Microsoft 365 apps. *This process can take up to 10 minutes*:

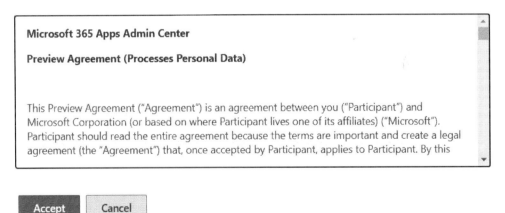

Figure 8.46 – License terms for preview features

Once provisioning is complete, the following dashboard screen appears. Here's where we should start creating one of the two profiles for auto-updating and configuring Microsoft 365 apps:

- **Devices information**: This profile includes devices that are assessed to be a low business risk in terms of app compatibility. Edit the profile to add or remove devices.

- **Update frequency, rollout schedule, and rollout throttling**: Updates are delivered from the Monthly Enterprise Channel. The daily limit on download size, delivery optimization, and preferred download times ensures that automatic updates are network-friendly:

Figure 8.47 – Servicing profile

Scroll down the page and click on the **Get started** button to (yes, you know the drill) get started:

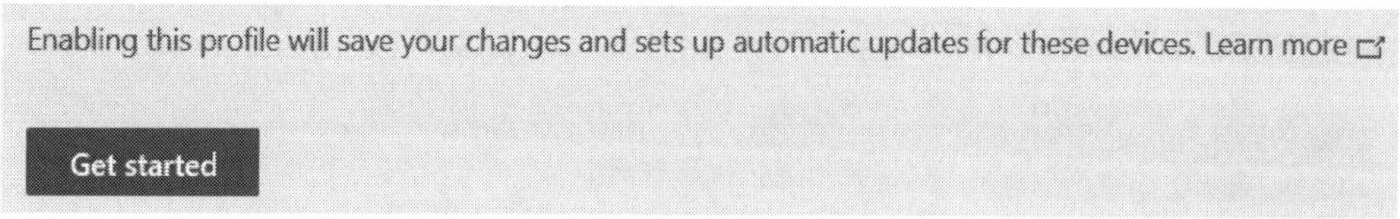

Figure 8.48 – Get started

Getting started

The following wizard will guide you through creating the servicing profile.

The servicing profile automates the monthly updates for Office apps while providing you with control. Apps will be updated from the Office CDN and be placed on the Monthly Enterprise Channel. The setup wizard will walk you through the process of selecting devices that you would like to add to the profile along with other settings.

You can also set up other features, such as client-side update deadlines and update exclusion dates. You can revisit these options once the profile has been created through the **Settings** tab:

Create profile

Getting started
Device selection criteria
Update exclusion dates
Update deadline
Review and enable

Getting started

This setup wizard will guide you through creating the servicing profile.

The servicing profile automates the monthly updates for Office apps while providing you with control. Apps will be updated from the Office CDN and be placed on the **Monthly Enterprise Channel**. The setup wizard will walk you through the process of selecting devices that you would like to add to the profile along with other settings.

You can also optionally setup other features such as client-side update deadlines and update exclusion dates. You can revisit these options after the profile has been created through the settings tab. Click on the Next button below to begin.

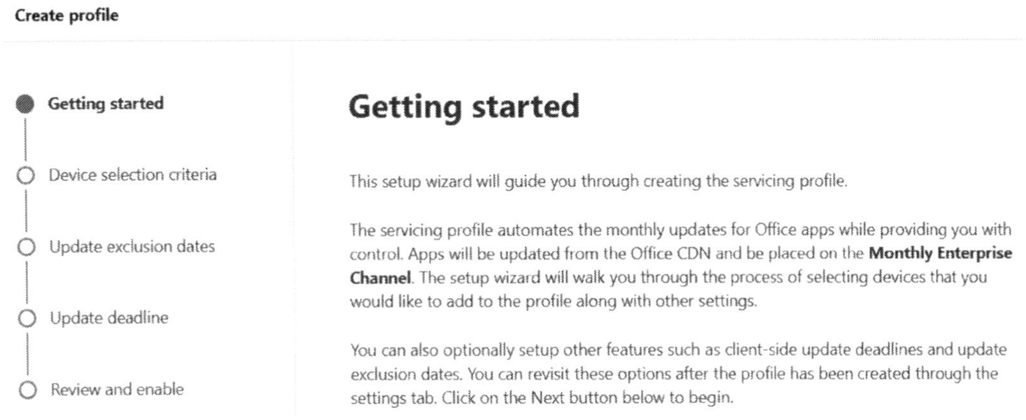

Figure 8.49 – Getting started

Click on the **Next** button to begin.

Device selection criteria

You can go configure your set of endpoints by adding additional criteria through the following filters.

Channels

In the **Channels** section, you define what devices will be moved from their current update channel to the Monthly Enterprise Channel.

For security purposes, you could exclude add-ins and macro usage.

Current Channel will be the default selection when you sign in to the Microsoft 365 admin center. To change this, you must go to **Settings** | **Org settings** | **Services** | and the Office installation options.

Device selection criteria

We have identified candidates for automatic updates in your environment. You can further narrow down this set of devices by adding additional criteria through the filters below.

Devices selected to be added to profile

Channels

Devices will be moved from their current update channel to the Monthly Enterprise Channel

0 devices

Include devices on:

Device count based on total number of devices in your environment, limited by selection criteria

☐ Beta Channel	**Channels** ... 0
☐ Current Channel (Preview)	**Disk space** ... 0
☑ Current Channel	**Macros** ... 0
☑ Monthly Enterprise Channel	**Add-ins** ... 0
☐ Semi-Annual Enterprise Channel (Preview)	**Devices** ... 0
☐ Semi-Annual Enterprise Channel	

Disk space

○————————————— more than 5 GB

Macros

◉ Include all devices

○ Exclude devices with macro usage (last 28 days)

Figure 8.50 – Device selection criteria

When you have selected the update channel, you can proceed to set up the update exclusion dates, as covered in the next section.

Update exclusion dates

Update exclusions can be used to prevent devices from downloading security and feature updates during specific moments. You can create different sets of exclusions that allow you to reduce the change in your environment during busy periods.

Click on **No exclusion dates** if you want to add them at a later date:

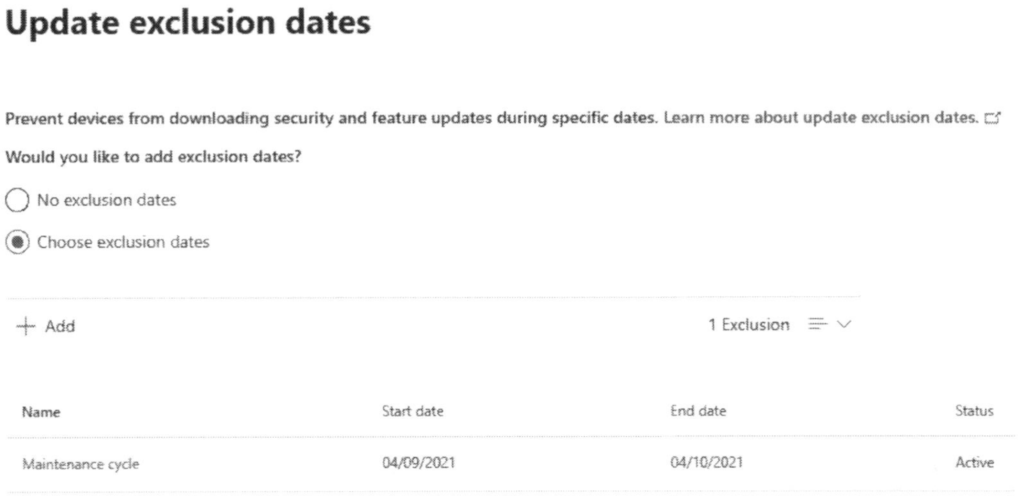

Update exclusion dates

Prevent devices from downloading security and feature updates during specific dates. Learn more about update exclusion dates. ⧉

Would you like to add exclusion dates?

◯ No exclusion dates

◉ Choose exclusion dates

＋ Add   1 Exclusion ☰ ⌄

Name	Start date	End date	Status
Maintenance cycle	04/09/2021	04/10/2021	Active

Figure 8.51 – Update exclusion dates

When you have selected the update exclusion dates, you can proceed to update deadlines, covered in the next section.

Update deadline

Within the **Update deadline** menu, you can manage how updates are applied to Microsoft 365 apps for enterprise. This will help you to adjust the update cycle of your Office applications as well as offer capabilities to enforce updates or let users do it at their own pace.

There is also the option to give the user some spare days before the updates are enforced on the endpoint.

Click on **Next**:

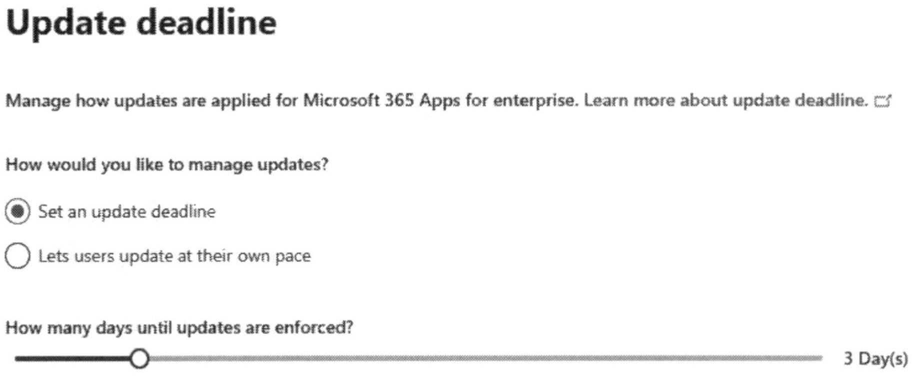

Update deadline

Manage how updates are applied for Microsoft 365 Apps for enterprise. Learn more about update deadline. ☐

How would you like to manage updates?

◉ Set an update deadline

○ Lets users update at their own pace

How many days until updates are enforced?

3 Day(s)

Figure 8.52 – Update deadline

Review all your settings and click on **Create profile** to publish the settings to your devices:

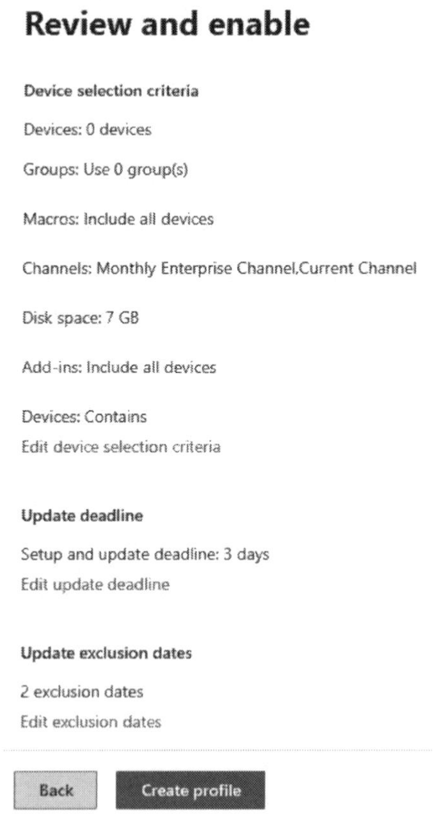

Review and enable

Device selection criteria

Devices: 0 devices

Groups: Use 0 group(s)

Macros: Include all devices

Channels: Monthly Enterprise Channel,Current Channel

Disk space: 7 GB

Add-ins: Include all devices

Devices: Contains
Edit device selection criteria

Update deadline

Setup and update deadline: 3 days
Edit update deadline

Update exclusion dates

2 exclusion dates
Edit exclusion dates

Back   Create profile

Figure 8.53 – Review and enable

The profile has been created successfully:

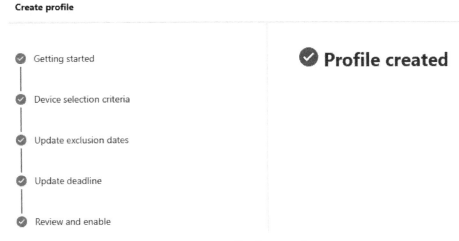

Figure 8.54 – Profile created

The **Servicing profile** enrollment will now happen with the specifics you just defined in the profile.

You can modify the existing **Servicing Profile** easily by clicking on the settings in the following menu later on:

Figure 8.55 – Monthly Enterprise Channel

This completes the configuration of Microsoft 365 app updates. In the next section, we will cover Microsoft 365 app customization.

Microsoft 365 apps – customization

The other great feature within the **Apps Admin Center** portal is **Customization**. Here, you can provide default policy settings to your endpoints, all centrally managed:

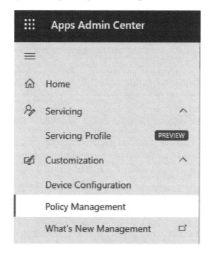

Figure 8.56 – Policy Management

The **Create policy configuration** menu allows you to create different configuration sets within Office that you'd normally do as either an administrative template or group policies:

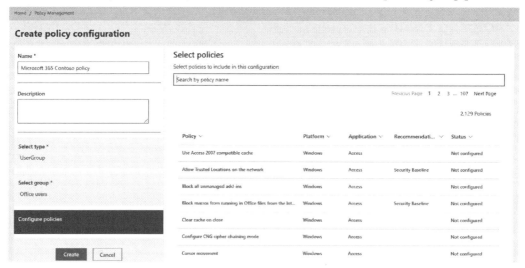

Figure 8.57 – Create policy configuration

We'll go deeper into this in *Chapter 10, Advanced Policy Management*.

Deploying Microsoft Teams

Microsoft Teams will be installed as a machine-wide installer via the aforementioned Microsoft 365 apps settings. It's good to mention that Teams is a per-user basis application. The Microsoft 365 setup will add the installer to your Windows 10 Enterprise endpoints and will auto-install when a new user logs on to the endpoint. Teams will then install inside the user profile.

Inside the Microsoft 365 apps settings in Microsoft Intune, you can select Teams to be installed alongside the rest of the apps:

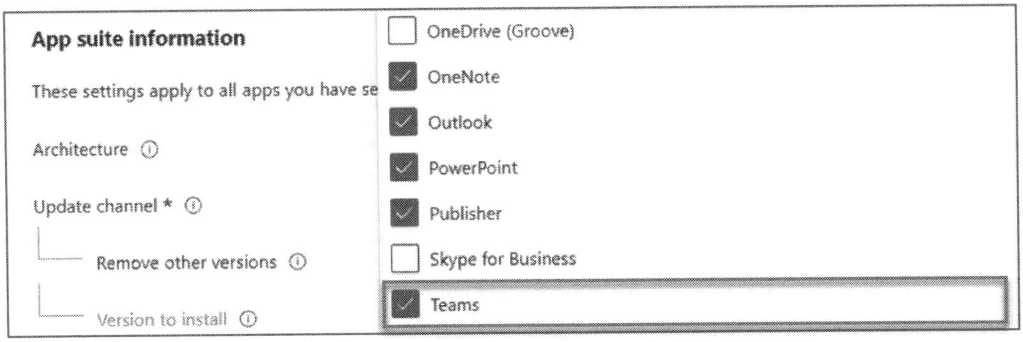

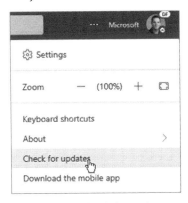

Figure 8.58 – App suite information

The Teams application is updated every 2 weeks after testing through internal update programs such as the **Technology Adoption Program** (**TAP**).

The machine-wide desktop app, which is installed inside the user profile, is updated automatically and doesn't require any user or IT admin interaction to do so.

You could also manually update the Teams app via the three-dot menu in the top right-hand corner. Clicking on **Check for updates** will trigger the update process with the *"We will check and install any updates while you continue to work"* notification at the top of the screen:

Figure 8.59 – MS Teams Check for updates menu option

Microsoft Teams follows its own update process and does not follow the update process of other Microsoft 365 apps.

OneDrive

OneDrive isn't part of the Microsoft 365 app delivery process for the simple reason that OneDrive is mandatory for Windows 10 Enterprise and is therefore included in the OS following enrollment.

OneDrive auto-updates based on either the **Insiders**, **Standard**, or **Deferred** ring cycle. OneDrive checks for available updates every 24 hours when it's running as part of your endpoint.

The production ring (which is the default) receives updates every 20 days, whereas the deferred ring gives you a bit more flexibility as it updates every 2–3 months. During this timeframe, customers can deploy updates on their own, allowing them to record precisely when their software is updated. When the number of days is exceeded, the update will apply automatically:

> **Important Note**
> Microsoft reserves the right to bypass the 60-day grace period for critical updates.

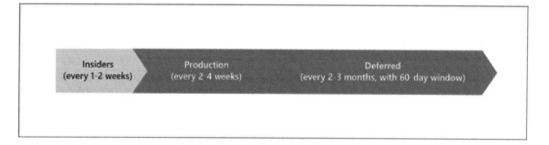

Figure 8.60 – OneDrive update schedule

You can put your OneDrive client inside the **Deferred** ring via designated OneDrive policies, which we will explain in the next chapter.

When you want to force updates to your endpoint via Microsoft Endpoint Manager, you could send the following command to your endpoints to make this possible. The restart parameter performs a reboot of your Windows 10 Enterprise desktop:

```
Execute C:\<location>\OneDriveSetup.exe /update /restart
```

The OneDrive client is installed in each user's profile under `%localappdata%`.
Beginning with the OneDrive sync client builds `19.174.0902.0013`, and later, you can
install OneDrive per machine. You only need to run `OneDriveSetup.exe/allusers`
to convert the installation from per-user to per-machine:

```
This can be done by creating a Powershell Script and run it
from Microsoft Intune to the device where you want the change.
#>
####################################################################
##################################

$url = "https://go.microsoft.com/fwlink/?linkid=2083517"
$output = "$ENV:temp" + '\OneDriveSetup.exe'
$O4BPath = "$ENV:localappdata" + 'Microsoft/OneDrive/
OneDriveSetup.exe'
#write $O4BPath
#write $output
IF(Test-Path $output)
{
}
 ELSE {
 Invoke-WebRequest -Uri $url -OutFile $output
    }
IF(!(Test-Path $O4BPath))
  {
     & "$output" + '/allusers'
  }
 ELSE {
    }
```

This script will download the latest version of the OneDrive sync client and convert the
installation to per-machine in `Program Files (x86)\Microsoft OneDrive`.

Deploying Microsoft Edge

Microsoft Edge has been fairly easy to distribute to your endpoints ever since update 79 – it completely integrates within Microsoft Endpoint Manager, and this also applies to most of the policies that we'll cover in the next chapter.

In the **Intune apps** menu, you must add Microsoft Edge for Windows to install the Microsoft Edge browser on managed Windows 10 devices – as **App type** to start the configuration:

Figure 8.61 – Microsoft Edge for Windows 10

When you want to test new features earlier than others that are active in the **Stable** ring, you can simply change the **Channel** setting to whatever best suits your use case.

You could also deploy all the different channel versions separately from your Windows 10 Enterprise endpoints:

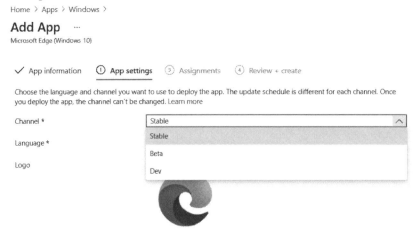

Figure 8.62 – Microsoft Edge for Windows 10 Stable

The same applies to language settings. Pick the OS default settings when you want to drive language settings from within the Windows OS, or overwrite them when you want to separate the browser language:

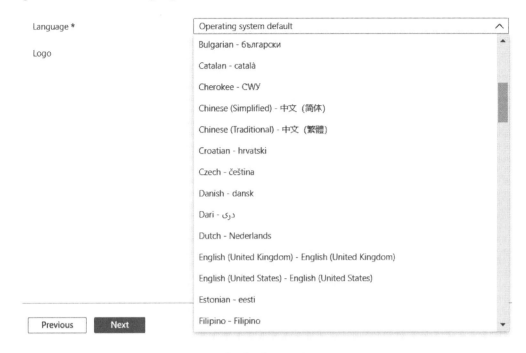

Figure 8.63 – Microsoft Edge for Windows 10 Language menu

Microsoft Edge is part of every new release of Windows, so this app type will be redundant sometime in the future.

What is MSIX?

MSIX is a Windows app package format that provides a modern packaging experience to all Win32, UWP, and Windows apps. It's a new way of doing application virtualization compared to technologies such as App-V.

Separating the applications from the images to update and assign applications without doing an image update sounds like a solution, right? Well, that's exactly what MSIX can accomplish. Let me explain how you could package an application here:

1. Declarative install via the manifest file.

2. The app signature needs to be trusted on the device.

3. Tamper protection via BlockMap and signature.

4. The OS manages the installation, updates, and removal:

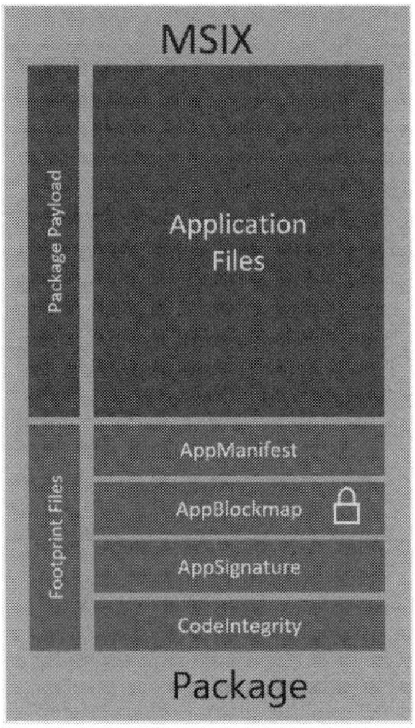

Figure 8.64 – MSIX package

AppxManifest.xml

The package manifest is an XML document that contains the information the system needs to deploy, display, and update an MSIX app. This info includes package identity, package dependencies, required capabilities, visual elements, and extensibility points.

AppxBlockMap.xml

The package block map file is an XML document that contains a list of the app's files along with indexes and cryptographic hashes for each block of data that is stored in the package. The block map file itself is verified and secured with a digital signature when the package is signed. The block map file allows MSIX packages to be downloaded and validated incrementally, and also works to support differential updates to the app files after they're installed.

AppxSignature.p7x

`AppxSignature.p7x` is generated when the package is signed. All MSIX packages are required to be signed prior to installation. With `AppxBlockmap.xml`, the platform can install the package and it can be validated.

How to create MSIX packages

The process of creating MSIX packages looks pretty similar to what you may have done in the past with App-V. The app developer creates the application and creates the MSIX package (this could be the **Independent Software Vendor (ISV)**), after which you customize the application for deployment via Intune – Microsoft Endpoint Manager and assign it to the correct AAD group or users.

Let's explain the following steps so you get a good feeling for the process:

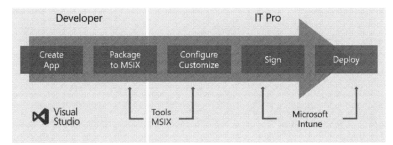

Figure 8.65 – MSIX tools

First, search for `MSIX Packaging Tool` in the Microsoft Store and install it on your Windows 10 virtual machine:

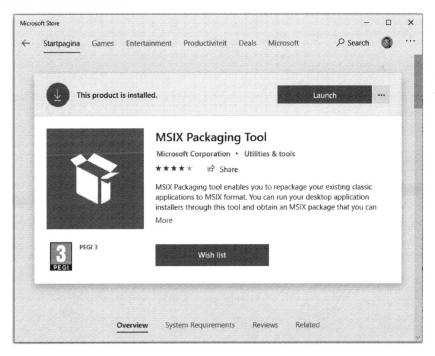

Figure 8.66 – MSIX Packaging Tool

Start the packaging tool:

Figure 8.67 – Start the MSIX Packaging Tool

Click on **Create your app package**:

Figure 8.68 – Application package

Click **Create package on this computer**:

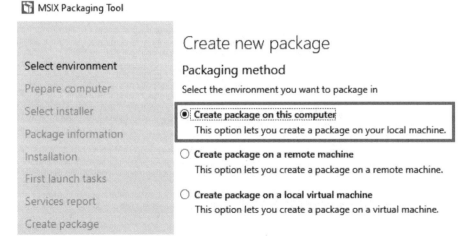

Figure 8.69 – Create package on this computer

Make sure that the status is the same on your image/session host as in the screenshot for the different action items.

Then, click on **Next**:

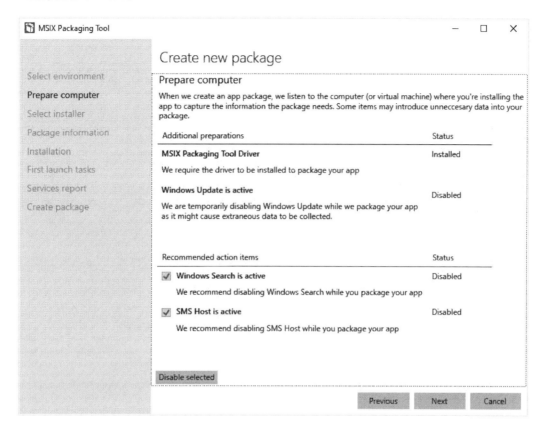

Figure 8.70 – Create new package

Browse for the application installer. This could be any of your Win32 applications. I'll use Notepad++ for the exercise.

Assign your certificate with the correct Common Name (CN, for example, Contoso) that we will require later. This could be a self-signed certificate as well (for PoC testing purposes):

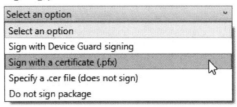

Figure 8.71 – Signing preference

> **Important Note**
>
> Make sure that the CN=Contoso (organization name) is correct on the certificate as well as in the package configuration.

Then, click on **Next**:

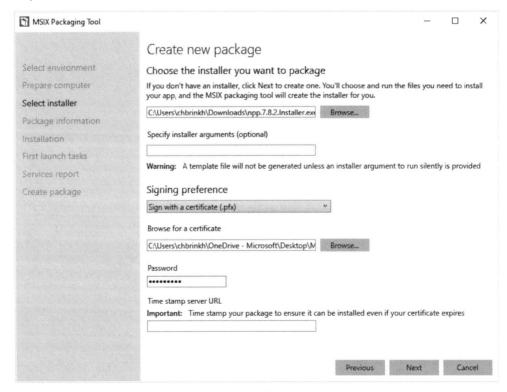

Figure 8.72 – Select installer

Enter in the application-specific requirements. The publisher's name is the certificate CN (for example, `Contoso`) of the organization. Make sure that the certificate is injected into your image, otherwise, the application cannot register and will fail.

> **Important Note**
> If the CN is detected correctly, you'll see the **Subject of the certificate provided** notification. The certificate could be self-signed, public, or internally created via a root CA. The private key and CN must be matching later in the process.

Click on **Next**:

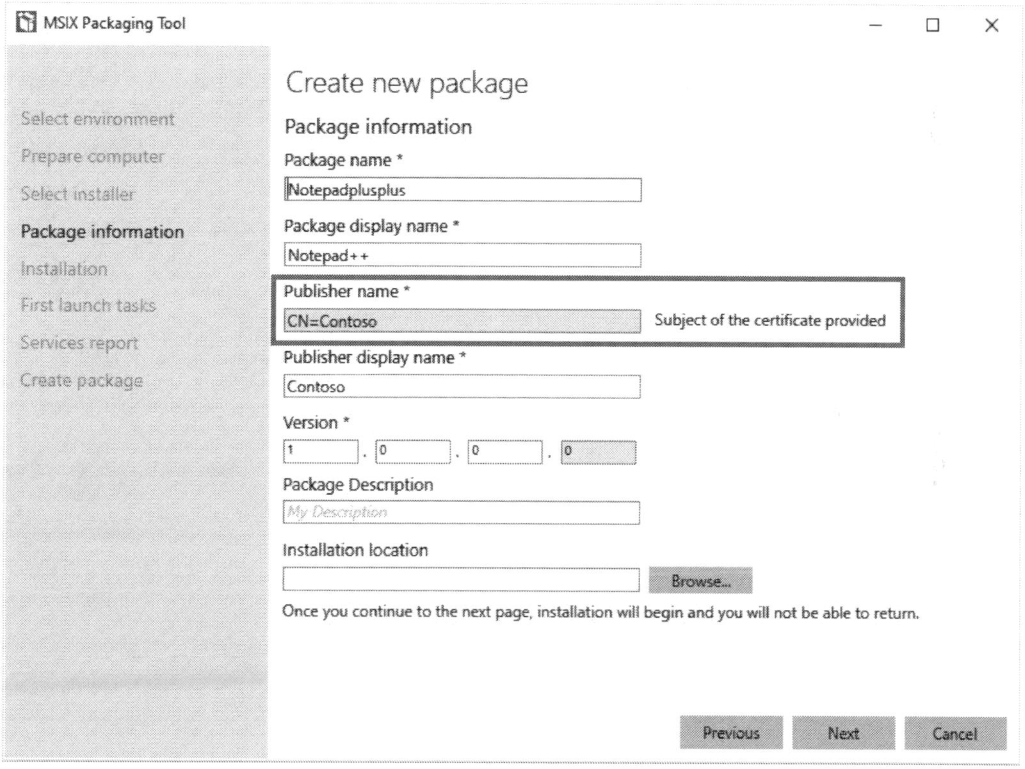

Figure 8.73 – Publisher name

Now, run through the installation process of your application:

Figure 8.74 – Installer Language

Make sure to disable **Auto-update** as the MSIX will be read-only.

Start the application to make sure that everything has been installed correctly.

If the application is installed correctly, you will see the following screen. Make sure to reboot your machine if required before moving on to the next step:

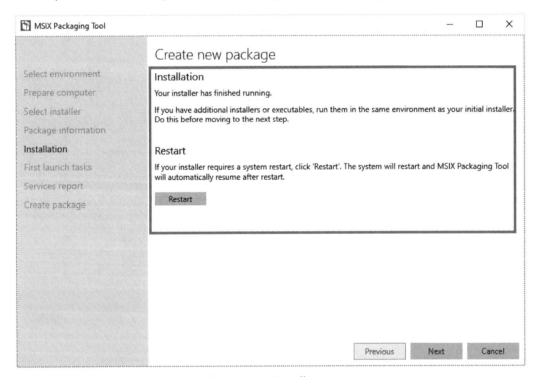

Figure 8.75 – Installation

We are almost ready. Click on **Next**.

Important Note

When you want to package extra plugins or other additional applications in the same MSIX package, please click on **No, I'm not done**.

I'm done, so I click on **Yes, move on**:

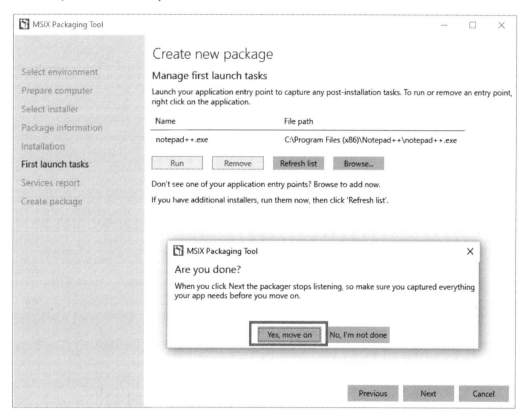

Figure 8.76 – Yes, move on

Then, click on **Next**:

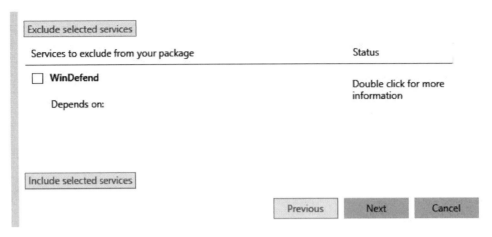

Figure 8.77 – Depends on

Save the `.msix` package file somewhere on your computer or network. Then, click on
Create:

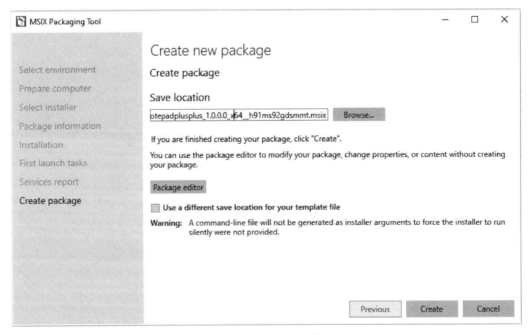

Figure 8.78 – Create package

The package is ready for the next step. When you want to edit things in the package, please click on **Package editor**:

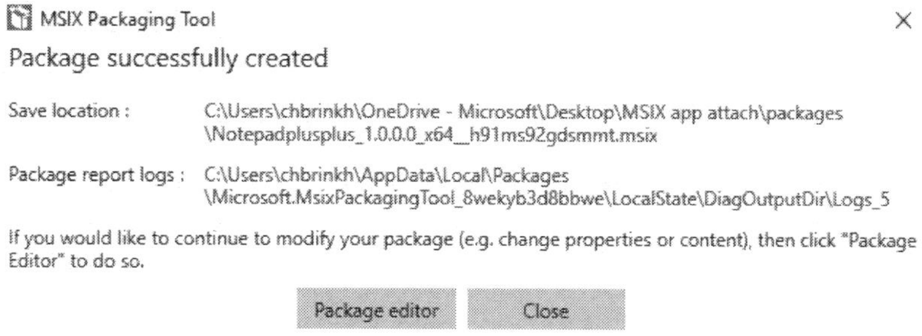

Figure 8.79 – Package successfully created

Pushing the MSIX package application to your endpoints

As explained at the start, to deploy MSIX applications, you must use the **Line-of-business app** as **App type** setting:

> **Important Note**
> The deployment of MSIX happens via the Intune SideCar agent.

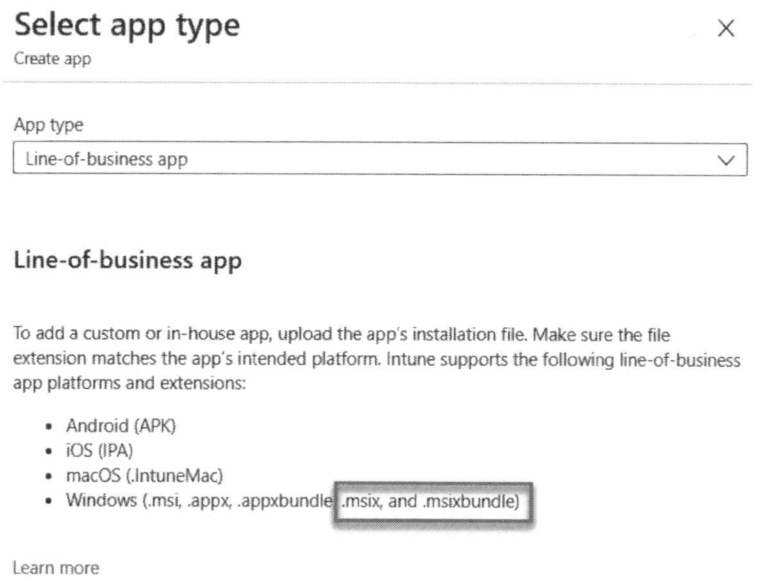

Figure 8.80 – Line-of-business MSIX

It will prompt you for the .msix package file that will be uploaded to Microsoft Endpoint Manager and distributed to your Windows 10 Enterprise endpoints:

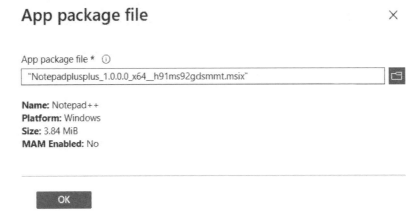

Figure 8.81 – MSIX App package

The application settings are pretty much the same as for other application formats – very straightforward:

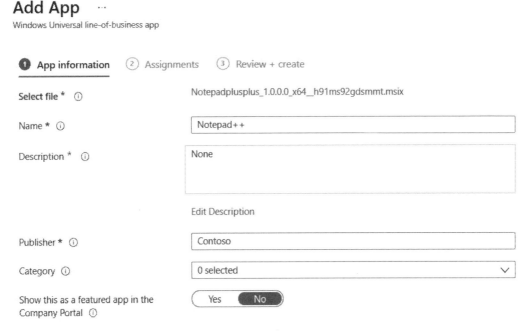

Figure 8.82 – App information MSIX

Once done, you should assign the MSIX application to the correct AAD groups and the application will be injected inside Windows 10 Enterprise without installing it:

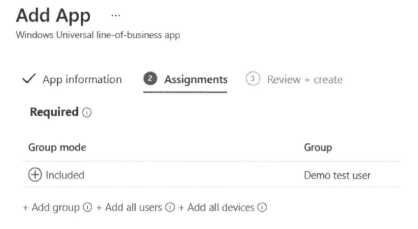

Figure 8.83 – App Assignments MSIX

This concludes the section regarding application virtualization with MSIX and delivery to your endpoints with Microsoft Endpoint Manager. There is no need to switch to the Azure portal – everything is consolidated from one unified management experience.

Summary

In this chapter, you've learned about all the different options to configure and distribute applications as regards both your physical and cloud endpoints. As this is a very important factor of the modern desktop, you are one step closer to becoming a modern workplace rockstar.

In the next chapter, we will deep dive into the other important element of the modern desktop, which is policy management!

Questions

1. What is the preferred and most comprehensive application deployment type for Windows applications (Win32)?

    A. Line-of-business app

    B. Windows app (Win32)

    C. Web link

    D. Microsoft Store app

2. What is the Edge release channel called for production usage workloads?

    A. Canary

    B. Stable

    C. Dev

    D. Beta

Answers

3. (B)

4. (B)

Further reading

If you want to learn more about Microsoft Endpoint Manager – Intune application deployment options, please use one of the following free online resources:

- Windows 10 app deployment by using Microsoft Intune | Microsoft Docs: `https://docs.microsoft.com/en-us/mem/intune/apps/apps-windows-10-app-deploy`

- Assign apps to groups with Microsoft Intune | Microsoft Docs: `https://docs.microsoft.com/en-us/mem/intune/apps/apps-deploy`

9

Understanding Policy Management

In this chapter, you will learn about how policy management from Microsoft Intune is different from **Group Policy Object** (**GPO**) and the different policy options to customize and secure your Windows 10/11 Enterprise desktops in your environment. This chapter will be very broad in terms of content, but it will give you the basic information to understand how policy management works between Windows and Microsoft Intune.

We have divided policy management into three chapters in this book; following this first one, *Chapter 10, Advanced Policy Management*, deals with advanced policy management with different scenarios, and *Chapter 11, Office Policy Management*, is about office policy management from the office cloud policy service.

In this chapter, we'll cover the following topics:

- Policy management
- What is a **Content Security Policy (CSP)** policy?
- **Windows Push Notification Services (WNS)**
- Getting started with policy design
- Policy management within Microsoft Endpoint Manager
- Migrating existing policies from **Azure Directory (AD)** – Group Policy management (preview)

Policy management

Using Microsoft Endpoint Manager – Intune to manage your Windows 10/11 Enterprise desktops is all about standardizing and simplifying the management layer of your environment. As explained in the previous chapter, everything is centered around layering your configuration sets (and applications) separately for the guest OS to remove the need to create custom images that include these things from the get-go.

Policy management within Microsoft Endpoint Manager – Intune makes it possible to configure the following options from within the **Devices** menu:

- **Compliance policies**
- **Conditional access**
- **Configuration profiles**
- **Settings catalog**
- **Scripts**
- **Group policy analytics (preview)**
- **Enrollment restrictions**
- **Policy sets**

Group policy management has been around for over 20 years and has been a way to configure the behavior of a group of users or computers in a domain. This is still possible with an on-premises domain today, but if you want to start modernizing your policy and settings management, you should start looking at Microsoft Intune and the feature set it provides for policy management. There are some disadvantages associated with using GPO, one of these being that it requires a line of sight to a domain controller. Another is that GPO is fire-and-forget, but what do we mean by this? A GPO is assigned to a specific group of users and devices, and they are applied when a device is connecting to a domain controller on a regular basis. There is no reporting back to the domain controller if the device received and applied the policy correctly, if no domain controller can be contacted, or if no new or changed policies are applied.

Sometimes, due to misconfiguration, a Windows device can contact a domain controller far away on the internal network with very slow connectivity, which can result in very long boot and sign-in times. Many of these issues can be avoided with a pure cloud-joined and managed device.

With COVID-19 hitting the world at the beginning of 2020, many companies were forced to have their employees work from home, something that many companies were not ready for. This also drove a new approach with MDM management of devices from the cloud. Microsoft Intune is a perfect match for this new way of working, as it just requires internet connectivity following the initial onboarding into Microsoft Intune.

In this chapter, we will focus on pure cloud management of Azure Active Directory Windows 10 devices, but the same will also apply to hybrid domain-joined devices that are managed from Microsoft Intune, also in a co-managed state. One important thing to note here is that GPO and MDM settings management is on the identity layer, either users or devices, whereas co-management between Microsoft Intune and **System Center Configuration Manager** (**SCCM**) is on the management plane.

First, we need to look back at traditional Windows management, where all Windows devices were on-premises in the office, in production, or with end users working at home with VPN. Modern policy management is still an option on those devices if they are hybrid-joined to Azure Active Directory. The best option moving forward with new devices is pure Azure Active Directory joined and onboarded with Windows Autopilot. What we are covering in this chapter covers both scenarios. This book is dedicated to cloud management, and certain scenarios do not apply to a hybrid-joined device, so you need to make some decisions to go to Azure AD-joined devices to get the best end user experience. Start small, start with a **Proof of Concept** (**POC**), and showcase the benefits of modern policy management. A best practice approach is to block on-premises devices in your POC from getting GPOs from the local Active Directory; otherwise, you can end up in a situation where you are not 100% sure where the settings are being applied from.

A **Configuration Service Provider** (**CSP**) is an interface for reading, setting, modifying, or deleting configuration settings on the device. These settings map to registry keys or files. Some CSPs support WAP format, some support SyncML, and some support both. SyncML is only used over the air for **Open Mobile Alliance Device Management** (**OMA DM**). On the other hand, WAP can be used over the air for OMA client provisioning, or it can be included in the phone image as a `.provxml` file that is installed during boot.

What is a CSP policy?

Some policies can only be configured at the device level, whereas other policies can be configured at the user level. This means that device-level policies will have an effect independent of the user logging into the device, whereas user-level policies will have an effect depending on the user logging into the device.

User scope is where the policy only applies to the user who logs into the device, and the policy can vary depending on who is logging on to the device. The following is an example of what the CSP tree looks like when configuring a user policy:

- `./User/Vendor/MSFT/Policy/Config/AreaName/PolicyName` to configure the policy
- `./User/Vendor/MSFT/Policy/Result/AreaName/PolicyName` to get the result

Device scope is where the policy only applies to the device itself, regardless of the user who logs into the device. The following is an example of what the CSP tree looks like when configuring a device policy:

- `./Device/Vendor/MSFT/Policy/Config/AreaName/PolicyName` to configure the policy
- `./Device/Vendor/MSFT/Policy/Result/AreaName/PolicyName` to get the result

The biggest difference between a GPO and a CSP policy is that a CSP policy has a result channel as well, so every setting that is being configured in the device will report back to the MDM system – in this case, Microsoft Intune.

If we take a closer look at the policy structure, it looks like the Windows registry is arranged in a tree structure:

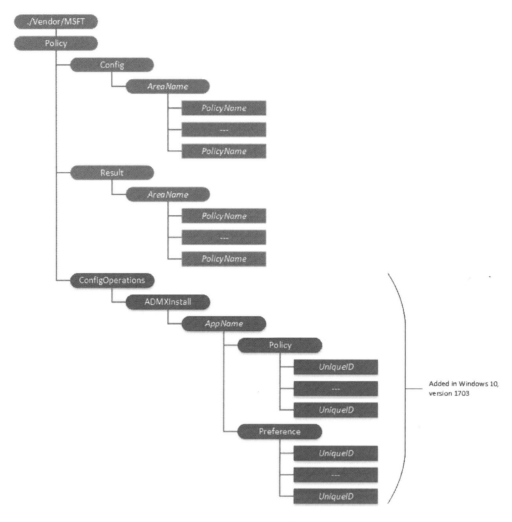

Figure 9.1 – CSP policy tree

By using ADMXInstall, you can add ADMX-backed policies for those Win32 or Desktop Bridge apps that have been added between OS releases. ADMX-backed policies are ingested in your device by using the CSP policy URI: `./Vendor/MSFT/Policy/ConfigOperations/ADMXInstall`.

The OMA-URI string needs to go into the CSP policy URI:

- `./Vendor/MSFT/Policy/ConfigOperations/ADMXInstall/Applicationname/Policy/ADMXFileName`.

- `./Vendor/MSFT/Policy/Config/` remains the same for all machine policies that you are deploying to the device.

`Applicationname` and `ADMXFileName` are user-defined. In this case, `Applicationname` is `App1`, and you can use the same name as `ADMXFileName`. Just remember that `ADMXFileName` needs to be unique, which means you cannot deploy two ADMX files with the same name on a device.

Here is the content of the ADMX file in my case – this could also have been Google Chrome, Microsoft Office, Internet Explorer, or others:

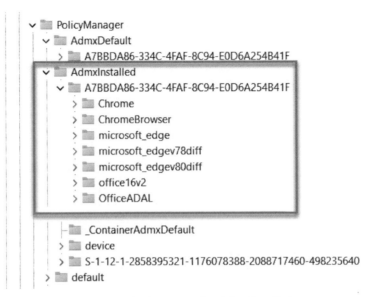

Figure 9.2 – Registry entry for AdmxInstalled

Then, if you take a closer look at the registry, the first place where they are written is `HKLM\SOFTWARE\MICROSOFT\PolicyManager\AdmxInstalled`.

The policy is always declared under a GUID and with the name you gave the policy in Microsoft Intune when you created the policy.

Then, you will be able to see the naming of the policy category that you are using when creating a policy setting:

`HKLM\Software\Microsoft\PolicyManager\AdmxDefault`

If the policy is a device policy, you will be able to see the direct results that apply to the devices in the following location: `HKEY_LOCAL_MACHINE\SOFTWARE\Microsoft\PolicyManager\current\device`.

In the end, all a policy does on a Windows device is set some registry keys, and it is the same with MDM policies. All the policy settings go here: `HKEY_LOCAL_MACHINE\SOFTWARE\Policies\`.

MDM policies are applied when a device syncs, either from Microsoft Intune or as part of the 8-hour schedule when a Windows device is running with MDM sync on.

For an IT admin to sync a device from Microsoft Intune, start the Microsoft Endpoint Manager admin center and follow these steps:

1. Click **Home | Devices | Windows | Windows devices**.

2. Search for the device you want to sync, and then you can select a single device and click **Sync**. Intune will then try and reach out to the device through the **Windows Push Notification Services** (**WNS**):

Figure 9.3 – Device sync

3. In the same view, where you just selected a single device, you can also leverage **Bulk Device Actions**:

Figure 9.4 – Bulk Device Actions

4. Select **Windows** for **OS** and **Sync** for **Device action**:

Bulk device action   ...

① **Basics**   ② Devices   ③ Review + create

OS * | Windows   ⌄ |

Device action * | Sync   ⌄ |

ⓘ Intune will attempt to check with this device. If successful, it will sync current actions or policies to the device.

Figure 9.5 – Bulk device action – Windows

5. Then, you can select up to 100 devices that Microsoft Intune will reach out to and perform the sync:

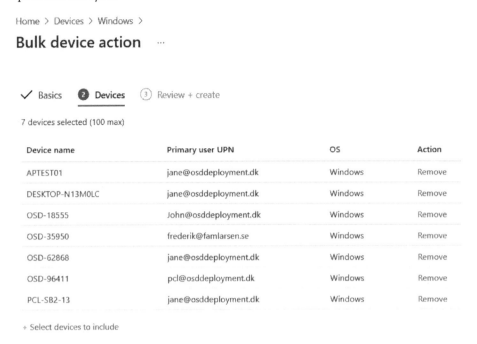

Home > Devices > Windows >

Bulk device action   ...

✓ Basics   ② Devices   ③ Review + create

7 devices selected (100 max)

Device name	Primary user UPN	OS	Action
APTEST01	jane@osddeployment.dk	Windows	Remove
DESKTOP-N13M0LC	jane@osddeployment.dk	Windows	Remove
OSD-18555	John@osddeployment.dk	Windows	Remove
OSD-35950	frederik@famlarsen.se	Windows	Remove
OSD-62868	jane@osddeployment.dk	Windows	Remove
OSD-96411	pcl@osddeployment.dk	Windows	Remove
PCL-SB2-13	jane@osddeployment.dk	Windows	Remove

+ Select devices to include

Figure 9.6 – Bulk device action

When leveraging bulk device actions, Microsoft Intune uses WNS. In the next section, you will learn about how WNS works.

Windows Push Notification Services (WNS)

WNS enables Microsoft Intune to send toast, tile, badge, and raw updates from Microsoft Intune to MDM-enrolled devices. This provides a mechanism to deliver new updates to your users in a power-efficient and dependable way:

1. Microsoft Intune makes an **HTTP POST** to the channel URI. This request is made over SSL and contains the necessary headers and the notification payload.

2. WNS responds to indicate that the notification has been received and will be delivered at the next available opportunity.

    WNS does not provide end-to-end confirmation that your notification has been received by the device or application. Microsoft Intune provides this option by showing the status in the **Device actions** status view on the **Overview** blade for a specific device:

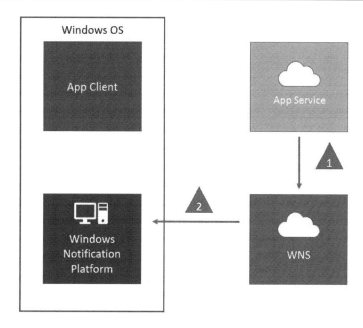

Figure 9.7 – WNS workflow

There is also an option for an end user to do this from the client side. On the client side, you can do a sync from **Company portal** or the settings app.

In the start menu, you can search for **Company Portal**, which will give you the option to sync this device:

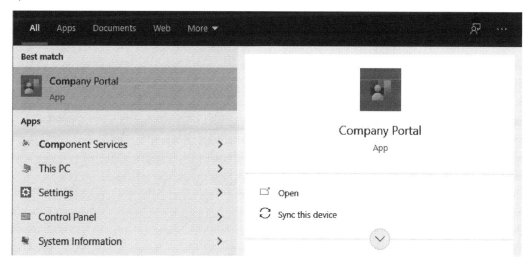

Figure 9.8 – Company Portal

If **Company Portal** is pinned to the start menu, you can right-click and sync this device:

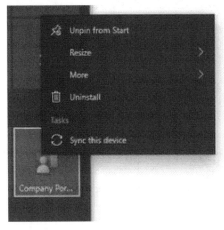

Figure 9.9 – Sync this device

In **Company Portal**, go to settings, and then click **Sync**:

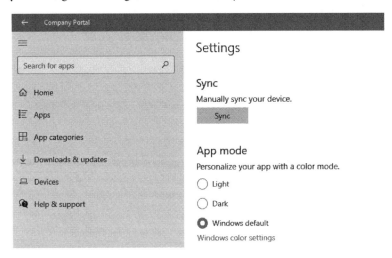

Figure 9.10 – Manually sync your device

In the Windows settings app, you can go to **Accounts | Access work or school**.

Select the identity from Azure Active Directory, and then click **Info**.

You are then able to see the policy areas managed by your company.

On Windows 11, you also have the same option as on Windows 10, but you can perform an export of your management log files directly from the **Access work or school** page in the settings app:

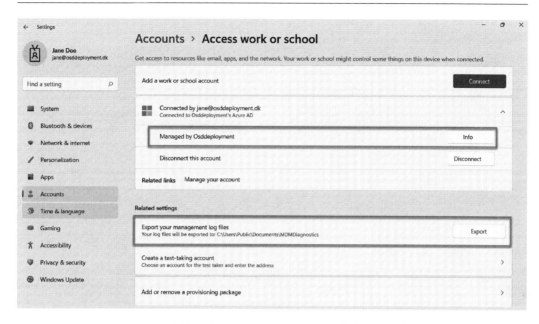

Figure 9.11 – Managed by your company (Windows 11)

Here's how this information looks on Windows 10:

⌂ Managed by Osddeployment

Connecting to work or school allows your organization to control some
things on this device, such as settings and applications.

Areas managed by Osddeployment

Osddeployment manages the following areas and settings. Settings
marked as Dynamic might change depending on device location, time,
and network configuration.

More information about Dynamic Management

Policies
•Experience
•InternetExplorer
•Update
•Authentication
•microsoft_edge~Policy~microsoft_edge~NativeMessaging
•microsoft_edge~Policy~microsoft_edge~Startup
•msteamsADMX~Policy~L_Teams
•microsoft_edgev80diff~Policy~microsoft_edge
Show more

Applications
•Company Portal: Succeeded
•VLC for Windows Store: Succeeded
•Microsoft.OneNoteWebClipper_8wekyb3d8bbwe
•Office 365 Admin: Succeeded
•{f9ff6a79-3bd1-464b-a224-165b746f4451}
•{2b802c36-cfc3-4d90-8d0b-75275dd684a0}
•{{e4dc7b28-2245-404f-a9e9-cf96254033ae}}: EnforcementCompleted
•{e4dc7b28-2245-404f-a9e9-cf96254033ae}: EnforcementCompleted

Figure 9.12 – Managed by your company (Windows 10)

It looks slightly different on Windows 11, but it displays the same information:

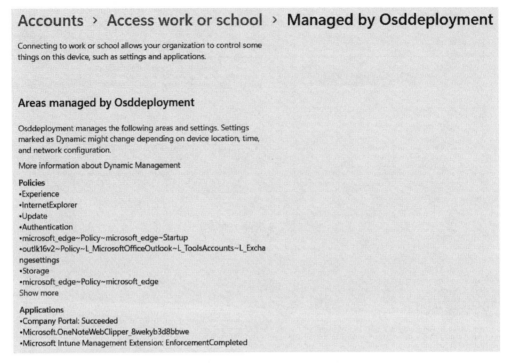

Figure 9.13 – Managed by your company (Windows 11)

If you scroll to the bottom of this settings page, you will see **Device sync status**, where you can see **Last Attempted Sync** and the **Sync** button:

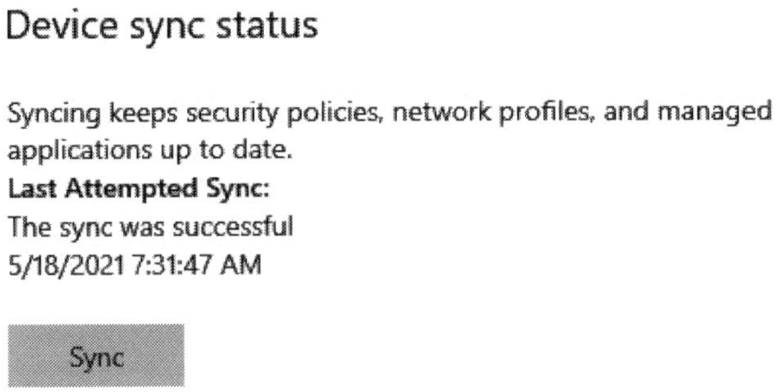

Device sync status

Syncing keeps security policies, network profiles, and managed applications up to date.

Last Attempted Sync:
The sync was successful
5/18/2021 7:31:47 AM

Sync

Figure 9.14 – Device sync status (Windows 10)

When a user is doing an MDM sync, all new policies will be applied to the device and all existing policies will be verified that they have been applied.

Getting started with policy design

When designing your strategy on policy management with Microsoft Intune, it is important to take the right approach. There are several policy types in Microsoft Intune. In the following list, you can see the different policy types and the order in which you should start creating policies:

1. Configure the security baseline.
2. Configure policy from the **Endpoint Security** blade.
3. Configure policy from the **Settings** catalog.
4. Configure the administrative template.
5. Configure the device configuration.
6. Leverage a custom policy as the last resort.

Just remember that there are no rights and wrongs, but if you're undertaking a migration from AD GPO to MDM settings management, it might be a good time to start afresh and see what you need to configure instead of taking your history of GPO setting in your on-premises environment with you. Sometimes, organizations do not even know why they implemented a specific policy setting back when they did. Perhaps the person responsible for implementing this policy setting is no longer even with the company and did not leave any documentation on why this setting was configured the way it was in the first place.

As there is no conflict handling incorporated in the MDM stack, you may inadvertently create a conflict between two settings coming from two different policies to the same user or device.

This can be from the same policy type or different policy types, so it is important to notice and monitor any conflicting policies.

In the Microsoft Endpoint Manager admin center, under each device, go to **Monitor |
Device configuration**:

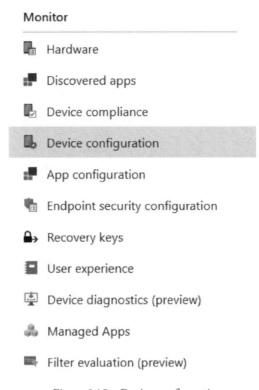

Figure 9.15 – Device configuration

You can see the policy that has conflicts and the work required to remediate the conflict:

Windows 10 - General Policy new   jane@osddeployment.dk   Conflict

Figure 9.16 – Policy conflict

When drilling down into the policy, you can see which settings are in conflict. In this
case, I know that it is a conflict between a policy in the **Endpoint Security** blade and the
Antivirus – Windows Defender Antivirus policy type:

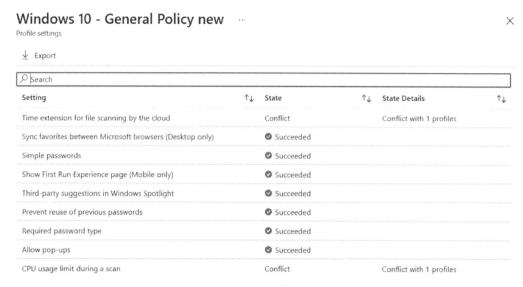

Figure 9.17 – Profile settings

Going to that policy, you can see in the **Per-setting status** blade that the top line, **CPU usage limit per scan**, has conflicts:

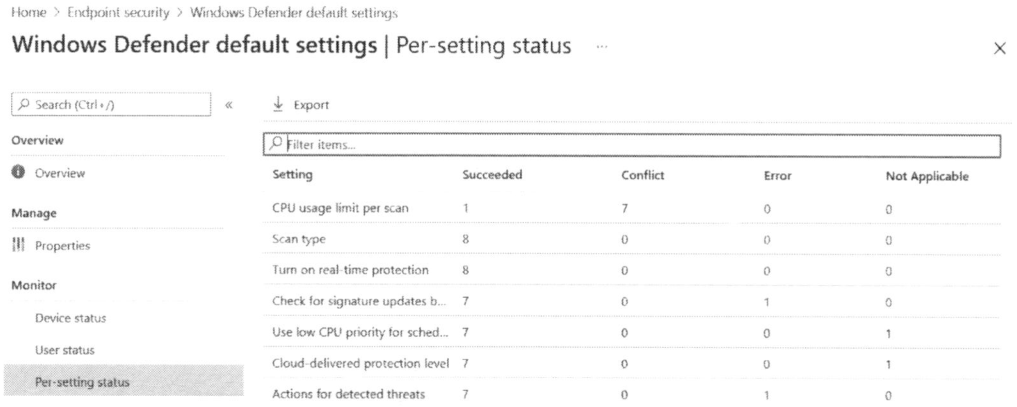

Figure 9.18 – Per-setting status

Let's now have a look at how to implement different policy types.

Policy management within Microsoft Endpoint Manager

Policy sets allow you to create a bundle of references to already existing management entities that need to be identified, targeted, and monitored as a single conceptual unit. A policy set is an assignable collection of apps, policies, and other management objects you've created. Creating a policy set enables you to select many different objects at once and assign them from a single place. As your organization changes, you can revisit a policy set to add or remove its objects and assignments. You can use a policy set to associate and assign existing objects, such as apps, policies, and VPNs, in a single package.

You can use policy sets to do the following:

- Group objects that need to be assigned together.
- Assign your organization's minimum configuration requirements on all managed devices.
- Assign commonly used or relevant apps to all users.

You can include the following management objects in a policy set:

- App configuration policies
- App protection policies
- Device configuration profiles
- Device compliance policies
- Device type restrictions
- Windows Autopilot deployment profiles
- Enrollment status page

Migrating existing policies from AD – Group Policy management (preview)

It's possible to migrate your existing Active Directory-based group policies into Microsoft Endpoint Manager – Intune. This can be done with the Group Policy analytics feature.

Many businesses that are looking at Microsoft Endpoint management need a good path to the new modern workplace. The translation of existing policy settings to Endpoint Manager could be tricky. This service will make life much easier for IT admins. Let me explain in more detail what it does and how you can use it yourself; it can be found on the **Devices** blade:

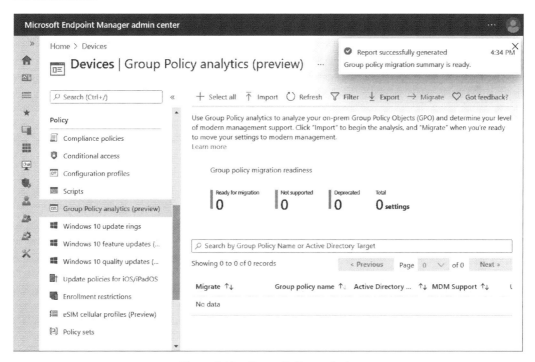

Figure 9.19 – Group Policy analytics

First, make sure to perform an export of your existing policy settings from within your Group Policy Management console, on-premises.

Export the policies by right-clicking, followed by **Save Report**.

Save the files somewhere centralized, as we need to upload them to Endpoint Manager:

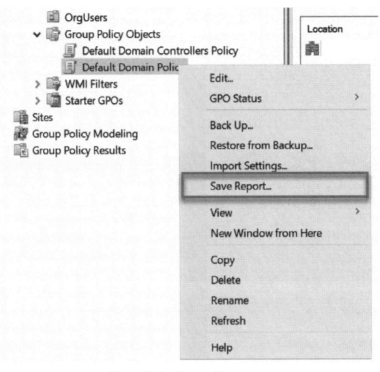

Figure 9.20 – Save policy report

Click on **Import**:

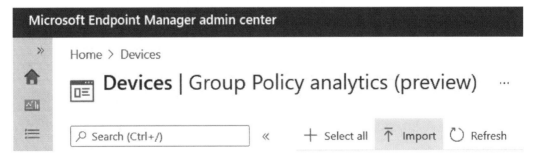

Figure 9.21 – Import – Group Policy

Search for the policy report file you exported:

Figure 9.22 – Import GPO files

> **Important Note**
> When you have multiple policies, you can upload them all here, too, for the
> purpose of further analysis.

After you run the policy analysis, you will see the **MDM Support** rate (which also applies
to Windows), showing how many of your settings/policies are also available in Endpoint
Manager to migrate from GPO to Intune settings 1:1:

Figure 9.23 – MDM Support

You will get the information back to proceed. The GPOs you imported are now all listed with the following information:

- **Group policy name**: The name is automatically generated using the information in the GPO.

- **Active Directory Target**: The target is automatically generated using the **Organizational Unit (OU)** target information in the GPO.

- **MDM Support**: This shows the percentage of group policy settings in the GPO that has the same setting in Intune.

- **Targeted in AD**: **Yes** means the GPO is linked to an OU in on-premises group policy. **No** means the GPO isn't linked to an on-premises OU.

- **Last imported**: This shows the date of the last import.

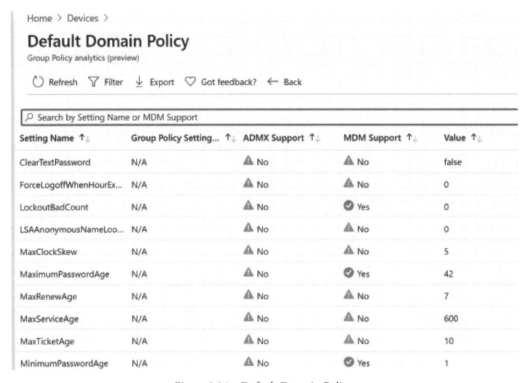

Figure 9.24 – Default Domain Policy

This concludes the section on Group Policy analytics that can help you with your policy migration from on-premises GPO to Microsoft Intune MDM policies.

Summary

In this chapter, you've learned about the basic policies in Microsoft Intune and how they apply to your Windows endpoints. This is knowledge that you can use to better understand what happens on a Windows device when you first start to deploy policies to your endpoint from Microsoft Intune.

In the next chapter, we will go more in-depth on how to configure different policy types from within Microsoft Intune.

Questions

1. Do CSP and ADMX policies write to the local registry in the same way?

   a) No

   b) Yes

2. What is the maximum number of devices for bulk action in MEM?

   a) 10

   b) 50

   c) 100

   d) 1000

3. What is a policy set?

   a) A group of guided scenario management objects

   b) A set of policies

   c) A template to configure a device

   d) A group of management objects

Answers

1. (b)

2. (c)

3. (d)

Further reading

If you want to learn more after reading this section, please use one of the following free online resources:

- Manage endpoint security in Microsoft Intune | Microsoft Docs: `https://docs.microsoft.com/en-us/mem/intune/protect/endpoint-security`

- Device compliance policies in Microsoft Intune – Azure | Microsoft Docs: `https://docs.microsoft.com/en-us/mem/intune/protect/device-compliance-get-started`

- Use templates for Windows 10 devices in Microsoft Intune – Azure | Microsoft Docs: `https://docs.microsoft.com/en-us/mem/intune/configuration/administrative-templates-windows`

- Restrict device features using policy in Microsoft Intune – Azure | Microsoft Docs: `https://docs.microsoft.com/en-us/mem/intune/configuration/device-restrictions-configure`

10
Advanced Policy Management

This is the second chapter on policy management in this book. You will learn about the different policy options available to customize and secure the Windows 10 Enterprise desktops in your environment. This chapter will be very broad in terms of content and topics related to Windows OS customizations, Microsoft 365 apps (Office, OneDrive, and so on), and group policy management.

We will cover different scenarios – some partial scenarios and some end-to-end scenarios. The most important part of this chapter will give you an insight into all the different policy options that exist in Microsoft Intune, and when and how you can leverage the different policy types in the best way to accomplish the task you need for your enterprise.

In this chapter, we'll be covering the following topics:

- Configuring a policy from the Endpoint Manager Security blade
- Configuring your Endpoint security profile
- Windows 10 unhealthy endpoints
- Configuring a policy from the Settings catalog
- Configuring administrative templates
- OneDrive Known Folder Move configuration

- OneDrive – block syncing specific file extensions
- Configure device configuration (template)
- Leveraging a custom policy as the last resort
- Pushing PowerShell scripts – scripted actions to endpoints
- Compliance policies
- Organizational compliance report

Policy management

Using Microsoft Intune, a part of Microsoft Endpoint Manager, to manage your Windows 10 or 11 Enterprise desktops is all about standardizing and simplifying the management layer of your environment. In *Chapter 9, Understanding Policy Management*, we covered the basics of how MDM policies work on the client side. We also learned how to get started with MDM policy management either from scratch or with Group Policy analytics.

In this chapter, we will look at different ways to configure settings within Microsoft Intune. We will start with security baselines as those are best practices for securing your desktops.

Configuring a policy from the Endpoint Manager Security blade

You should start with a security baseline if your organization is ready for it. Let's say that your organization is already leveraging a Microsoft security baseline such as **Center for Internet Security** (**CIS**) Benchmarks. With GPOs today, you already know the impact that a security baseline can have on your Windows production environment. There are multiple different baselines in Microsoft Intune:

- **Windows 10 Security Baseline**: Use the Windows 10 security baseline to help you secure and protect your users and devices. This baseline consists of recommendations for settings that impact security and is created by the Windows Security team. If you are already using some kind of security baseline in your **Group Policy Object** (**GPO**) today, it is highly recommended to adopt the Intune Windows 10 security baseline as well.

- **Microsoft Defender for Endpoint Baseline**: The Microsoft Defender for Endpoint baseline represents the default recommended configuration for Defender for Endpoint and might not match baseline defaults for other security baselines. This means that if you are leveraging this baseline in conjunction with the Windows 10 Security baseline, you can create conflicts between the different policy settings.

- **Windows 365 Security Baseline (Preview)**: The Windows 365 Security baseline provides a set of policy templates built on security best practices and experience from real-world implementations. You can use security baselines to get security recommendations that can help lower risks. The Windows 365 baseline is one baseline for Cloud PC with security settings for Windows, Microsoft Edge, and Microsoft Defender for Endpoints. This also means that you should not assign other security baselines to the same group of devices as it can end up in a policy conflict.

- **Microsoft Edge Baseline**: The Microsoft Edge baseline sets the recommended configuration for the Microsoft Edge browser. The Microsoft Edge security baseline has a very small footprint and only sets security-related settings, so it is easy to test out in your organization. If you are allowing your users to use different browsers on company-owned Windows 10 devices, you should also create a security baseline on those third-party browsers; otherwise, there is a risk that your end users will always use the least secure browser.

Be aware that when a baseline changes its version, the old one will be read-only. You can continue to use those profiles but you won't be able to edit them. You should change the baseline version to take advantage of the newest recommendations every time a new version is released.

The Microsoft Edge baseline defaults represent the recommended configuration for Microsoft Edge browsers, so they might not match the baseline defaults of other security baselines.

In this example, we are going to create a Microsoft Edge baseline policy:

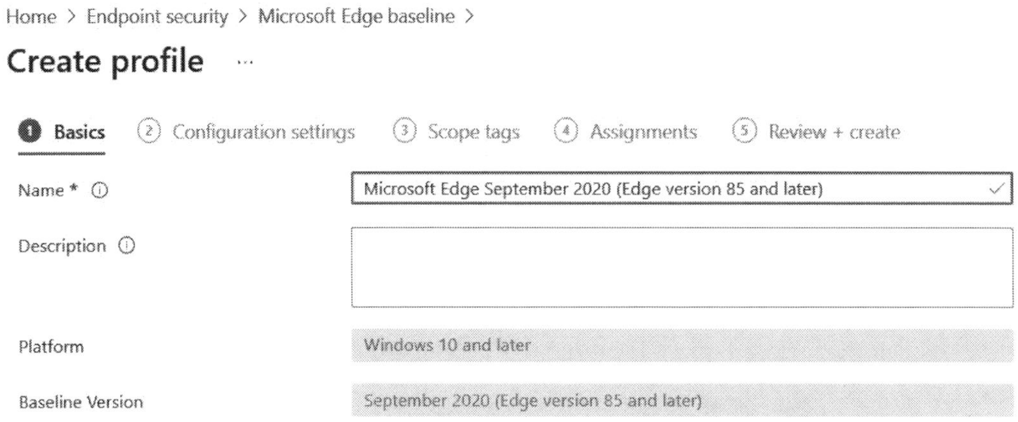

Home > Endpoint security > Microsoft Edge baseline >

Create profile   ...

| ● Basics | ② Configuration settings | ③ Scope tags | ④ Assignments | ⑤ Review + create |

Name * ⓘ

Microsoft Edge September 2020 (Edge version 85 and later)   ✓

Description ⓘ

Platform

Windows 10 and later

Baseline Version

September 2020 (Edge version 85 and later)

Figure 10.1 – Microsoft Edge baseline – Create profile screen

You can change the settings within a security baseline if your tests have concluded that the settings in the baseline will not break apps or productivity in your environment. If you are happy with the settings, you can keep all the recommended values as-is:

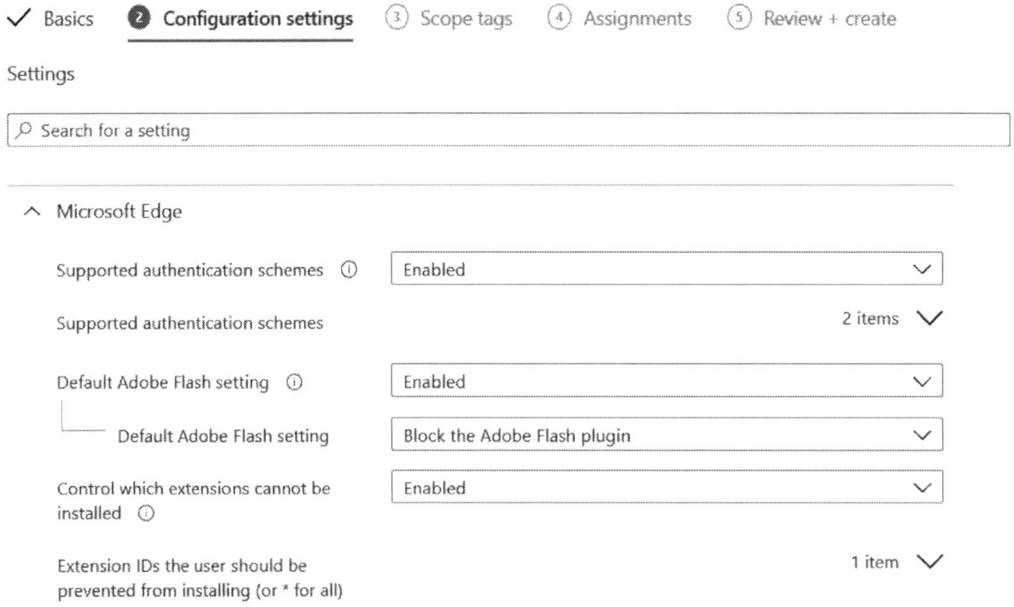

| ✓ Basics | ② Configuration settings | ③ Scope tags | ④ Assignments | ⑤ Review + create |

Settings

🔎 Search for a setting

∧ Microsoft Edge

Supported authentication schemes ⓘ   Enabled   ⌄

Supported authentication schemes   2 items ⌄

Default Adobe Flash setting ⓘ   Enabled   ⌄

└── Default Adobe Flash setting   Block the Adobe Flash plugin   ⌄

Control which extensions cannot be
installed ⓘ   Enabled   ⌄

Extension IDs the user should be
prevented from installing (or * for all)   1 item ⌄

Figure 10.2 – Microsoft Edge baseline – Configuration settings

This concludes this section on Microsoft Security baselines. Next, we will cover Endpoint security policies.

Configuring your Endpoint security profile

The **Endpoint security** node of Microsoft Intune was built to allow IT or security admins to configure device security. By using these security-focused policies, you will only see security-related policies in this blade view and not regular policies for other types of settings. Policies in the Endpoint Security blade can be applied to Windows or macOS. These policies can be Windows 10 MDM (Microsoft Intune) or Windows 10 and Windows Server (ConfigMgr). The last one is for tenant-attached devices that are not onboarded to Microsoft Intune.

Microsoft Defender policy

Antivirus policies include the same settings as endpoint protection or device restriction profiles for device configuration policies.

However, those policy types include additional categories of settings that are unrelated to antivirus policies. While the Windows Defender policy types in the **Endpoint security** blade only contain Windows Defender settings, you can see the three different policy types here:

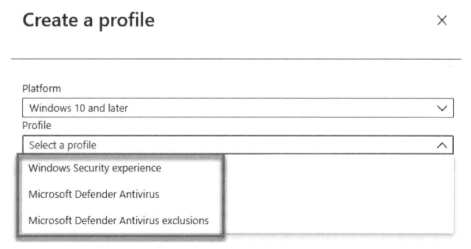

Figure 10.3 – Windows Defender policy types

Profile: **Windows Security experience**

The Windows Security app is used by several Windows security features to provide notifications about the health and security of a machine. Security app notifications include firewalls, antivirus products, and Windows Defender SmartScreen.

The Windows Security experience profile can be used to turn off areas in the Windows Security app, such as family options if you don't want to show family options on your Intune-managed devices:

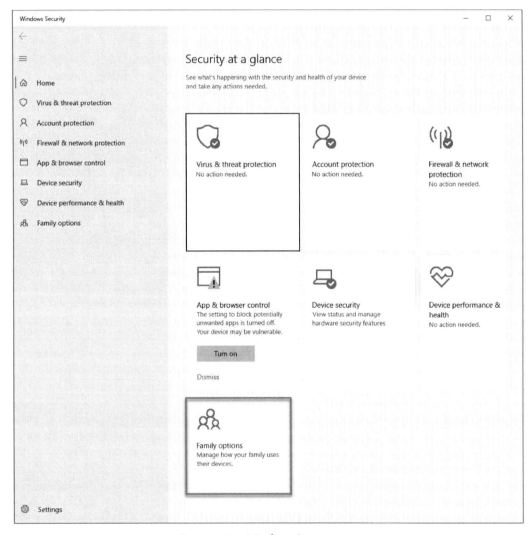

Figure 10.4 – Windows Security app

Profile: **Microsoft Defender Antivirus**

Microsoft Defender Antivirus is a next-generation antivirus solution that brings together technologies such as machine learning and cloud infrastructure to protect devices in your enterprise organization.

Profile: **Microsoft Defender Antivirus exclusions**

These **configuration service providers** (**CSPs**) for Microsoft Defender Antivirus exclusions are also managed by the Microsoft Defender Antivirus policy, which includes identical settings for exclusions. Settings from both policy types (antivirus and antivirus exclusions) are subject to policy merging. This means that you can create as many policies as you like and assign them to the same user or device without causing a conflict.

This concludes this section on Windows Defender policies. Next, we'll learn how to monitor Windows Defender in Microsoft Intune.

Antivirus reporting in Endpoint security

In the **Endpoint security** blade, you will also find antivirus reports displaying status details about your Endpoint security antivirus policies and devices:

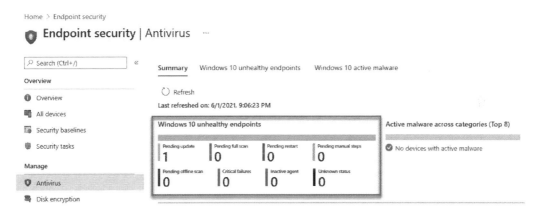

Figure 10.5 – Windows 10 unhealthy endpoints

The **Summary** tab gives you an overview of the Windows Defender status of your devices so that you can dive deeper into the reports.

Windows 10 unhealthy endpoints

The **Windows 10 unhealthy endpoints** tab gives you an overview of devices that are unhealthy. Within this report, you can leverage the device actions that are related to Microsoft Defender for unhealthy endpoints. As an example, if you have devices that have **Antivirus (AV)** signatures that are out of date, you can invoke a remote action on the affected client devices. The devices will then start the process of updating Windows Defender signatures:

Figure 10.6 – Windows 10 unhealthy endpoints – remote action

This concludes our look at the basic Windows Defender AV settings. From a security perspective, you need to look at other security postures on devices as well. First, we will look at attack surface reduction, which is also part of the Windows Defender security stack on a Windows device.

Attack surface reduction

This is another big, important area with multiple policy types that you can configure:

Figure 10.7 – Attack surface reduction

A great example is the **Application control** policy type.

The **Application control** policy can help mitigate security threats. It does this by restricting the applications that users are allowed to run and the code that runs in the system's core (kernel). Application control policies can also block unsigned scripts and Windows Installer (MSI) and restrict Windows PowerShell to run in Constrained Language mode.

With a few settings, you can easily harden your Windows operating system:

Create profile ⋯
Application control

✓ Basics   ❷ **Configuration settings**   ③ Scope tags   ④ Assignments   ⑤ Review + create

Settings

🔎 Search for a setting

∧ Microsoft Defender Application Control

App locker application control ⓘ | Enforce Components, Store Apps, and Smartlocker   ∨ |

Block users from ignoring SmartScreen warnings ⓘ   (**Yes**   Not configured)

Turn on Windows SmartScreen ⓘ   (Yes   Not configured)

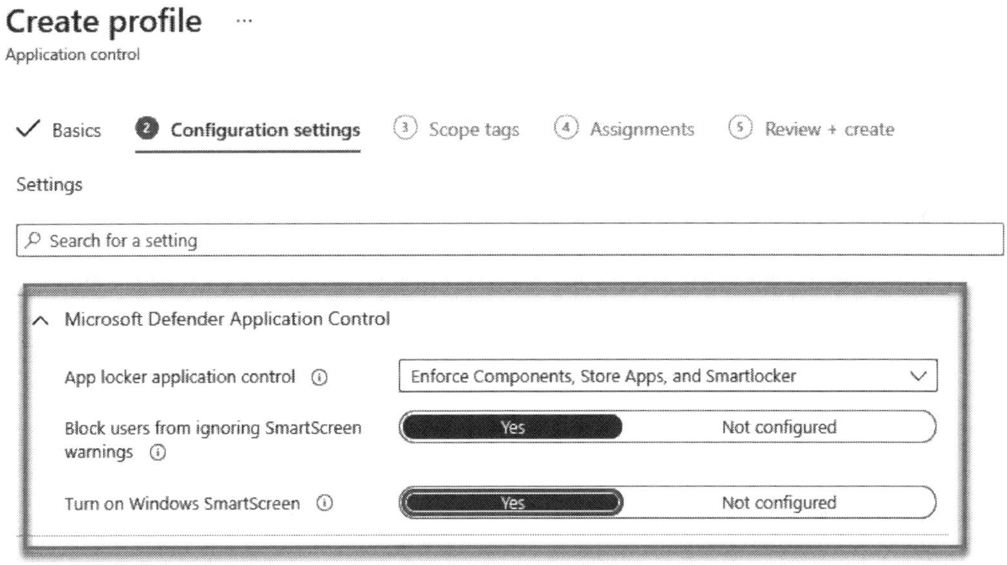

Figure 10.8 – Microsoft Defender Application control policy

Now, let's enable Windows SmartScreen (not only for Microsoft Edge, as we will show later in this chapter).

Set **App locker application control** to **Enforce Components, Store Apps, and Smartlocker** – this will enable **Windows Defender Application Control** (**WDAC**) so that only the following can be executed on the Windows operating system:

- Windows components
- Third-party hardware and software kernel drivers
- Microsoft Store-signed apps
- [Optional] Reputable apps, as defined by the **Intelligent Security Graph** (**ISG**)

WDAC policies apply to the managed computer as a whole and affect all users of the device.

Configuring a policy from the Settings catalog

The settings catalog works in conjunction with other policy types in Microsoft Intune:

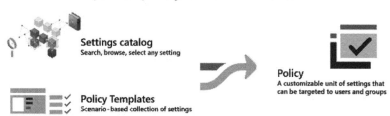

Figure 10.9 – Simplified policy creation workflow

When you create a new policy from the **Settings** catalog, no settings are configured initially, and the policy only contains the settings you specify. You have the option to remove one or more settings from a category with the settings picker. The settings picker will allow you to search or browse to select any settings available in the settings catalog for configuration in your policy, and even allows you to add filters to search for a specific OS edition such as HoloLens, IoT Enterprise, or Windows Professional:

Figure 10.10 – Settings picker – Add filter

The settings in the settings catalog are generated directly from Windows CSPs, and the settings experience in the catalog is dynamically generated based on the type of setting and its metadata, such as tooltips. The settings catalog continues to add new Windows settings and reduces the need to deploy custom policies from Microsoft Intune (OMA-URI-based). One of the new things in the settings catalog is that if a setting is not in your policy, then it will be considered not configured. Editing a policy later on and removing a setting from an existing settings catalog policy will not only remove that setting from the policy, but it will also remove the previously set enforcement from assigned devices on the next device check-in.

There are thousands of settings to choose from in the settings catalog, including settings that are not in any other policy type in Microsoft Intune and have not been available before in the console. You can also configure Administrative Templates in the settings catalog. As Windows adds or exposes more settings to MDM providers, these settings are quickly added to the Microsoft Intune settings catalog to be configured.

To create a profile with the settings catalog, you open the Microsoft Endpoint Manager admin center:

1. Go to **Home** > **Devices** > **Windows** > **Configuration profiles** and apply the following:

   - **Platform**: Select **Windows 10 and later**

   - **Profile type**: Select **Settings catalog (preview)**:

Figure 10.11 – Create a profile

2. As part of the profile creation, you need to fill out the wizard:

   - **Name**: Enter a descriptive name for the profile, such as Settings Catalog Policy.

- **Description**: Enter a description for the profile. This setting is optional, but it is highly recommended to enter a description so that you can go back at a later point and see what the intent of this policy is:

Home > Devices > Windows >

Create device configuration profile ⋯
Windows 10 and later - Settings catalog (preview)

| ① **Basics** | ② Configuration settings | ③ Assignments | ④ Scope tags | ⑤ Review + create |

Name *   Settings Catalog Policy   ✓

Description

Platform   Windows 10 and later   ⌄

Figure 10.12 – Create device configuration profile

3. In **Configuration settings**, select **Add settings**. In the settings picker, select the **User Rights** category or another category to see all the available settings:

Home > Devices > Windows >

Create device configuration profile ⋯
Windows 10 and later - Settings catalog (preview)

| ✓ Basics | ② **Configuration settings** | ③ Assignments | ④ Scope tags | ⑤ Review + create |

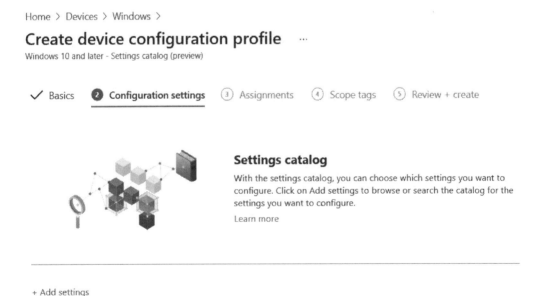

Settings catalog

With the settings catalog, you can choose which settings you want to configure. Click on Add settings to browse or search the catalog for the settings you want to configure.

Learn more

+ Add settings

Figure 10.13 – Create device configuration profile

4. The UI will automatically expand with the settings that you have just selected – in this case, the **User Rights** policy. Before the setting catalog was released, this was a policy where IT admins were forced to leverage a custom policy in Microsoft Intune, which required a lot of specialized knowledge:

> **Pro Tip**
> The tooltip always gives you the required information on what the policy does. This is a part of the metadata from the Windows **Configuration Service Providers** (**CSPs**). The tooltip also includes a **Learn more** link to the Microsoft Windows docs page for the underlying CSP.

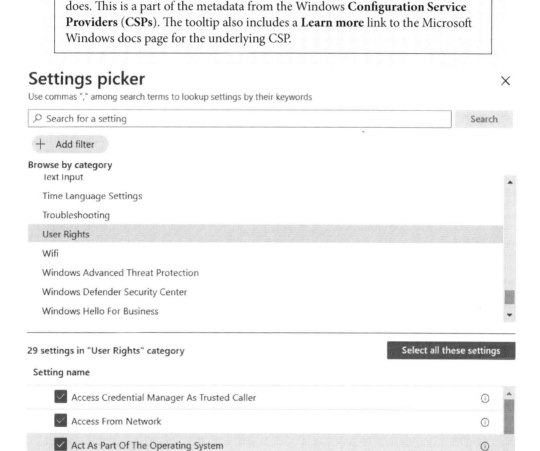

Figure 10.14 – Settings picker

> **Pro Tip**
> If you are not configuring all settings, you can remove individual settings by clicking the *not configured* icon, and the setting will be removed when saving the settings catalog. This means that it will not affect users or devices when deployed.

5. When configuring an individual setting, you can expand it with multiple values by clicking **Add**:

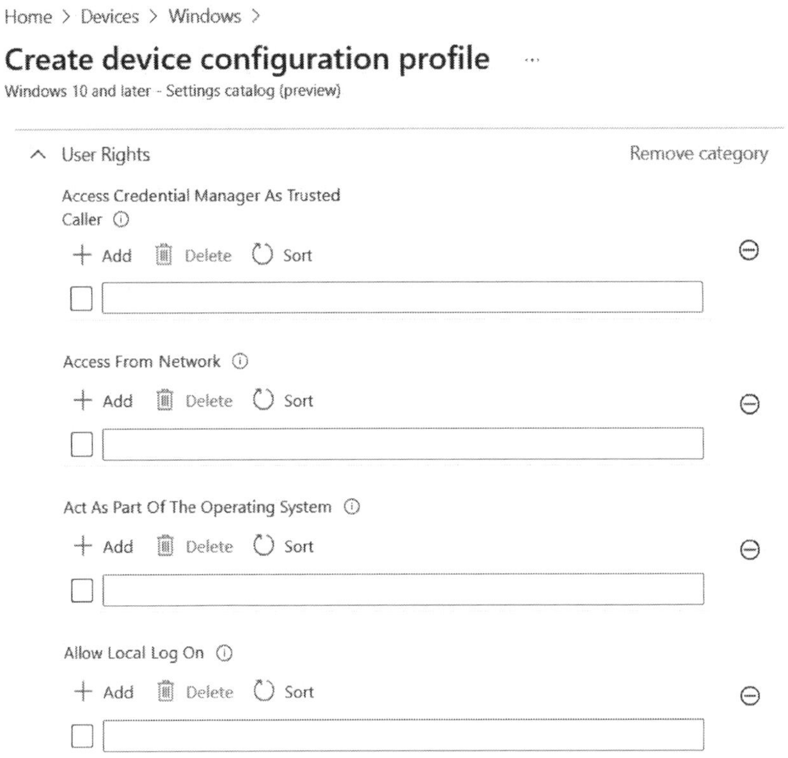

Home > Devices > Windows >

Create device configuration profile   ...

Windows 10 and later - Settings catalog (preview)

∧   User Rights   Remove category

Access Credential Manager As Trusted
Caller ⓘ

   + Add   🗑 Delete   ⟳ Sort   ⊖

   ☐ [   ]

Access From Network   ⓘ

   + Add   🗑 Delete   ⟳ Sort   ⊖

   ☐ [   ]

Act As Part Of The Operating System   ⓘ

   + Add   🗑 Delete   ⟳ Sort   ⊖

   ☐ [   ]

Allow Local Log On   ⓘ

   + Add   🗑 Delete   ⟳ Sort   ⊖

   ☐ [   ]

Figure 10.15 – Create device configuration profile

6. In this case, we are allowing users and administrators the right to local log on:

Figure 10.16 – Allow Local Log On

7. You don't need any separator in the settings catalog, as you did in the past when creating the same policy as a custom policy in Microsoft Intune.

    In this case, we will also deny users with the Azure AD Global Admin role or Device administrator from logging into the devices. So, I will check the **security identifier** (**SID**) in the local administrator group on my Azure AD joined devices:

Deny Local Log On ⓘ

+ Add   🗑 Delete   ↻ Sort

☐ | S-1-12-1-388599465-1267877230-482940842-3474507461 | ✓ |

☐ | S-1-12-1-4259618714-1306471581-2343542420-3443586765| | ✓ |

Figure 10.17 – Deny Local Log On

8. From Windows 10 version 2004, you can leverage SID for an Azure AD group:

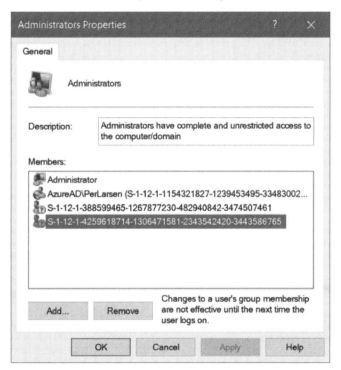

Figure 10.18 – Administrators Properties

9. The SID can be found in the local administrator group on Windows 10 devices that are joined to your organization's Azure Active Directory.

Another example in the settings catalog is administrative templates for **Microsoft Edge Update**. The new Microsoft Edge is a Win32 app, so it leverages an ADMX policy instead of a CSP OMA-URI.

By browsing by category, you can find **Microsoft Edge Update**:

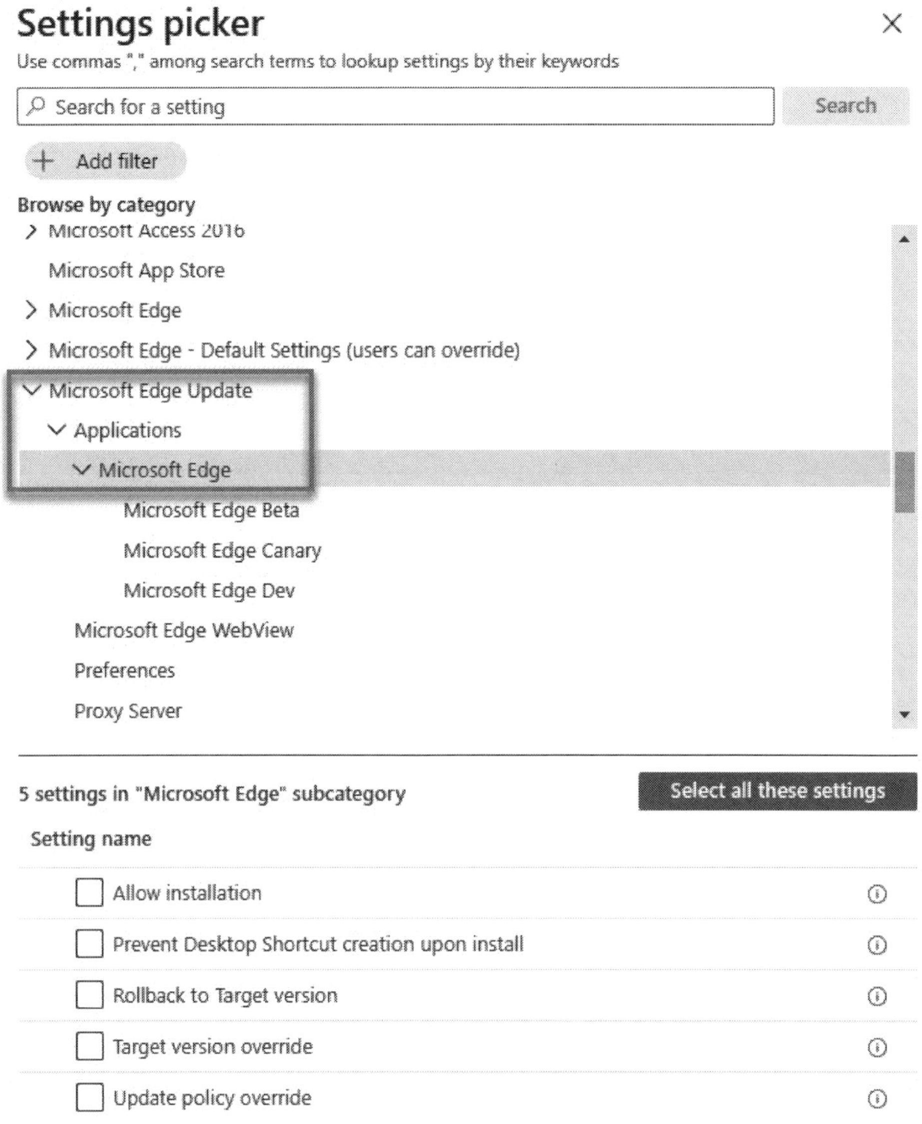

Settings picker   ×

Use commas "," among search terms to lookup settings by their keywords

🔍 Search for a setting	Search

➕ Add filter

Browse by category
> Microsoft Access 2016

Microsoft App Store

> Microsoft Edge

> Microsoft Edge - Default Settings (users can override)

∨ Microsoft Edge Update

   ∨ Applications

      ∨ Microsoft Edge

         Microsoft Edge Beta

         Microsoft Edge Canary

         Microsoft Edge Dev

   Microsoft Edge WebView

Preferences

Proxy Server

---

5 settings in "Microsoft Edge" subcategory   **Select all these settings**

Setting name

☐ Allow installation   ⓘ

☐ Prevent Desktop Shortcut creation upon install   ⓘ

☐ Rollback to Target version   ⓘ

☐ Target version override   ⓘ

☐ Update policy override   ⓘ

Figure 10.19 – Settings picker – Browse by category

10. Find the policy category you want to configure and *select all these settings* or *select one or more individual settings*. In this case, we will select **Microsoft Edge Update**:

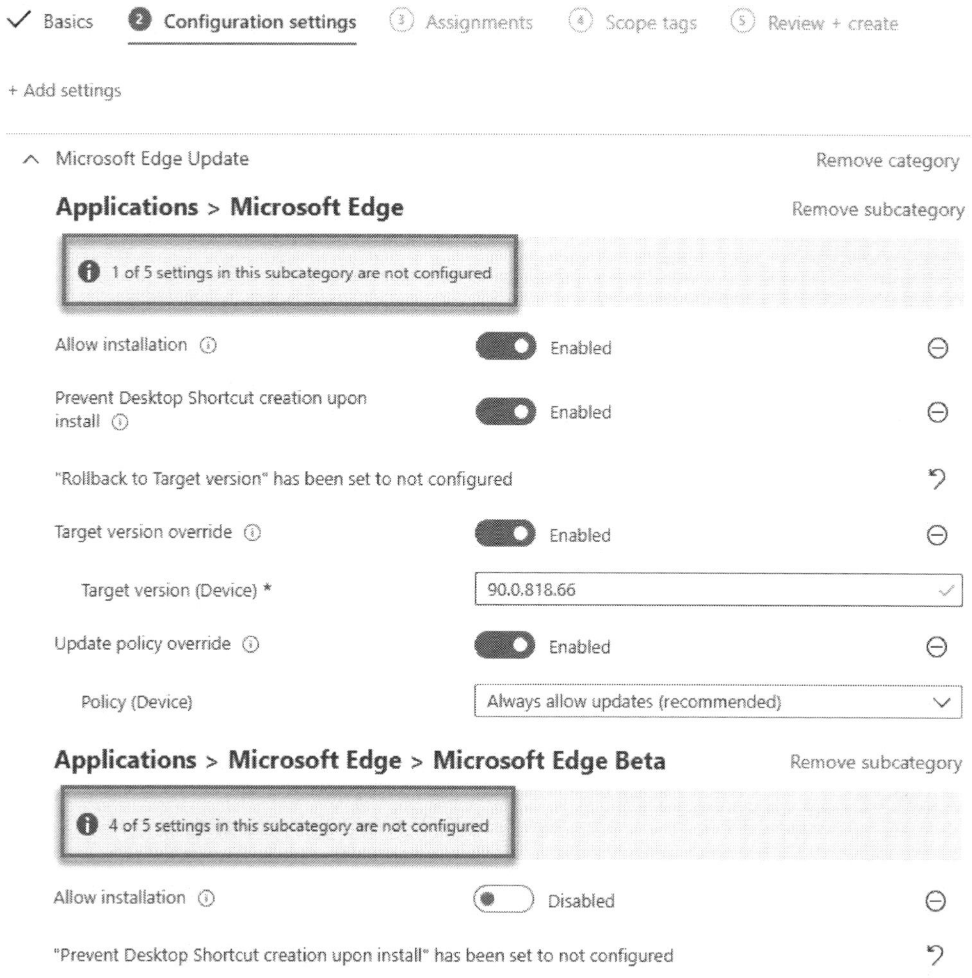

✓ Basics   ② **Configuration settings**   ③ Assignments   ④ Scope tags   ⑤ Review + create

+ Add settings

∧ Microsoft Edge Update   Remove category

Applications > Microsoft Edge   Remove subcategory

ℹ 1 of 5 settings in this subcategory are not configured

Allow installation ⓘ   Enabled ⬤   ⊖

Prevent Desktop Shortcut creation upon   Enabled ⬤   ⊖
install ⓘ

"Rollback to Target version" has been set to not configured   ↺

Target version override ⓘ   Enabled ⬤   ⊖

Target version (Device) *   90.0.818.66   ✓

Update policy override ⓘ   Enabled ⬤   ⊖

Policy (Device)   Always allow updates (recommended)   ∨

Applications > Microsoft Edge > Microsoft Edge Beta   Remove subcategory

ℹ 4 of 5 settings in this subcategory are not configured

Allow installation ⓘ   Disabled ◯   ⊖

"Prevent Desktop Shortcut creation upon install" has been set to not configured   ↺

Figure 10.20 – Settings in this subcategory are not configured

11. Configure the settings you want to set and remove the ones you do not want to configure on your devices.

In this case, we have configured all the settings in **Applications | Microsoft Edge** except for one, called **Rollback to Target version**, which we have removed. This means that the setting has been set to not configured. This is a different behavior than some of the other profile types in Microsoft Intune, where settings are either enabled or disabled.

12. In **Applications | Microsoft Edge | Microsoft Edge Beta**, we have configured one setting and removed the rest:

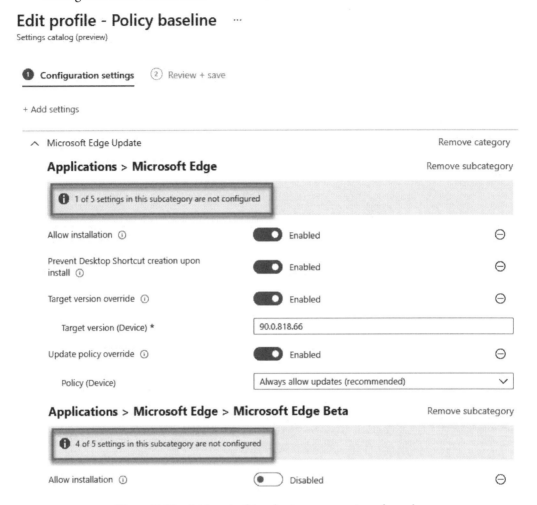

Figure 10.21 – Settings in this subcategory are not configured

13. When we, at a later point in time, edit the settings catalog policy, we will only see the settings that we configured in the first place.

Now, we can add a new subcategory and continue to build on existing policies in Microsoft Intune. In this case, we will add the **Microsoft Edge Canary** subcategory:

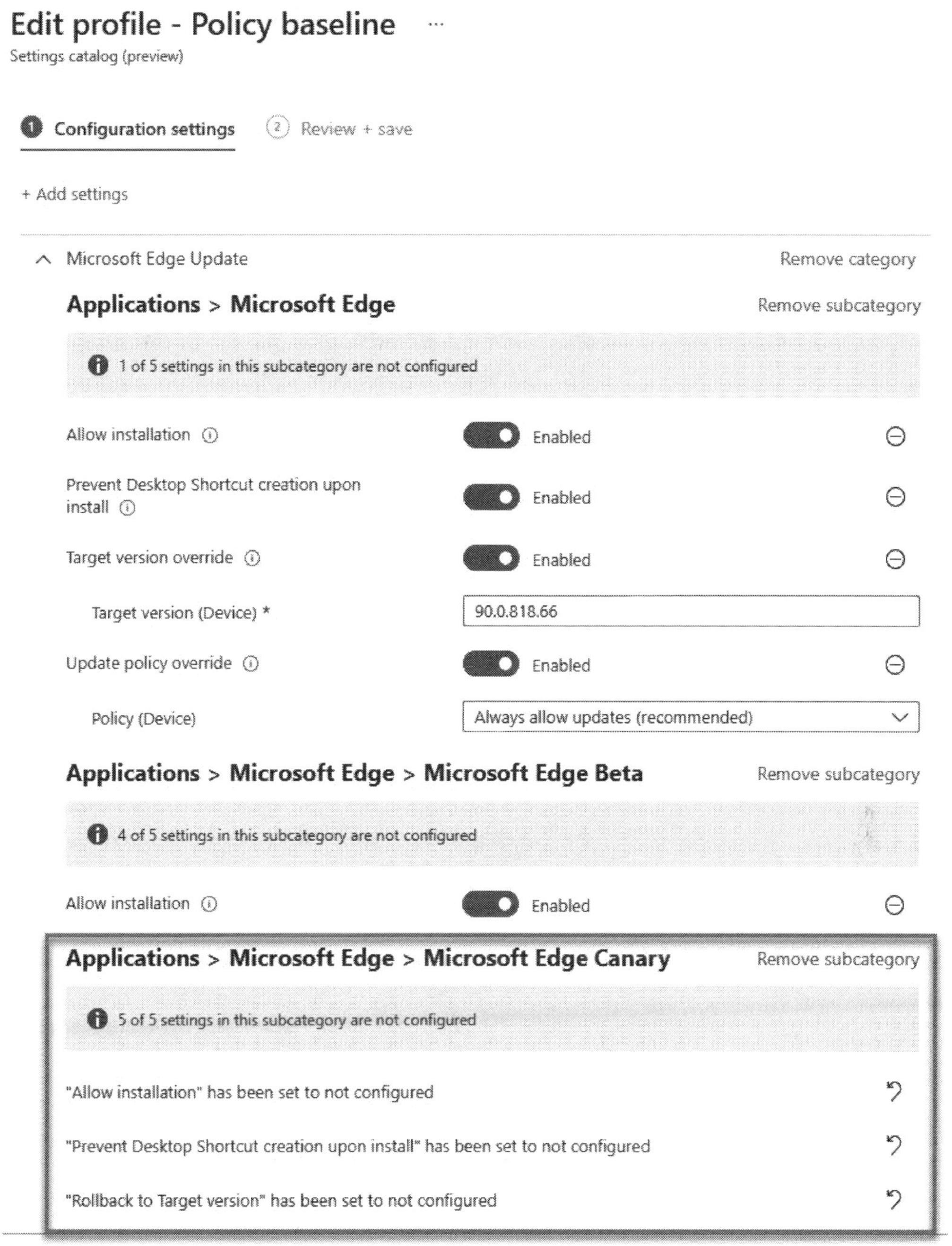

Edit profile - Policy baseline ···

Settings catalog (preview)

1 **Configuration settings**   ② Review + save

\+ Add settings

∧ Microsoft Edge Update   Remove category

Applications > Microsoft Edge   Remove subcategory

ℹ 1 of 5 settings in this subcategory are not configured

Allow installation ⓘ	**◉** Enabled	⊖
Prevent Desktop Shortcut creation upon install ⓘ	**◉** Enabled	⊖
Target version override ⓘ	**◉** Enabled	⊖
Target version (Device) *	90.0.818.66	
Update policy override ⓘ	**◉** Enabled	⊖
Policy (Device)	Always allow updates (recommended) ∨	

Applications > Microsoft Edge > Microsoft Edge Beta   Remove subcategory

ℹ 4 of 5 settings in this subcategory are not configured

Allow installation ⓘ	**◉** Enabled	⊖

Applications > Microsoft Edge > Microsoft Edge Canary   Remove subcategory

ℹ 5 of 5 settings in this subcategory are not configured

"Allow installation" has been set to not configured	↺
"Prevent Desktop Shortcut creation upon install" has been set to not configured	↺
"Rollback to Target version" has been set to not configured	↺

Figure 10.22 – Microsoft Edge Canary subcategory

This concludes this section on the settings catalog. In the next section, we will cover how to configure administrative templates from Microsoft Intune.

Configuring administrative templates

Administrative templates include thousands of settings that control features in Microsoft Edge version 77 and later, Internet Explorer, Microsoft Office, Remote Desktop, OneDrive, passwords, PINs, and more. These settings allow IT pro administrators to manage group policies using Microsoft Intune in the cloud.

The Windows settings are GPO settings that you already know about from **Active Directory (AD)**. These settings, which are built into Windows, are ADMX-backed settings that use XML. The Office and Microsoft Edge settings are ADMX-ingested and use the ADMX settings in Office administrative template files and Microsoft Edge administrative template files.

Administrative Templates are built into Intune and do not require a custom policy with OMA-URI. This is still necessary for third-party ADMX policies, and this will be covered later in this chapter. As part of your Microsoft Intune solution, use these template settings as a one-stop-shop to manage your Windows 10 devices.

Not all ADMX policies are whitelisted in all Windows 10 versions, so it is a good idea to keep your version of Windows 10 as current as possible in your organization. To verify what ADMX policies are supported on the Windows 10 build you are running, check the Windows policy CSP documentation: `https://docs.microsoft.com/en-us/windows/client-management/mdm/policy-configuration-service-provider#policies-supported-by-group-policy-and-admx-backed-policies`.

To configure the template, follow these steps:

1. In the Microsoft Endpoint Manager admin center, go to **Home | Devices | Windows | Configuration profiles** and apply the following:

    - **Platform**: Select **Windows 10 and later**
    - **Profile type**: Select **Templates**

- **Template Name**: Select **Administrative Templates**:

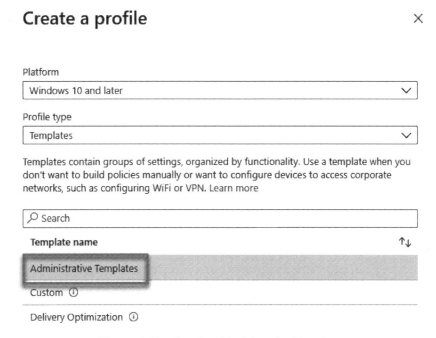

Figure 10.23 – Creating Administrative Templates

2. When creating a profile in Microsoft Intune, the name is a mandatory field. You should enter a name that indicates what the policy does:

- **Name**: Enter `Microsoft Edge Policy`:

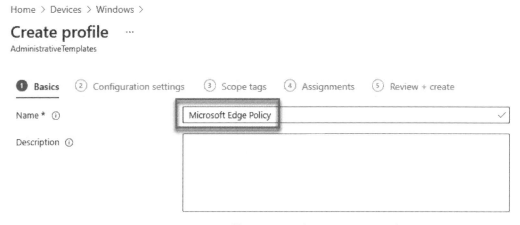

Figure 10.24 – Create profile screen – Administrative Template

3. Now you can select **All Settings**, **Computer Configuration**, or **User Configuration**, depending on what you want to configure. In this use case, we will configure the Microsoft Edge browser.

4. Under **Computer Configuration**, you can find all the top-level categories, such as **Microsoft Edge**:

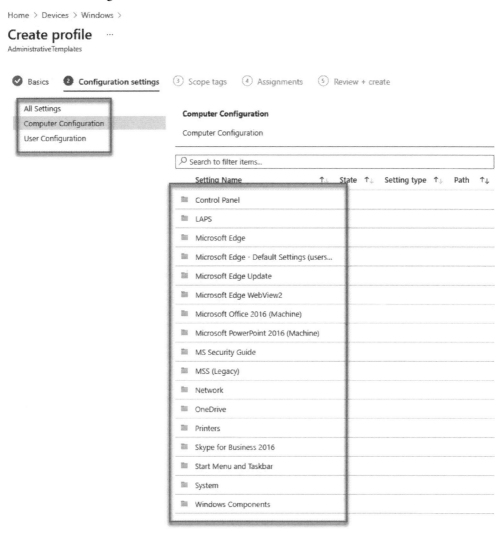

Figure 10.25 – Computer Configuration

5. In this case, we will configure **SmartScreen settings** for **Microsoft Edge**:

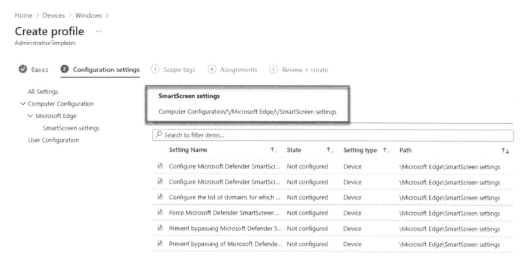

Figure 10.26 – SmartScreen settings

6. For each setting, there is a description of what the policy does.

7. Most policies have options for **Enabled**, **Disabled**, and **Not configured** – in this case, we will *enable* SmartScreen:

Figure 10.27 – Configure Microsoft Defender SmartScreen

8.   We are going to configure all the settings that we need in this policy and leave the ones we don't want to be configured as **Not configured**:

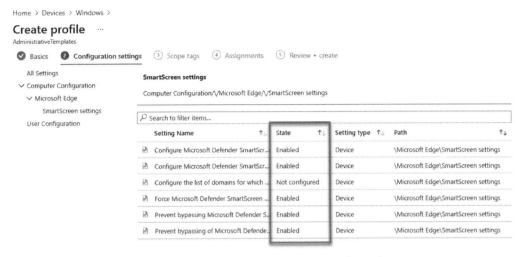

Figure 10.28 – SmartScreen settings – configured

Computer Configuration can be assigned to a user or device groups in Microsoft Intune. Consider leveraging device groups for your device policy.

Once you have deployed the policy to your devices, you can test the Microsoft SmartScreen functionality via Microsoft Defender Testground, at `https://demo.wd.microsoft.com/`:

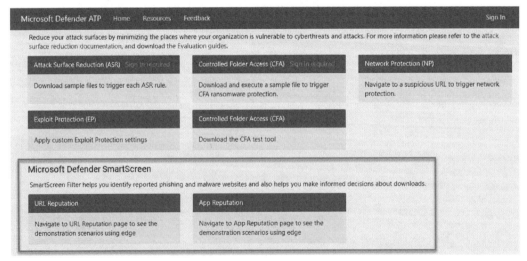

Figure 10.29 – Microsoft Defender SmartScreen Testground

With Microsoft Defender Testground, you can test the policies you have deployed, but also the end user experience and whether or how they are blocked from performing certain actions. Let's have a closer look at the available test settings.

URL reputation

With this test site, you can test Microsoft Defender SmartScreen and see the end user experience:

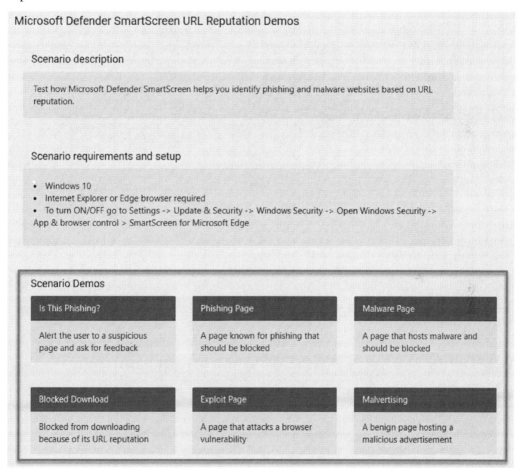

Figure 10.30 – Scenario Demos

By clicking **Phishing Page** underneath **Scenario Demos**, you can see whether Microsoft SmartScreen has been configured correctly and what the end user experience is like:

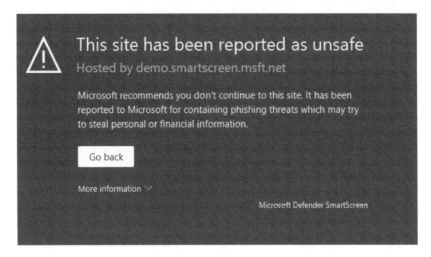

Figure 10.31 – SmartScreen end user blocked

Phishing sites can impersonate trusted sites to trick you into revealing personal or financial information. Even if it looks and feels trustworthy, the site you are trying to visit could be a phishing site in disguise. By continuing to this site, you might be putting your sensitive information – such as passwords, credit card numbers, contact info, or software activation keys – at risk.

This concludes the Edge browser policy configuration for SmartScreen. Next, we will cover how to leverage administrative templates in Microsoft Intune to configure OneDrive Known Folder Move.

OneDrive Known Folder Move configuration

Administrative templates could also be used to configure Microsoft OneDrive **Known Folder Move (KFM)**.

Here are the two primary advantages of leveraging Windows known folders (Desktop, Documents, Pictures, Screenshots, and Camera Roll) in Microsoft OneDrive for the users in your Microsoft 365 environment:

- Your end users can continue using the folders they are familiar with. They do not have to change the way they do their daily work to save files to OneDrive.

- Saving files to OneDrive backs up your users' data in the Microsoft 365 backend in OneDrive, and the end user can access their data from anywhere on any device:

Figure 10.32 – Manage protection of important folders

To configure OneDrive KFM, you can create an administrative template profile in Microsoft Intune. Start by giving the profile a name:

- **Name**: Enter `OneDrive Know Folder Move`:

Home > Devices > Windows >

Create profile   ⋯
AdministrativeTemplates

| ❶ Basics | ② Configuration settings | ③ Scope tags | ④ Assignments | ⑤ Review + create |

Name * ⓘ   OneDrive Know Folder Move   ✓

Description ⓘ

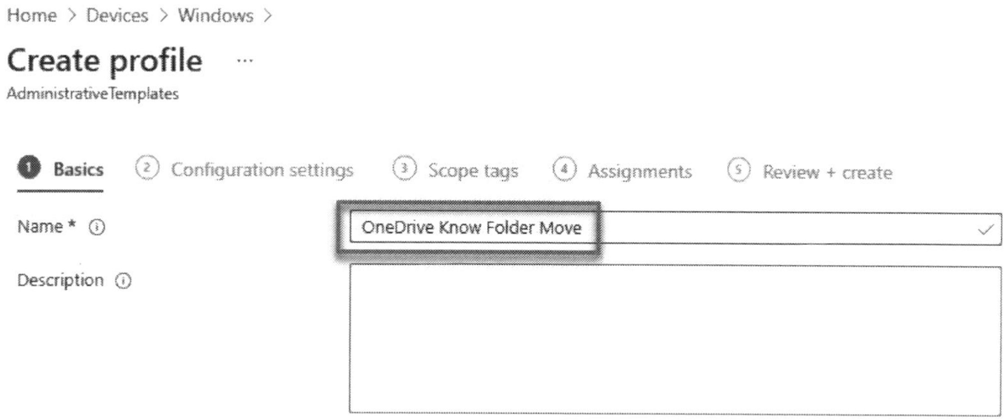

Figure 10.33 – Administrative Templates – OneDrive KFM

There are a few settings that you need to configure to silently configure OneDrive KFM for the end user:

- **Silently sign in users to the OneDrive sync app with their Windows Credentials**: Select **Enabled**:

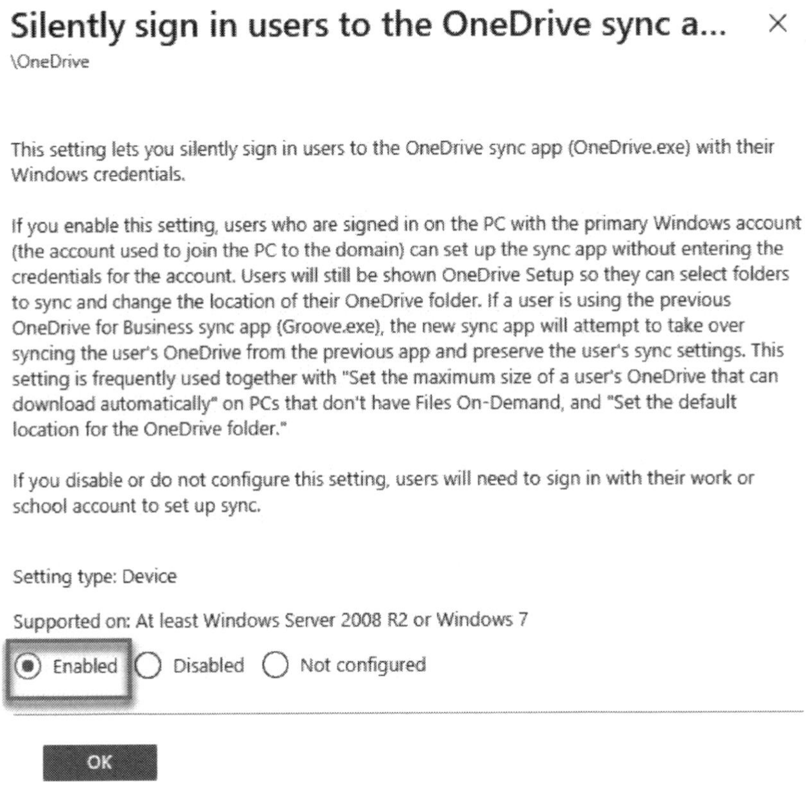

Figure 10.34 – Silently sign in users to OneDrive

- **Silently move Windows known folders to OneDrive**: Select **Enabled**.

- **Tenant ID**: Use the tenant ID from your Microsoft 365 tenant.

- **Show notification to users after folders have been redirected**: No:

Silently move Windows known folders to O...   ×

\OneDrive

This setting lets you redirect known folders to OneDrive without any user interaction. In sync client builds below 18.171.0823.0001, this setting only redirects empty known folders to OneDrive (or known folders already redirected to a different OneDrive account). In later builds, it redirects known folders that contain content and moves the content to OneDrive. We recommend using this setting together with "Prompt users to move Windows known folders to OneDrive." If moving the known folders silently does not succeed, users will be prompted to correct the error and continue.

If you enable this setting and provide your tenant ID, you can choose whether to display a notification to users after their folders have been redirected.

If you disable or do not configure this setting, your users' known folders will not be silently redirected and/or moved to OneDrive.

Setting type: Device

Supported on: At least Windows Server 2008 R2 or Windows 7

◉ Enabled   ○ Disabled   ○ Not configured

Tenant ID: *

3f10ff99-fa9a-4af2-b352-85803031ff83

Show notification to users after folders have been redirected:

No   ⌄

OK

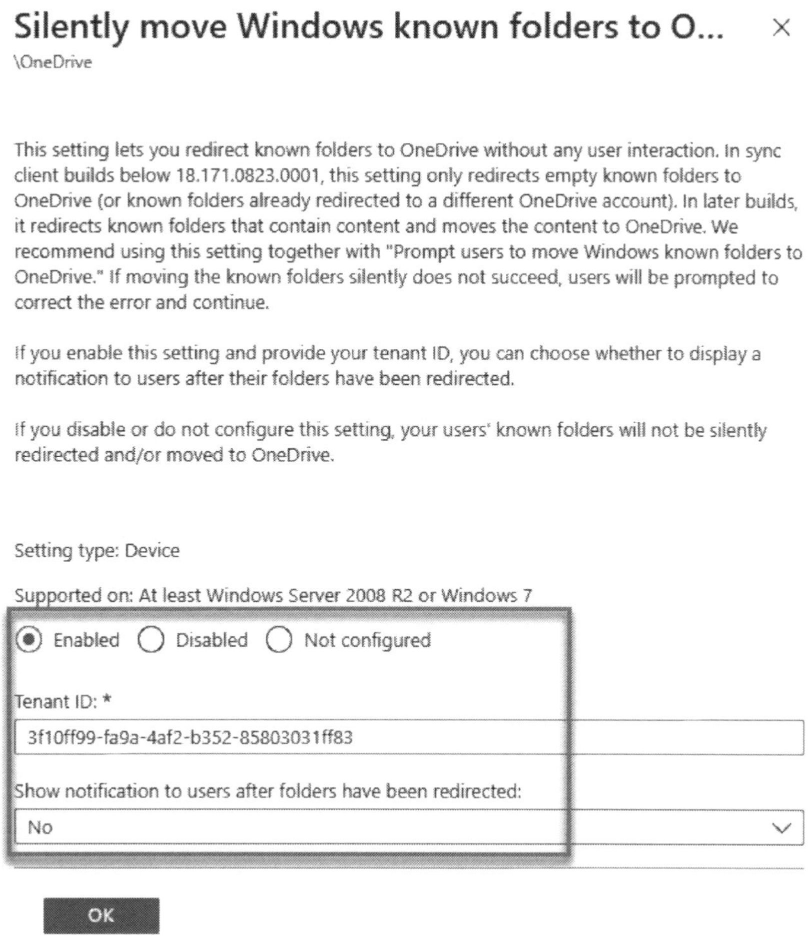

Figure 10.35 – Silently move Windows known folders to OneDrive

To find your Tenant ID, you can go to the Azure Active Directory admin center (`https://aad.portal.azure.com`). You can find it under **Azure Active directory** | **Properties** | **Tenant ID**.

You can also find your Tenant ID, which is unique for your organization:

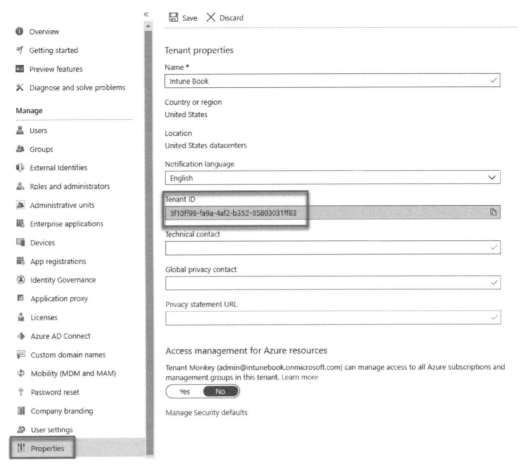

Figure 10.36 – Tenant ID in Azure AD

OneDrive – block syncing specific file extensions

One of the main key releases customers have been waiting for has been the possibility to exclude files, folders, and extensions from syncing. This is something I will explain in more depth in this section, plus some more tips and tricks for the use of OneDrive.

This setting lets you enter keywords to prevent OneDrive from uploading certain files to OneDrive. You can enter complete names, such as `setup.exe`, or use the asterisk (`*`) as a wildcard character to represent a series of characters:

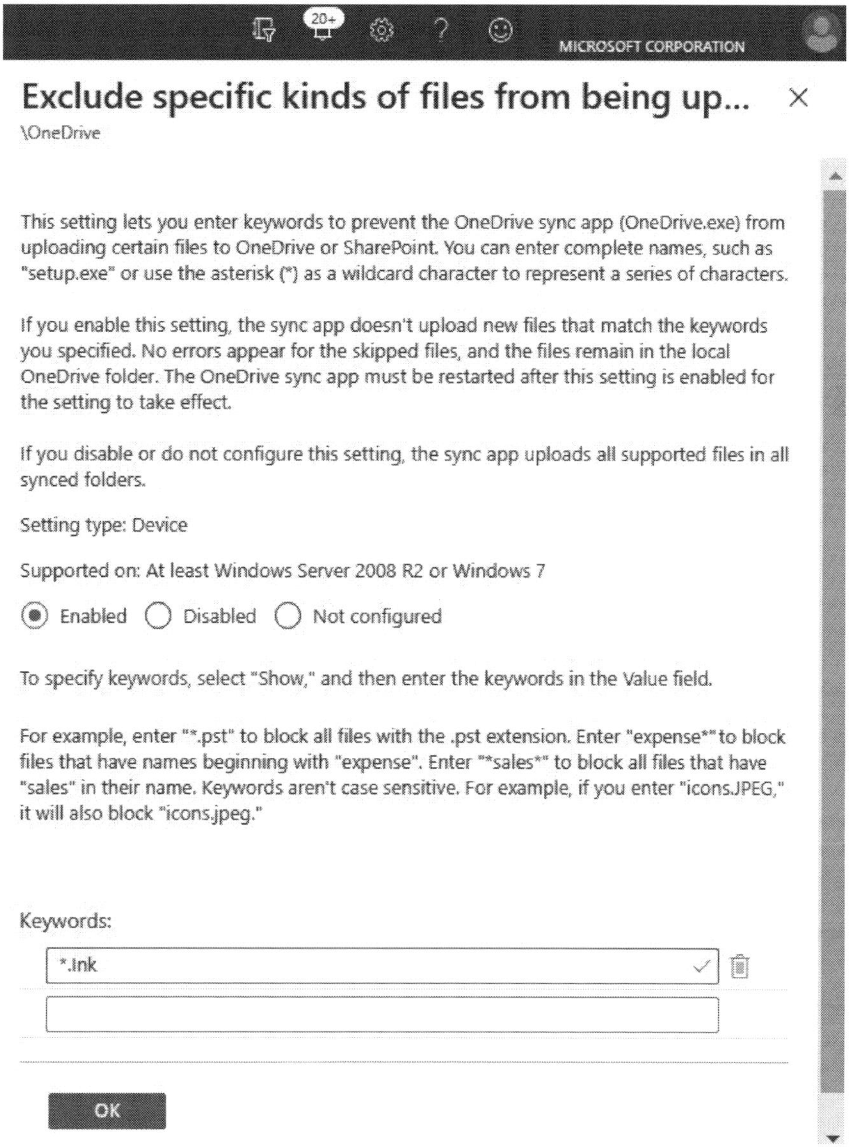

Figure 10.37 – Exclude specific kinds of files from being uploaded

You can assign your OneDrive KFM policy to a device group.

This concludes this section on administrative templates. Next, we will walk through some of the many different options for device configuration with templates in Microsoft Intune.

Configure device configuration (template)

Templates contain groups of settings, organized by functionality. You should use a template when you don't want to build policies manually or want to configure devices to access corporate networks, such as configuring Wi-Fi or VPN.

We will show some examples, along with use cases, in this section.

The first one is **Delivery Optimization**. Here, it is recommended that you configure it on all Windows devices, but especially if Windows Update for Business is running:

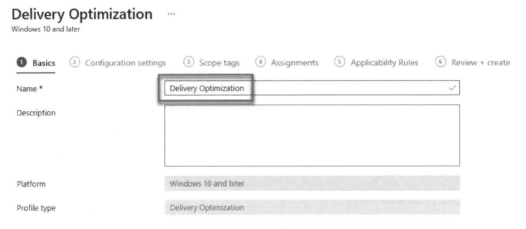

Figure 10.38 – Templates – Delivery Optimization

View the information in the **i** icon, which will give you the recommended values for each setting:

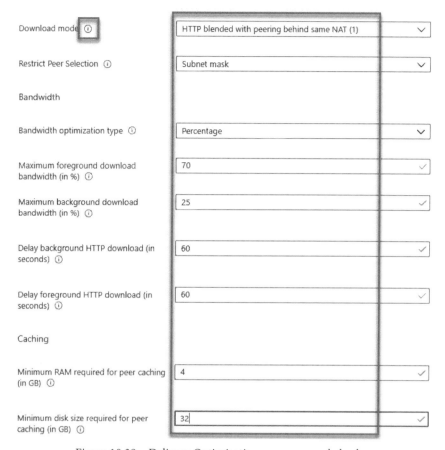

Figure 10.39 – Delivery Optimization – recommended values

Then, configure all the settings, test them, and evaluate whether all the recommended settings are working as expected in your organization.

Another great example of a device configuration template is **Shared multi-user device**, which is used to configure access, account deletion, maintenance, and power management settings for a shared Windows 10 device used by multiple users in your organization:

Shared PC mode ⓘ	Enable / Not configured
Guest account ⓘ	Domain ⌄
Account management ⓘ	Enabled ⌄
Account Deletion ⓘ	At storage space threshold and inactive threshold ⌄
Start delete threshold(%) ⓘ	15 ✓
Stop delete threshold(%) ⓘ	25 ✓
Inactive account threshold ⓘ	15 ✓
Local Storage ⓘ	Disabled ⌄
Power Policies ⓘ	Enabled ⌄
Sleep time out (in seconds) ⓘ	Enter number of seconds ✓
Sign-in when PC wakes ⓘ	Enabled ⌄
Maintenance start time(in minutes from midnight) ⓘ	Enter number of minutes from midnight ✓

Figure 10.40 – Shared multi-user device

End users can sign into these shared devices with an AAD account. Once they've signed in, their credentials are cached. As they use the device, end users only get access to features you allow. For example, you choose when the device goes into sleep mode and whether users can see and save files locally, enable or disable power management settings, and more. You also control whether the AAD account will be deleted by setting a certain threshold; the user account will be deleted when it is reached. This feature uses the same local user profile that has been optimized for shared use, so the login time for a first-time user on the device will only be a few seconds.

Leveraging a custom policy as a last resort

Only use a custom policy as a last resort. It is not always easy to create a custom policy. You need to know where, how, and why the CSP is working.

In this scenario, we will create a custom OMA-URI policy that configures devices with the correct commercial ID for Update Compliance solutions.

You must configure the identifier that's used to uniquely associate the telemetry data of this device as belonging to a given organization. If your organization is participating in a program that requires this device to be identified as belonging to your organization, this setting can be used to provide that identification. The value for this setting will be provided by Microsoft as part of the onboarding process for the program. Microsoft will not be able to use this identifier to associate this machine and its telemetry data with your organization if you disable or do not configure this policy setting.

Follow these steps to create a custom profile with a template in Microsoft Intune:

1. For **Profile type** and select **Templates**. For **Template name**, select **Custom**. Then, click **Add**:

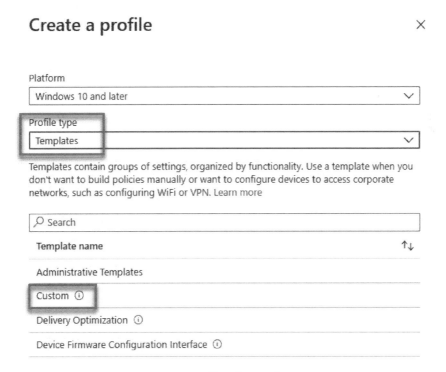

Figure 10.41 – Templates – Custom

2. By clicking **Add**, you can fill out all the required values in the **Add row** blade. You can add as many rows as you need to the policy you are creating:

    - **Name**: Update Compliance Commercial ID.

    - **Description**: Configure devices with the Commercial ID for Update Compliance solutions.

    - **OMA-URI**: Enter the following path, which is case-sensitive, and avoid trailing spaces: ./Vendor/MSFT/DMClient/Provider/ProviderID/ CommercialID

    - **Data type**: Select **String**.

    - **Value**: Specify the GUID for your Commercial ID, which you can get from your Update Compliance settings in Microsoft Azure:

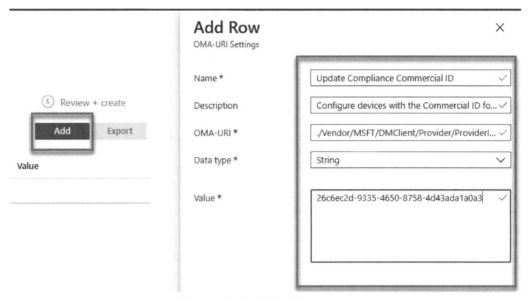

Figure 10.42 – OMA-URI settings

This concludes this section on custom policies. The need for custom policies will reduce as the capacity of the settings catalog is built out in the future. In the next section, we will cover the option of running PowerShell scripts from Microsoft Intune to set device configurations.

Pushing PowerShell scripts – scripted actions to endpoints

If there is no policy for the configuration change that you need to make on your corporate devices, you can leverage PowerShell scripts in Microsoft Intune. This is also a good way of publishing one-time installations or custom scripted actions to both your physical and cloud endpoints:

1. In the Microsoft Endpoint Manager admin center, browse to **Home | Devices | Windows | PowerShell scripts** and click **Add**:

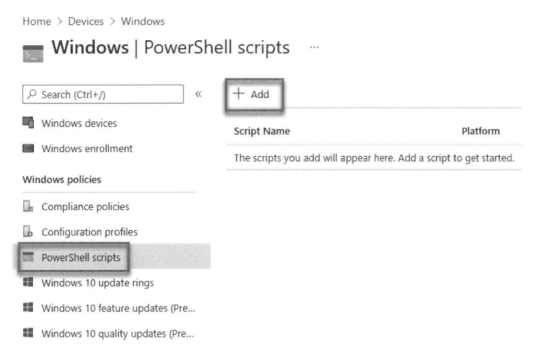

Figure 10.43 – PowerShell scripts

2. Click **Select a file** to upload your PowerShell script to Microsoft Intune:

> **Important Note**
> Make sure to select **Run script on the 64-bit PowerShell host** for the right
> registry location.

Figure 10.44 – Uploading a PowerShell script

Assign the script to the user or device groups. The script will then run once on each
assigned device. Here are some script examples:

- **Enable Reserved Storage**:

```
$Storage = Invoke-Command {DISM /Online /
Get-ReservedStorageState}
$Output = $Storage | Select-String "Reserved storage is
disabled."
Write-Host $Output
If ($Output -like "Reserved storage is disabled."){
    Invoke-Command {DISM /Online /
Set-ReservedStorageState /State:Enabled}
}
```

- **Enable ADAL for OneDrive**:

```
$registryPath = "HKCU:\SOFTWARE\Microsoft\OneDrive"
$Name = "EnableADAL"
$value = "1"
IF(!(Test-Path $registryPath))
    {
    New-Item -Path $registryPath -Force | Out-Null
    New-ItemProperty -Path $registryPath -Name $name
-Value $value `
    -PropertyType DWORD -Force | Out-Null}
  ELSE {
    New-ItemProperty -Path $registryPath -Name $name
-Value $value `
    -PropertyType DWORD -Force | Out-Null}
```

These are just examples of leveraging PowerShell scripts to configure an Intune-managed Windows device. Next, we will cover compliance policies.

Compliance policies

Microsoft Endpoint Manager can set a compliance state on a device. There are two possible outcomes for a device: compliant or noncompliant.

In Microsoft Intune, you can define the rules and settings that users and devices must meet to be compliant. If Conditional Access has been configured, then users and devices that are noncompliant can be blocked from accessing resources that contain corporate data.

> **Important Note**
> Conditional Access requires an Azure AD Premium license.

Include actions that apply to noncompliant devices. Actions for noncompliance can alert users to the conditions of noncompliance and safeguard data on noncompliant devices.

There are two types of compliance policies in Microsoft Intune:

- **Compliance policy settings**: Tenant-wide settings that act like a built-in compliance policy that every device receives. The compliance policy settings set a baseline for how the compliance policy will work in your Microsoft Intune environment.

  These settings configure the way the compliance service treats devices. Each device evaluates these as a *Built-in Device Compliance Policy*, which is reflected in device monitoring.

  The following are the options you can configure in the built-in policy:

  - Mark devices with no compliance policy assigned as **Default value is Compliant**. This means that this security feature is disabled by default. It is recommended that you change this setting to **Not Compliant** so that all devices without a compliance policy will automatically be marked as non-compliant.

  - Enhanced jailbreak detection: **Default value Disabled** (applies only to iOS/iPadOS).

  - Compliance status validity period (days): The default value is 30 days.

  Specify a period in which devices must successfully report on all their received compliance policies. If a device fails to report its compliance status for a policy before the validity period expires, the device is treated as non-compliant. You can configure a period so that it ranges from 1 to 120 days.

  To manage the compliance policy settings, sign into the Microsoft Endpoint Manager admin center and go to **Endpoint security | Device compliance | Compliance policy settings**.

- **Device compliance policy**: Platform-specific rules you configure and deploy to groups of users or devices. These rules define requirements for devices, such as the minimum number of operating systems or the use of disk encryption. Devices must meet these rules to be considered compliant.

Windows

The **Device Health Attestation (DHA)** service validates the **Trusted Platform Module (TPM)** and **Platform Configuration Register (PCR)** logs for a device and then issues a DHA report. Microsoft offers the DHA cloud service, a Microsoft-managed DHA service that is free, geo-load-balanced, and optimized for access from different regions of the world.

DHA enables enterprises to raise the security bar of their organization to hardware monitored and attested security, with minimal or no impact on operation costs.

The DHA service integrates with MDM solutions and does the following:

- Combines the info DHA service that's received from devices (through existing MDM device management communication channels) with the DHA report.

- Makes more secure and trusted security decisions, based on attested hardware and protected data.

- When leveraging DHA in a compliance policy, Windows 10 must be rebooted before it gets into a compliant state in Microsoft Intune.

In the **Device Health** section of the Windows compliance policy, there are three settings:

Home > Endpoint security > Compliance policies >

Windows 10 compliance policy   ···
Windows 10 and later

✓ Basics   ❷ **Compliance settings**   ③ Actions for noncompliance   ④ Assignments   ⑤ Review + create

∧ Device Health

Windows Health Attestation Service evaluation rules

Require BitLocker ⓘ	Require	Not configured
Require Secure Boot to be enabled on the device ⓘ	Require	Not configured
Require code integrity ⓘ	Require	Not configured

Figure 10.45 – Compliance policy – Device Health

Update these settings as follows:

- **Require BitLocker**: **Require** – The device can protect data that's stored on the drive from unauthorized access when the system is off or hibernating.

- **Require Secure Boot to be enabled on the device**: **Require** – The system is forced to boot to a factory trusted state. The core components that are used to boot the machine must have correct cryptographic signatures that are trusted by the organization that manufactured the device. These signatures are verified by UEFI firmware before it lets the machine start. If any files are tampered with, which breaks their signature, the system doesn't boot.

In the **System Security** section, there is a subsection for the **Device Security** section of the Windows compliance policy. Here, you can configure four settings:

- **Firewall**: Turn on the Microsoft Defender Firewall and prevent users from turning it off.

- **Trusted Platform Module (TPM)**: **Require** – Intune checks the TPM chip version for compliance. The device is compliant if the TPM chip version is greater than 0. The device isn't compliant if there isn't a TPM version on the device.

- **Antivirus**: **Require** – Check compliance using antivirus solutions that are registered with Windows Security Center, such as Symantec or Microsoft Defender.

- **Antispyware**: **Require** – Check compliance using antispyware solutions that are registered with Windows Security Center, such as Symantec or Microsoft Defender:

Figure 10.46 – Compliance policy – Device Security

In the **Defender** section of the Windows compliance policy, you can configure four settings, as shown here:

- **Microsoft Defender Antimalware**: **Require** – Turn on the Microsoft Defender antimalware service and prevent users from turning it off.

- **Microsoft Defender Antimalware minimum version**: Minimum version of Microsoft Defender (for example, 4.11.0.0).

- **Microsoft Defender Antimalware security intelligence up-to-date**: **Require** – Force the Microsoft Defender security intelligence to be up-to-date.

- **Real-time protection**: **Require** – Turn on real-time protection, which scans for malware, spyware, and other unwanted software:

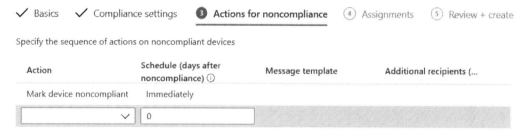

Figure 10.47 – Compliance policy – Defender

You can also configure an action for noncompliance to send an email to the primary user of the device or retire a noncompliant device:

Figure 10.48 – Actions for noncompliance

As an IT admin, you can monitor different parts of the compliance state:

- **Compliance Operational report**: Provides real-time operational reports that can help the IT admin take action based on the data they find in this report.

  Go to **Home | Devices | Monitor | Windows health attestation report**. Here, you have the option to see how many of your devices do not have BitLocker and secure boot enabled, as an example:

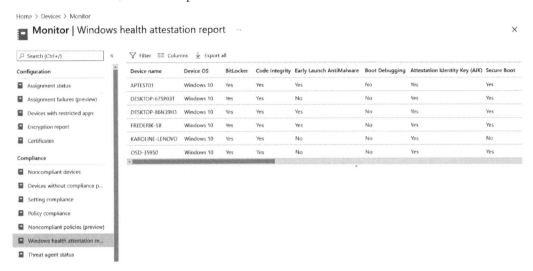

Figure 10.49 – Windows health attestation report

- **Noncompliant devices report**: Go to **Home | Devices | Monitor | Noncompliant devices**.

In this report, you have the option to see all your noncompliant devices. If you apply the **OS == Windows** filter, you will only see the noncompliant Windows devices:

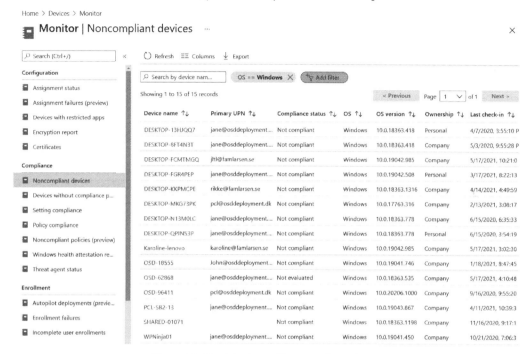

Figure 10.50 – Monitor – Noncompliant devices

- **Noncompliant policies (preview)**: Go to **Home | Devices | Monitor | Noncompliant policies (preview)**.

  In this report, you get a quick overview of your compliance policies in Microsoft Intune and how many devices are not compliant with a specific compliance policy:

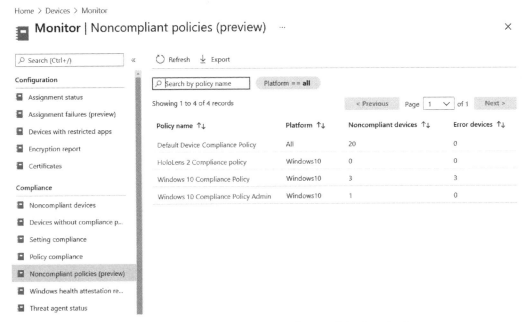

Figure 10.51 – Monitor – Noncompliant policies (preview)

This concludes this section on compliance policies and how to do operational monitoring on compliance policies. Next, we will cover organizational reporting on compliance.

Organizational compliance report

This is a summary report that gives an overall view of, in this case, the compliance status of your devices. This report gives you a quick overview of the compliance status of all devices in Microsoft Intune.

Go to **Home | Report | Device compliance**. In this report, you will be given a quick overview of the compliance statuses of your devices in Microsoft Intune:

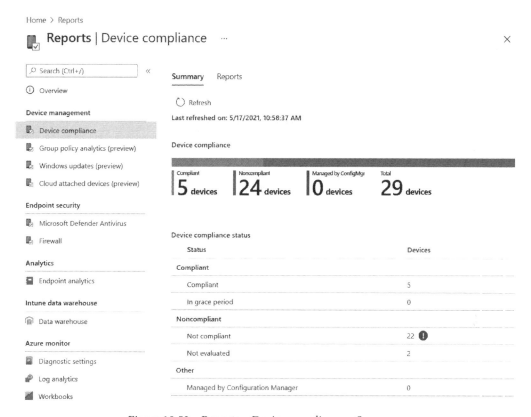

Figure 10.52 – Reports – Device compliance – Summary

By clicking on **Reports**, you will get the **Device compliance** and **Device compliance trends** options:

Figure 10.53 – Reports – Device compliance

With **Device compliance**, by leveraging the filters, you can select Windows devices and get a report on those alone. You can also filter based on the compliance's status and/or ownership:

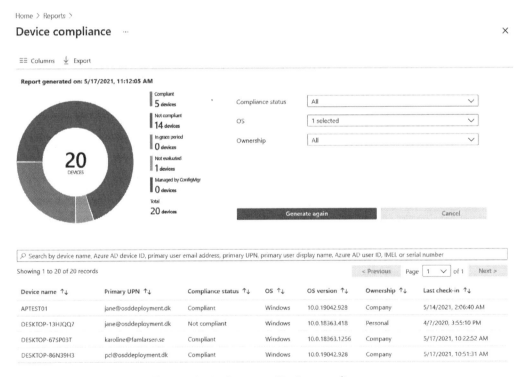

Figure 10.54 – Reports – Device compliance

Device compliance trends

This report will provide you with a historical view of your compliance status for the last 60 days.

In this view, we have a filter for setting Windows as the OS again:

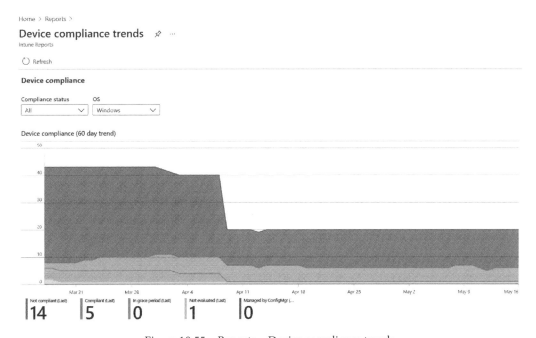

Figure 10.55 – Reports – Device compliance trends

This concludes this section on device compliance organizational reporting.

Summary

In the chapter, you've learned about the different policy types and looked at scenarios for configuring Windows in a more modern way via Microsoft Endpoint Manager for both physical and cloud endpoints. We have looked at some scenarios and policy configurations that you can leverage. In the policy management area, you need to figure out what kind of approach you want to take in your enterprise environment. When looking at pure cloud-managed devices and policies, it would be the perfect time to look forward and not backward. As examples, start by deploying policies that have a security impact, such as the Edge security baseline, Windows Defender policies, and so on. Then, look at deploying policies that will help your end users be more productive, such as configuring OneDrive Known Folder Move, policies that help end users start working in their apps better, such as autoconfiguring Microsoft Edge, removing prompts from applications, and so on. When you are done with those two big areas, you might be done or at least in a good place to start. After testing with your end users regarding their experience and any feedback they have, you can go back and change your policies to fit the business requirements. The same goes for when you are talking to application owners in your business, or your security department has specific requirements that certain policies or settings to be on your devices. This is an ongoing process to evaluate whether you are using the correct policies in your environment, just as you probably had a similar process when your policy configuration was done with GPO.

After this chapter, you will be able to manage your physical and cloud endpoints and know when to follow which configuration path moving forward. The next chapter is part three of policy management. The last part looks at a cloud service that you can leverage if you have Office 365 to configure Microsoft 365 apps, both with and without Microsoft Intune.

Questions

1. What is Storage Sense?

   a) A service to optimize the performance of your SSD.

   b) A service with a sense of humor.

   c) A service to clean up your endpoints from the OneDrive cache and the Downloads folder in your profile.

   d) A service to block services from running.

2. What is the recommended option to start configuring settings on your Windows endpoints?

    a) Settings Catalog

    b) Administrative templates

    c) Security baseline

    d) Device restriction profile

3. What policy type can you use to configure Microsoft Edge?

    a) Shared multi-user device

    b) Administrative templates

    c) Kiosk profile

    d) Device restriction profile

Answers

1. (c)
2. (a)
3. (b)

Further reading

If you want to learn more after reading this chapter, please take a look at the following free online resources:

- Device compliance policies in Microsoft Intune – Azure | Microsoft Docs: `https://docs.microsoft.com/en-us/mem/intune/protect/device-compliance-get-started`

- Use templates for Windows 10 devices in Microsoft Intune – Azure | Microsoft Docs: `https://docs.microsoft.com/en-us/mem/intune/configuration/administrative-templates-windows`

- Restrict device features using policies in Microsoft Intune – Azure | Microsoft Docs: `https://docs.microsoft.com/en-us/mem/intune/configuration/device-restrictions-configure`

11
Office Policy Management

You'll learn about the Office cloud policies in this chapter, and how you can use this cloud service to configure the Microsoft 365 apps that your end users have installed either on their Windows devices at home or their company-issued Windows devices that are managed by a management tool such as Microsoft Intune. This is not a replacement for GPO, administrative templates, or settings catalog policies in Microsoft Intune, but in some scenarios, you can leverage the Office cloud policy service.

We will also show how the Office Cloud policy service has Security Policy Advisor, which can help you and your enterprise to get insights into whether you have the correct security policy recommendations implemented. These recommendations are based on Microsoft best practices and information about your existing environment.

Security Policy Advisor can only be used in combination with the Office Cloud policy service.

In this chapter, we will cover the following topics:

- The Office cloud policy service
- Creating a policy configuration with the OCP service
- Security Policy Advisor

The Office cloud policy service

The Microsoft 365 Apps admin center (`https://config.office.com`) provides cloud-based policy management of Microsoft 365 enterprise apps. Policies deployed from the **Office cloud policy** (**OCP**) service will work on devices that are managed and unmanaged, so basically, all devices that users in your Office 365 organization are logging in to, both corporate and personally owned.

When a user signs into Microsoft 365 Apps for enterprise on a device, the policy settings roam to that device. You can also enforce some policy settings for Office web apps, iOS, macOS, and Android.

The Office cloud policy service includes many of the same user-based policy settings that are available in Group Policy or in Microsoft Intune. Conflict handling between the OCP service and policy settings from **Group Policy Object** (**GPO**) or Microsoft Intune is done so that Microsoft Intune or GPO will always win. A user can be a member of multiple Azure Active Directory groups with conflicting policy settings. By setting a priority on the Office policy in OCP, you can control which policy setting is applied. The highest priority is applied, with 0 being the highest priority that you can assign to a policy in the OCP service.

Requirements for using the Office cloud policy service are as follows:

- At least version 1808 of Microsoft 365 Apps for enterprise (and for the subscription versions of the Project and Visio desktop apps).

- User accounts must be created in or synchronized to **Azure Active Directory** (**AAD**). The user must be signed in to Office 365 ProPlus with an AAD-based account.

- Security groups must be created in or synchronized to **AAD**, with the appropriate users added to those groups.

Pros of cloud-based policy management are as follows:

- It works on all devices – managed and unmanaged, both Microsoft Intune and SCCM.

- It works on BYOD and personal devices.

- The settings are always up to date and as it is a service from the Microsoft Office team, there is no need to download updated Administrative Template files (ADMX/ADML).

Cons of cloud-based policy management are as follows:

- It only involves user policies and not device settings.
- It works with BYOD and personal devices – so if a user is using Office ProPlus on a private device, they will have the same policies as they do at work.

You can get started using the Office cloud policy service at `https://config.office.com`:

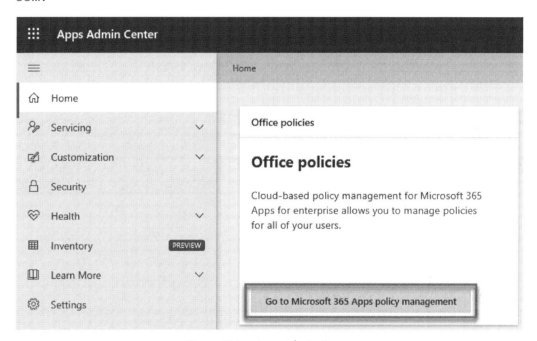

Figure 11.1 – Apps Admin Center

Office policies from OCP can also be accessed from the Microsoft Endpoint Manager admin center, under **Apps | Policies for Office apps**.

Creating a policy configuration with the OCP service

The following are the basic steps for creating a policy configuration from the MEM admin center.

To create a policy configuration, you must be assigned one of the following roles in AAD: Global Administrator, Security Administrator, or Office Apps Admin. Intune Service Administrators do not have the right to create OCP policies.

1.   Go to **Home | Apps | Policies for Office apps**.

     You won't have any policy configurations if this is the first time you are looking at the Office cloud policy service.

     Click **Create** to create your first policy configuration.

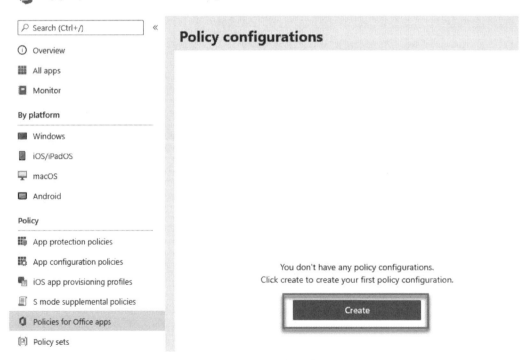

Figure 11.2 – Policies for Office apps

2. Enter `Office policy` in the **Name** field, then click on **Select type** to expand into the view you see in the following screenshot. Select **This policy configuration applies to users**.

    When selecting this option, you are able to select a target user group from AAD. If you select **This policy configuration applies to users that access documents anonymously using Office web apps**, it will apply to Office online if the documents are being accessed anonymously. An IT admin can always set up external sharing so that a guest user must sign in or provide a verification code:

Figure 11.3 – Create policy configuration – Select type

3. For the **Select group** option, choose **Office 365 Users** (a custom group).

Then click on **Select group** to expand into the view you see in the following screenshot. You can select AAD security groups, but a security group can only have one OCP service policy assigned:

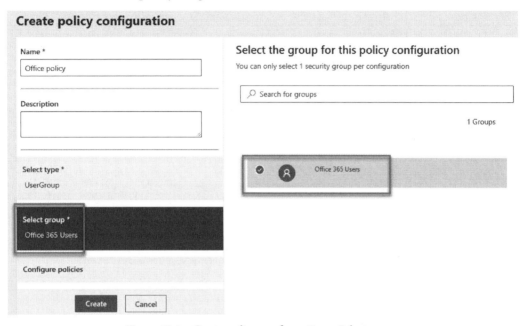

Figure 11.4 – Create policy configuration – Select group

4.   If an OCP is already assigned to an AAD group, it will be grayed out in the UI as you can only assign one Office cloud policy per group in Azure AD:

Figure 11.5 – Select the group for this policy configuration

Configuring policies

As of this moment, there are 2,133 different policy settings within the Office cloud policy service.

Configure the policy settings to be included in the policy configuration. You can search for the policy setting name to find the policy setting that you want to configure. You can also filter on the application, on whether the policy is a recommended security baseline, and on whether the policy has been configured. The **Platform** column indicates whether the policy is applied to Microsoft 365 Apps for enterprise for Windows devices, Office for the web, or both.

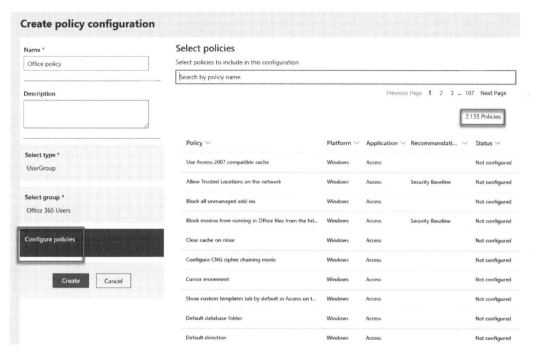

Figure 11.6 – Create policy configuration

In this case, we are going to configure the default file format for all Microsoft 365 enterprise apps:

1. Search for Default file format.
2. Select Word for **Default file format**.
3. Change from **Not configured** to **Enabled**:

Figure 11.7 – Default file format

Do the same for the rest of the Microsoft 365 enterprise apps.

Click **Create**.

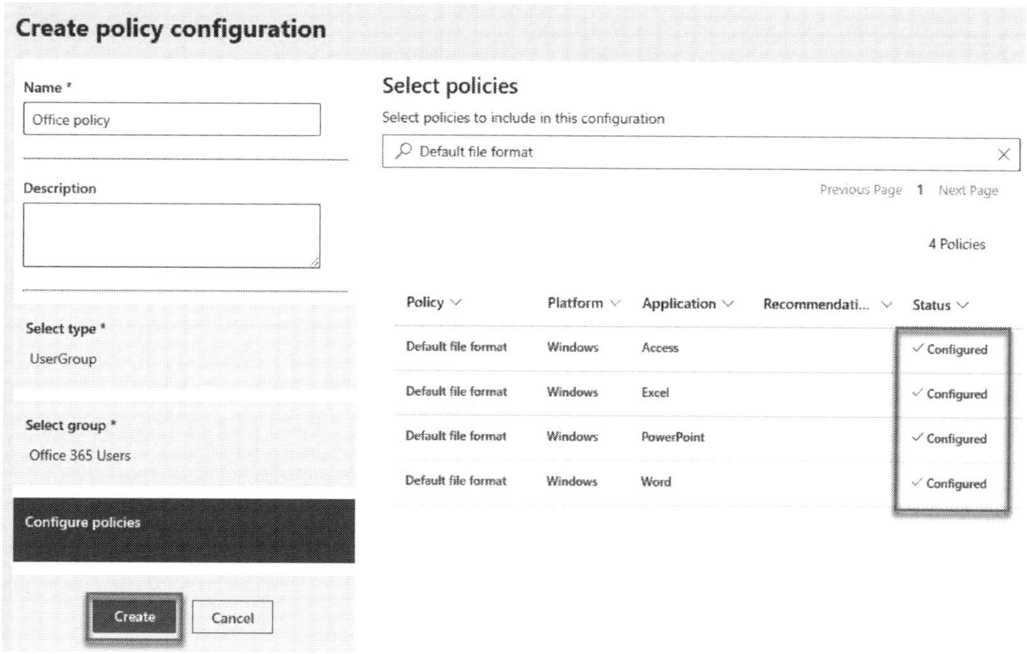

Figure 11.8 – Create policy configuration

This concludes the section on Office cloud policies in Microsoft Endpoint Manager. We showed you how to create Office policies that can be deployed to all endpoints in your organization. In the next section, we will show you some tips and tricks in the OCP service.

Tips and tricks in the OCP service

When choosing between the many settings you want to configure, it can be hard to find the setting that you are looking for. Filtering is a great way to find the settings you are looking for. Filtering is done on the different columns.

If you enter Windows, you will only see policies that are applicable to Windows:

Figure 11.9 – Filters on Platform

If you enter Word, you will only see policies that are applicable to Word:

Figure 11.10 – Filters on Application

If you select **Security Baseline**, you will only see policies that are applicable to Windows; there are no security baselines for other operating systems:

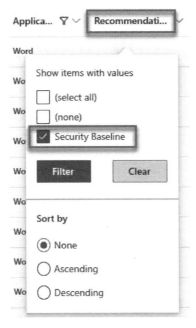

Figure 11.11 – Filters on Recommendations

When you select a policy setting that is in the security baseline, you just need to select **Microsoft recommended security baseline** to get the policy configured to the correct value:

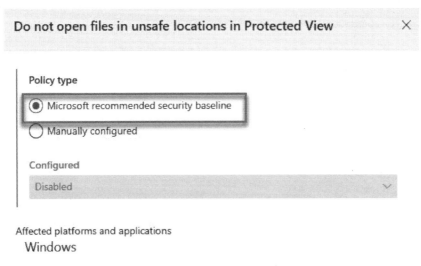

Figure 11.12 – Microsoft recommended security baseline

If you check **Configured**, you will only see policies that are configured in the policy:

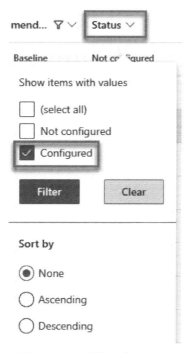

Figure 11.13 – Filters by Status

If you use **Configured** as a filter, you can see all the policy settings that are configured:

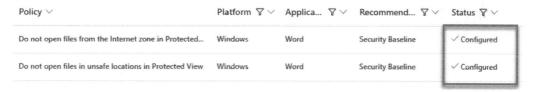

Policy ⌄	Platform ⊽⌄	Applica... ⊽⌄	Recommend... ⊽⌄	Status ⊽⌄
Do not open files from the Internet zone in Protected...	Windows	Word	Security Baseline	✓ Configured
Do not open files in unsafe locations in Protected View	Windows	Word	Security Baseline	✓ Configured

Figure 11.14 – Filter – Configured

If you want to create a new policy configuration with the same settings as an existing policy configuration, you can select the existing policy configuration on the **Policy configurations** page, and then choose **Copy**. Make the appropriate changes and then choose **Save**:

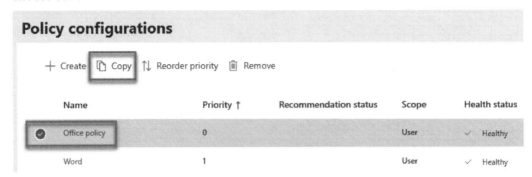

Figure 11.15 – Policy configurations – Copy

In this section, we covered all the tips and tricks on filtering in Office cloud policies. In the next section, we will cover how the policies are applied.

How are Office cloud policies applied?

The Click-to-Run service used by Microsoft 365 Apps for enterprise checks with the Office cloud policy service when a user signs into an Office application for the first time. If the user has no assigned policy configuration, the next check-in will happen after 24 hours.

If a user is in a group that has a policy configuration assignment, then policies are applied, and a check-in will happen after 90 minutes again.

If an error occurred, a check-in would happen the next time the end user opens an Office app, such as Word or Excel. If no Office apps are running when the next check is scheduled, then the check-in will happen the next time the end user opens an Office app.

Policies from the Office cloud policy service are applied only when the Office app is restarted. This is the same behavior as Group Policy. For Windows devices, policies are enforced based on the primary user that is signed into Microsoft 365 Apps for enterprise. If there are multiple Azure Active Directory accounts signed in, only policies for the primary account are applied. If the primary account is switched, most of the policies assigned to that account will not apply until the Office apps are restarted.

> **Note**
> If you are only installing Microsoft Teams on your device, the Click-to-Run
> service is not installed and Office cloud policies are not applied to the devices.

It is possible to switch accounts in an Office application by going to **File** | **Account** | **Switch account**:

Figure 11.16 – Office – Account

Microsoft Intune ADMX policies or GPO user policies can be located in the local registry, `HKCU\software\policies\Microsoft\Office\16.0\`:

Figure 11.17 – Registry path for Office ADMX

Many policies from GPO or Microsoft Intune ADMX policies are set per device. That is also the case in this example and the reason for only one policy value showing up.

Policy settings retrieved from the Office cloud policy service are stored in the registry at `HKEY_CURRENT_USER\Software\Policies\Microsoft\Cloud\Office\16.0`. This key is overwritten each time a new set of policies is retrieved from the policy service during the check-in process.

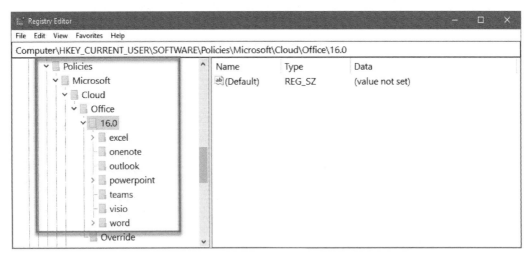

Figure 11.18 – Registry path for Office cloud policy

Policy service check-in activity is stored in the registry at `HKEY_CURRENT_USER\Software\Microsoft\Office\16.0\Common\CloudPolicy`. Deleting this key and restarting the Office apps will trigger the policy service to check in the next time an Office app such as Word or Excel is launched:

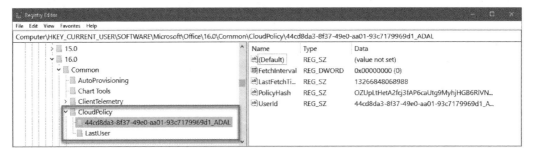

Figure 11.19 – Registry path for Office cloud policy check-in

This concludes the section about configuring policies with the Office cloud policy service. In the next section, we will cover how Security Policy Advisor in the Apps admin center helps you improve the security settings of the policies you have configured in the Office cloud policy service.

Security Policy Advisor

Outside of Microsoft Intune, directly in the Microsoft 365 Apps admin center, there are more options for Office policy management.

Sign into the Apps Admin Center at `https://config.office.com`:

Figure 11.20 – Welcome to the Microsoft 365 Apps Admin Center

You have the option to use Security Policy Advisor, where you will be given intelligent recommendations for security policies based on how Microsoft 365 apps for enterprise are used:

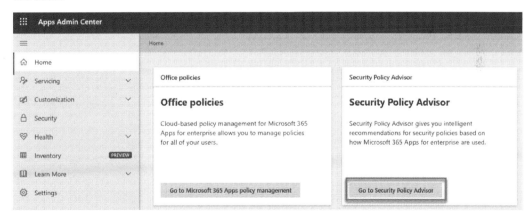

Figure 11.21 – Apps Admin Center – Security Policy Advisor

Security Policy Advisor is turned *Off* by default and needs to be turned *On*:

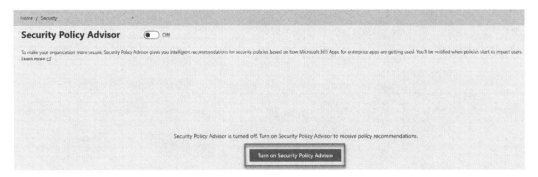

Figure 11.22 – Turn on Security Policy Advisor

After the policies have been assigned and applied to your users, you will start to see recommendations coming up in Security Policy Advisor. It will display **New recommendations available** in the **Status** column, and in the **Recommended Policies** column, you can see how many policy settings that Microsoft recommends you look at, so you can verify whether they need to be configured in your environment:

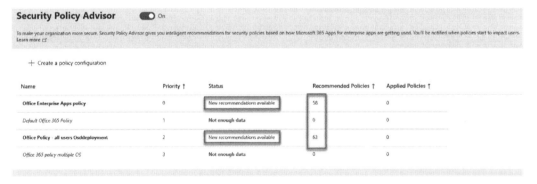

Figure 11.23 – Security Policy Advisor

You can then go through each setting and then **Apply** or **Ignore** it, and it will be reflected in your policy:

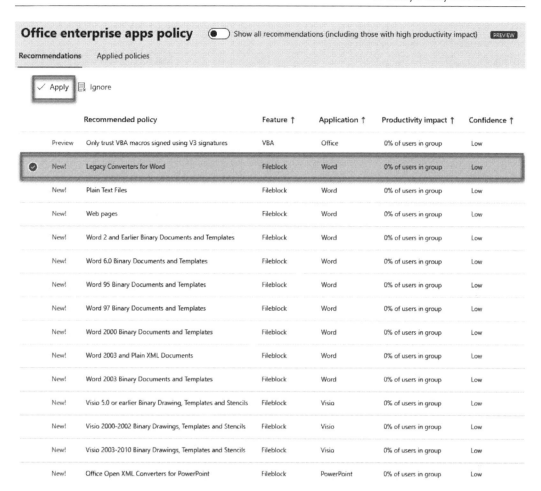

Figure 11.24 – Office enterprise apps policy

Going to the **Applied policies** blade, you can see or roll back the policy setting you just applied:

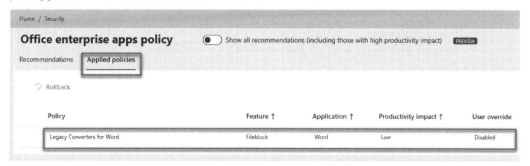

Figure 11.25 – Office enterprise apps policy – Applied policies

Enable **Show all recommendations (including those with high productivity impact)**:

Figure 11.26 – Office enterprise apps policy – Show all recommendations

You will get an overview of recommended policy settings and the productivity impact for your end users. This can help you make the right decision before changing the policy settings:

	Recommended policy	Feature ↑	Application ↑	Productivity impact ↓	Confidence ↑
New!	Office Open XML Converters for Word	Fileblock	Word	100% of users in group	High
New!	Excel 2007 and later Binary Workbooks	Fileblock	Excel	100% of users in group	High
Preview	Only trust VBA macros signed using V3 signatures	VBA	Office	0% of users in group	High
New!	Legacy Converters for Word	Fileblock	Word	0% of users in group	High

Figure 11.27 – Office enterprise apps policy – Recommended policy

You will also see policy recommendations that have a high user impact, in this case, **100% of users in group**.

Summary

This concludes the last of the chapters relating to policy management in this book. In the chapter, you've learned about the Office cloud policy service, which you can use either from its management portal or from within Microsoft Intune. Office cloud policies apply to all kinds of endpoint, including Windows (both desktop and Windows 365), macOS, iOS, and Android. The last three OS types are not covered in this book, but it is important to know that the Office cloud policy service works on multiple OSes, not only on Windows. One point to take away from this chapter is that Office cloud policies only apply in the user context, which means that you are not able to set policies that only exist at the device level at this point in time.

In the next chapter, you will learn about the different tools that are available for profile management.

Questions

1. What is the Office cloud policy service?

    A. An on-premises service

    B. A set of group policies

    C. A cloud service that helps you configure policies for Microsoft 365 apps

    D. A service for configuring Microsoft Edge

2. Can you configure Office cloud policy services from the Microsoft Endpoint Manager admin center?

    A. Yes

    B. No

3. Can you configure Office 2016 with the Office cloud policy service?

    A. Yes

    B. No

Answers

1. (C)
2. (A)
3. (B)

Further reading

If you want to learn more after reading this chapter, please use the following free online resource:

-   Overview of the Office cloud policy service for Microsoft 365 Apps for enterprise: `https://docs.microsoft.com/en-us/deployoffice/overview-office-cloud-policy-service`

12
User Profile Management

Profile management is a very important factor in ensuring a good user experience. Your Windows profiles contain a baseline of settings to make your Windows 10 experience personal. Therefore, it's very important to use technology that meets your needs to make sure that the same experience you have on Windows follows you on your other devices and endpoints too.

Luckily, with cloud services, profile management is a lot easier these days – thanks to services such as **Azure Active Directory** (**Azure AD**), OneDrive, and Microsoft Edge, it's almost a piece of cake!

After this chapter, you will know everything about the configuration of modern profile management on both physical and cloud endpoints.

In this chapter, we'll go through the following topics:

- Windows profiles
- **Enterprise State Roaming** (**ESR**)
- Microsoft Office's roaming settings
- OneDrive for Business Known Folder Move

- Microsoft Edge
- ESR + OneDrive + Edge + Office

Windows profiles

The Windows profile is a very important component of Windows 10 Enterprise.

There are different types of profiles that you could use within your desktop environment. The first, local user profiles, is mostly used as part of Microsoft Endpoint Manager. To modernize it, we will be adding cloud services to the profile (explained later).

The other versions were used in the past to simplify the profile. Let's see some more details about the different profile versions used as part of Microsoft Endpoint Manager:

- **Local user profiles**: These are user profiles stored locally on the OS disk and created when you log on to Windows 10 Enterprise for the first time. Everything stored in the local profile is specific to the user and not to the computer. Local profiles are the solution that we use within both physical endpoints and Windows 365.

- **Temporary user profiles**: A temporary profile is issued in case of a profile error, with the temporary profile being used to avoid the user loading a new empty profile that overwrites the existing one. Temporary profiles are flushed after the user logs on as a safety mechanism. Temporary profiles are only used in error scenarios when your normal local profile cannot be loaded.

Profile types we don't recommend using at the time of writing this book are roaming and mandatory profiles:

- **Roaming user profiles**: This is a relatively old technology that makes it possible to replicate your local profile during logon and logoff to a central file server share. This profile copy process is file-based and can drag out the duration of the logon process for the user when the profile is large in size. With Office 365 services being used with caching enabled, this technology isn't the best option. Local profiles are the best solution as an alternative when you are the owner of the physical or cloud endpoint – as a persistent end user experience.

- **Mandatory user profiles**: A mandatory profile is a template of a local profile with many custom settings or modifications applied. Every time the user logs on, a new Windows local profile is created based on this mandatory profile template. This makes it possible to provide a consistent and brand-new profile experience for the end user. Profile settings are not saved after logging off. Therefore, this profile type is only applicable in non-persistent use cases.

Here's a list of the high-level differences of the current profile management options available while writing this book. Some will be explained more deeply in this chapter:

Technology	Modern settings	Win32 settings	OS settings	User data	Browser settings and cache
Enterprise State Roaming (ESR)	Yes	No	Yes	No	Yes
OneDrive	No	No	No	Yes	No
Microsoft Edge	No	No	No	No	Yes
Roaming profiles	No	Yes	Yes	Yes	Yes

Modern profile management

While profile management is one of the most important factors in successfully creating a good user experience, it's also important to simplify the processes around profile management.

As you've learned earlier in the book, Windows 365 Cloud PCs are personal desktops with the same capabilities as you would find on a physical desktop. Therefore, we don't use FSLogix Profile Container, as this is designed for non-persistent environments most likely based on multi-session OSes. In traditional **Virtual Desktop Infrastructure** (**VDI**) deployments, all kinds of complex solutions are used to match the physical and virtual worlds together. With the Windows 365 Cloud PC, we don't have this challenge as we work with native local profiles and leverage other technology to modernize our user profile while also making our personal documents available across all our devices.

Enterprise State Roaming

ESR provides users with a unified experience across their Windows devices and reduces the time needed to configure a new device.

To be more specific, ESR offers the following:

- **ESR separates your corporate and consumer data**: You as a business are in control of your corporate data; ESR does not sync end user personal data into the Azure cloud.

- **Highly secure**: The profile data being synced to Azure with ESR is automatically encrypted while sending it to the Azure cloud from your Windows device. Once your settings are synced to the cloud, the data remains encrypted.

- **Simplified management and monitoring**: Provide easy access, control, and visibility of who is able to sync their Windows profile settings to ESR and who isn't. In the Azure portal, you can filter access based on Azure AD groups.

When you have a mixture of physical and virtual devices in your environment, ESR could be utilized to transfer parts of your profile across your devices for a unified profile settings experience. See the following screenshot for how to activate the setting for all your users or for a selected (Azure AD) group of people:

Figure 12.1 – ESR settings

What specific profile data is included in ESR?

Here's a list of profile settings for the Azure AD users that are stored within the ESR data and that will be restored every time the user logs on to a clean Windows 10 Enterprise device to provide a unified experience:

Profile component	Description
Windows themes	Your desktop themes and taskbar settings are saved.
Language settings	Keyboard layouts, system language, date and time settings, and more.
Cached password	Your passwords are stored in both Windows and your browsers.
Ease of access features	High-contrast theme preferences and Narrator and Magnifier settings are saved.
Other Windows settings	Mouse properties and settings are saved.

Once you enable ESR, log on to your Windows 10 Enterprise desktop and open **Accounts** under the **Settings** menu. You'll see all the activated settings synced as part of your Windows profile!

It's pretty common that you as an IT admin create a policy that enforces the following settings, so end users cannot disable the settings. This would ensure that the profile settings data is always safely stored in the Microsoft cloud:

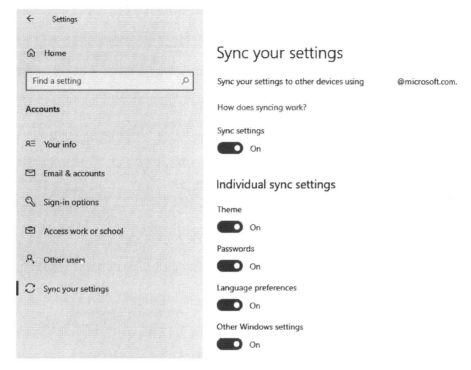

Figure 12.2 – ESR settings in Windows

In the next section, we will explain more about how Microsoft Office products automatically synchronize settings to the cloud for a seamless end user experience.

Microsoft Office's roaming settings

Office's roaming feature enables experiences across Microsoft 365 apps and devices to improve productivity and make Office more personalized to you across any device. Some examples of settings and features are the list of most recently used files, the last reading position in a document, the first-run experience for Office add-in, autocorrect preferences, and themes.

Here's the full list of settings:

- Most recently used files (all apps)
- Most recently used locations (all apps)

- Most recently used templates (all apps)
- Custom dictionary
- Outlook signature
- Office personalization
- Word's Resume Reading feature
- PowerPoint's Last Viewed Slide feature
- Mounted services
- OneNote notebook name
- Visio device settings

The roaming feature is another layer on top of local profiles to ensure you have a unified user experience and consistent data access across your Windows 10 Enterprise devices, whether you are using a physical or Cloud PCs endpoint:

Figure 12.3 – Word's Recent documents pane

In the next section, we explain how Outlook signatures can be synced to the cloud.

Outlook's signature cloud settings

Another cool new enhancement provided by Office's roaming feature is the ability to store your Outlook settings on the cloud as part of your Azure AD/Office 365 account. We explained in the previous section the different Office services, such as most recently used files, and the other components that are saved.

One of the Outlook settings that has been a challenge for a while is Outlook signatures. This has now been fixed as signature settings are stored in the cloud, so your experience is consistent when you access Outlook for Windows on any computer.

To enable this feature, you simply open the **Outlook Options** menu, followed by choosing **General**. On this pane, you check the box next to **Store my Outlook settings in the cloud**.

Your Outlook signature will now follow you, even after a local profile reset, which is pretty cool, right?

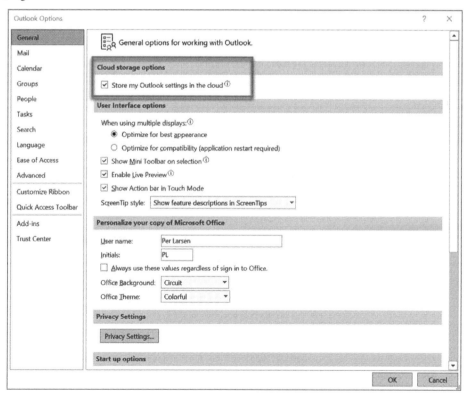

Figure 12.4 – Outlook's cloud storage options

In the next section, you will learn about OneDrive for Business **Known Folder Move** (**KFM**).

OneDrive for Business Known Folder Move

OneDrive for Business KFM is a simple way to back up your important folders (the **Desktop**, **Documents**, and **Pictures** folders) within your virtual Windows 365 PC, so they're protected and available on other devices without any user interaction required.

OneDrive PC folder backup is **enabled by default on Windows 365** and is therefore an easy way to continue your work on other devices, such as your physical endpoint or mobile device, as all the folders will instantly become available on those devices too.

With OneDrive Files On-Demand enabled by default, the storage allocation within your Cloud PC profile will also be low, as this feature within OneDrive gives you access to your files without taking up storage space on your computer.

As part of Windows 365, OneDrive is silently configured, and PC folder backup (KFM) is also activated by default to ensure your data for business continuity and disaster recovery purposes with your Windows 10/11 Enterprise desktop environment.

You can find the OneDrive KFM setting in the OneDrive client installed on your Windows device to sync your **Desktop**, **Documents**, and **Pictures** folders to the OneDrive cloud, as follows:

Manage folder backup

These folders are syncing in OneDrive. New and existing files will be added to OneDrive, backed up, and available on your other devices, even if you lose this PC.

Desktop	Documents	Pictures
Files backed up	Files backed up	Files backed up
Stop backup	Stop backup	Stop backup

Space left in OneDrive after selection: 4,639 GB

Figure 12.5 – OneDrive KFM

Important note

The setting shown in the following screenshot allows you to configure OneDrive PC folder backup silently on your Windows 10 Enterprise endpoints. As you can see, it's relatively easy...

As a side note, there is a new error message built into OneDrive to warn you about deleting files locally on your PC while using KFM. Luckily, the files are automatically backed up into the Recycle Bin for 30 days. So, no worries at all.

When you want to use this setting on your Windows 10 Enterprise endpoints, please activate the following option directly in Microsoft Endpoint Manager as a policy setting:

Figure 12.6 – Excluding OneDrive files and extensions from syncing

If you accidentally delete a file in your Windows profile, OneDrive automatically takes a file snapshot – and will always provide the option to restore within the next 30 days. See the following new message that appears:

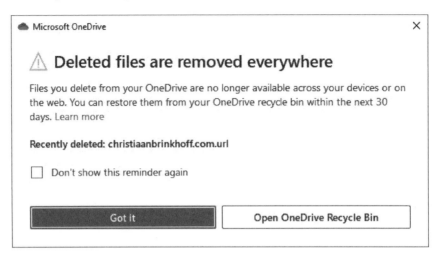

Figure 12.7 – The new prompt for accidentally deleted files in OneDrive

In the next section, we will explain how you can carry out maintenance and cleanup actions on your OneDrive cache from Windows.

Windows 10 Storage Sense

Windows 10 Storage Sense works with OneDrive to automatically free up space by taking locally available OneDrive files that you haven't used recently and making them online-only again.

Any files you haven't used in the last 30 days can be set to online-only when your device runs low on free space. You will also be able to schedule and define how often Storage Sense should run:

Figure 12.8 – Storage Sense

OneDrive and Storage Sense

With Storage Sense, you are able to silently assist your Windows device in managing your storage, for example, to free up OneDrive caching space. OneDrive uses Files On-Demand to sync only the necessary data to your endpoint. As OneDrive caches the data locally, you might want to free up this caching space after a while. Storage Sense makes it possible to do this in line with your business preferences.

OneDrive data always remains visible inside your profile, and only has to be downloaded again if you need to access it again and make changes.

You can find Storage Sense in the **System** settings menu of Windows, under **Storage**. You can clean up data with the dropdown under **Content will become online-only if not opened for more than**:

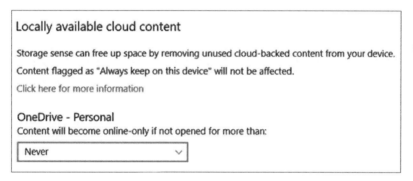

Figure 12.9 – Cleaning the cache

You could also do this only in the event of low space on the OS disk – in case of emergency:

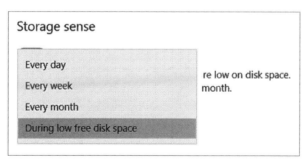

Figure 12.10 – Clean up schedules

You could also use the feature to clean up your **Downloads** folder within your Windows profile. This is also very handy:

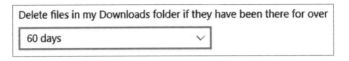

Figure 12.11 – Downloads folder cleanup

Microsoft Edge

Microsoft Edge is more and more becoming the mainstream browser for the vast majority of users. This is the result of hard work by the Edge engineering team within Microsoft as many features have been added lately to address customer feedback and make Edge ready for enterprise adoption.

In the context of profile management, Microsoft Edge offers great things as well, because it supports the synchronization of all your browser-related data as part of your Azure AD credentials. This means that your history, favorites, password collections, settings, extensions, and open tabs will be stored for you in the Microsoft cloud.

For example, you can have OneDrive KFM configured for your profile-related data inside your Windows profile to redirect your **Documents**, **Pictures**, and **Desktop** folders as a backup layer – and Edge does the same thing with your browser settings. Also, it's important to note that the Edge browser-specific profile data is shared across all your devices that use Edge as the browser. Imagine switching from your physical or virtual endpoint to your Surface Duo or iPhone and continuing where you left off.

During the initial configuration process, or at the first launch of Edge, you'll be asked to log on with your Azure AD credentials. After that, it'll ask you to sync your profile. After this first launch, it'll now start saving your Edge profile data – from the second time you launch Edge, all your browser settings will be pre-loaded, and your Edge browser will look and feel exactly the same as on your other devices.

You could also pre-set silent logons and auto-sync activation within Edge using group policies to enforce this setting to ensure profile synchronization.

The setting to enable profile syncing manually in Edge looks as in the following screenshot:

Figure 12.12 – Edge profile sync option

The following Edge-specific profile data will synchronize automatically after enabling the sync setting:

- Favorites

- Passwords

- Form-fill data

- History

- Open tabs (sessions)

- Settings (preferences)

- Extensions

Another option to highlight is the use of multiple profiles. For example, say you have your personal account for private usage, and your business account. You can simply create another profile and the personal profile will be completely isolated from the other one. Say goodbye to the limit of opening only one private mode session, or other browsers that you only use for this reason.

You can also use the **Browse as a guest** option to use an isolated session without profile creation when you prefer not to save it to the online profile storage of your Azure AD account credential.

As you can see in the following screenshot, the **Sync is on** status is green, meaning that my Edge-related profile settings and data are being synchronized as explained previously:

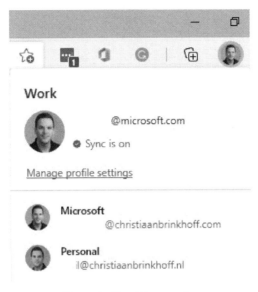

Figure 12.13 – Edge syncing

Now, let's go ahead and understand how we can use some cloud-related sync services to our advantage.

ESR + OneDrive + Edge + Office

Throughout the journey of modernizing your Windows profiles as part of your Windows 10 Enterprise devices, you want to leverage as many of the cloud-related sync services as possible to ensure user data and settings are being roamed. This is what you can do with the combination of all the different products outlined in the preceding sections.

With all three products activated in your environment, you can ensure that the profile components shown in the following diagram are synced and saved to ensure a unified experience across multiple devices.

ESR and Microsoft Edge will take care of your Windows and browser-related settings while OneDrive syncs your **Documents**, **Pictures**, and **Desktop** folders directly to the cloud:

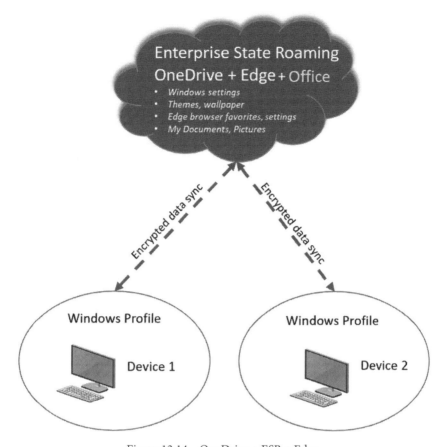

Figure 12.14 – OneDrive + ESR + Edge

Migrating from legacy to modern profile management

All the sections in this chapter explained how you could modernize your profile management configuration as part of your physical or cloud endpoint.

The ease of configuring everything also applies to the migration paths from any other profile management solution, whether that's roaming profiles or any other solution on the market.

The steps to perform on your legacy environment before migrating are as follows:

1. If you are working on a roaming profile, the only thing you must do is activate OneDrive PC folder backup (KFM) and ESR, and make sure that Edge and OneDrive silent configuration is turned on.

2. When you configure this on top of your existing profile solution, the syncing of data will happen while your users remain working on the existing solution.

3. The IT admin can then (after successfully configuring all the modern parts) schedule a cutover moment to remove the roaming profile elements and continue using local profiles instead. This approach also applies to FSLogix.

This could be an option to choose when you currently use a traditional VDI solution and want to leverage Windows 365, but also when you use Endpoint Configuration Manager or any other management solution for physical endpoint management and want to migrate them to physical endpoints managed by Microsoft Endpoint Manager.

Summary

In the chapter, you've learned about all the different options to modernize and optimize your Windows profile with products such as OneDrive and Microsoft Edge as part of your Windows 10 Enterprise environment.

In the next chapter, we're going to explain everything about the world of identity and security management.

Questions

1. What is the name of the feature that allows you to redirect your profile folders within OneDrive?

    A. PC folder backup

    B. Folder snapshot

    C. Folder copy

    D. OneDrive profile backup

2. What is the main benefit of using Edge in the context of modernizing your Windows profile?

    A. Edge can be enrolled via Microsoft Endpoint Manager.

    B. It is included by default in Windows 10 Enterprise and therefore doesn't require installation inside your Windows profile.

    C. Edge supports the synchronization of your Edge profile-related data, including your favorites, history, and password cache.

Answers

1. (A)
2. (C)

Further reading

If you want to learn more about Windows profiles after reading this chapter, please consult the following free online resources:

- Enterprise State Roaming FAQ – Azure Active Directory | Microsoft Docs: `https://docs.microsoft.com/en-us/azure/active-directory/devices/enterprise-state-roaming-faqs`

- Microsoft Edge and Enterprise State Roaming | Microsoft Docs: `https://docs.microsoft.com/en-us/deployedge/microsoft-edge-enterprise-state-roaming`

13
Identity and Security Management

In this chapter, you will learn everything about **Azure Active Directory** (**AAD**) and security. We will cover the history of AAD and the different security aspects that you can configure to secure your Windows 10 Enterprise devices within your organization.

In this chapter, we'll go through the following topics:

- Microsoft Identity
- AAD
- Users and groups
- Hybrid AAD
- Conditional Access
- BitLocker disk encryption
- Self-service password reset
- AAD password protection
- Password-less authentication
- What is and isn't supported in each password-less scenario
- Microsoft Defender for Endpoint

Microsoft Identity

Active Directory Domain Services (**AD DS**) has been on the market since the year 2000. As some of you might remember, it arrived with the first release of Windows 2000 Server.

The way it works is, you join your Windows client or server devices to **Active Directory** (**AD**) to take over the management layer of it via either group policies or security settings, or you use it to chain different AD environments to each other to delegate organization permissions to resources that are stored in a different AD environment – in different forests.

Within the context of **Microsoft Endpoint Manager** (**MEM**), it's possible to connect to Windows devices that are both AD DS- and AAD-joined. Devices that are joined to AD DS and need to become available in AAD as well are known as **hybrid AAD-joined** (**HAADJ**). Before your business is ready to work natively in AAD, hybrid AAD might be the best option to use as an interim solution. Let's talk more about this in the next sections of this chapter.

If your devices are enrolled into AAD directly and listed in **All Devices** within MEM, you can see the AAD domain properties in your Windows 10 Enterprise **Settings** menu.

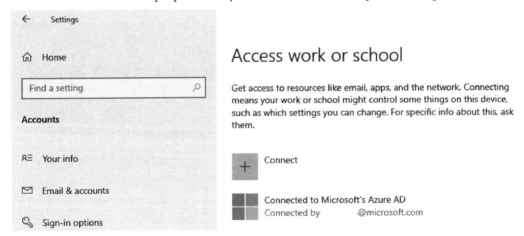

Figure 13.1 – Access work or school

Devices can be in different states, but common for them all is that you can see them in the settings app under **Accounts | Access work or school**.

Let's look at AAD next.

AAD

AAD provides **single sign-on (SSO)** and **multi-factor authentication (MFA)** to Windows 10 Enterprise and MEM to help protect your users from 99.9 percent of cybersecurity attacks.

AAD is the evolution of traditional AD (AD DS) and makes it possible to do the following:

- SSO simplifies access to your apps from anywhere.

- Conditional Access and MFA help to protect your environment from outside intruders.

- As a single identity platform, it lets you engage with internal and external users more securely.

- Developer tools make it easy to integrate identity into your apps and services.

Let's look at AAD users next.

AAD users

AAD users include the account settings of a user in your organization and only live in the Microsoft Azure cloud. Creating and deleting users can be done by using either the AAD Global Administrator role or an account that has the account administrator **role-based access control (RBAC)** role assigned.

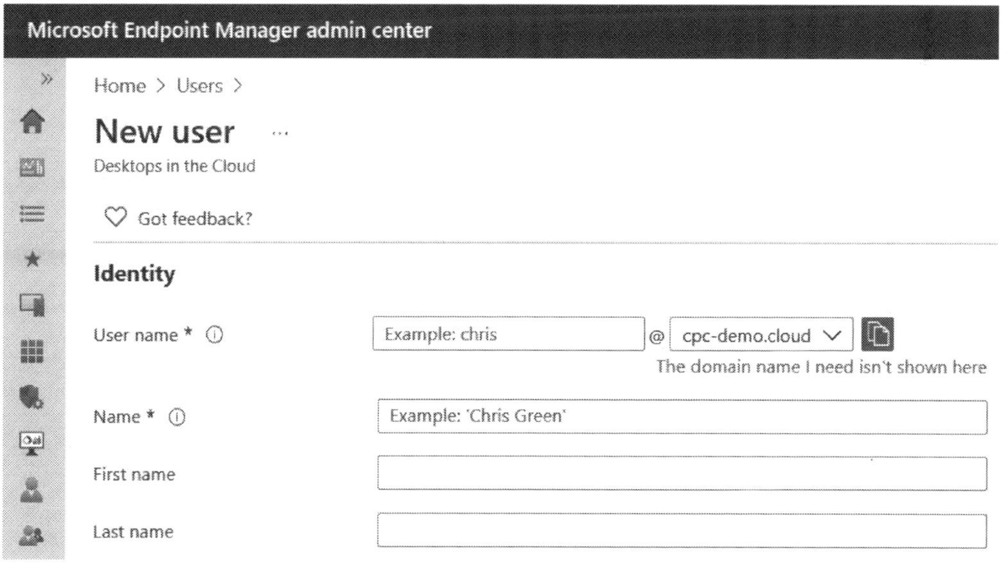

Figure 13.2 – New user in the MEM admin center

Creating new users directly in AAD is for cloud-only identities; hybrid identities still need to be created in the on-premises AD and synced to AAD with AD Connect. Let's look at AAD guest users next.

AAD guest users

Guest user accounts are designed to collaborate with other organizations outside of your AAD tenant environment without creating a normal AAD user account that contains your organization's domain. One example is to allow access to a SharePoint site. If an end user has permission to share documents in OneDrive for Business, it can also be done with a guest user.

Be aware that a guest user cannot enroll a device into AAD or Microsoft Intune.

In the **Create a new user** workflow, the IT admin can choose to invite a user instead of creating one in the corporate AAD, as seen in this workflow:

Figure 13.3 – Inviting guest users

In the **Invite user** workflow, the IT admin can also assign groups or roles in AAD. This means that a guest user can be assigned the role of Intune administrator, so you can give the role to an external consultant, as an example.

Let's look at different options for groups in AAD next.

AAD group types

There are two types of AAD groups, as follows:

- **Security**: This is the most commonly used type as it is used to add members to a group to gain access to a folder share, applications, RBAC, a security policy, or a cloud desktop environment.

- **Microsoft 365**: This is the group type used within other Microsoft cloud services, such as Exchange Online and SharePoint, to collaborate better. This group type also allows customers to share access to members outside the organization's AAD tenant environment.

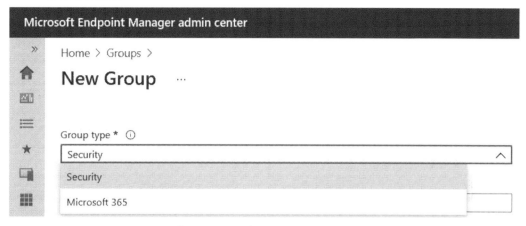

Figure 13.4 – Creating a new group

Security groups can be used for both users and devices but not a mix. Next, we will look at the different membership types.

AAD membership types

In the previous section, we explained the differences in types of AAD groups. There are three ways to make users or devices members of an AAD group:

- **Assigned**: This is the most common way of assigning access to a specific group. You add specific users to an AAD group to gain access, for example, to a security policy.

- **Dynamic user**: This type makes it possible to automatically add users to a group based on conditions that you define. There is no interaction needed to add – as well as remove – the users to the AAD group when the user no longer meets the requirements to be part of the group.

- **Dynamic device**: This type is somewhat the same as the dynamic user membership type; however, now it is used to automatically add or remove devices from the AAD group.

Pick the type that fits your use case best, as dynamic membership could provide a more scalable method for larger organizations. Dynamic groups are only supported as either the user or device type – not both.

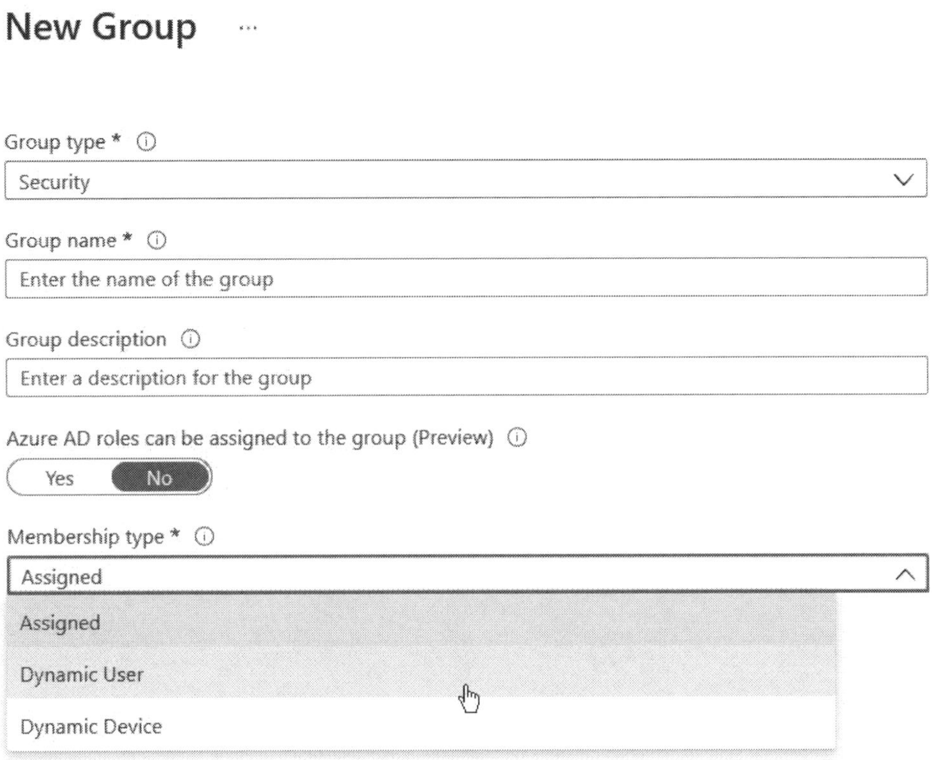

New Group   ···

Group type * ⓘ

Security	∨

Group name * ⓘ

Enter the name of the group

Group description ⓘ

Enter a description for the group

Azure AD roles can be assigned to the group (Preview) ⓘ

(Yes   **No**)

Membership type * ⓘ

Assigned	∧

Assigned
Dynamic User
Dynamic Device

Figure 13.5 – Creating a new group

Within the dynamic membership rules, you can create complex attribute-based rules to enable dynamic membership for groups, which you could use to add and remove users from the AAD group.

For example, you can add all users that have `@contoso.com` as `proxyAddresses` configured in AAD automatically by adding the following rule. You can imagine that any number of options will be available through this approach.

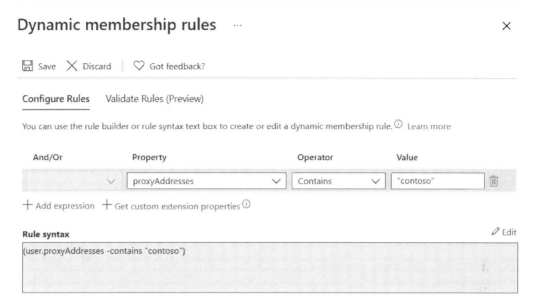

Figure 13.6 – Dynamic membership rules

You can easily test the expressions as well with the **Validate Rules** option now. If the validation turns red, it means that the user isn't part of the allowed filtering property and therefore will not be added to the AAD group dynamically:

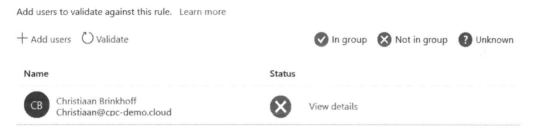

Figure 13.7 – Dynamic rule validation

Dynamic groups can help you be more agile in your Microsoft Intune assignment. Dynamic devices have several attributes that can help group similar device types as one example.

Next, we will look at hybrid AAD and why it can be important.

Hybrid AAD

Devices that are HAADJ are part of your organization and are signed in with an AD (AD DS) account belonging to the organization. They exist in the cloud and on-premises to make the translation possible between traditional AD DS and AAD. This is needed for different scenarios within MEM as well as *Windows 365*.

To use hybrid AAD, you must replicate your on-premises environment to bring/sync your identities and devices to AAD. You do that with the Microsoft AAD Connect software.

The software has been built on **Microsoft Identity Management (MIM)** and is preconfigured with all the configuration items to replicate your on-premises users, groups, and devices to AAD.

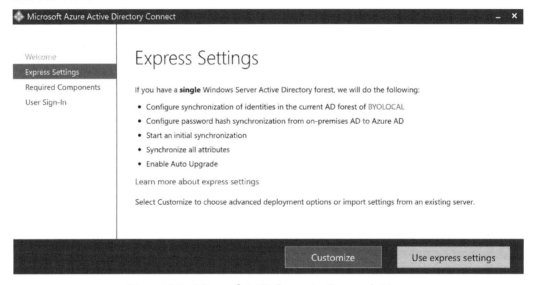

Figure 13.8 – Microsoft AAD Connect – Express Settings

If you have configured AAD Connect in the past, you must change the configuration to HAADJ for services such as Windows 365. Hybrid AAD could also be beneficial in the following alternative scenarios:

- You have Win32 apps deployed to these devices that rely on AD machine authentication.

- You want to continue to use Group Policy to manage device configuration.

- You want to continue to use existing imaging solutions to deploy and configure devices.

- You must support down-level Windows 7 and 8.1 devices in addition to Windows 13.

Make sure that the server where you configure AAD Connect – HAADJ – can connect to all the following URLs:

- `https://enterpriseregistration.windows.net`
- `https://login.microsoftonline.com`
- `https://device.login.microsoftonline.com`
- `https://autologon.microsoftazuread-sso.com`

Follow these steps to align with the prerequisites of the service. For physical PCs, do the following:

1. Go to your AAD Connect server, most likely running on-premises in your own private cloud data center environment.
2. Open the Microsoft AAD Connect program.
3. Open the **Configure device options** task.

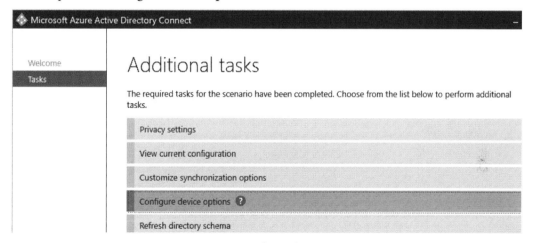

Figure 13.9 – Configure device options

4. Verify that you are the owner of this AAD tenant by logging on with your
    organization's Global Administrator account.

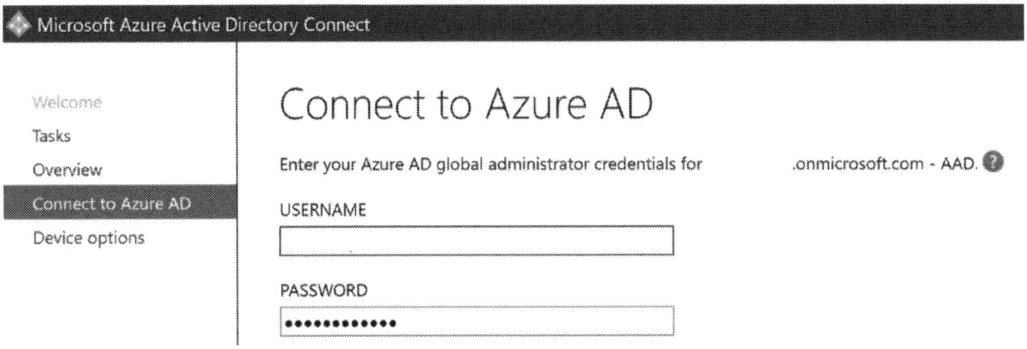

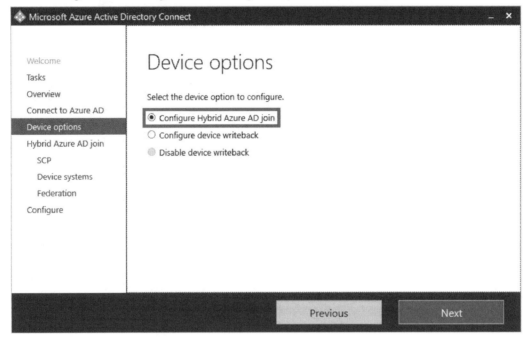

Figure 13.10 – Connecting to AAD

5. After that is done, you will be asked to change the device options of your AAD
    configuration. Change this to **Configure Hybrid Azure AD join**.

Figure 13.11 – Configure Hybrid Azure AD join

6. Make sure to select the **Windows 10 or later domain-joined devices** option.

Figure 13.12 – Device OSes

7. After clicking **Next**, you must configure the **service connection point** (**SCP**) to your AD forest.

    You must click on the green **Add** button to add the right Enterprise Administrator credentials of your on-premises AD to the AAD authentication service.

Figure 13.13 – SCP configuration

8. Once done, click the **Next** button.

    You are now ready to change your AAD Connect configuration to a hybrid AAD.

9. Click **Configure** to start the configuration.

Next, let's read about Conditional Access.

Conditional Access

Conditional Access is the tool used by AAD to bring signals together, make decisions, and enforce organizational policies. It is at the heart of the new identity-driven control plane.

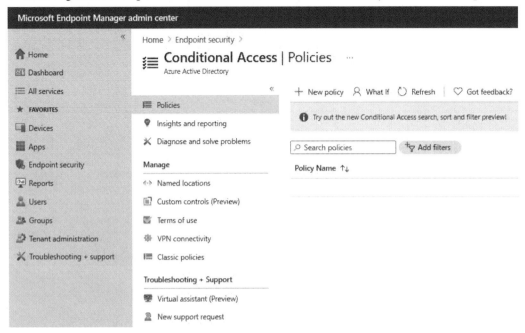

Figure 13.14 – Conditional Access

Administrators must have two primary goals:

- Empower users to be productive wherever and whenever.
- Protect the organization's assets.

You can apply the right access controls when needed to keep your organization secure and stay out of your users' way when not needed with the help of Conditional Access policies.

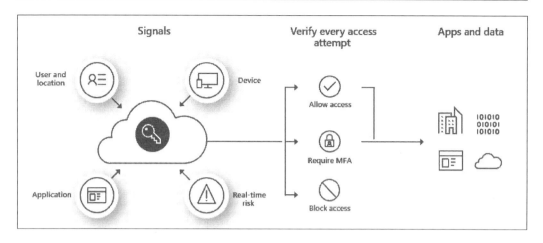

Figure 13.15 – Conditional Access workflow

Next, we will look at user and group scoping in a Conditional Access policy.

Users and groups

Conditional Access allows you to control user access based on user and group assignments. The creation of a Conditional Access policy starts with filtering based on the following conditions:

- **None**
- **All users**
- **Select users and groups**:
    - **All guest and external users**
    - **Directory roles**
    - **Users and groups**

The following screenshot is an example of configuring filters based on AAD groups:

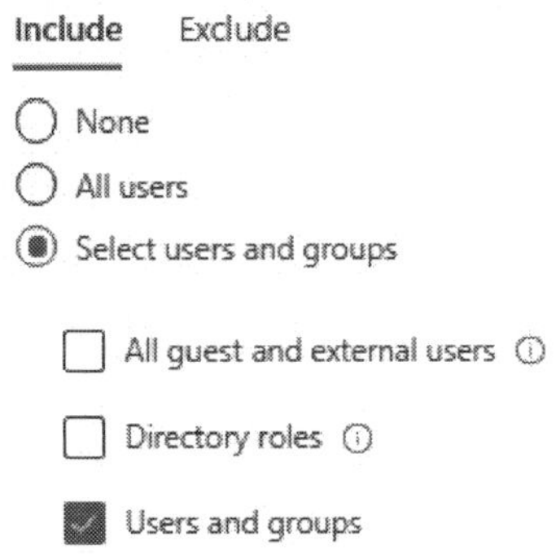

Figure 13.16 – Including users and groups

Including and excluding users and group assignments can be configured to fit the access control your company needs.

Next, we will look at cloud apps in a Conditional Access policy.

Cloud apps

Cloud apps are AAD Enterprise applications that represent the Microsoft cloud or third-party applications. This could be, for example, Windows 365, a **Software as a Service (SaaS)** application, or Office 365 services.

To enforce different Conditional Access settings per cloud app(s), you can create different policies that only apply to that specific application to customize access:

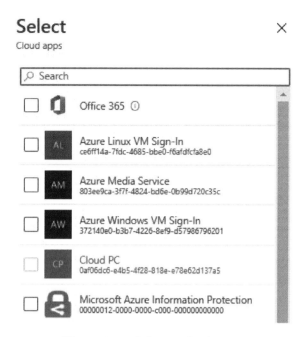

Figure 13.17 – Selecting cloud apps

Cloud apps most likely are named after the service; otherwise, you have to select them according to the right app ID, such as `0af06dc6-e4b5-4f28-818e-e78e62d137a5`.

Aside from filtering on cloud apps, you could also apply Conditional Access settings during actions, for example, the process of registering and joining devices to MEM. You must then select user actions instead of cloud apps:

- **Register security information**
- **Register or join devices**

Control user access based on all or specific cloud apps or actions. Learn more

Select what this policy applies to

User actions ⌄

Select the action this policy will apply to

☐ Register security information

☐ Register or join devices

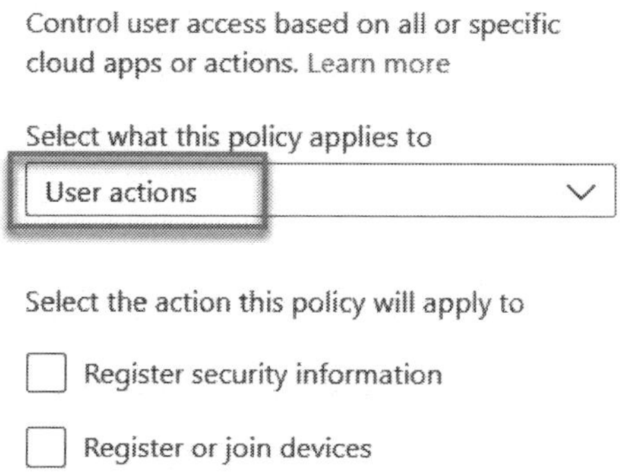

Figure 13.18 – User actions

Next, we will look at conditions in a Conditional Access policy.

Conditions

There are four different types of conditions to configure:

- **Device platforms**: Control user access from different device platforms; for example, this policy should only apply when users log on from Android, Windows, macOS, iOS, or a Windows phone.

Figure 13.19 – Including/excluding a platform

- **Locations**: Control user access based on their physical location, for example, based on public IP allow-listing.

Figure 13.20 – Include/exclude locations

You can configure IP authorization – IP lists in Conditional Access – in the **Named locations** menu.

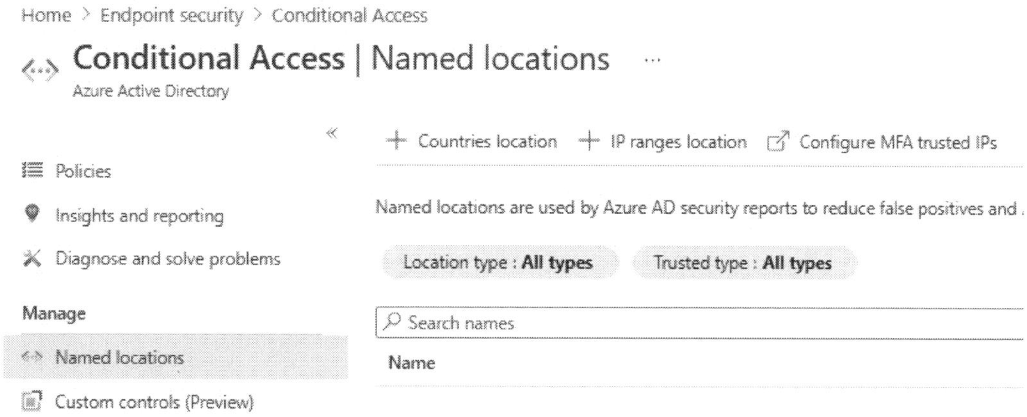

Home > Endpoint security > Conditional Access

Conditional Access | Named locations   ...
Azure Active Directory

+ Countries location   + IP ranges location   ☑ Configure MFA trusted IPs

▤ Policies

Named locations are used by Azure AD security reports to reduce false positives and .

♥ Insights and reporting

✕ Diagnose and solve problems

Location type : **All types**   Trusted type : **All types**

Manage

⌕ Search names

⟨·⟩ Named locations

Name

⊠ Custom controls (Preview)

Figure 13.21 – Conditional Access – Named locations

- **Client apps**: Control user access to target specific client applications not using modern authentication.

Select the client apps this policy will apply to

Modern authentication clients

☑ Browser

☑ Mobile apps and desktop clients

Legacy authentication clients

☑ Exchange ActiveSync clients ⓘ

☑ Other clients ⓘ

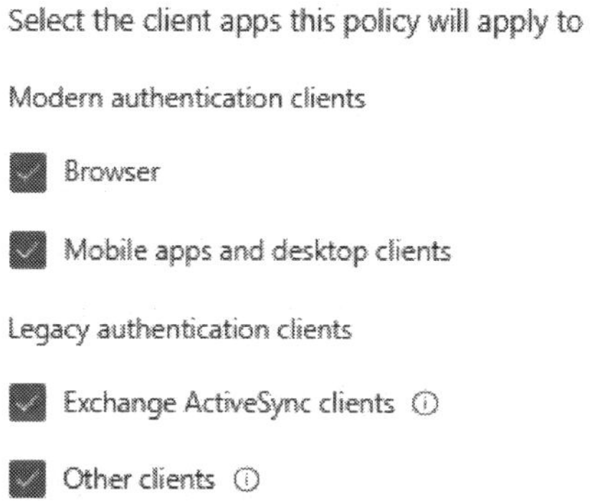

Figure 13.22 – Select the client apps this policy will apply to

- **Device state (preview)**: Control user access when the device the user is signing in from is not HAADJ or marked as compliant.

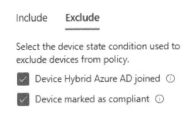

Figure 13.23 – Excluding a device state

After assignments have been configured, you can continue to the access control.

Grant

You can select the following options as Conditional Access grant settings, of which MFA is the most common one to use:

- **Require MFA**: Users must complete additional security requirements such as a phone call or text.

- **Require device to be marked as compliant**: Device must be Intune-compliant. If the device is non-compliant, the user will be prompted to bring the device under compliance.

- **Require HAADJ device**: Devices must be HAADJ to get access.

- **Require approved client app**: Device must use these approved client applications.

- **Require app protection policy**: The devices that you connect from must use policy-protected apps.

You could also select multiple controls, to force either multiple requirement options or one of multiple options, to provide access if multiple endpoint scenarios apply:

- **Require all the selected controls**

- **Require one of the selected controls**

> **Note**
> When selecting MFA and devices marked as compliant, you could lock yourself out, so please be careful!

Setting **Grant access** can be configured to have either all or some controls.

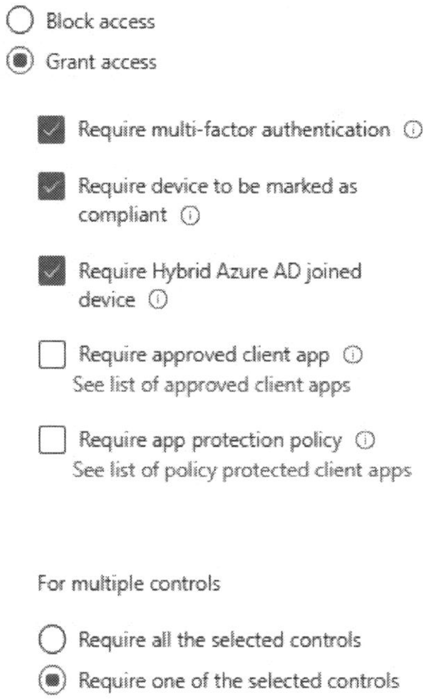

Figure 13.24 – Grant access

MFA should be mandatory; add other settings as you like, for example, controlling access from devices that aren't MEM-managed.

Control user access based on session controls to enable limited experiences within specific cloud applications:

- **Use app-enforced restrictions**: App-enforced restrictions might require additional admin configurations within cloud apps. The restrictions will only take effect for new sessions.

- **Access control settings**: Conditional Access App Control enables user app access and sessions to be monitored and controlled in real time based on access and session policies. Access and session policies are used within the cloud app security portal to further refine filters and set actions to be taken on a user.

- **Sign-in frequency**: This is the time period before a user is asked to sign in again when attempting to access a resource. The default setting is a rolling window of 90 days, that is, users will be asked to re-authenticate on the first attempt to access a resource after being inactive on their machine for 90 days or longer.

> **Tip**
> This setting could be beneficial in enforcing MFA every hour on **bring-your-own-device (BYOD)** devices to ensure that access expires after that time!

- **Persistent browser session**: A persistent browser session allows users to remain signed in after closing and reopening their browser window:

> **Note**
> Persistent browser session only works correctly when **All cloud apps** is selected

- This does not affect token lifetimes or the sign-in frequency setting.

- This will override the **Show option to stay signed in** policy on company branding.

- **Never persistent** will override any persistent SSO claims passed in from federated authentication services.

- **Never persistent** will prevent SSO on mobile devices across applications and between applications and the user's mobile browser.

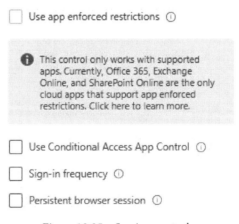

Figure 13.25 – Session control

This concludes the walk-through of the Conditional Access policies that you can configure to secure your corporate data. Next, we will show an option to prevent users from carrying out AAD device registration on their BYOD devices.

Preventing users from carrying out AAD device registration

To block your users from adding additional work accounts to your corporate domain-joined, AAD-joined, or HAADJ Windows 10 devices, enable the following registry key. This policy can also be used to block domain-joined machines from inadvertently getting AAD registered with the same user account: `HKLM\SOFTWARE\Policies\Microsoft\Windows\WorkplaceJoin`, `"BlockAADWorkplaceJoin"=dword:00000001`.

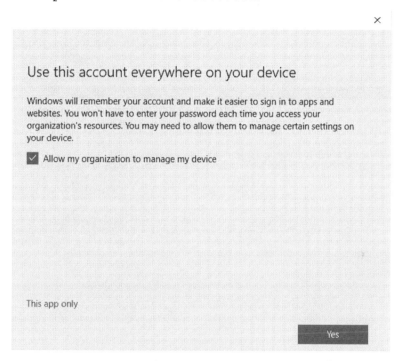

Figure 13.26 – Use this account everywhere on your device

There is no central way to prevent a user from registering their BYOD device in AAD. If AAD automatic MDM enrollment is configured and the checkmark for **Allow my organization to manage my device** is set, the device will be enrolled into Microsoft Intune. Next, we will take a look at **self-service password reset (SSPR)**.

Self-service password reset

The SSPR feature allows businesses to give users the ability to reset their own passwords without any interaction with the service desk. This could massively reduce the number of support tickets in your organization as most users can recover themselves.

When a user enters their password too many times incorrectly, the account will go into a locked state. With the SSPR service, the end user can then change the password and will be prompted for MFA during that process.

> **Note**
> Before users can unlock their account or reset a password, they must register their contact information.

SSPR requires an AAD Premium P1 license, which comes with Microsoft 365 E3 or higher.

You must go to AAD in the Azure portal (`https://portal.azure.com/#home`) to activate the feature.

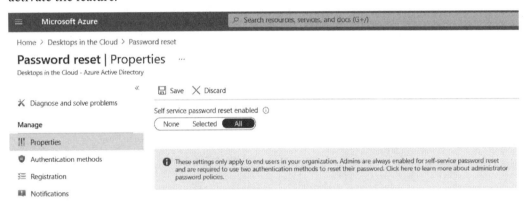

Figure 13.27 – Self service password reset enabled

It's also possible to make SSPR available for AAD group members only – via the **Selected** option in the menu.

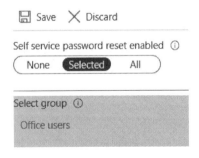

Figure 13.28 – Password reset – selecting a group for scoping

Next, we will take a look at AAD password protection.

AAD password protection

Azure MFA keeps most intruders out – and proactively prevents other people from getting access to your environment with only the password. This isn't enough, as there are more Microsoft services to leverage in order to secure your user accounts....

Avoid bad passwords with the AAD password protection feature. With AAD password protection, default global banned password lists are automatically applied to all users in an AAD tenant. You can define entries in a custom banned password list to support your own business and security needs.

Adding this feature would assure you, as an IT administrator, that the most common passwords – which are no different every year – stay in the past!

You can find the **Password protection** feature under **Authentication methods** in the Azure portal. You can also change the lockout thresholds here.

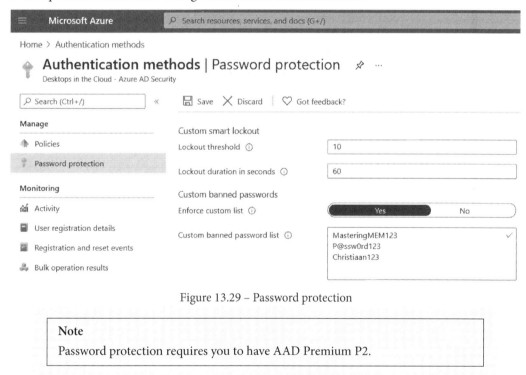

Figure 13.29 – Password protection

> **Note**
> Password protection requires you to have AAD Premium P2.

Next, we will look at password-less authentication.

Password-less authentication

While reading the previous section, you might have thought, what about password-less sign-in authentication? Good point!

Microsoft aims to make setting passwords easier; our strategy is a four-step approach where we deploy replacement offerings, reduce the password surface area, transition to password-less deployment, and finally, eliminate passwords.

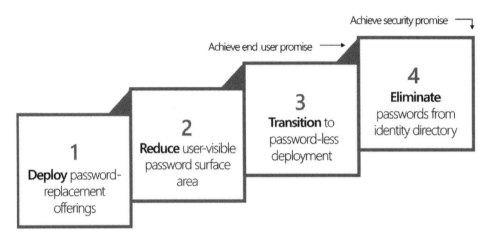

Figure 13.30 – Password-less phases

Password-less authentication is a way to log on to your Windows 10 Enterprise endpoint without entering your password. One of the most common approaches to do this is via a so-called YubiKey security key. You have them for USB-C, USB, and other devices, such as an Apple device. Other options are to use text messages or the Microsoft Authenticator app.

Figure 13.31 – YubiKey

Let's talk about the YubiKey. The end user experience looks very similar to how you normally log on to Windows. While you are normally logging on with either Windows Hello or your password, you can now select a USB key, as shown:

Figure 13.32 – Windows sign-in options

After that, Windows will ask you to inject the security key into the USB port that holds the passphrase to log on to your Windows 10 device without a password.

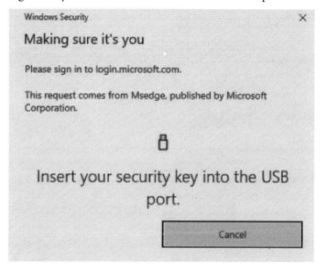

Figure 13.33 – FIDO2 authentication

First, you need to enable password-less authentication in your AAD tenant.

Enabling password-less authentication

To enable password-less authentication, you have to go to the Azure portal and open AAD. Then, follow these steps:

1. Go to **Security**.

2. Open **Authentication methods**.

3.   Under the **Manage** menu, select **Authentication methods**.

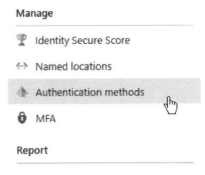

Figure 13.34 – Authentication methods

4.   Click on **FIDO2 Security Key**.

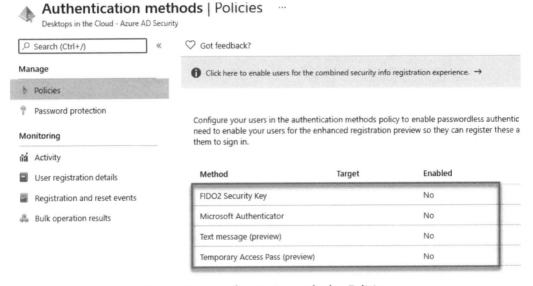

Figure 13.35 – Authentication methods – Policies

5. Enable the settings for (at least) sign-in and strong authentication.

ENABLE	TARGET			GENERAL
(Yes No)	(All users Select users)			Allow self-service set up
				(Yes No)
USE FOR:	Name	Type	Registratior	
• Sign in				Enforce attestation
• Strong authentication	All users	Group	Optional	(Yes No)

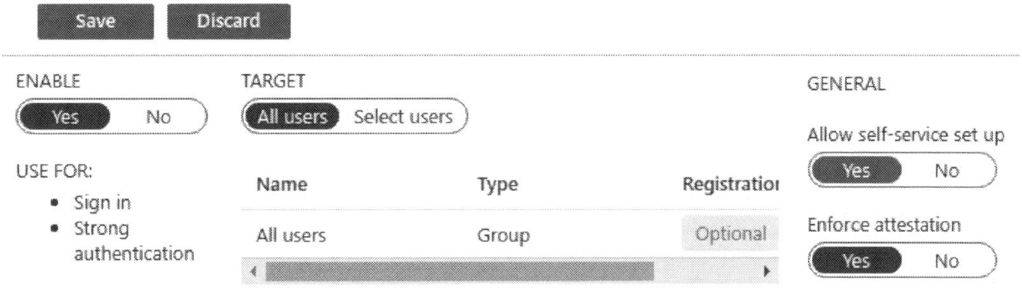

Figure 13.36 – FIDO2 security key configuration

You can also use a key restriction policy to specify what FIDO2 keys your end users can leverage in your tenant, by entering an allow or block list of devices with an **Authenticator Attestation GUID (AAGUID)**.

The FIDO2 specification requires each security key provider to provide an AAGUID during attestation. An AAGUID is a 128-bit identifier indicating the key type, such as the make and model.

You're now done with the prerequisites and are ready to use FIDO2 keys. You should see the following log-on screen for AAD while using password-less authentication via the Microsoft Authenticator mobile application, and all without entering the password.

← balas@contoso.com

Approve sign in

🛡 To sign in with balas@contoso.com, please follow the instructions on your phone and enter the number you see below.

69

Use your password instead

Figure 13.37 – Password-less sign-in

Password-less sign-in is more secure and the end user rarely has to enter their password anywhere.

Next, we will show a table of where the end user can leverage password-less sign-in.

What is and isn't supported in each password-less scenario

Microsoft's password-less authentication methods enable different scenarios. The organizational needs, prerequisites, and capabilities of each authentication method need to be considered before selecting your password-less authentication strategy.

> **Note**
> There is no additional cost for password-less authentication.

In the following table, you can see the options based on different scenarios:

Scenario	Phone authentication	Security keys	Windows Hello for Business
Computer sign-in: From an assigned Windows 10 device	No	Yes With biometric recognition and/or PIN	Yes With biometric recognition and or PIN
Computer sign-in: From a shared Windows 10 device	No	Yes With biometric recognition and/or PIN	No
Web app sign-in: From a user-dedicated computer	Yes	Yes Provided SSO to apps is enabled by computer sign-in	Yes Provided SSO to apps is enabled by computer sign-in
Web sign-in: From a mobile or non-Windows device	Yes	No	No
Computer sign-in: From a non-Windows computer	No	No	No

This concludes the section about password-less sign-on. Next, we will cover BitLocker disk encryption.

BitLocker disk encryption

BitLocker has been available since the first release of Windows Vista and gives the option to encrypt the drives attached to the endpoint. In most cases, BitLocker can work in conjunction with your endpoint that has a **Trusted Platform Module (TPM)** chip.

As long as you can authenticate to your device and you are not moving the OS disk out of the endpoint and exchanging it for another device, it's unlikely that you will ever need the BitLocker key that is associated with your device disk to decrypt everything. The help desk operator role will be able to access all the keys to restore:

1. To enable BitLocker for your Windows 10 or Windows 11 endpoints, you have to go to **Endpoint security**, followed by **Disk encryption**.

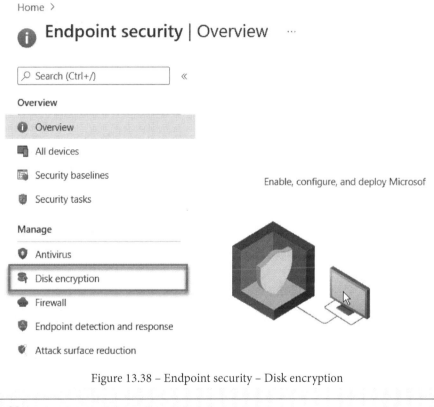

Figure 13.38 – Endpoint security – Disk encryption

> **Note**
> BitLocker is not supported on Windows 365 as of yet.

2. Click on **Create Policy**.

3. Select **Windows 10 and later** as the platform with **BitLocker** for **Profile**.

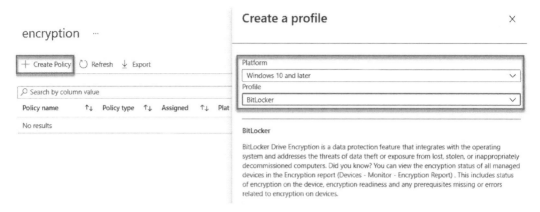

Figure 13.39 – BitLocker profile

4. Enter a name for the policy.

5. Change the BitLocker base settings to align them with your needs. Here's a rundown of what every setting means:

   - **Enable full disk encryption for OS and fixed data drives**: If not configured, no BitLocker enforcement will take place. If the drive was encrypted before this policy was applied, no extra action will be taken. If the encryption method and options match that of this policy, the configuration should return success.

   - **BitLocker fixed drive policy**: This policy setting is used to control the BitLocker for the fixed drive. The values of this policy determine the strength of the cipher that BitLocker uses for encryption.

   - **BitLocker system drive policy**: This policy setting is used to control BitLocker for the system drive. The values of this policy determine the strength of the cipher that BitLocker uses for encryption.

   - **BitLocker removable drive policy**: This policy setting is used to control BitLocker for the removal drive. The values of this policy determine the strength of the cipher that BitLocker uses for encryption.

Most likely, you want to enable full disk encryption for the OS and fixed drives, including potentially the rotation of the recovery password to increase security.

Consider the following best practices when configuring silent encryption on a Windows 10 device:

- Creating the BitLocker policy with the recommended settings.

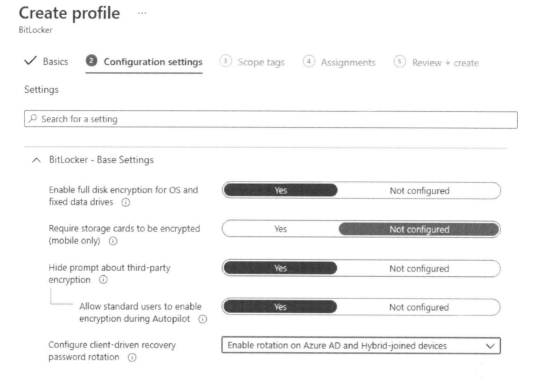

Figure 13.40 – Configuration settings

- In the **Fixed Drive** Settings and **OS Drive** Settings sections, you can adjust the base settings to make them stricter.

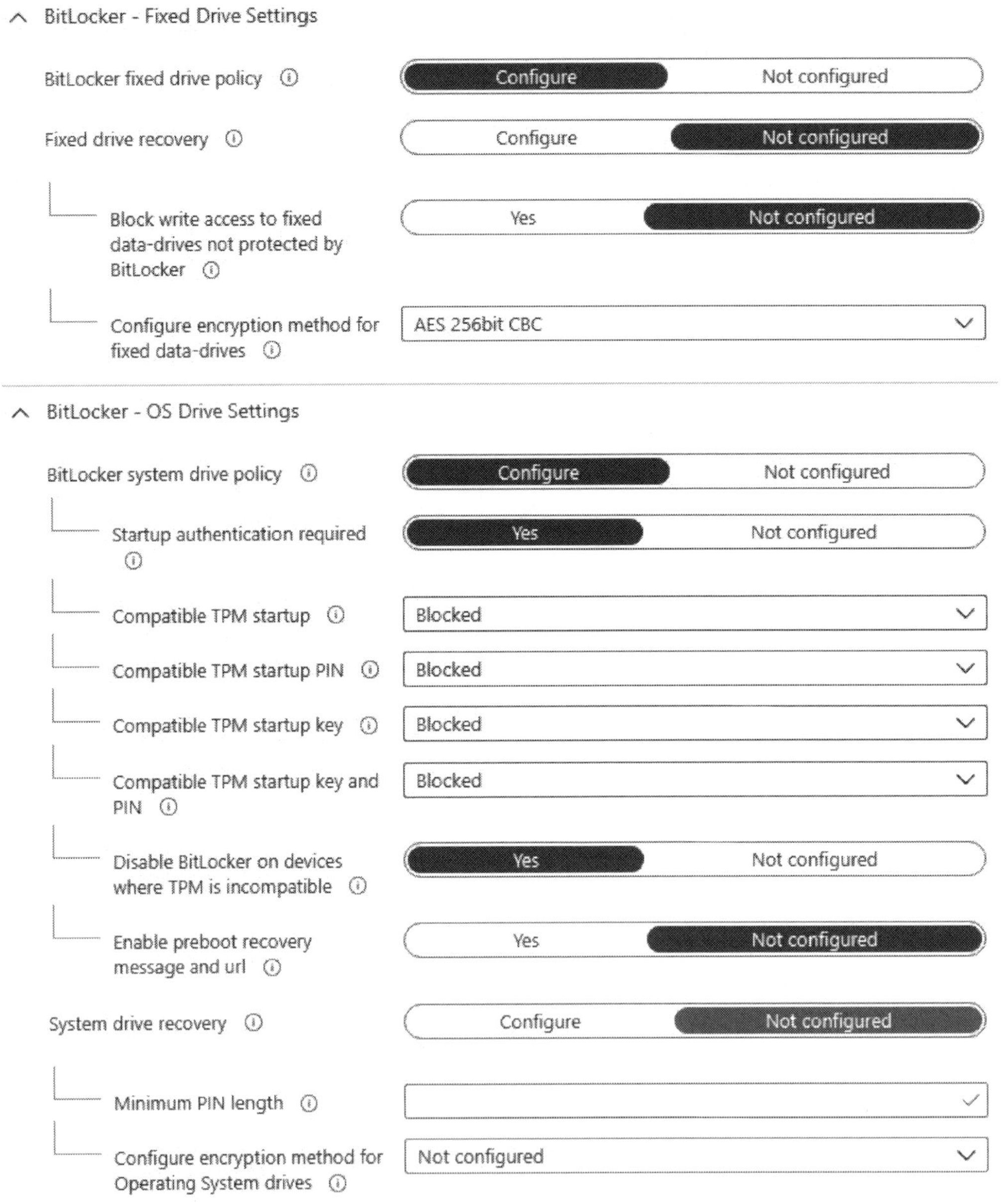

∧ BitLocker - Fixed Drive Settings

BitLocker fixed drive policy ⓘ   [**Configure** | Not configured]

Fixed drive recovery ⓘ   [Configure | **Not configured**]

  └─ Block write access to fixed   [Yes | **Not configured**]
     data-drives not protected by
     BitLocker ⓘ

  └─ Configure encryption method for   [AES 256bit CBC   ⌄]
     fixed data-drives ⓘ

∧ BitLocker - OS Drive Settings

BitLocker system drive policy ⓘ   [**Configure** | Not configured]

  └─ Startup authentication required   [**Yes** | Not configured]
     ⓘ

  └─ Compatible TPM startup ⓘ   [Blocked   ⌄]

  └─ Compatible TPM startup PIN ⓘ   [Blocked   ⌄]

  └─ Compatible TPM startup key ⓘ   [Blocked   ⌄]

  └─ Compatible TPM startup key and   [Blocked   ⌄]
     PIN ⓘ

  └─ Disable BitLocker on devices   [**Yes** | Not configured]
     where TPM is incompatible ⓘ

  └─ Enable preboot recovery   [Yes | **Not configured**]
     message and url ⓘ

System drive recovery ⓘ   [Configure | **Not configured**]

  └─ Minimum PIN length ⓘ   [✓]

  └─ Configure encryption method for   [Not configured   ⌄]
     Operating System drives ⓘ

Figure 13.41 – BitLocker fixed drive settings

> **Important Note**
> BitLocker cannot silently encrypt the device if these settings are configured to required because these settings require user interaction.

After you are done with the BitLocker-specific configuration, you have to finish the assignment, most likely based on AAD users or groups.

BitLocker recovery keys

When a problem happens with your endpoint and you need to recover your drives, you most likely need your recovery key. Luckily, the BitLocker keys are automatically saved to MEM.

You can find the device's BitLocker recovery keys under **Devices** | *the user's devices* | **Recovery keys** in MEM:

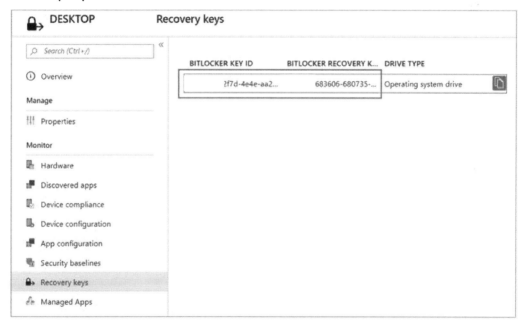

Figure 13.42 – BitLocker recovery keys

Enter the recovery key in the key field of Windows 10 and you are good to go!

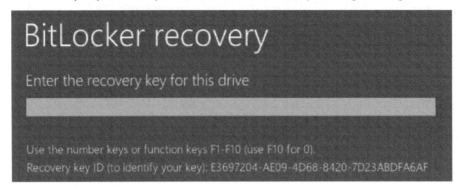

Figure 13.43 – BitLocker recovery

You can search the device's BitLocker recovery keys under **Devices | BitLocker keys** without knowing the device name, in the AAD admin center.

Figure 13.44 – Searching for BitLocker keys

This concludes the section on BitLocker management in Microsoft Intune. Next, we will cover Microsoft Defender for Endpoint.

Microsoft Defender for Endpoint

Microsoft Defender for Endpoint is Microsoft's Enterprise endpoint security platform that was created to help businesses prevent, investigate, detect, and respond to threats. This serves to increase the level of security of your whole endpoint configuration.

Microsoft Defender for Endpoint is a security solution that includes risk-based vulnerability management and assessment, attack surface reduction, behavioral-based and cloud-powered next-generation protection, **endpoint detection and response (EDR)**, automatic investigation and remediation, managed hunting services, rich APIs, and unified security management.

Integration with MEM

MEM becomes more and more prominent for customers who are using Windows 365/ Azure Virtual Desktop as it provides a unified way of configuring and maintaining your physical and virtual cloud endpoint as well as other devices such as mobile.

Microsoft Defender for Endpoint integrates seamlessly into MEM. You only need to activate the Intune integration once during the initial setup and your reports will flow into MEM.

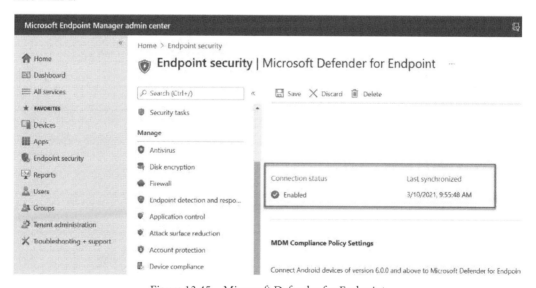

Figure 13.45 – Microsoft Defender for Endpoint

This concludes the overview on Microsoft Defender for Endpoint. Next, we will give you an overview of the security baselines.

Security baselines

Security baselines are preconfigured groups of Windows settings that help you apply the security settings that are recommended by the relevant security teams. The baselines you deploy can be customized to enforce only the settings and values required by you.

There are multiple security-related settings in Windows as well as for Microsoft Edge for your endpoints. Another great asset is the option to do versioning and filtering based on different OSes or scenarios that have to be stricter. You no longer have to use GPOs to ensure the security settings on your endpoints – just create a security baseline profile and you're all set.

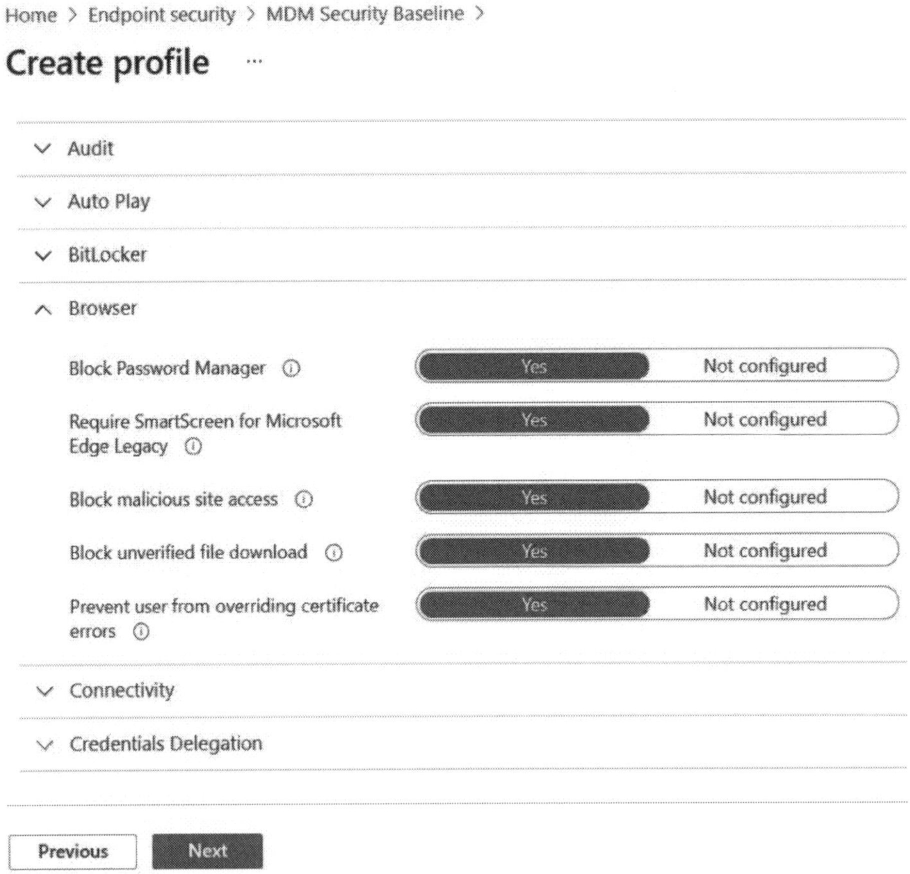

Home > Endpoint security > MDM Security Baseline >

Create profile   ⋯

∨   Audit

∨   Auto Play

∨   BitLocker

∧   Browser

Block Password Manager ⓘ	Yes	Not configured
Require SmartScreen for Microsoft Edge Legacy ⓘ	Yes	Not configured
Block malicious site access ⓘ	Yes	Not configured
Block unverified file download ⓘ	Yes	Not configured
Prevent user from overriding certificate errors ⓘ	Yes	Not configured

∨   Connectivity

∨   Credentials Delegation

[Previous] [Next]

Figure 13.46 – MDM security baselines

This concludes this security baseline overview. Next, we will cover compliance policies.

Compliance policies

We can define the rules and settings that users and devices must meet to be compliant. This can include actions that apply to noncompliant devices. Actions for noncompliance can alert users to the conditions of noncompliance and safeguard data on noncompliant devices.

See the following example of how you can set the risk level within Microsoft Defender when your endpoint does not meet the compliance expectations. Your device will show up as a risk in Microsoft Defender for Endpoint as well as in Intune – marked as non-compliant.

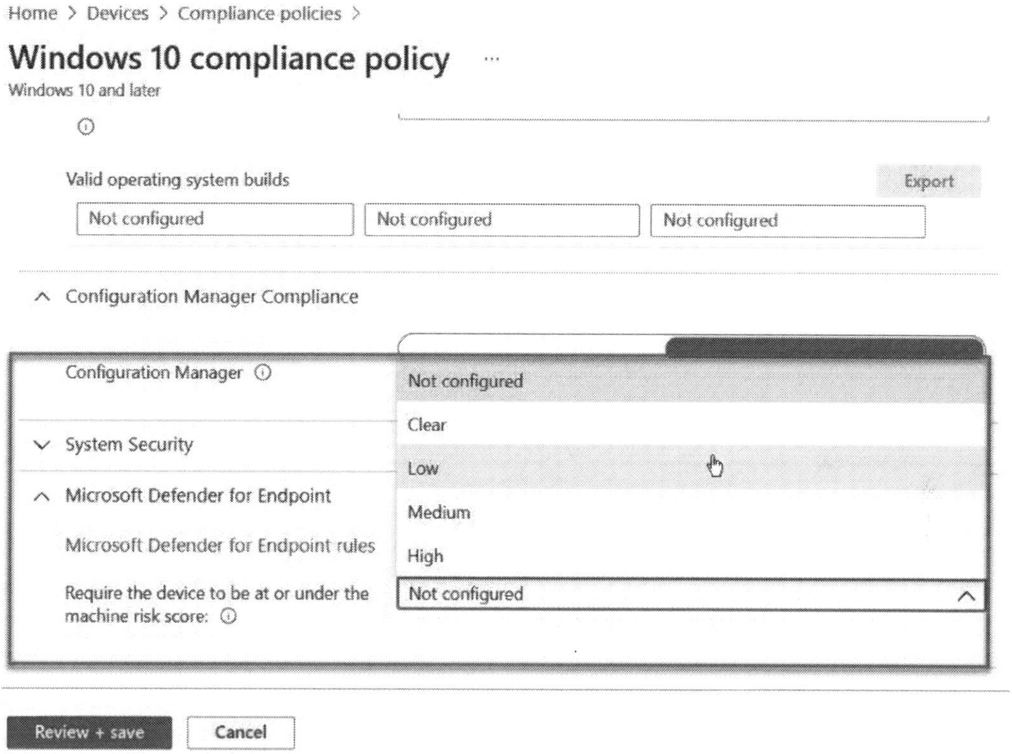

Figure 13.47 – Microsoft Defender for Endpoint compliance settings

> **Note**
>
> More information on compliance policies can be found in *Chapter 10, Advanced Policy Management*.

Windows 365 security baselines

Windows 365 delivers its own branded set of security baselines that include different best practices that are optimized for cloud PC virtualized scenarios.

We highly recommend customers use these as they come from experience from real-world implementations. You can use these policies to lower the risk while increasing the security boundaries of your cloud PCs.

You can use security baselines to get security recommendations that can help lower risk. The Windows 365 baselines enable security configurations for Windows 10, Edge, and Microsoft Defender for Endpoint. They include versioning features and help customers choose when to update user policies to the latest release.

Figure 13.48 – Security baselines

Requirements for Defender for Endpoint

In the next part of this section, I'm going to explain how you configure Microsoft Defender for Endpoint via MEM to secure your virtual or physical Windows endpoints:

1. Go to the MEM admin center via `https://endpoint.microsoft.com/#home`.

2. Go to **Endpoint security**.

Figure 13.49 – Endpoint security

3. Click on **Open the Microsoft Defender Security Center**.

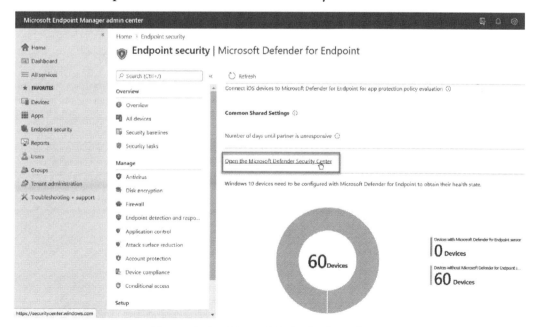

Figure 13.50 – Microsoft Defender for Endpoint

4. Click on **Next**.

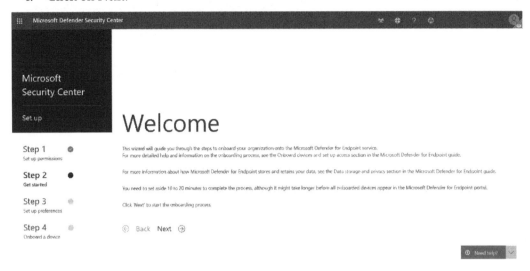

Figure 13.51 – Microsoft Defender Security Center – Step 2

5. Fill in your region, data retention policy time, and org size.

> **Note**
>
> You could also select the **Preview features** option to be among the first to try upcoming features.

Click **Next**.

Figure 13.52 – Microsoft Defender Security Center – Step 3

6. Make sure all the settings are correct, as there is no way back. Click on **Continue**.

Create your cloud instance

You won't be able to change some of your preferences
(such as the data storage location) after clicking 'Continue'.
If you want to check or make any changes, click 'Back to
preferences' and review your preferences. Click 'Continue' if
you want to set up your account.

Figure 13.53 – Create your cloud instance

7. Your Microsoft Defender for Endpoint account is being created. Please wait.

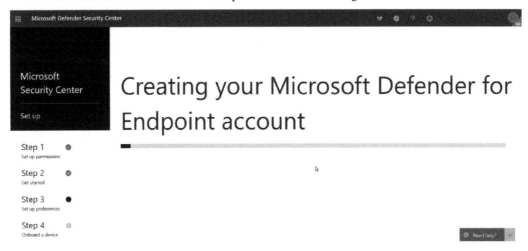

Figure 13.54 – Microsoft Defender Security Center – Step 3

Now you are ready to create the Microsoft Defender for Endpoint integration with Microsoft Intune.

Connecting to Intune – MEM integration

Follow these steps to proceed with the integration:

1. Open the Security Center portal: `https://securitycenter.windows.com/`.

2. Go to **Settings**.

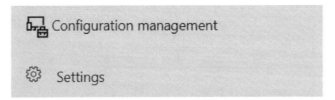

Figure 13.55 – Settings

3. Turn the slider next to **Microsoft Intune connection** to **On**.

Settings

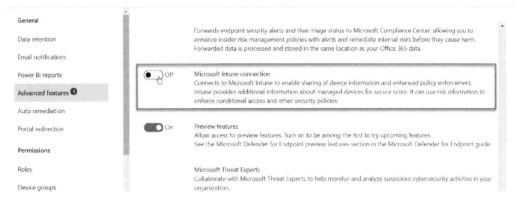

Figure 13.56 – Microsoft Intune connection

4. Click on **Save preferences**.

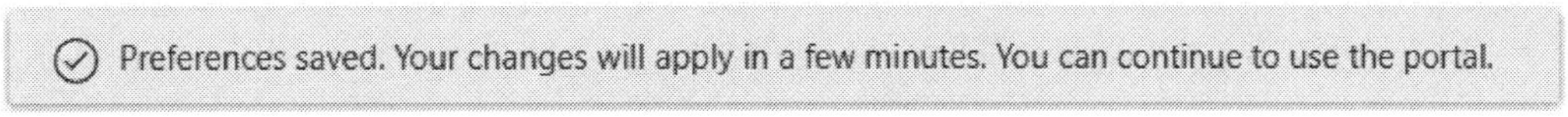

⊘ Preferences saved. Your changes will apply in a few minutes. You can continue to use the portal.

Figure 13.57 – Preferences saved

5. At this point, Microsoft Defender integrates into MEM. You can check the status in the **Endpoint security** menu.

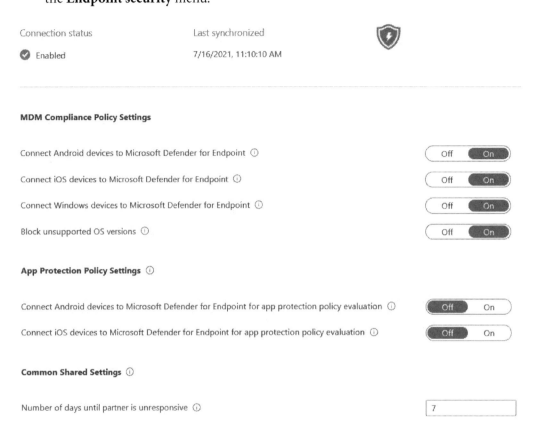

Figure 13.58 – Connectors and tokens – Microsoft Defender for Endpoint

> **Note**
>
> When on, compliance policies using the device threat level rule will evaluate devices, including data from this connector. When off, Intune will not use device risk details sent over this connector during device compliance calculation for policies with a device threat level configured. Existing devices that are not compliant due to risk levels obtained from this connector will also become compliant.

MDM Compliance Policy Settings: When on, compliance policies using the Device Threat Level rule will evaluate devices, including data from this connector, which is recommended to leverage the device threat level as part of the compliance policy for Windows devices.

When off, Intune will not use device risk details sent over this connector during device compliance calculations for policies with a Device Threat Level configured. Existing devices that are not compliant due to risk levels obtained from this connector will also become compliant.

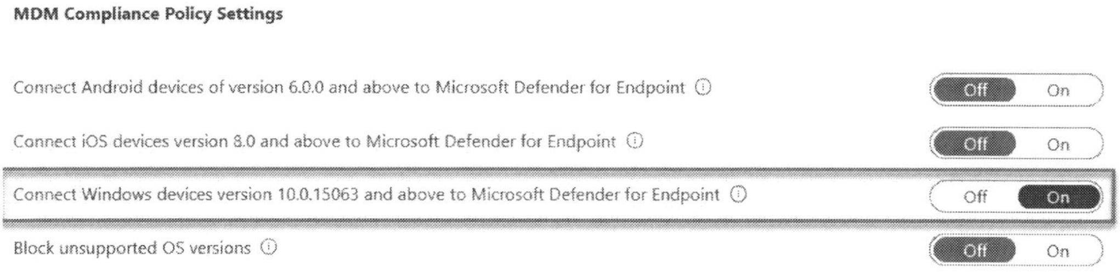

MDM Compliance Policy Settings

Connect Android devices of version 6.0.0 and above to Microsoft Defender for Endpoint ⓘ   Off On

Connect iOS devices version 8.0 and above to Microsoft Defender for Endpoint ⓘ   Off On

Connect Windows devices version 10.0.15063 and above to Microsoft Defender for Endpoint ⓘ   Off On

Block unsupported OS versions ⓘ   Off On

Figure 13.59 – MDM Compliance Policy Settings

6. We now need to enroll our Windows endpoints into Defender.

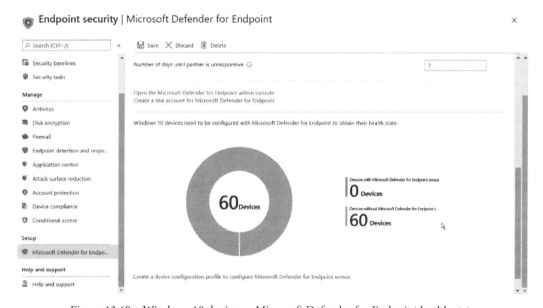

Figure 13.60 – Windows 10 devices – Microsoft Defender for Endpoint health state

7. Switch back to the MEM portal.

8. Go to **Endpoint security**, followed by **Endpoint detection and response**.

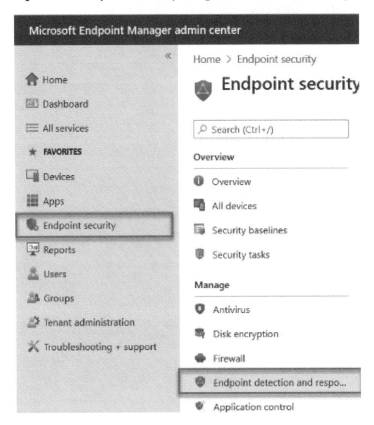

Figure 13.61 – Endpoint detection and response

Before you start, download your Defender onboarding file. You can find it in
Defender, under **Settings | Onboarding**: `https://securitycenter.`
`windows.com/preferences2/onboarding`.

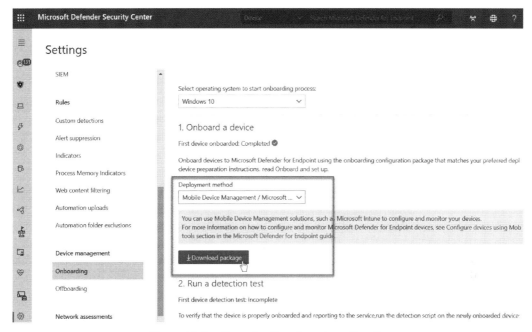

Figure 13.62 – Downloading the onboarding file

9. Store it somewhere on your computer and unzip the folder.

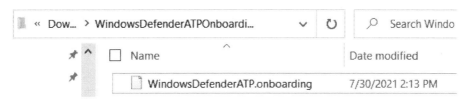

Figure 13.63 – Saving the onboarding file

10. Select **Windows 10 and later** and **Endpoint detection and response (MDM)** for the respective fields.

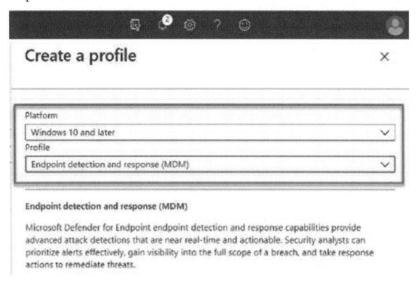

Figure 13.64 – Endpoint detection and response (MDM) profile creation

11. Enter a name. Then, click **Next**.

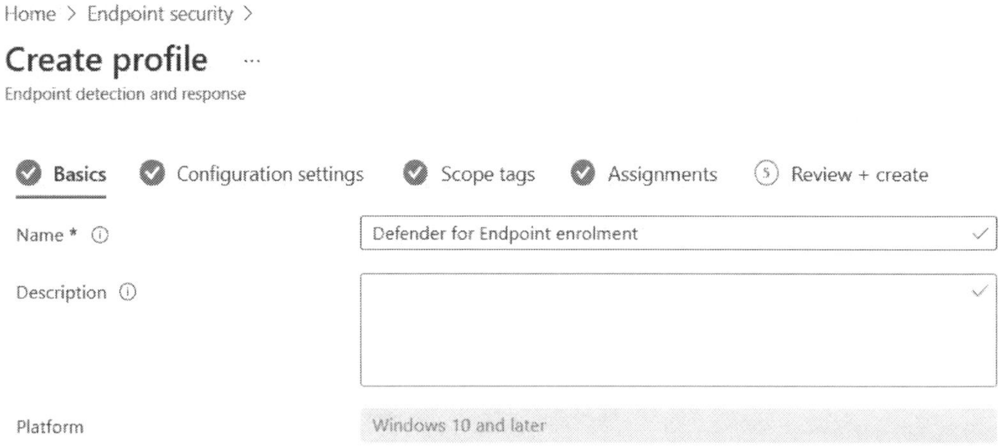

Home > Endpoint security >

Create profile   ...
Endpoint detection and response

✅ **Basics**	✅ Configuration settings	✅ Scope tags	✅ Assignments	⑤ Review + create

Name * ⓘ   Defender for Endpoint enrolment   ✓

Description ⓘ

Platform   Windows 10 and later

Figure 13.65 – Create profile 1

12. Enable the **Onboarding blob** setting.

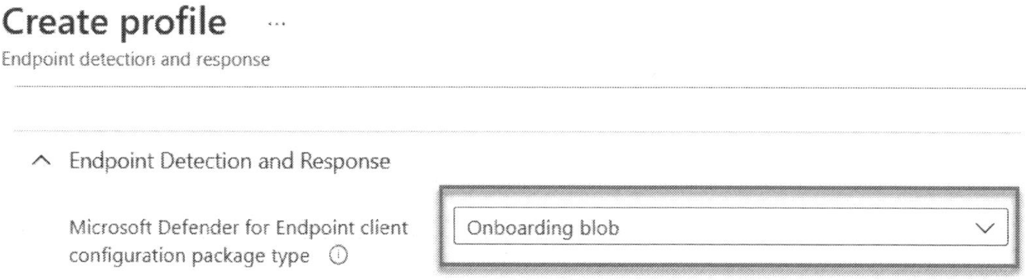

Create profile ...
Endpoint detection and response
Endpoint Detection and Response
Microsoft Defender for Endpoint client configuration package type
Onboarding blob

Figure 13.66 – Create profile 2

13. Select the `WindowsDefenderATP.onboarding` file you downloaded earlier and upload it to your tenant.

Select file
Select file
"WindowsDefenderATP.onboarding"
select

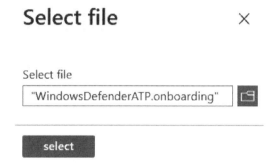

Figure 13.67 – Uploading the onboarding file

14. Confirm that the onboarding file has been added correctly. This file includes the configuration that will be pushed to the endpoints so they know how to connect to your Defender for Endpoint tenant.

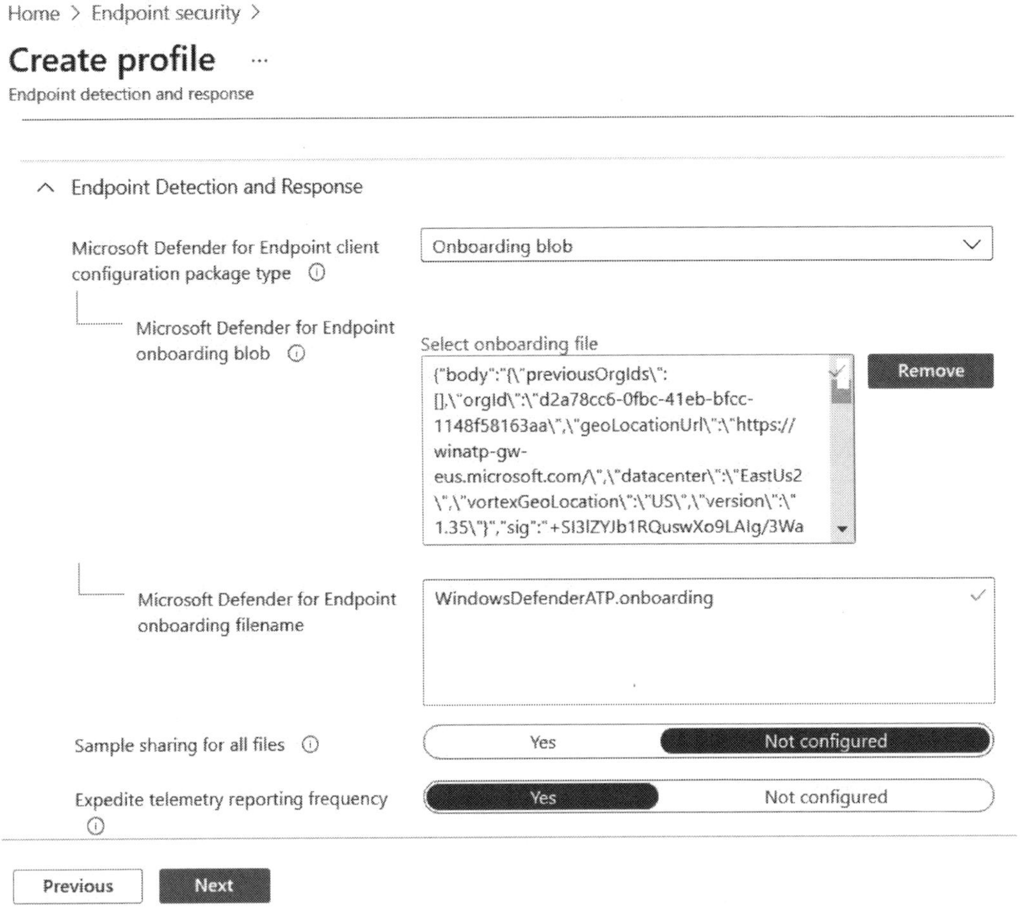

Home > Endpoint security >

Create profile   ...

Endpoint detection and response

∧ Endpoint Detection and Response

Microsoft Defender for Endpoint client configuration package type ⓘ

Onboarding blob   ⌄

    Microsoft Defender for Endpoint onboarding blob ⓘ

Select onboarding file

{"body":"{\"previousOrgIds\":
[],\"orgId\":\"d2a78cc6-0fbc-41eb-bfcc-
1148f58163aa\",\"geoLocationUrl\":\"https://
winatp-gw-
eus.microsoft.com/\",\"datacenter\":\"EastUs2
\",\"vortexGeoLocation\":\"US\",\"version\":\"
1.35\"}","sig":"+SI3lZYJb1RQuswXo9LAIg/3Wa

Remove

    Microsoft Defender for Endpoint onboarding filename

WindowsDefenderATP.onboarding   ✓

Sample sharing for all files ⓘ

| Yes | Not configured |

Expedite telemetry reporting frequency ⓘ

| Yes | Not configured |

Previous   Next

Figure 13.68 – Creating an endpoint onboarding profile

15. Click **Next**.

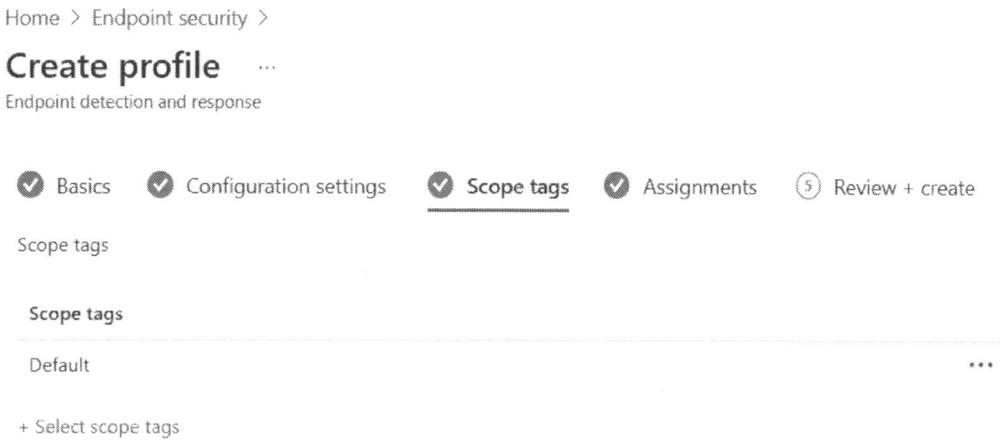

Home > Endpoint security >

Create profile   ···
Endpoint detection and response

✓ Basics   ✓ Configuration settings   ✓ **Scope tags**   ✓ Assignments   ⑤ Review + create

Scope tags

Scope tags

Default   ···

+ Select scope tags

Figure 13.69 – Scope tags

16. Click on **Add all devices**. Then, click **Next**.

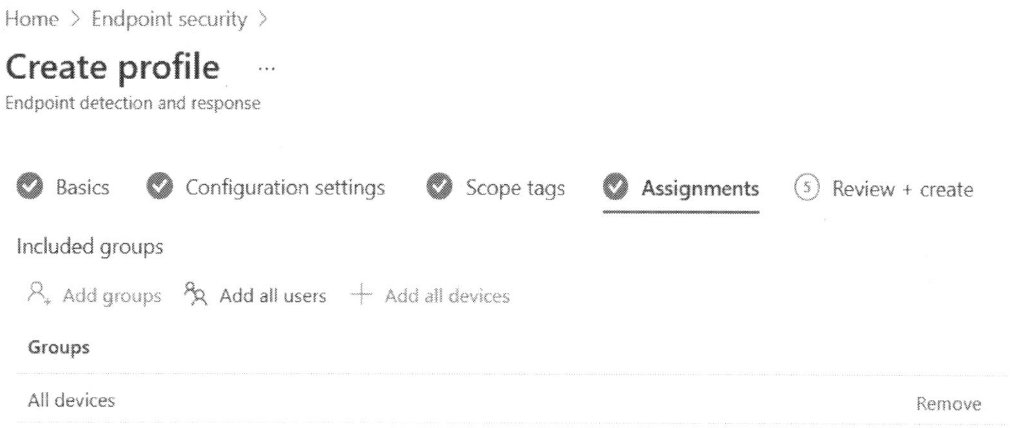

Home > Endpoint security >

Create profile   ···
Endpoint detection and response

✓ Basics   ✓ Configuration settings   ✓ Scope tags   ✓ **Assignments**   ⑤ Review + create

Included groups

👤₊ Add groups   👥 Add all users   ＋ Add all devices

Groups

All devices   Remove

Figure 13.70 – Assignments

17. Click on **Create**.

Home > Endpoint security >

Create profile ...

Endpoint detection and response

✓ Basics   ✓ Configuration settings   ✓ Scope tags   ✓ Assignments   ⑤ **Review + create**

Summary

Basics

Name	Defender for Endpoint enrolment
Description	--
Platform	Windows 10 and later

Configuration settings

Auto populate Microsoft Defender for Endpoint onboarding blob	Not configured
Microsoft Defender for Endpoint client configuration package type	Onboarding blob
Microsoft Defender for Endpoint onboarding blob	

{"body":"{\"previousOrgIds\":[],\"orgId\":\"d2a78cc6-0fbc-41eb-bfcc-1148f58163aa\",\"geoLocationUrl\":\"https://winatp-gw-eus.microsoft.com/\",\"datacenter\":\"EastUs2\",\"vortexGeoLocation\":\"US\",\"version\":\"1.35\"}","sig":"+SI3lZYJb1RQuswXo9LAlg/3Wadr4b4rEX7F5ScLS1w
Vhr5+SHir6qZmqtwW/0yUJrWiwbONU2O0PbQN0AHdzNntXMPNZDrH8dl0sh
9KYgIbXgTRdeEk7LDV0X1wAtdq/4v7ViomqZxaZnxJkvbZnKxdF7WKxNZHWt/J6
LUhNLRZ2Ay89Do2u/HP99n2xKjq6CaB53bGKlQCLtdVnICqNwFJ2GyDEloDktJ1/
DoUdlMZ8+Vcg3zv4o9TddBdp9P1GyRcH0TZzX1RHsBiZ/4fgUcbuwUmE5fk5Ho
ly1EhCXHek/KZNxOh7w2pRAvEGEiMSbCMzbchvSRBGiigkptNA==","sha256sig
":"9pg1ISSxq8f59T2dU71IymGNTLjFI+kfP4BsWRkuvmHLPwPppS+3+N19pyyE0

[Previous]   [**Create**]

Figure 13.71 – Creating the policy

18. Confirm that the rule is saying **Yes** under **Assigned**.

Home > Endpoint security

🛡 **Endpoint security** | Endpoint detection and response

🔍 Search (Ctrl+/)	«
Overview	
ⓘ Overview	
🖥 All devices	
🗂 Security baselines	
🛡 Security tasks	

+ Create Policy   ○ Refresh   ⬇ Export

🔍 Search by column value

Policy name	↑↓	Policy type	↑↓	Assigned	↑↓	Platform	↑↓	Target
Defender for Endpoint Enr		Endpoint detection and r...		Yes		Windows 10 and later		MDM

Figure 13.72 – Endpoint detection and response

You should now see the status of your Windows 10 virtual or physical endpoint changing from **Devices without Microsoft Defender for Endpoint Sensor** to **Devices with Microsoft Defender for Endpoint Sensor**.

> **Note**
> The number of devices in this view only shows devices onboarded from the Microsoft Intune onboarding profile, not devices onboarded from scripts, Microsoft Endpoint Configuration Manager, or third-party tools.

Next, we will cover different options in Microsoft Defender Security Center.

Alerts and security assessments

Once the rollout and activation are done, and you have configured some security baselines and compliance profiles and assigned them to your desktops, you are ready to review your devices in the Microsoft Defender Security Center console. When you click on devices, you're able to drill down into the different assessments and alerts (if any) being detected.

Security recommendations

Microsoft Defender also recommends activating different features to increase the security level of your desktops in the **Security recommendations** tab. In there, you can find multiple settings that you can directly enable and push into Intune when you set up the connection correctly to your Intune tenant environment.

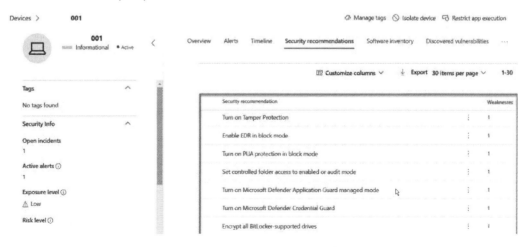

Figure 13.73 – Security recommendations

Summary

In this chapter, you've learned about the history of AD and about AAD, and what the options are to secure your identities better with Conditional Access and Microsoft Defender for Endpoint.

You learned how you can combine the force of Microsoft 365 E5 with device compliance on Microsoft Intune-managed devices with a Microsoft Defender for Endpoint risk score in a compliance policy to only allow access to corporate data by leveraging conditions all in the Microsoft zero-trust security model.

In the next chapter, we're going to take a deeper dive into how to monitor your Windows 10 Enterprise endpoints with Endpoint analytics.

Questions

1. Do you need a license in order to use Azure MFA?

    A. Yes

    B. No

2. What configuration profile setting is required to configure your Windows 10 devices for Microsoft Defender for Endpoint?

    A. Endpoint collections and response

    B. Security assessment

    C. Endpoint detection and response

    D. Sample sharing for all files

Answers

1. (B)
2. (C)

Further reading

If you want to learn more about AAD, Conditional Access, and Microsoft Defender for Endpoint after reading this chapter, please use one of the following free online resources:

- *Microsoft Defender for Endpoint – Microsoft Tech Community*: `https://techcommunity.microsoft.com/t5/microsoft-defender-for-endpoint/bg-p/MicrosoftDefenderATPBlog`

- *Practice security administration – Learn | Microsoft Docs*: `https://docs.microsoft.com/en-us/learn/modules/m365-security-threat-protect/practice-security-administration`

14
Monitoring and Endpoint Analytics

After deploying your desktops, it's important to ensure the performance and quality level of Windows and the applications that are part of your physical and Windows 365 cloud PCs in your environment.

You will learn in this chapter how you can achieve this with Endpoint analytics, Productivity Score, and other monitoring capabilities of Microsoft Endpoint Manager.

In this chapter, we'll go through the following topics:

- Monitoring and analytics
- Monitoring your physical and virtual cloud endpoints
- Endpoint analytics – advanced monitoring
- Top 10 impacting start up processes
- OS restart history
- Resource performance
- Insights and recommendations – score trends

- Application reliability

- Windows 365-specific metrics

- Insights and recommendations

- Customizing your baselines

- Productivity Score

- Service health

Monitoring and analytics

Monitoring your Windows 10 Enterprise environment is just as important as the implementation of it. User experience is the most important part of a successful implementation.

Microsoft Endpoint analytics and Productivity Score as built-in services make it possible for you to stay ahead of problems that you might encounter in your environment before they occur. You don't need to make an additional environment or pay for consumption-based resources as part of this service; everything is included in your Microsoft 365 license. *You'll read about everything you need to know in this regard in this chapter!*

Monitoring your physical and virtual cloud endpoints

If you are an existing Microsoft Endpoint Manager customer, you'll already use the **Monitor** option inside the **Devices** menu. As Windows 365 is equal to a physical Windows 10 Enterprise desktop, you can monitor both your virtual and physical devices here for one unified experience.

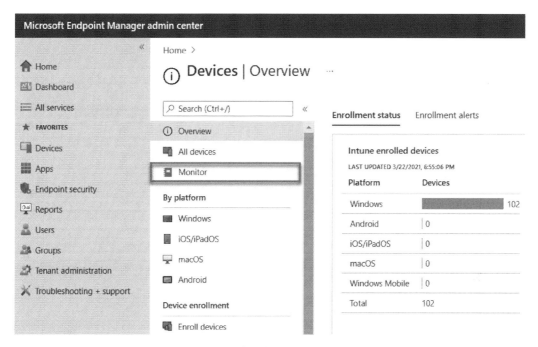

Figure 14.1 – Microsoft Endpoint Manager admin center

You can gather insights about your environment as well as think about metrics such as **app licenses**, **discovered apps**, **app install**, and **app protection statuses**.

Here's a full rundown of the different monitoring dashboards available:

- **Configuration:**

  - Assignment status

  - Assignment failures

  - Devices with restricted apps

  - Encryption report

  - Certificates

- **Compliance:**

  - Non-compliant devices

  - Devices without compliance policy

  - Setting compliance

  - Policy compliance

  - Non-compliant policies

  - Windows Health Attestation report

  - Threat agent status

- **Enrollment:**

  - Autopilot deployments

  - Enrollment failures

  - Incomplete user enrollments

- **Software updates:**

  - Per-update ring deployment state

  - Installation failures for iOS devices

  - Feature update failures

  - Windows expedited update failures

- **Other:**

  - Device actions

You could, for example, easily find out what apps are being deployed and how many are successful, as in the example in the following section.

Endpoint analytics – advanced monitoring

The main purpose of Endpoint analytics is to proactively optimize the user experience and track your progress along the way. It's your main dashboard as an IT administrator to track the quality level of both your physical and virtual desktop environments.

The metrics that you can find show the value of all Microsoft Endpoint Manager-managed devices in your environment, for example, of your physical and Windows 10 or 11 cloud PCs combined.

Here's a list of the reports/dashboards currently available in Endpoint analytics:

Figure 14.2 – Overview of your environment

Start up performance – logon duration

Improving start up performance to optimize the time from powering on your physical computer to productivity is best for consistent performance in terms of increasing the speed to productivity.

Review your current score and see how it compares to the selected baseline. Refer to the list of different insights and recommendations to learn how to improve your device start up times and score; this can be found in the Endpoint analytics dashboards.

Here's a list of the metrics available in Endpoint analytics, per organization, and per user device level, to dig deeper into specific scenarios:

- **Core boot**: Average time it takes to reach the sign-in prompt after a device is turned on. Excludes the OS update time:

  - **Group Policy**: Average time spent processing Group Policy during the device's core boot

  - **To sign-in screen**: Core boot time minus the time spent processing Group Policy

- **Core sign-in**: Average time it takes to get to a responsive desktop after a user signs in. Excludes new user sign-in and first sign-in following a feature update:

  - **Group Policy**: Average time spent processing Group Policy during the device's core sign-in

  - **To desktop**: Average time between sign-in and when the desktop renders, minus the time spent processing Group Policy

  - **To responsive desktop**: Average time between when the desktop renders and when CPU usage falls below 50%

The start up performance score gives the IT department insight into the end user experience from power-on to productivity. With these insights come recommendations on what to change to improve end users' experience. Next, we will cover the performance score breakdown.

Performance score breakdown

To calculate our tenant's score, we look at how long it takes each device to complete the core boot phase and score each experience from 0 (poor) to 100 (exceptional). We then calculate the average score of all devices to get the core boot score.

In the following screenshot, you can find an example breakdown of the full logon process, from booting up and the logon process of your physical, to even further in your cloud PC, your Windows 10 Enterprise endpoint.

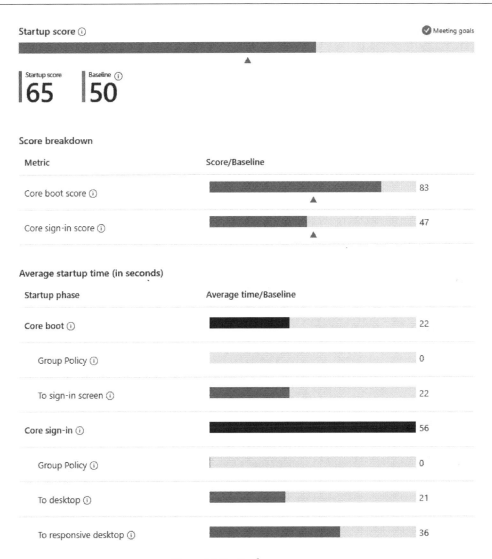

Figure 14.3 – Performance score

If you need to see the individual status of a single Windows 10 physical or cloud PC, you can go to **Endpoint Analytics | Reports | Startup performance | Device performance**.

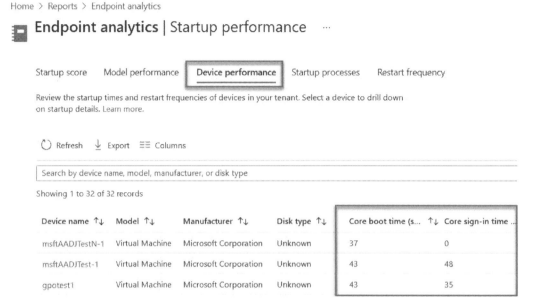

Figure 14.4 – Device performance

Once you click on the device name, different individual metrics are shown. Here, you can find the logon duration and boot history of your endpoints.

> **Important note**
> The sign-in history is segmented to make it easier to find the potential root cause of the delay.

Boot history

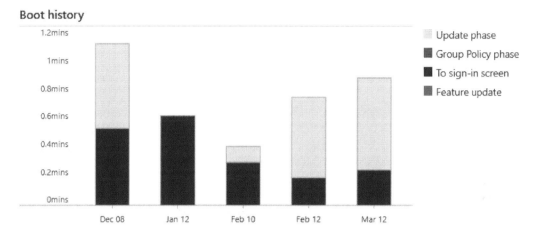

Figure 14.5 – Boot history

You could also find the sign-in history here if you scroll a little further down. This is the easiest method to track whether performance has decreased (or not).

Sign-in history

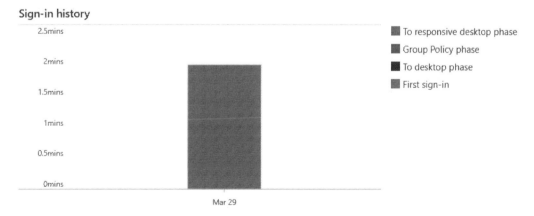

Figure 14.6 – Sign-in history

If your cloud PC is performing badly and is causing a lot of CPU spikes, Endpoint analytics will suggest you resize your cloud PC. This is a new, proactive method to ensure the performance of your end users.

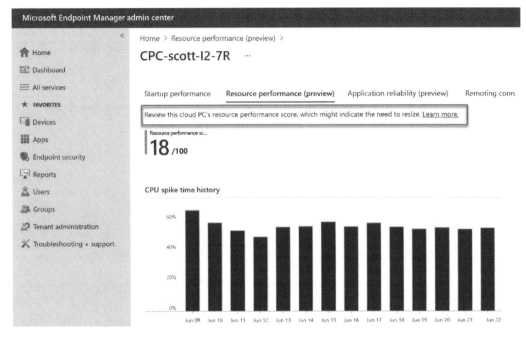

Figure 14.7 – Resource performance

You can find this feature (in preview) in the Microsoft Endpoint Manager portal, under **Devices**; select the **Resize** button, as seen in the following screenshot:

Figure 14.8 – Resize feature

When you click **Resize**, you will be taken to the following screen:

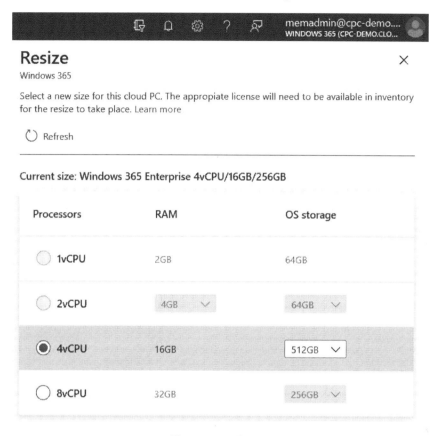

Figure 14.9 – Resize

In this section, we covered Endpoint analytics reporting for Windows 365. Next, we will look closer into some of the detailed data you can get on your Windows devices with Endpoint analytics.

Top 10 impacting start up processes

In **startup performance** under the **device performance** blade, you can select a single device where you can show the top 10 processes that have the most impact on the device's start up performance.

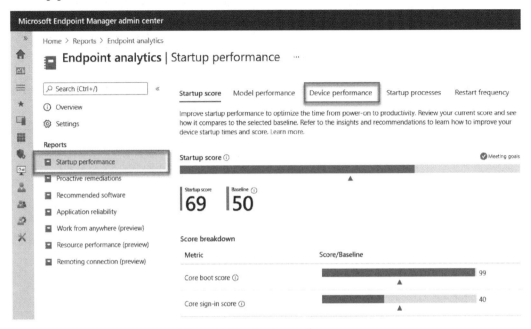

Figure 14.10 – Startup performance

This data is also visible in the **Device** blade if you go into a specific device and then to **Monitor | User Experience**.

Top 10 impacting startup processes ⓘ

Process name	Description	Publisher	Impact (seconds)
WmiPrvSE	WMI Provider Host	Microsoft Corporation	6
omadmclient	Windows MDM Client	Unknown	5
svchost-netsvcs	Service Host: netsvcs	Microsoft Corporation	1
svchost-RPCSS	Service Host: RPCSS	Microsoft Corporation	1
svchost-UnistackSvcGroup	Service Host: UnistackSvcGroup	Microsoft Corporation	1
svchost-DcomLaunch	Service Host: DcomLaunch	Microsoft Corporation	1
svchost-LocalSystemNetworkRestricted	Service Host: LocalSystemNetworkRestri...	Microsoft Corporation	1
svchost-LocalServiceNetworkRestricted	Service Host: LocalServiceNetworkRestri...	Microsoft Corporation	1
svchost-AppReadiness	Service Host: AppReadiness	Microsoft Corporation	1
svchost-LocalServiceNoNetwork	Service Host: LocalServiceNoNetwork	Microsoft Corporation	1

Figure 14.11 – Top 10 impacting start up processes

OS restart history

Last but not least, you can also find the restart actions on each physical and cloud PC in the last section of the dashboard:

OS restart history ⓘ

Date	OS version	Restart category	Stop code	Failure bucket Id
03/30/21	10.0.19042.867	Update		
04/15/21	10.0.19042.928	Update		

Figure 14.12 – OS restart history

Resource performance

In this dashboard, it's possible to see the application events on your physical and cloud PCs. This gives you insights into one of the most important indicators of bad user experience – CPU and RAM utilization.

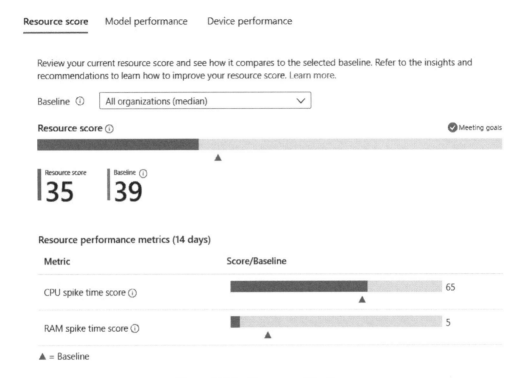

Figure 14.13 – Resource utilization

Insights and recommendations – score trends

It's also possible to see the last 30 days of resource consumption and whether there's a trend. This would make it easy, when you provide a fix, to see whether the improvement affects all your users.

Also, the other way around, when issues occur or you install an update that requires way more resources than before, you can start correlating your results with the time of enrollment of that patch or update. Very insightful.

Daily metric trends (30 days)

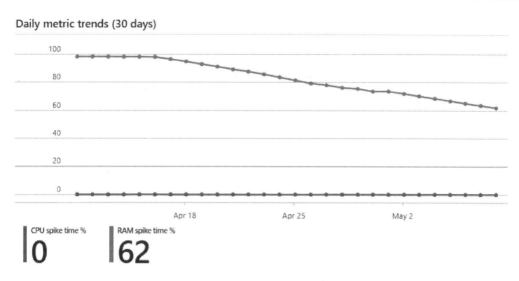

Figure 14.14 – Score trends

Application reliability

Healthy, performant applications enable users in your organization to be productive. Review your current app reliability score and see how it compares to the selected baseline. Refer to the insights and recommendations to learn how to improve your app reliability score.

Figure 14.15 – App reliability score

App reliability score provides IT admins with a high-level view of desktop application robustness across your environment. App reliability score is a number between 0 and 100. The score is calculated from the app reliability scores of each desktop application in your environment that's found in the **App performance** tab.

Each application on the **App performance** tab is assigned an App reliability score based on the following:

- **Crash frequency**: For each app, there are two metrics:

  - The total number of app crashes.

  - The total usage duration over a 14-day rolling window is used to calculate the Mean time to failure value in the **App performance** tab.

- **Total usage duration**: Is a factor in the usage duration across all enrolled devices in Endpoint analytics. This ensures that you get the data for the most disruptive application issues that are prioritized in the App reliability score.

Windows 365-specific metrics

Another huge benefit is that Endpoint analytics is also the tool you use to check the status of your physical endpoints. This means that you can create one single pane of glass to check the status of your physical endpoint and cloud PC endpoint altogether at once.

There are six new Windows 365 Endpoint analytics categories to measure the performance of your environment:

- **Resource performance:**

  - CPU spike time percentage

  - RAM spike time percentage

- **Remoting connection:**

  - RD client login time

  - RD client login failure

  - **Round Trip Time (RTT)**

The following screenshot is an example of measuring the latency of the connection to your Windows 365 cloud PC environment:

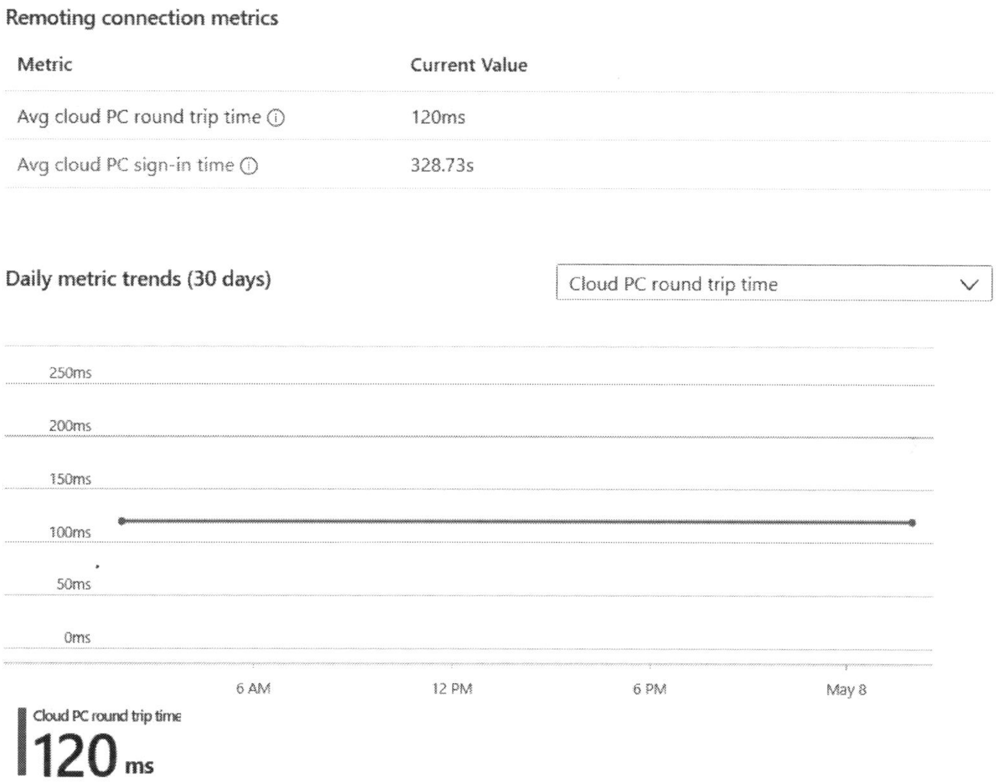
Remoting connection metrics
Metric
Current Value
Avg cloud PC round trip time
120ms
Avg cloud PC sign-in time
328.73s
Daily metric trends (30 days)
Cloud PC round trip time
250ms
200ms
150ms
100ms
50ms
0ms
6 AM
12 PM
6 PM
May 8
Cloud PC round trip time
120 ms

Figure 14.16 – Remoting connection metrics

The following are the kinds of metrics that are available to measure start up performance and logon duration:

- **Start up performance:**
    - Boot time for Windows 365 cloud PC endpoint
    - Login time for Windows 365 cloud PC endpoint

The following are insights on both the boot time, logon duration, and round-trip time (RTT – latency) of both your physical and cloud PC environment.

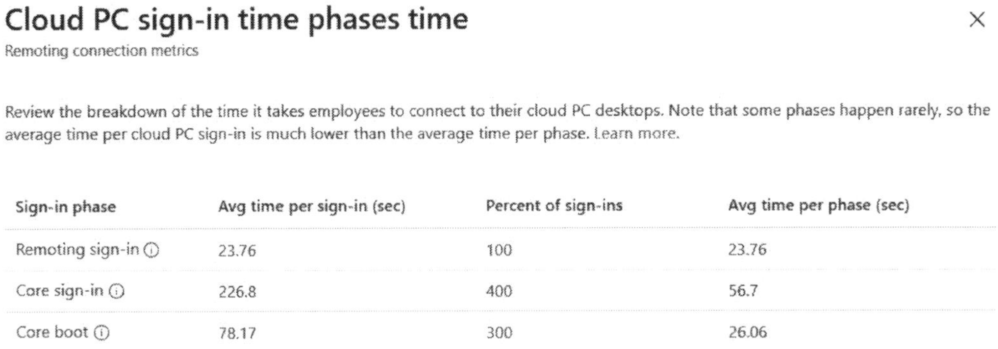

Cloud PC sign-in time phases time   ×

Remoting connection metrics

Review the breakdown of the time it takes employees to connect to their cloud PC desktops. Note that some phases happen rarely, so the average time per cloud PC sign-in is much lower than the average time per phase. Learn more.

Sign-in phase	Avg time per sign-in (sec)	Percent of sign-ins	Avg time per phase (sec)
Remoting sign-in ⓘ	23.76	100	23.76
Core sign-in ⓘ	226.8	400	56.7
Core boot ⓘ	78.17	300	26.06

Figure 14.17 – Start up performance

- **Proactive remediations:**

    - Automated actions to remediate common issues with a Windows 365 cloud PC

- **Recommended software:**

    - Windows 10 version

    - **Azure Active Directory (AAD)** devices

    - Intune devices

- **Application health:**

    - Cloud PC app usage and crashes

Insights and recommendations

Endpoint analytics also gives you advice when it detects performance issues in your environment. For example, if, on the resource performance dashboard, over 90% CPU usage is being detected, it recommends upgrading your cloud PC. This could also apply to physical PCs.

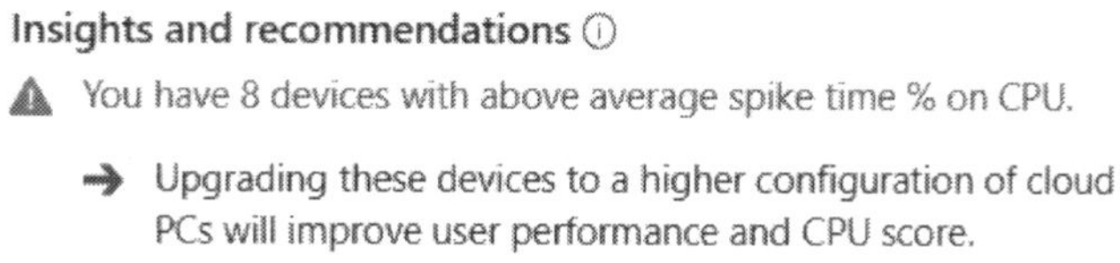

Insights and recommendations ⓘ

⚠ You have 8 devices with above average spike time % on CPU.

➔ Upgrading these devices to a higher configuration of cloud PCs will improve user performance and CPU score.

Figure 14.18 – Recommendation

Configuration Manager data collection

You could also collect user experience data from devices managed by Microsoft Endpoint Configuration Manager to calculate scores and insights. We explain the steps to enable tenant attach and co-management in *Chapter 6, Windows Deployment and Management*.

In the **Endpoint analytics | Settings** menu, you can find out whether the connection works properly. If not, as in the following example, no data will be shown in Endpoint analytics coming from Configuration Manager.

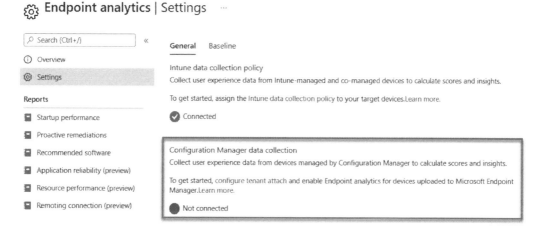

Figure 14.19 – Settings menu

Customizing your baselines

Change your baselines to your own values via the **Settings** menu, as you could have higher or lower principles as the default settings. This would allow organizations to adjust the scorings to standards that match the expectations of their environment and applications.

Baselines define the score and whether indicators show up in green or red in Endpoint analytics. Be careful when defining your own baselines to ensure the quality and performance level of your Windows 10 physical and cloud PCs.

You can see in the following screenshot how you can change the baseline regression thresholds. You can find this setting under **Endpoint analytics | Settings**.

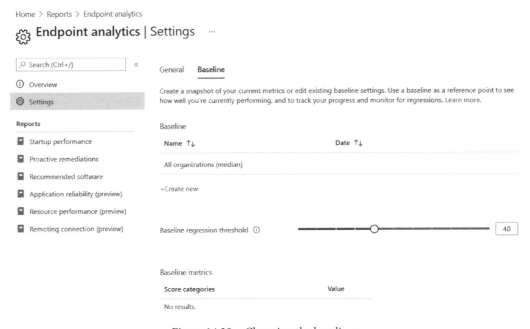

Figure 14.20 – Changing the baselines

Proactive remediations

Another great benefit of using Endpoint analytics is that you can create and run script packages on devices to proactively find and fix the top support issues in your organization.

For example, you can create detection scripts that search for settings on your Windows 10 endpoint – if the setting or registry key no longer exists, it fires off the remediation script to get the setting back in. This is a very unique and proactive way to make sure that your environment remains consistent.

The section shown in the following screenshot allows you to see the status of your deployed script packages and monitor the detection and remediation results. Results are shown as the number of devices affected.

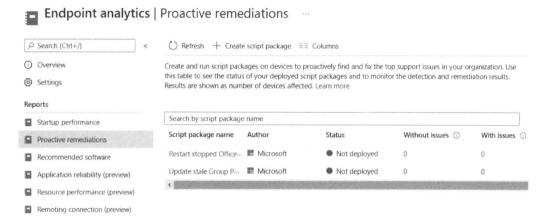

Figure 14.21 – Proactive remediations

If you want to create a proactive remediation script package action yourself, you simply click on **+ Create script package**.

Enter a name for the script and configure the detection and remediation script with the right settings, as in the following example.

> **Important note**
> If you are adding registry keys to a 64-bit Windows endpoint, make sure to enable **Run script in 64-bit PowerShell** to ensure it is at the correct location!

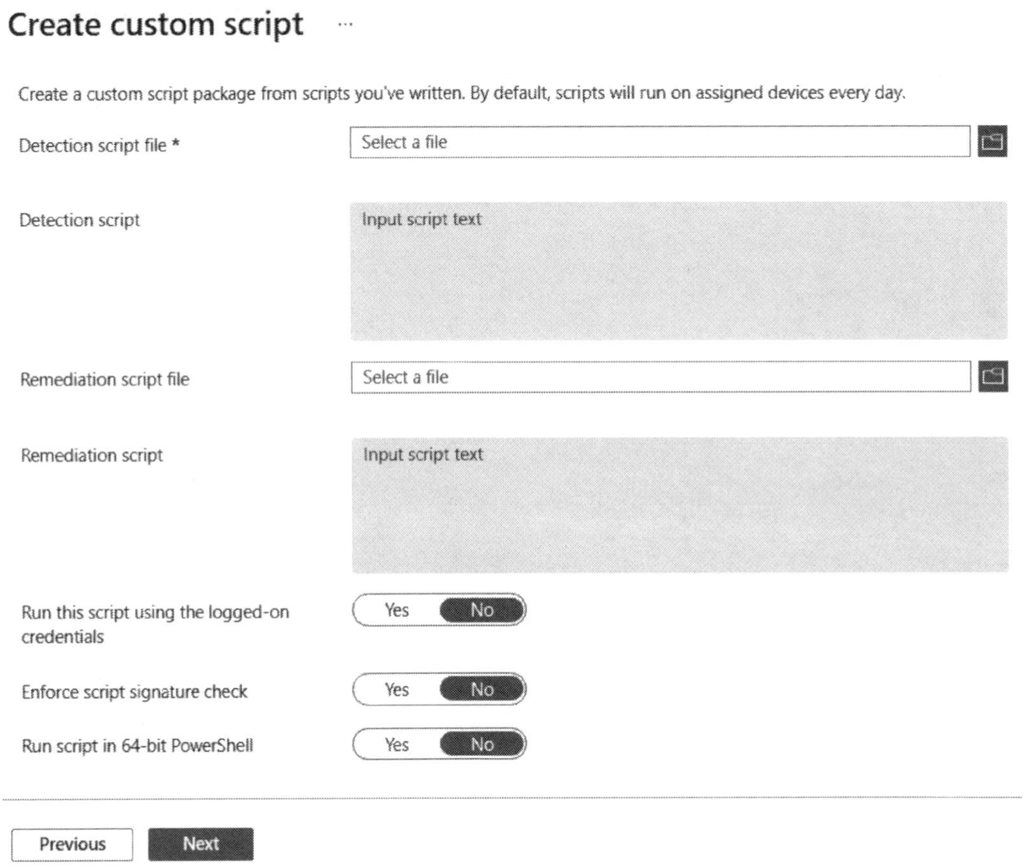

Create custom script   ⋯

Create a custom script package from scripts you've written. By default, scripts will run on assigned devices every day.

Detection script file *	Select a file

Detection script

Input script text

Remediation script file	Select a file

Remediation script

Input script text

Run this script using the logged-on credentials   Yes   No

Enforce script signature check   Yes   No

Run script in 64-bit PowerShell   Yes   No

Previous   **Next**

Figure 14.22 – Create custom script

Assign the custom script actions to the right groups/users either via AAD or on a device basis and the detection will start directly:

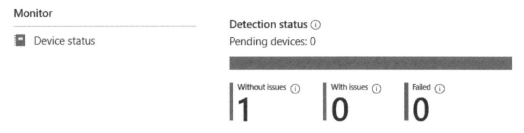

Figure 14.23 – Detection status

Azure Monitor integration

It's also possible to export diagnostics to Azure Monitor so you can query the data and do whatever you want with it. For example, you can create workbooks to map the status of your environment.

To enable this, you activate one of the diagnostic settings. There are also additional costs involved as it requires a storage account and a Log Analytics workspace.

The following list of logs can be automatically exported to a Log Analytics workspace:

- **AuditLogs**
- **OperationalLogs**
- **DeviceComplianceOrg**
- **Devices**

By enabling log analytics integration for Microsoft Endpoint Manager in the diagnostic settings, as seen in the following screenshot, you will be able to create queries and a custom dashboard based on the telemetry data that is being collected in Azure Monitor:

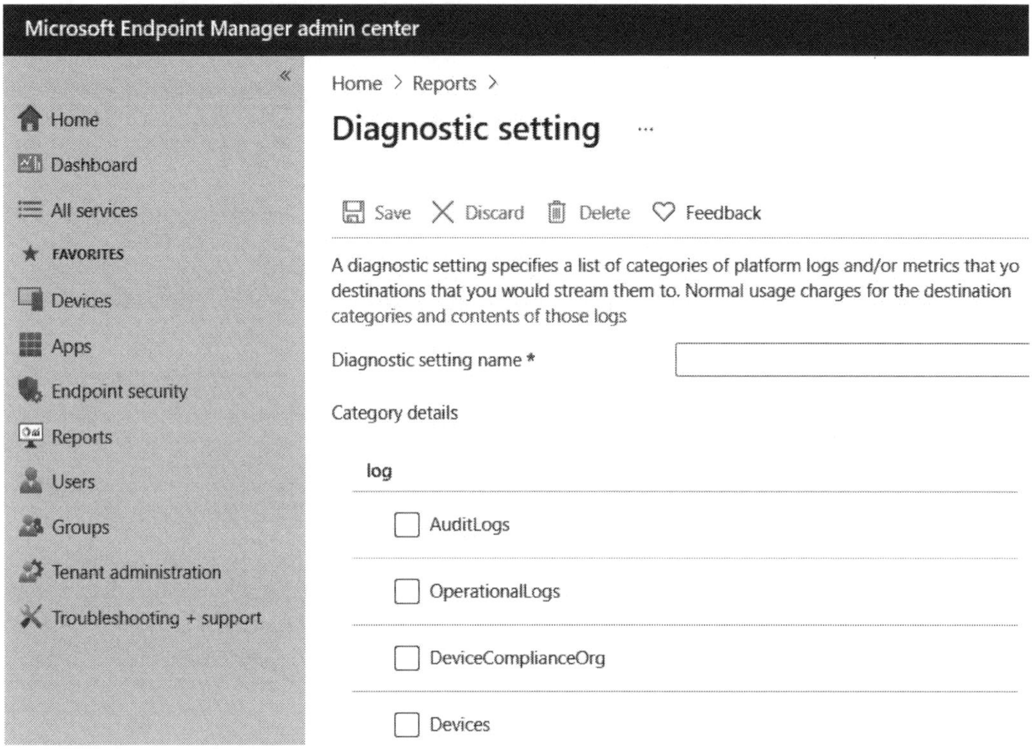

Figure 14.24 – Diagnostic setting

Productivity Score

Endpoint analytics contains great insights, but most people are not able to see them since it requires access to the Microsoft Endpoint Manager admin center. If you are an Intune admin or have the Global Administrator role, you could display the analytics.

With Productivity Score, you can quantify how Microsoft Endpoint Manager enables productivity in your environment.

Here are some important indicators within Productivity Score:

- Understand how user productivity is impacted by underlying technology performance factors.

- Focus on areas for improvement.

- Assign points across technology areas based on the overall experience impact.

See the following example of the active health of Microsoft 365 as part of your Windows 10 endpoints.

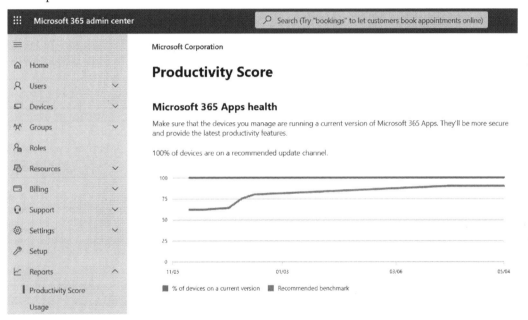

Figure 14.25 – Productivity Score

Service health

Next to Endpoint analytics and the other monitoring capabilities explained in the previous section within Microsoft Endpoint Manager, you can also monitor the service availability at a high level.

If you experience issues or other problems within Windows 365, Microsoft 365, or Microsoft Endpoint Manager, you can check the service health to determine whether this is a known issue with a resolution in progress before you call support or spend time troubleshooting.

To *find* the **Service health** dashboard, you must *open* the Microsoft 365 admin center portal.

Go to **Health** followed by **Service health**.

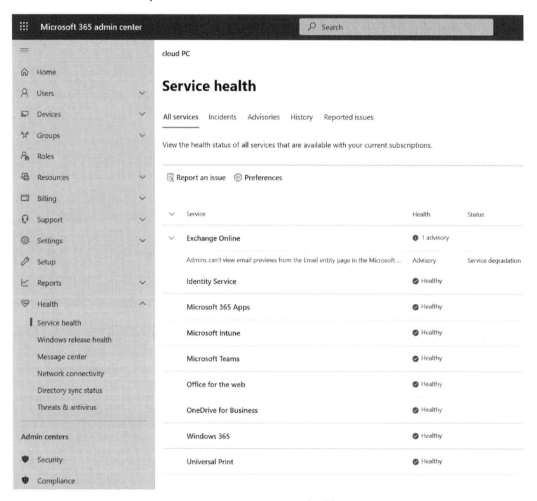

Figure 14.26 – Service health

This concludes the chapter on monitoring and Endpoint analytics. As we have shown, you will only benefit from enabling Endpoint analytics in your environment to get more insight into your Windows estate.

Summary

In this chapter, you've learned about the different monitoring, analytics, and reporting capabilities within Microsoft Endpoint Manager. Endpoint analytics gives you great insights that you can react to, but remediation scripts have the option to detect issues before the end user notices and remediate them. This is the best way to keep your end users productive and keep support calls to a minimum. Endpoint analytics is part of the Microsoft Intune and Windows Enterprise license, at no additional cost; you should just enable it to start getting data on your devices, which includes information on app crashes and reasons for reboots, including a blue screen.

In the next chapter, we're going to explain to you how you can simplify your traditional printing environment with Microsoft Universal Print.

Questions

1. Is it possible to measure the logon duration of your physical and cloud PCs?

   A. Yes

   B. No

2. What does the service health dashboard show?

   A. The availability of the different Microsoft cloud services

   B. The SLA of the different Microsoft cloud services

   C. The downtime of the different Microsoft cloud services

Answers

1. (A)
2. (A)

Further reading

If you want to learn more about monitoring and analytics after reading this chapter, please use one of the following free online resources:

- What is Endpoint analytics? Microsoft Endpoint Manager | Microsoft Docs: `https://docs.microsoft.com/en-us/mem/analytics/overview`

- Endpoint analytics page in Microsoft Productivity Score – Microsoft Endpoint Manager | Microsoft Docs: `https://docs.microsoft.com/en-us/mem/analytics/productivity-score`

15
Universal Print

Businesses are doing more and more things digitally; however, printing on physical paper remains important. Universal Print is a relatively new platform-as-a-service on Azure that can simplify the whole printing configuration and maintenance process compared to a traditional print server environment.

After reading this chapter, you will be able to connect both legacy printers and modern printers that are Universal Print ready to the Microsoft cloud. We'll also take a closer look at how you can assign printers to physical PCs and cloud PCs as endpoints via Microsoft Endpoint Manager.

Long story short, you will become an expert in printing!

In this chapter, we'll go through the following topics:

- What is Universal Print?
- Configuring Universal Print

What is Universal Print?

Universal Print is a new cloud-based print solution that allows IT admins to share printers through the cloud. Universal Print eliminates the need for on-premises print servers and lets you easily manage and deploy printers directly with Microsoft Endpoint Manager to use them as part of your cloud and physical desktops.

It enables you to manage printers directly through a centralized portal in Microsoft Azure. Say goodbye to installing (and maintaining) printer drivers on devices and/or base images. Also, everything works with Azure **Active Directory** (**AD**). This means that users can use the same set of credentials they use for other Microsoft services, whether they log on to a physical or a virtual desktop running in the cloud.

Another great benefit of the service is that you most likely already have the licenses – most customers that are eligible to use Microsoft Endpoint Manager also get Universal Print licenses. You can find the licenses you need for Universal Print in the requirements section later in this chapter.

Universal Print – architecture explained

The core print services run in the cloud as a platform service running on Azure, while the Universal Print connector(s) must be installed on a device running Windows Server or the Windows client OS. The connector device may be a physical device, virtualized on-premises, or hosted on Azure:

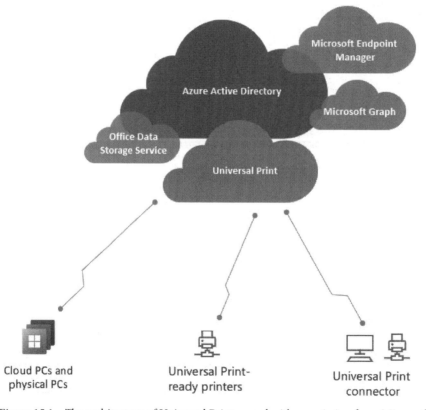

Figure 15.1 – The architecture of Universal Print – used with permission from Microsoft

When your printer is Universal Print-ready, you can then connect the printer directly to the cloud! There's no need for an ExpressRoute or a site-2-site VPN connection in all scenarios. Did you share and connect your printers correctly? You can then start assigning printers via Microsoft Endpoint Manager to your virtual (and physical) Windows 10 Enterprise desktops!

See the following example – the settings menu of a Lexmark printer that is Universal Print ready:

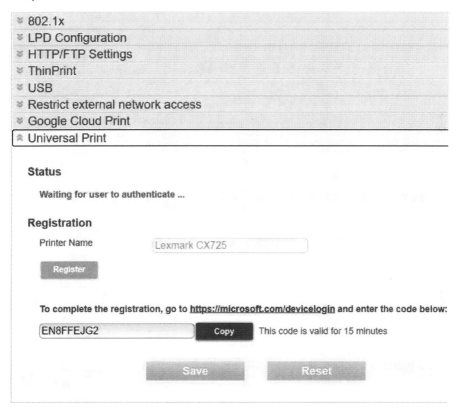

Figure 15.2 – Universal Print – Lexmark printer settings

This section explained how you can connect directly from your printer to the Universal Print service. Now, we will switch to the Universal Print connector process and explain how you can connect non-Universal Print-ready printers to Universal Print.

The print connector

The print connector is the proxy between your on-premises location and the Universal Print service. If your printer doesn't support Universal Print, this makes every printer scenario supported.

See the following print connector connection process. We'll explain more about this process later on in this chapter:

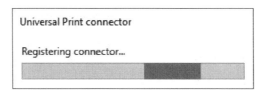

Figure 15.3 – Universal Print – print connector

Now you know how to connect your printers, we can start explaining how the data flow works.

Where does my printed data go?

Universal Print stores all print queues in Office data storage. This is the same storage that stores customers' Office 365 mailboxes and OneDrive files. A job stays in the print queue for a few days. If the job is not claimed at the printer within 3 days, it gets marked as aborted. Even after printing, a job may stay in Universal Print for a few more days (up to a total of 10 days).

Printer defaults

All the management of Universal Print happens from within the Azure portal, and this also applies to changing the printer's default settings such as color mode, the size of the paper, the output bin, and so on. Normally, you would have logged on to a traditional print server; with Universal Print you can do it from the cloud from one management console (see the following example).

The settings you define are taken over by the Windows 10 physical or virtual desktop by default:

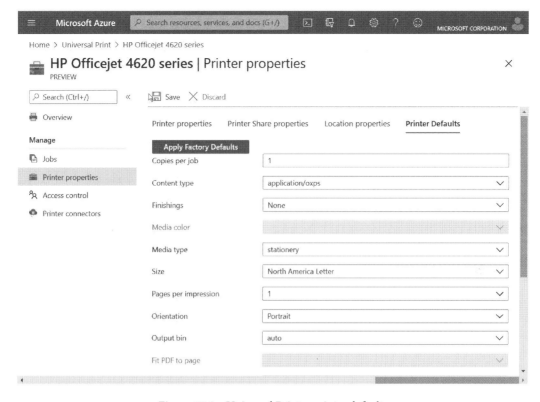

Figure 15.4 – Universal Print – printer defaults

Let's jump into the requirements of the service, now you've learned about all the basics to kick the tires.

Universal Print – service requirements

In this section, you will learn about all the prerequisites to use Universal Print:

- Your desktops should be joined to Azure AD. **Hybrid AAD joined (HAADJ)** device physical and virtual desktops are also supported.

- An *eligible* Microsoft 365 or Windows SKUs license.

- Universal Print licenses assigned to the Azure AD tenant via the Global Administrator.

- A Universal Print supported printer that can connect directly to the cloud – without a connector.

- A normal USB or network printer (via a connector).

- To configure Universal Print, the administrator doing the work should have either the Printer Administrator Azure AD role or should just be the Global Administrator.

- A Windows 10 client device – on version 1903 or later.

- A Universal Print connector host.

After these more functional and licensing requirements, let's look at the network requirements. As Universal Print is a cloud service, you can imagine that a network and firewalling are very important.

Network requirements

The connectors and your desktops should be able to connect to the following Universal Print service URLs:

- `https://login.microsoftonline.com`

- `https://aadcdn.msftauth.net`

- `*.print.microsoft.com`

Enough talking. Let's switch over to the deployment steps to deploy Universal Print in your environment.

Learning how to deploy Universal Print

Before we start, make sure that your environment is Hybrid Azure **Active Directory** (**AD**) enabled – or Azure AD only. Make sure the first **Windows 10 or later domain-joined devices** box has been ticked. You can find information about how to set up Hybrid Azure AD join and Azure AD join in *Chapter 13, Identity and Security Management*.

Also, make sure you have a Universal Print license assigned to your Azure AD tenant.

See the following screenshot to see how you can change your Azure AD Connect configuration to Hybrid Azure AD join during the setup flow:

Figure 15.5 – Azure AD Connect – enable Hybrid Azure AD join

Now, let's look at what rights you need in order to configure and maintain Universal Print.

Delegating printer access – custom roles

If you want to delegate access, for example, if you need to configure the Universal Print service with an account other than the Global Administrator, then to achieve this you need to assign Printer Administrator or Printer Tech rights to your user accounts.

See the following screenshot to see the roles in the admin center portal:

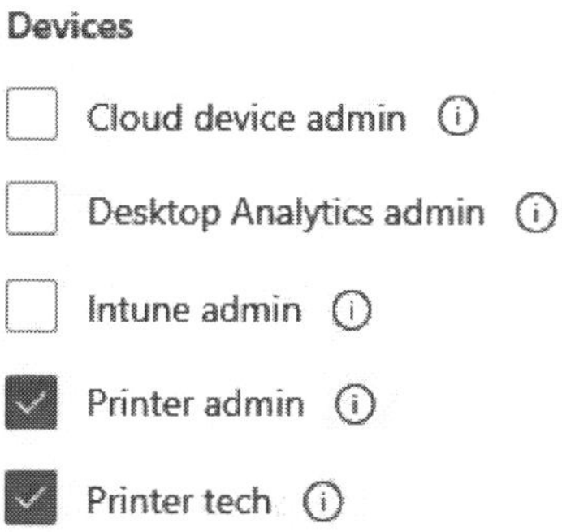

Devices

☐ Cloud device admin ⓘ

☐ Desktop Analytics admin ⓘ

☐ Intune admin ⓘ

☑ Printer admin ⓘ

☑ Printer tech ⓘ

Figure 15.6 – Universal Print role-based access controls

Now you've learned about role-based access delegation. Of course, Microsoft isn't doing Universal print all alone, and some features require partners to jump in. In the next section, you will find more information about this.

Connecting your existing printer to Universal Print

The following steps explain how you can connect your own printer to Universal Print. If your printer is Universal Print-ready, you can skip the connector installation and connect to the Universal Print service directly from the printer over the internet.

Here's a list of software and hardware partner solutions:

- Brother
- Canon
- Celiveo 365
- The ezeep Hub by ThinPrint
- HP Workpath
- Kofax ControlSuite
- Konica Minolta
- Kyocera
- Lexmark
- MPS Monitor
- MyQ X
- PaperCut
- Pharos Beacon
- PriApps
- Printix SaaS
- Ricoh
- Toshiba
- uniFLOW Online
- Xerox Workplace Cloud
- YSoft

More information about the value-adding solution briefs and contact details can be found here: `http://aka.ms/uppartners`.

Configuring Universal Print

Let's jump into the configuration flow of Universal Print. In this section, we explain everything you need to know to purchase licenses and configure and assign Universal Print printers to your end users. Let's start:

1. Go to the Azure portal via `portal.azure.com` and log on as either the Global Administrator or with the account with the Printer admin/tech role assigned.

2. Search for `Universal Print`:

Figure 15.7 – Universal Print – Azure portal

3. Are you getting this error? Make sure you have a Universal Print license assigned.

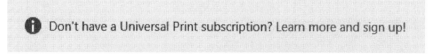

Figure 15.8 – Universal Print subscription prompt

4. Set up the Universal Print connector to connect to your on-premises location/printers.

   Your own printers are not able to connect with Universal Print directly and require a bridge/proxy, which has to be done with the Universal Print connector.

   > **Important note**
   > You can also install the software on one of your legacy print servers to connect it to the Universal Print service.

5. Install the Universal Print connector on your local physical desktop, that is, on the same network as your printers.

6. Download the latest Universal Print connector here: `https://aka.ms/UPConnectorMSI`.

7. To install the Universal Print connector, click **Install**:

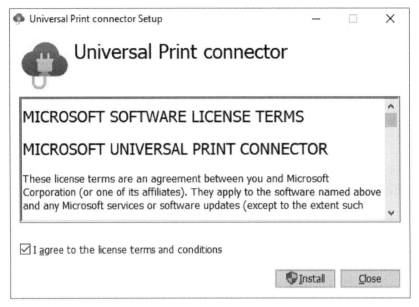

Figure 15.9 – Universal Print – print connector

Once the installation is ready, click on **Launch**:

Figure 15.10 – Universal Print – print connector

8. Click on **Ok** to confirm the diagnostic data prompt.

9. Click on **Login**:

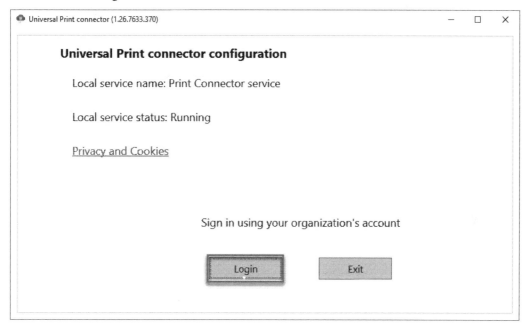

Figure 15.11 – Universal Print – print connector

10. Log on with your user's Azure AD credentials.

> **Important note**
> It is not necessary to use the Print Administrator/Global Administrator account.

11. Enter a name for the connector – the connector will show up later in the Universal Print admin portal as the proxy for the designated printer(s):

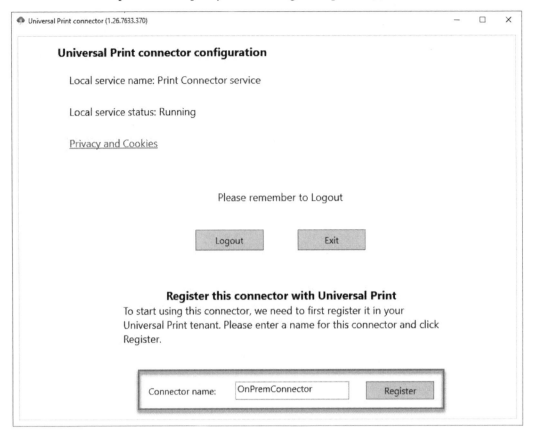

Figure 15.12 – Universal Print – print connector

The connector will now be registered to the Universal Print service.

12. In the **Connectors** menu, you'll see the connector name show up:

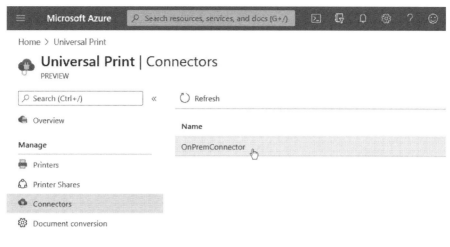

Figure 15.13 – Universal Print – print connector

> **Important note**
> The print connector will be created as a device in Azure Active Directory – as a device object with an object ID.

You can see an example of how that looks in the Azure portal here:

Microsoft Azure	🔍 Search resources, services, and docs (G+/)	

Home > Microsoft Corporation > Devices >

OnPremConnector

⚙️ Manage   ✓ Enable   🚫 Disable   🗑️ Delete

ℹ️ This device is a printer. Printers cannot be enabled, disabled, or deleted in the Azure AD portal. Learn more about managing printers. →

Name	OnPremConnector
Device ID	4476f28b-93bf-42ce-930f-88cdb7509f14
Object ID	32721fa1-0f61-4f60-abe6-253a2f7e5de6
Enabled	Yes
OS	Printer
Version	v1.0
Join Type	Azure AD joined

Figure 15.14 – Azure AD – print connector

13. You can click on the connector name to see some of the details of that specific machine and its status:

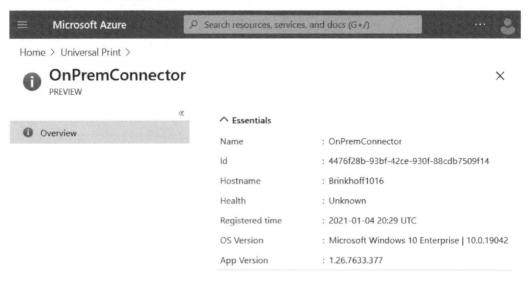

Figure 15.15 – Universal Print – print connector

After configuring the connector, we now have to prepare our domain configuration for Hybrid Azure AD join.

Enabling Hhybrid AD configuration – via the Universal Print connector

The following step to enable Hybrid AD configuration is only needed when an endpoint is Azure Hybrid AD joined. When your physical endpoint is active in Azure AD, you can skip the following step.

Activate Hybrid Azure AD in the Universal Print connector by ticking the **On** box:

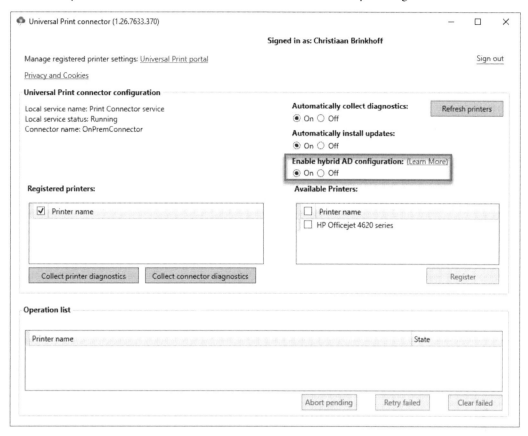

Figure 15.16 – Universal Print – print connector

Registering your own custom printers with Universal Print

We are finished with the connection part; we now need to make the printers available in the cloud as part of the Universal Print service:

1. Select the printers in the **Available Printers** list. Click on **Register**:

> **Important note**
>
> The list of available printers is detected from the printers attached to the desktop/server you install the printer connector on.

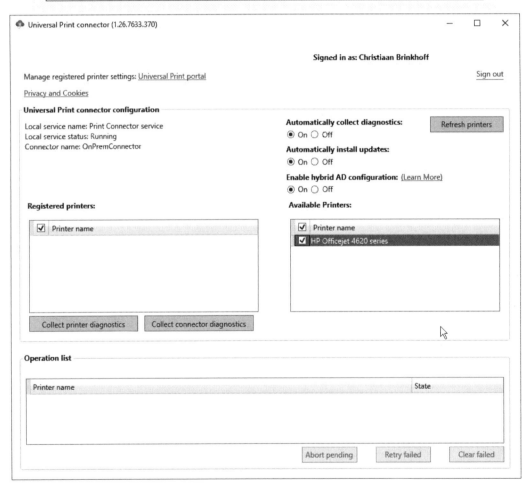

Figure 15.17 – Universal Print – print connector

2. The printers are added to the cloud. The status is **in progress**. This takes a minute or so.

We've done all the pre-steps now. The printers are now all visible in the **Registered Printers** list; however, as you can see, they aren't shared yet. That's something we are going to do now.

Sharing your printers with your users

Let's look at how you can share your printers with your end users:

1. Go to the Universal Print portal and open **Printers**.

> **Important note**
> As you can see, they have the status **Not shared**.

2. Select the printer(s) you want to share. Click on **Share**:

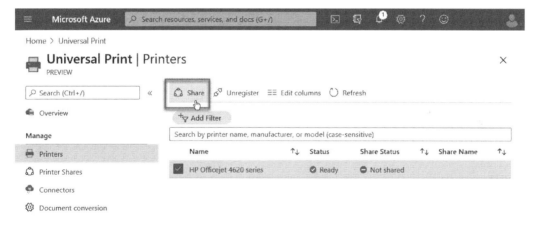

Figure 15.18 – Universal Print – management console

Now we are ready with the print sharing/publishing steps, the users are still not allowed to see and use the printers. Therefore, we need to add either an Azure AD group or the users directly to the list of members.

Assigning permissions to use a printer(s)

In this section, you'll learn how to assign the right level of permissions to your end users in order for them to print:

> **Tip**
>
> Did you know you can also select the **Allow access to everyone in my organization** option to allow all users to print?

1. Select your Azure AD users or groups. Once you're ready, click on **Share Printer**:

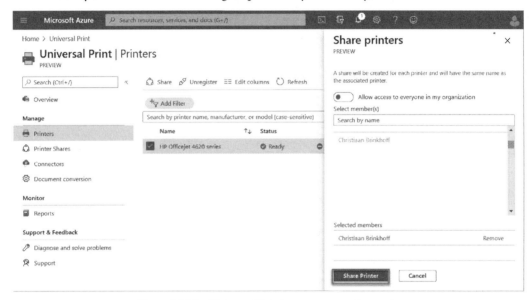

Figure 15.19 – Universal Print – management console

2. The printer is now ready to test within your desktop as the status is **Printer Shared**:

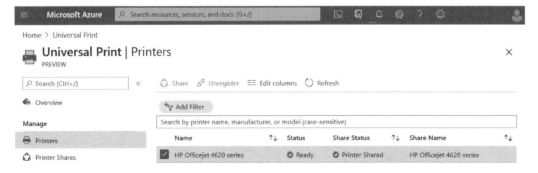

Figure 15.20 – Universal Print – management console

We are almost ready. Let's move on to the section that will explain how to test your printers!

Testing your Universal Print connected printer

In this section, you'll learn how to test your printers to confirm that the configuration happened successfully. After succeeding, you will be an official Universal Print expert:

1. First, you need to log on as an Azure AD user to your Windows 365 cloud or physical PC environment that is assigned to one of the previously shared printers within Universal Print.

2. Search for **Printers & scanners** in the Start menu:

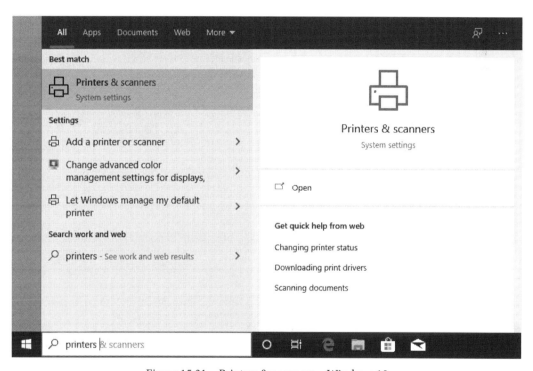

Figure 15.21 – Printers & scanners – Windows 10

3.   Click on **Add a printer or scanner**:

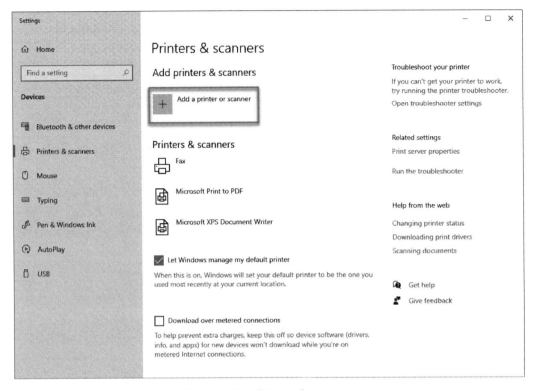

Figure 15.22 – Printers & scanners

4. Click on **Search Universal Print for printers**. Your assigned cloud printers should pop up automatically:

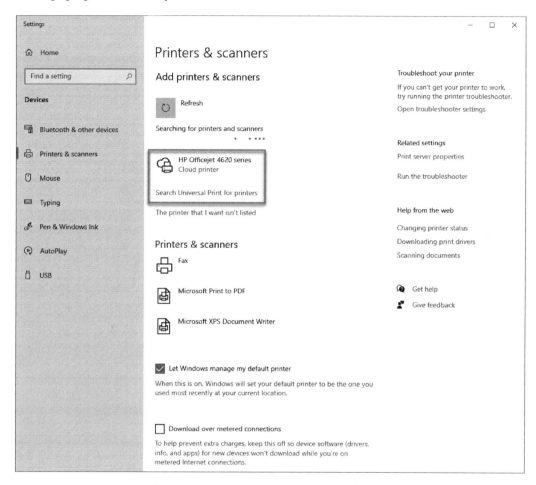

Figure 15.23 – Printers & scanners – Windows 10

5.   Click on **Add device** to add the cloud-based printer to your virtual or physical desktop:

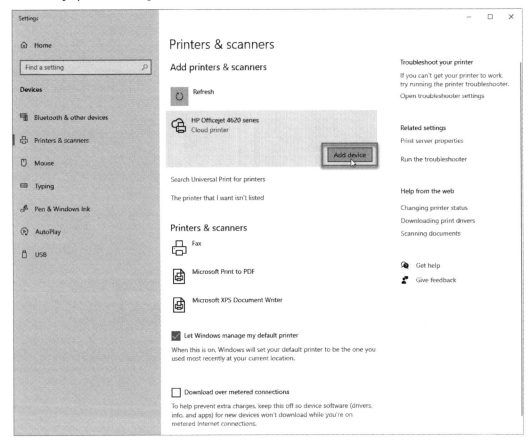

Figure 15.24 – Add device

6.   The printer has now been added and is ready to be tested:

Figure 15.25 – Printers & scanners – printer added

7. Open the cloud-based printer and click on **Manage**.

8. Click on **Print a test page**. The test page has been sent to the printer. You can open the print queue to see if something happens:

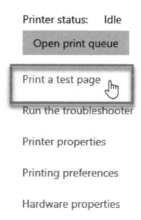

Figure 15.26 – Printers & scanners – Print a test page

9. The test print job has been sent to the printer.

10. If everything goes fine, the print job should be available and listed in the Universal Print admin portal too. You can find the jobs in the Universal Print portal by clicking on the printer, followed by **Jobs**. You should see the job with the status **Completed**. Great job:

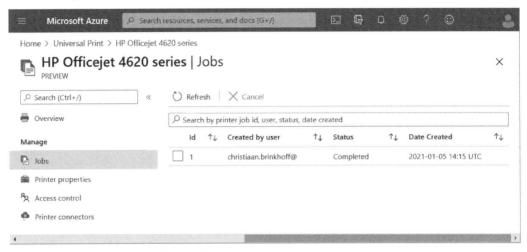

Figure 15.27 – Universal Print – print jobs

In the next section, you'll learn how to publish printers via Microsoft Endpoint Manager.

Assigning and deploying cloud printers with Microsoft Endpoint Manager

In the previous section, you learned about all the basics – as well as the manual process – of assigning printers. This process is also possible to perform via Microsoft Endpoint Manager (as explained earlier) as a more enterprise-ready approach to, for example, assign hundreds of printers across the globe to your users:

1. First, download the Universal Print provisioning tool via this link: `https://www.microsoft.com/en-us/download/details.aspx?id=101453`.

2. Make the CSV list ready for deployment as Microsoft Endpoint Manager enrolment will use a CSV file as the source. You can find the `printers.csv` file in the tool as part of `SamplePolicy.zip`.

3. Add all the Universal Print printer share name and share IDs and whether the printer should become the default printer in the CSV file in the following order, `SharedId, SharedName, IsDefault`:

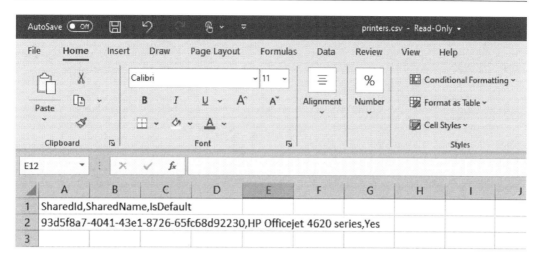

Figure 15.28 – Universal Print – Microsoft Endpoint Manager CSV config file

4. Look up the printer share names and share IDs that you want to add via Microsoft Endpoint Manager:

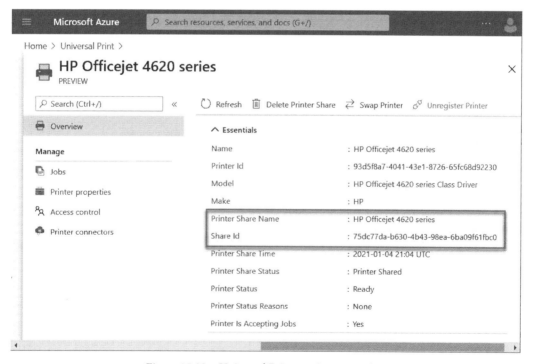

Figure 15.29 – Universal Print – printer overview

5. Generate the custom Win32 application package, which includes the new CSV file with the correct printer share names and IDs. You learned about creating a package in *Chapter 8, Application Management and Delivery*.

6. Download the Microsoft Win32 Content Prep Tool.

7. Unzip the tool, for example, on the `C:\` drive (you can pick the folder of your choice) from `https://github.com/Microsoft/Microsoft-Win32-Content-Prep-Tool`:

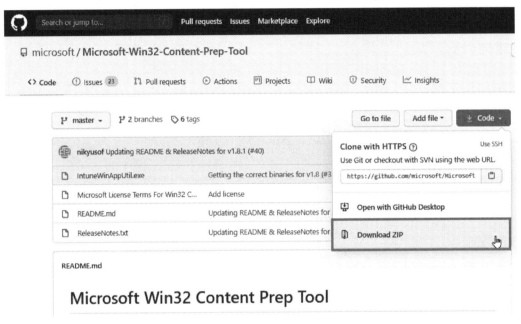

Figure 15.30 – Intune – Win32 Content Prep Tool

8. Open PowerShell and change directory to the Intune Prep Tool location, for example, `C:\Microsoft-Win32-Content-Prep-Tool-master`:

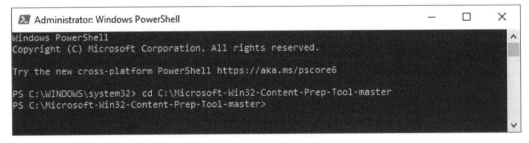

Figure 15.31 – PowerShell

9. Run `.\IntuneWinAppUtil.exe` and fill in the following requirements:

- **Source folder**: The folder where the list of printers (`printers.csv`) and `InstallPolicy.cmd` files are present.

- **Setup file**: The path of the `InstallPolicy.cmd` file (or any other script that will be used to copy the `printers.csv` file on users' devices).

- **Output folder**: The folder where you would like the generated `intunewin` package file to be stored.

- **Do you want to specify catalog folder (Y/N)**: Enter N.

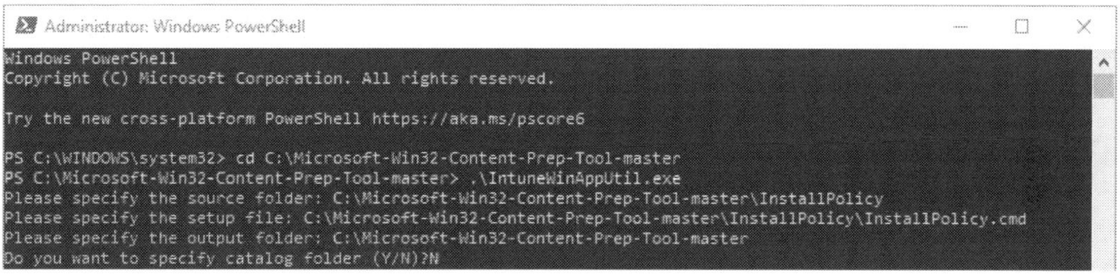

Figure 15.32 – PowerShell

10. The `.intunewin` package is ready to use within Microsoft Endpoint Manager:

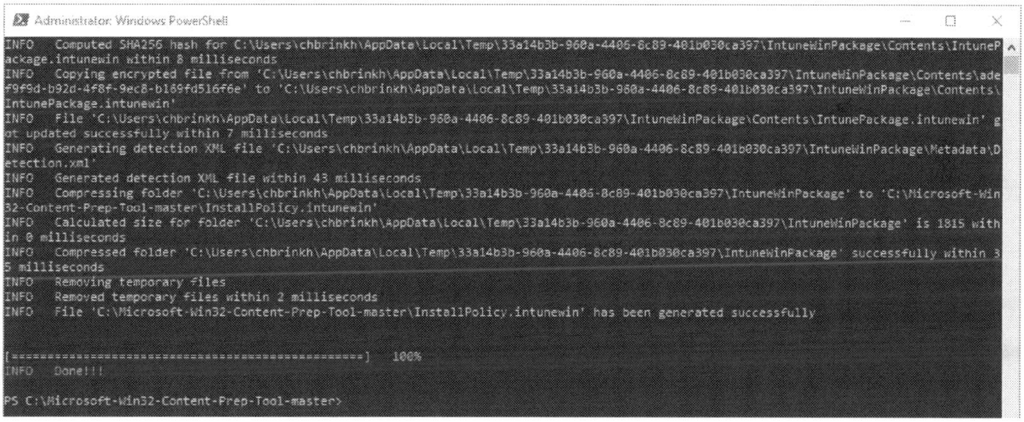

Figure 15.33 – The .intunewin package ready to use

11. Open the Microsoft Endpoint Manager console via `http://endpoint.microsoft.com/`. Then open the **Apps** menu and click on **Add**:

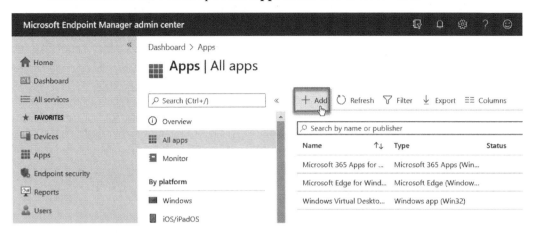

Figure 15.34 – Intune – Win32 configuration

12. Choose **Windows app (Win32)**:

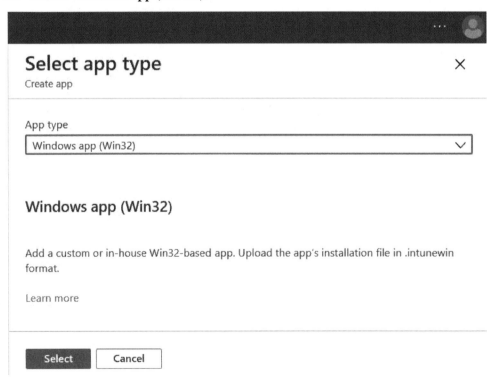

Figure 15.35 – Select app type

13. Click on **Select app package file** and browse to the `.intunewin` file output – for example, `InstallPolicy.intunewin` in the `C:\Microsoft-Win32-Content-Prep-Tool-master` folder:

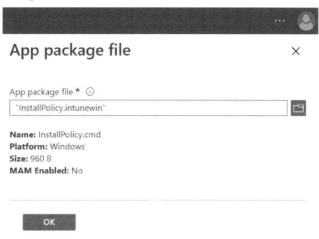

Figure 15.36 – App package file

14. Give the app a custom name such as `Install HP Printer`, as in the following example:

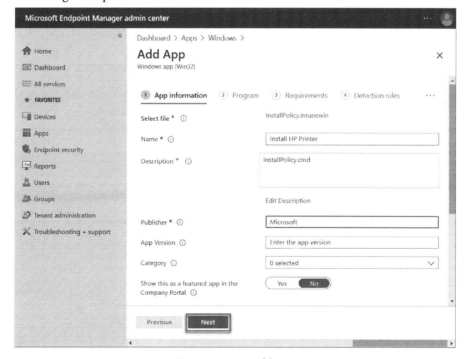

Figure 15.37 – Add app

15. Change the line that follows in the **Install command** and **Uninstall command** fields. Make sure it's a **User** installed application:

- `InstallPolicy.cmd user install`

- `InstallPolicy.cmd user uninstall:`

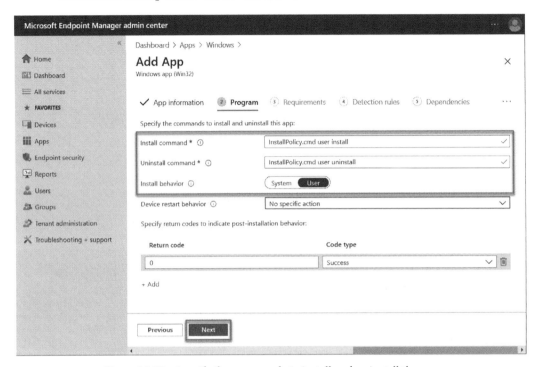

Figure 15.38 – Specify the commands to install and uninstall the app

16. Change the requirements in the screenshot to the baseline OS version and click **Next**. The baseline defines the minimum version of Windows to run in order to receive the printer assignment package:

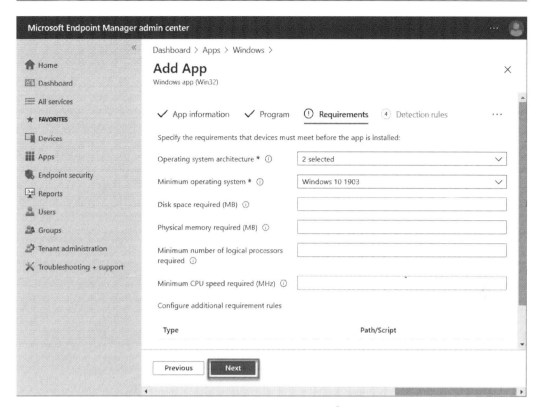

Figure 15.39 – Intune – Win32 configuration

17. Fill in the detection rule based on the CSV file that included the printers to be added. Add the following location in the **Path** field and `printers.csv` in the **File or folder** field: `%AppData%\UniversalPrintPrinterProvisioning\Configuration`.

18. Make sure **Detection method** is set to **File or folder exists**. Click **OK**:

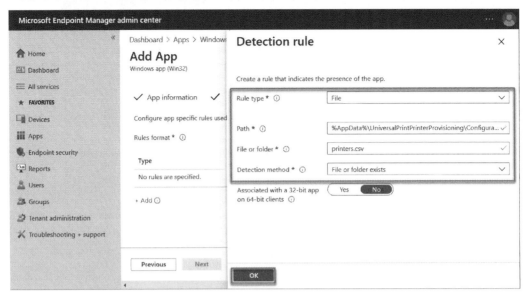

Figure 15.40 – Detection rule

19. Filter the list of printers in the **Assignments** menu to, for example, AD groups per department:

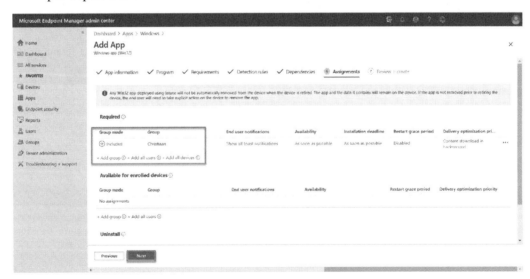

Figure 15.41 – Filter the list of printers

20. Confirm the settings by clicking on **Next** and then **Create**:

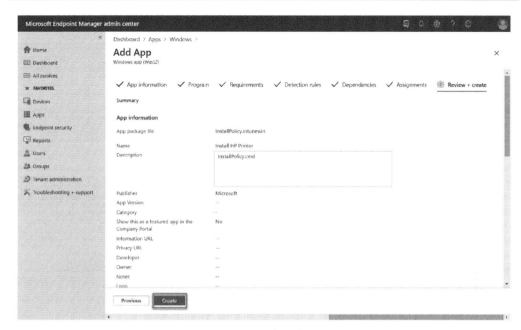

Figure 15.42 – Confirm the settings

21. Your printers will then be pushed to your physical and cloud desktops:

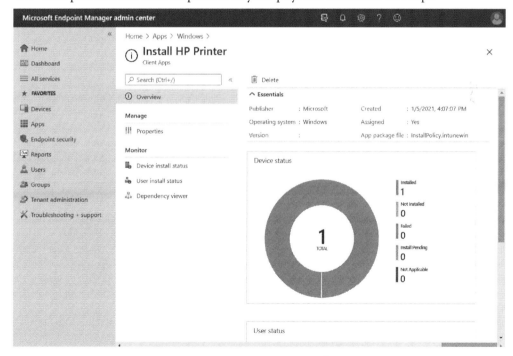

Figure 15.43 – Intune – Win32 configuration

You've now finished configuring Universal Print and have become a real expert in printing to the cloud. This will make your life as an IT professional a lot easier while maintaining your printers in comparison with a traditional printing environment.

Summary

In the chapter, you've learned about a new Microsoft 365 service called Universal Print, how to configure the service, and how to publish printers to your endpoints via Microsoft Endpoint Manager.

In the next chapter, we're going to talk about other managed devices that you can manage with Microsoft Endpoint Manager.

Questions

1. What port needs to be open in the firewall in order to use Universal Print?

   A. TCP - 443

   B. TCP - 445

2. Are print jobs with Universal Print sent to the cloud encrypted?

   A. Yes

   B. No

3. Does Universal Print support zero-trust?

   A. Yes, all traffic goes over the internet over SSL.

   B. No.

Answers

1. (A)
2. (A)
3. (A)

Further reading

If you want to learn more about Universal Print after reading this chapter, please use the following free online resources:

- Universal Print – Tech Community via `aka.ms/upcommunity`: `https://techcommunity.microsoft.com/t5/universal-print/ct-p/UniversalPrint`

- Universal Print – Get started via `aka.ms/updocs`: `https://docs.microsoft.com/en-us/universal-print/fundamentals/universal-print-getting-started`

Section 4: Tips and Tricks from the Field

Learn from the writers about the most common deployment- and networking-related errors they see in the field and learn how to counter and resolve them.

This part of the book comprises the following chapters:

16
Troubleshooting Microsoft Endpoint Manager

In this chapter, you will learn about the methods for requesting help while you are configuring your **Microsoft Endpoint Manager** (**MEM**) environment and, when you run into issues, learn how to resolve them either by yourself or with a little bit of help from Microsoft Support.

In this chapter, we'll go through the following topics:

- Troubleshooting MEM
- Service health and message center
- Troubleshoot blade in MEM
- Troubleshooting Windows 10 MEM enrollment
- Windows 10 device diagnostics
- Troubleshooting application delivery
- Troubleshooting Autopilot
- Windows 11 Autopilot diagnostics page

- Troubleshooting locating a Windows device
- Troubleshooting Microsoft Edge

Troubleshooting MEM

Under the **Tenant admin** blade, you have **Tenant status**. This is where some important information about your tenant is stored, such as the following:

- **Tenant name** and **Tenant location**: Here, you can see what part of the world your tenant is in—in this case, Europe.
- **MDM authority**: **MDM** stands for **mobile device management**. This is not as important as it was in the past.
- **Service release**: This is important. Here, you can follow whether your tenant has been upgraded to the latest service release.

Intune is a service that Microsoft updates monthly, so depending on where your tenant is located, you may see that your version of Intune is updated before others, based on this deployment schedule:

1. **Day 1**: **User interface** (**UI**) rolls out to the Asia Pacific region.
2. **Day 2**: UI rolls out to Europe, the Middle East, and Africa.
3. **Day 3**: UI rolls out to North America.
4. **Day 4+**: UI rolls out to Intune for Government.

The following screenshot shows an overview of the information stored in **Tenant status**:

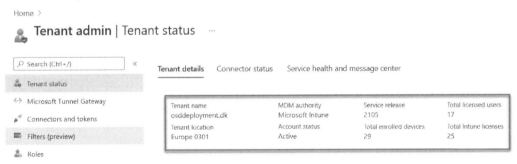

Figure 16.1 – Tenant status

Connector status is where you can see the status of Windows Autopilot sync, Microsoft Store for Business sync, and the Microsoft Defender for Endpoint connector, which all are Windows-related.

You can also see the status of all the other connector types. There are three different statuses a connector can have, as outlined here:

- **Unhealthy**:
  - The certificate or credentials have expired.
  - The last synchronization was 3 or more days ago.

- **Warning**:
  - The certificate or credentials will expire within 7 days.
  - The last synchronization was more than 1 day ago.

- **Healthy**:
  - The certificate or credentials won't expire within the next 7 days.
  - The last synchronization was less than 1 day ago.

You can see an overview of this in the following screenshot:

Tenant details   **Connector status**   Service health and message center

5 UNHEALTHY

Status	↑↓	Connector	↑↓	Time stamp
● Unhealthy		APNS expiry date		2/10/2021, 10:57:38 AM
● Unhealthy		DEP last sync date		8/19/2020, 11:26:00 AM
● Unhealthy		VPP last sync date		10/21/2020, 6:52:27 PM
● Unhealthy		VPP expiry date		9/7/2020, 9:28:03 AM
● Unhealthy		DEP expiry date		8/19/2020, 10:38:31 PM
⚠ Warning		Mobile Threat Defense Connectors		7/19/2019, 9:11:52 PM
✓ Healthy		Managed Google Play App Sync		9/1/2020, 3:16:18 PM
✓ Healthy		Windows AutoPilot last sync date		6/3/2021, 4:14:01 AM
✓ Healthy		Managed Google Play Connection		4/14/2021, 6:07:16 PM
✓ Healthy		Microsoft Store for Business last sync date		6/3/2021, 7:20:59 AM
✓ Healthy		Microsoft Defender for Endpoint Connector		6/3/2021, 6:27:31 AM
-- Not Enabled		Exchange ActiveSync Connections		N/A
-- Not Enabled		Certificate authority connector		N/A
-- Not Enabled		JAMF last sync date		N/A

Figure 16.2 – Connector status

Service health and message center

SERVICE HEALTH shows active incidents and advisories. This information is made easy to access in the MEM admin center, as you can see from the following screenshot representation. The same information is also available in the Microsoft 365 Service health dashboard in the Microsoft 365 admin center:

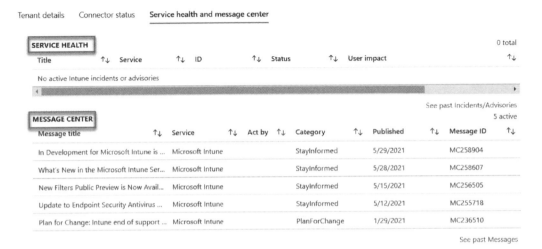

Figure 16.3 – Service health and message center

In the **Tenant admin** blade, you have an option to log a free support ticket when you have a Microsoft Intune subscription, as illustrated in the following screenshot:

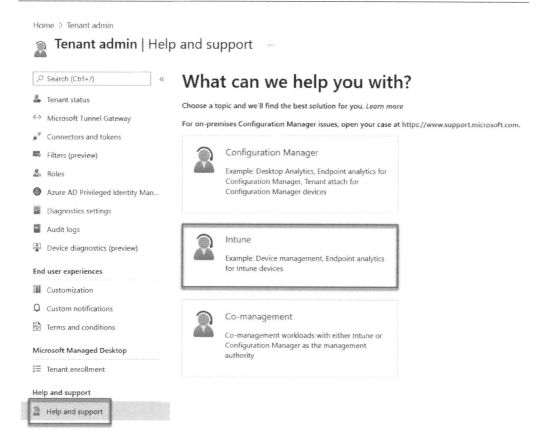

Figure 16.4 – Intune support

Click on **Intune** to start the Microsoft Intune support workflow. First, you will be guided through common scenarios or recommended support articles. If none of these help you to resolve your issue, you can create a support request, where you need to provide as much detailed information as possible.

Troubleshoot blade in MEM

Inside the **Troubleshoot** blade, the **information technology** (**IT**) admin can select the user from where the troubleshooting starts inside the MEM admin center.

Go to **Troubleshooting + support** and you are ready to start. If you instead want to troubleshoot a userless device, you can start the **Device** blade and locate the device directly to see which profiles and apps are assigned to the device. In this case, however, we want to find and help an end user by performing the following steps:

1. Select the user who you want to help by clicking the **Select user** button, as illustrated in the following screenshot:

Figure 16.5 – Troubleshooting: Select user button

2. The first section is **ASSIGNMENTS**, where you can see the applications that are available or needed by the user, as illustrated in the following screenshot:

Figure 16.6 – Troubleshooting assignments

3. By way of an example, you have an option to change the scope to **Configuration profiles**, as illustrated in the following screenshot:

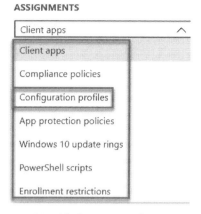

Figure 16.7 – Troubleshooting configuration profiles

4. With the new view you are shown, you can see all the policies assigned to this user, as illustrated in the following screenshot:

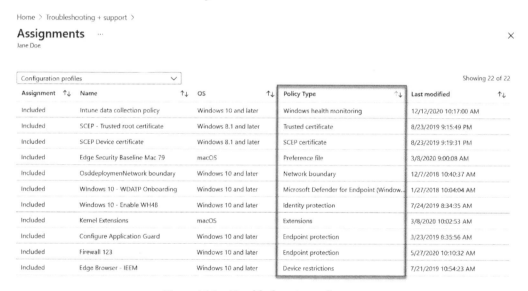

Figure 16.8 – Troubleshooting policy type

5. When you go deeper by selecting one of the policies, you will end up in the **Policy** blade where you can see the status, errors, and per-setting status for the policies.

    In this case, you can see that all devices that have this policy have the settings applied correctly:

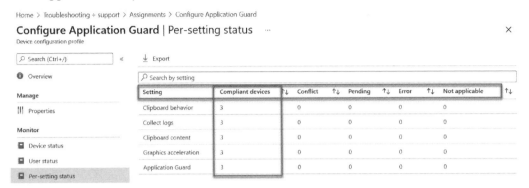

Figure 16.9 – Troubleshooting compliant settings per device

6. If there are errors on a policy, it will show up on the **Per-setting status** blade, as illustrated in the following screenshot:

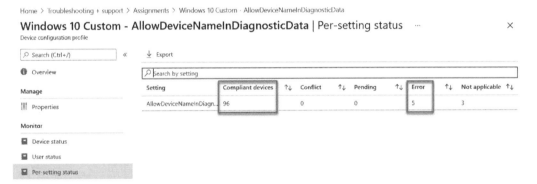

Figure 16.10 – Troubleshooting a compliant settings error

7. Then, you can go to the **Device status** blade where you can see which devices the errors are on, as illustrated in the following screenshot:

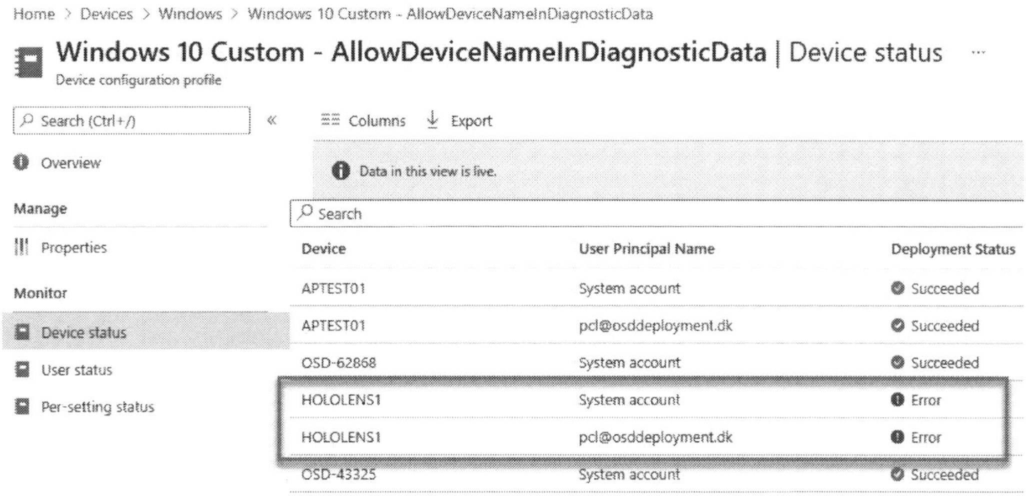

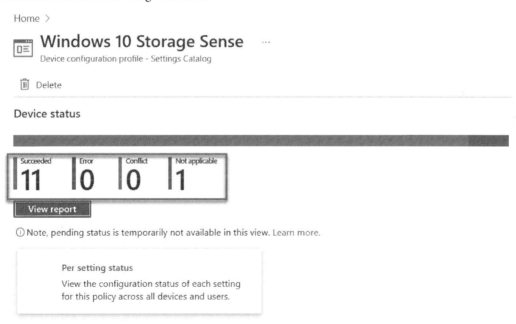

Figure 16.11 – Device status: policy error

If the policy is a Settings Catalog policy, you will see a much better reporting overview, as illustrated in the following screenshot:

Figure 16.12 – Troubleshooting the Settings Catalog

You still have the same option to see whether the individual settings are compliant or have errors or conflicts, as illustrated in the following screenshot:

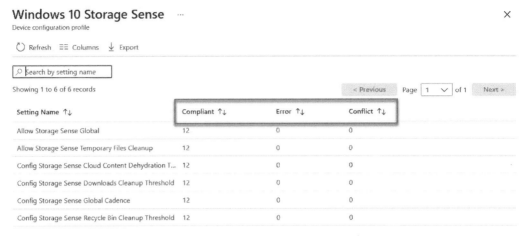

Figure 16.13 – Troubleshooting the Settings Catalog report

As we have demonstrated, you have more flexibility and a better overview of reporting by leveraging the Settings Catalog.

Troubleshooting Windows 10 MEM enrollment

You might get this error as part of the **out-of-box experience** (**OOBE**) when **Azure Active Directory** (**Azure AD**) joins a Windows 10 device (this is not a device known in the Autopilot service):

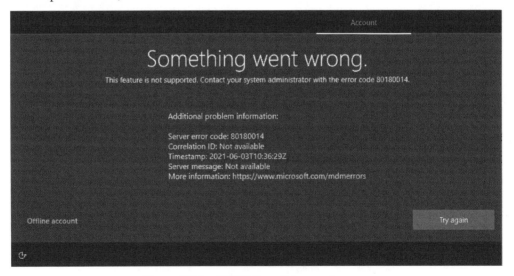

Figure 16.14 – OOBE: Something went wrong

You can follow these steps to troubleshoot your enrollment:

1. Go to **Devices | Monitor | Enrollment failures** in the MEM admin center, as illustrated in the following screenshot:

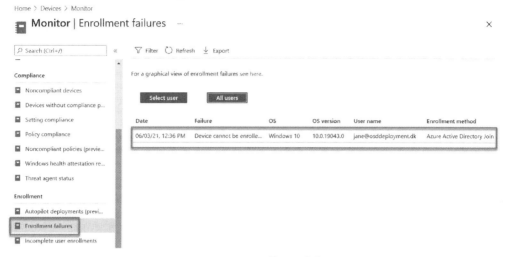

Figure 16.15 – Enrollment failures

> **Important note**
>
> If the user is blocked from enrolling in Azure AD, enrollment will never proceed to Microsoft Intune and will therefore not show up if the Intune report for enrollment fails.

2. In the MEM admin center, you can go to **Home | Devices | Windows | Windows enrollment**, as illustrated in the following screenshot:

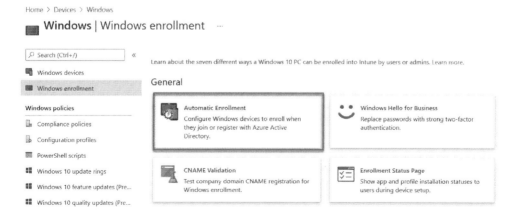

Figure 16.16 – MDM Automatic Enrollment

3. Click **Automatic Enrollment** to configure the MDM user scope, which will take you to the following screen:

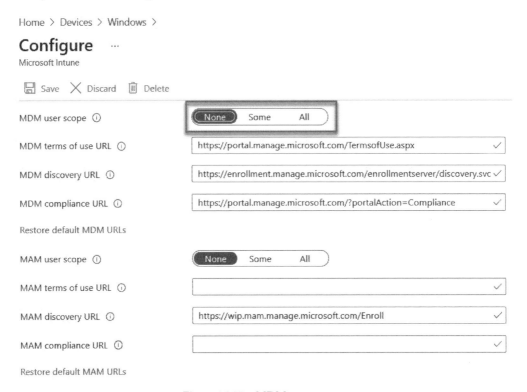

Figure 16.17 – MDM user scope

4. See whether your MDM user scope is set to **None**. The recommendation is to allow **All**; you also have a gate to control Windows MDM automatic onboarding in **System Center Configuration Manager** (**SCCM**) for co-management devices, as a device needs to be in a collection to go into Microsoft Intune.

    Inside Microsoft Intune, you have enrollment restrictions as well to ensure you can distinguish between personal and corporate-owned devices being enrolled in Microsoft Intun. This can also be scoped differently for different Azure AD user groups.

You can leverage the **Incomplete user enrollments** report to get a complete overview of enrollment failures in your tenant, as illustrated in the following screenshot:

Figure 16.18 – Incomplete user enrollments

5. Go and check whether the user is in a group with enrollment restrictions where personally owned **Windows (MDM)** enrollment is set to **Block**, as illustrated in the following screenshot:

Figure 16.19 – Enrollment restrictions

BitLocker failures

You can follow these steps to troubleshoot a BitLocker failure:

1. Under **Home | Devices | Monitor | Encryption report**, you can see an **Encryption readiness** column to ascertain whether a device is ready to be BitLocker-encrypted, as illustrated in the following screenshot:

Figure 16.20 – Encryption report

2. You can also dig into a specific device to see which policy the device has applied, as illustrated in the following screenshot:

Figure 16.21 – Device encryption status

This concludes our look at some of the monitoring capabilities in Microsoft Intune.

Windows 10 device diagnostics

By leveraging the DiagnosticLog **Configuration Service Provider** (**CSP**), Microsoft Intune can collect logs remotely on a Windows 10 device that is online and has internet connectivity.

Client requirements

There are some client requirements for remote log collection from the MEM admin center, including the Windows build version. These are outlined in more detail here:

- **Desktop**: Windows 10 1909/19H2 or later (build number 10.0.18363+)— Home, Pro, Enterprise, and Education versions supported.

- **HoloLens 2**: Windows 10 2004/20H1 or later (build number 10.0.19041+).

- Devices must be online and available via the internet, and **Windows Push Notification Service** (**WNS**) must have access to the machine.

The following screenshot shows the **Collect diagnostics** option:

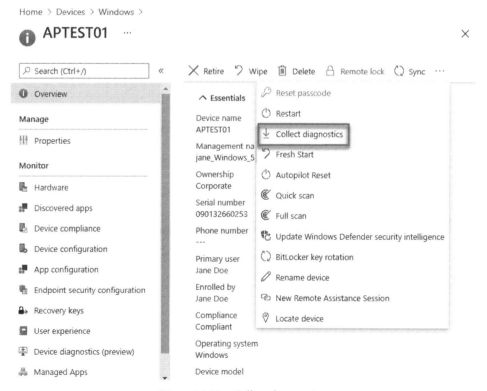

Figure 16.22 – Collect diagnostics

The IT admin will ask you to click **Yes** before Intune reaches out to the device and collects the logs, as illustrated in the following screenshot:

Collect diagnostics - APTEST01

Intune will attempt to collect the diagnostics that are on this device. To download and view the diagnostics, go to Monitor > Device diagnostics. Continue with diagnostics collection?

Yes   No

Figure 16.23 – Collecting diagnostics for a Windows device

You will be able to follow the status on the device (remember to refresh this page to get the updated status), as illustrated in the following screenshot:

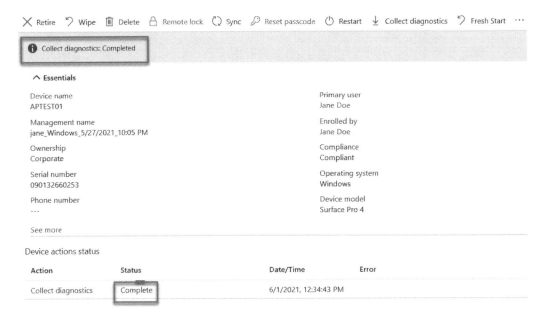

Figure 16.24 – Collecting diagnostics completed

There are three status messages for a diagnostic log collection, outlined as follows:

- **Complete**: Diagnostics were successfully collected from the device and are available for download under the **Device diagnostics** blade.

- **Pending diagnostics upload**: The device is running the diagnostics log collection and will finish shortly, or the device is offline/unreachable and has not received the request. The diagnostics collection action is good for 12 hours, after which time the IT admin needs to click the action again, so if the machine comes online and/or checks into the Intune service, the diagnostic log collection will be initiated on the device.

- **Failed**: The device ran diagnostics but failed to complete the task or failed to upload the logs to the backend service. To troubleshoot this issue, take a look at the **MDMDiagnostics** registry key at `HKEY_LOCAL_MACHINE\SOFTWARE\Microsoft\MdmDiagnostics` and the subkeys inside.

In the **Monitor** area on the device in MEM, you can find access to the **Device diagnostics (preview)** blade, as illustrated in the following screenshot:

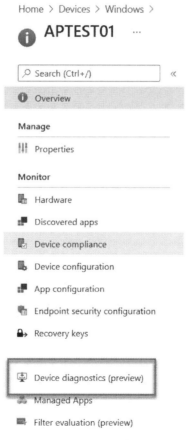

Figure 16.25 – Device diagnostics

Here, you can see the latest history for the diagnostics log collections, as illustrated in the following screenshot:

Figure 16.26 – Device diagnostics download

You can then download the logs that will come down to your local device in a `.zip` file. Extract the `.zip` file and this will give you a `result.xml` file and a list of folders containing the logs collected from the device, as illustrated in the following screenshot:

Figure 16.27 – Device diagnostics download results

There are limitations in terms of what can be collected with the DiagnosticLog CSP, which is described in the following documentation: `https://docs.microsoft.com/en-us/windows/client-management/mdm/diagnosticlog-csp`.

Remote log collection lets an IT admin collect and download Windows device logs without interrupting the end user or their productivity.

In the next section, we will cover application delivery troubleshooting.

Troubleshooting application delivery

There are different app types in Microsoft Intune that require different approaches for troubleshooting, listed as follows:

- Win32 apps
- **Line-of-business (LOB)** apps
- Microsoft Store apps

Win32

In the MEM admin center on a specific device, the **Managed Apps** blade provides the IT admin with information on the installation status of an app, and also includes installation failures.

The **Troubleshooting** pane within Intune provides failure details, including details about managed apps on a user's device. Details about the **end-to-end (E2E)** life cycle of an app are provided under each device in the **Managed Apps** pane. You can view installation issues, such as when an app was created, modified, targeted, and delivered to a device, as illustrated in the following screenshot:

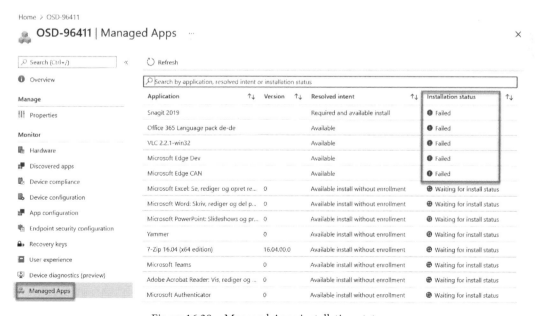

Figure 16.28 – Managed Apps installation status

By clicking on the failed app, Microsoft Intune will provide an error code along with a **Collect logs** option so that the IT admin can troubleshoot and fix the application installation issue if it persists, as illustrated in the following screenshot. The IT admin can only collect logs if the installation of the app has failed:

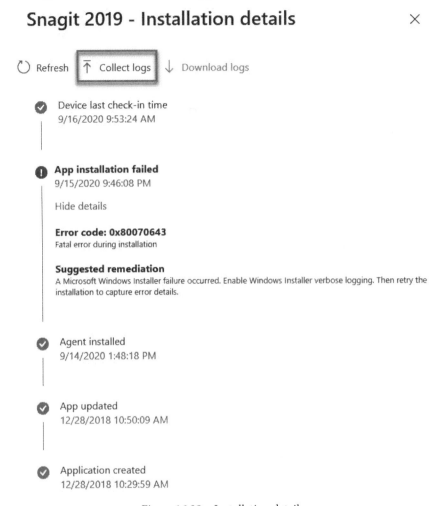

Figure 16.29 – Installation details

From the app itself, you can also see the installation status for both device installation and user installation before digging deep into the device/user to troubleshoot, as illustrated in the following screenshot:

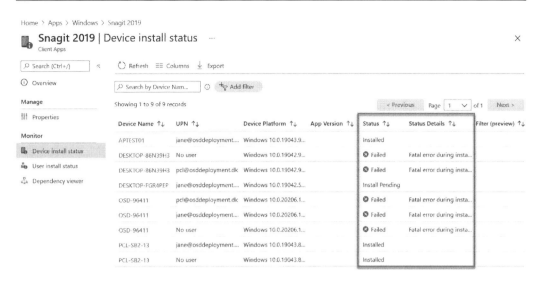

Figure 16.30 – Device install status

LOB

Microsoft Software Installer (**MSI**) LOB apps use the MDM stack to install apps. There is no ordering on application delivery to the Windows device of any kind, and no way of controlling conflicts between LOB MSI and Win32 MSI installation as both use the same trusted installer on the device.

It is not recommended to mix both LOB and Win32 app deployments on the same device with Microsoft Intune during the Windows Autopilot process.

Microsoft Store apps

The most common issue with installing apps from Microsoft Store is that a **Group Policy Object** (**GPO**) has blocked access to Microsoft Store or there is a network-related issue.

Be aware that offline apps should be assigned to devices and online apps should be assigned to users.

You can run the following PowerShell command on the device to see errors associated with the installation of Microsoft Store apps: `Get-Appxlog | Out-GridView`.

`Get-Appxlog` displays the logs associated with the most recent deployment operation.

Troubleshooting Autopilot

As part of the **Monitoring** blade in the MEM admin center, there is a report that shows the status of Autopilot deployments in the tenant. This report can be used as an example to monitor new devices that go through Windows Autopilot and give the IT admin an overview of the successes/failures and the total deployment time for devices.

When you are troubleshooting Windows Autopilot, it is important to be familiar with the following workflow:

1. A wireless (Wi-Fi) or wired (Ethernet) connection is established.

2. The Windows Autopilot profile is downloaded. When you use a wired connection or manually establish a wireless connection, the profile downloads from the Autopilot deployment service as soon as the network connection is in place. If you have an Ethernet connection, you may experience a situation where regional and language settings are bypassed. This can be configured in the Autopilot profile.

3. The next step is user authentication. When performing a **user-driven deployment** (**UDD**), the user will enter their Azure AD credentials and password. If a user is assigned to the Windows Autopilot object, the username will be completed automatically, leaving just the password to be validated.

4. The next step is Azure AD Join. For UDDs, the device will be joined to Azure AD using the specified user credentials. For self-deploying scenarios, the device will be joined without specifying any user credentials.

5. Automatic MDM enrollment occurs next. As part of the Azure AD join process, the device will enroll in Microsoft Intune when configured in Azure AD.

6. Settings, applications, and certificates are applied. If the **enrollment status page** (**ESP**) is configured, most settings will be applied while the ESP is displayed. If not configured or available, settings will be applied after the user has signed in.

Navigate to **Home | Devices | Monitor | Autopilot deployments**. Autopilot reporting will contain data from the last 30 days. Devices that are using Autopilot reset will not show up in this report. You can see an overview of the report here:

Data is retained for the last 30 days

Enrollment date	Enrollment met...	Serial number	Device name	User	Autopilot profile	Enrollment statu...	De
05/11/21, 4:35 PM	Self-deploying AAD	000206600856	HL2-00206600856		Autopilot HL2	Success	20
05/12/21, 7:31 AM	User-driven AAD	090132660253	APTEST01	jane@osddeployme...		Success	1 H
05/28/21, 12:05 AM	User-driven AAD	090132660253	APTEST01	jane@osddeployme...	Windows AutoPilot ...	Success	31
05/20/21, 12:53 PM	User-driven AAD	090132660253	APTEST01	jane@osddeployme...	Windows AutoPilot ...	Success	16

Figure 16.31 – Autopilot report

If you see the normal OOBE screens when Azure AD is joining a device, it is not going through the Autopilot workflow. Most likely, there is no Autopilot profile assigned to the device. You can find the Windows Autopilot device and see additional details by navigating to **Home | Devices | Windows | Windows Autopilot devices**, which will take you to the following screen:

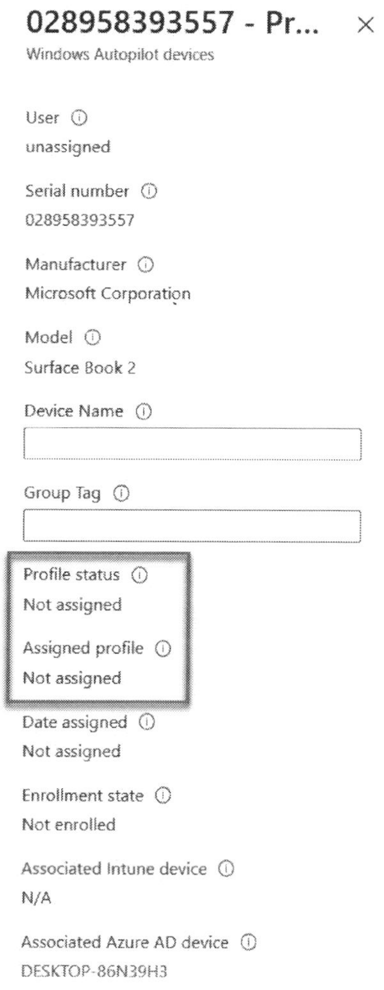

028958393557 - Pr...   ✕

Windows Autopilot devices

User ⓘ
unassigned

Serial number ⓘ
028958393557

Manufacturer ⓘ
Microsoft Corporation

Model ⓘ
Surface Book 2

Device Name ⓘ

Group Tag ⓘ

Profile status ⓘ
Not assigned

Assigned profile ⓘ
Not assigned

Date assigned ⓘ
Not assigned

Enrollment state ⓘ
Not enrolled

Associated Intune device ⓘ
N/A

Associated Azure AD device ⓘ
DESKTOP-86N39H3

Figure 16.32 – Autopilot profile not assigned

In this case, there is no profile assigned—the most likely reason is that the Autopilot device object does not belong to the right group where the Autopilot profile is assigned. You can also see that this device is in Azure AD but not in Intune. There is a lot of useful information on the Autopilot device object when you click on it.

You cannot assign an Autopilot profile directly to a device from Microsoft Intune; you can only do this for an Azure AD group. From Microsoft Store for Business, you can assign a profile directly to a device. This can break the expected Windows Autopilot onboarding experience and make troubleshooting harder for yourself.

Windows 11 Autopilot diagnostics page

When you deploy Windows 11 with Autopilot, you can enable users to view additional detailed troubleshooting information about the Autopilot provisioning process. A new **Windows Autopilot diagnostics** page provides IT admins and end users with a user-friendly view to troubleshoot Windows Autopilot failures.

If you set **Turn on log collection and diagnostics page for end users** to **Yes**, you will enable Windows Autopilot diagnostics on an Autopilot device, as illustrated in the following screenshot:

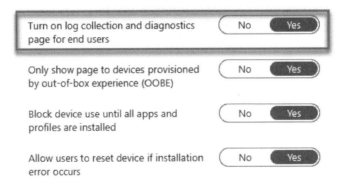

Figure 16.33 – ESP profile

If there are any errors during the Windows Autopilot process, the end user has an option to see more details by clicking **view diagnostics**, as illustrated in the following screenshot:

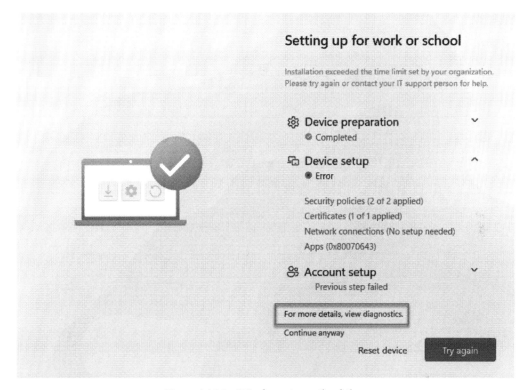

Figure 16.34 – Windows Autopilot failure

This will start the new **Windows Autopilot diagnostics** page for Windows 11, which is currently only available for the user-driven Windows Autopilot deployment mode.

The end user will then see clear icons that show statuses such as the following:

- **Task failed**
- **Task in progress**
- **Task unknown or incomplete**
- **Task successfully completed**

Under **Enrollment Status**, you can see all the checks that have been done, such as **Trusted Platform Module (TPM)** attestation and MDM enrollment, as illustrated in the following screenshot:

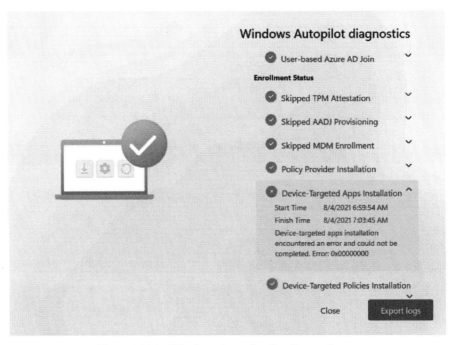

Figure 16.35 – Windows Autopilot Enrollment Status

With the **Windows Autopilot diagnostics** overview, you can expand **General** and **Hardware** to get more information on the device. You can also dig into **Apps and policies status** to get more information about different errors in this area, as illustrated in the following screenshot:

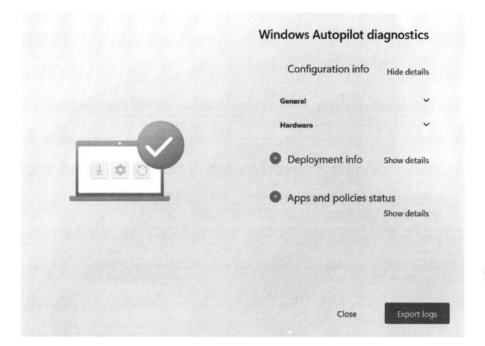

Figure 16.36 – Windows Autopilot diagnostics configuration information

You can see examples of different task messages for app failure in the following screenshot:

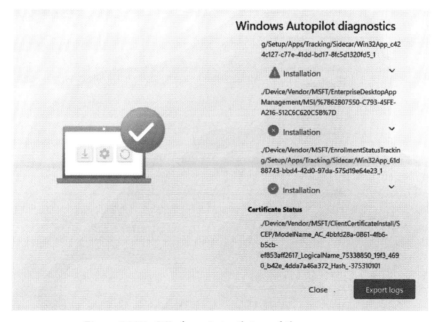

Figure 16.37 – Windows Autopilot app failure messages

You can see in this **Windows Autopilot diagnostics** screen that there is an incomplete installation for an LOB MSI and an error on a Win32 app. Once you have the app **identifier (ID)**, you can go back to Microsoft Intune and continue troubleshooting from the app side.

In the next section, we will cover how to ensure that your devices have enabled the location service so that you can find your Windows devices if they are lost.

Troubleshooting locating a Windows device

To get the location of a lost or stolen Windows device on a map, use the **Locate device** action in Microsoft Intune.

These are the Windows versions supported:

- Windows 10 version 20H2 (10.0.19042.789) or later

- Windows 10 version 2004 (10.0.19041.789) or later

- Windows 10 version 1909 (10.0.18363.1350) or later

- Windows 10 version 1809 (10.0.17763.1728) or later

The Windows **Location** service is off by default, as illustrated in the following screenshot:

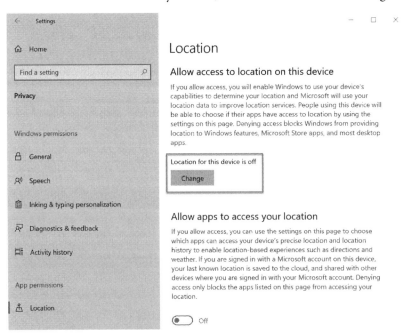

Figure 16.38 – Location service is off

It requires the user to turn it on if they want to leverage this feature or create a policy that turns the location service on. To do that, perform the following steps:

1. Create a policy in the Settings Catalog to enable the location service on your Windows devices, as illustrated in the following screenshot:

Home > Devices > Windows >

Create device configuration profile   ...
Windows 10 and later - Settings catalog (preview)

① **Basics**   ② Configuration settings   ③ Assignments   ④ Scope tags   ⑤ Review + create

Name *	Enable Location Service ✓
Description	
Platform	Windows 10 and later ⌄

Figure 16.39 – Enable Location Service profile

2. Search for `privacy` and select **Let Apps Access Location**, as illustrated in the following screenshot:

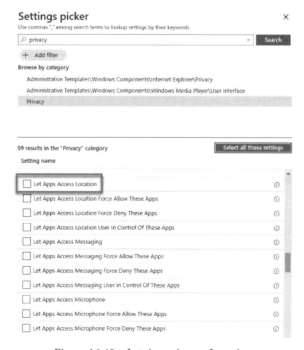

Figure 16.40 – Let Apps Access Location

3. Change the setting to **Force allow**, as illustrated in the following screenshot:

Figure 16.41 – Force allow

4. After deploying the policy to your devices, you will see the following message: **Some of these settings are hidden or managed by your organization**. In this case, the **Location for this device is on** field is activated and the end user cannot turn it off as it is configured from Microsoft Intune as a policy. This is illustrated in the following screenshot:

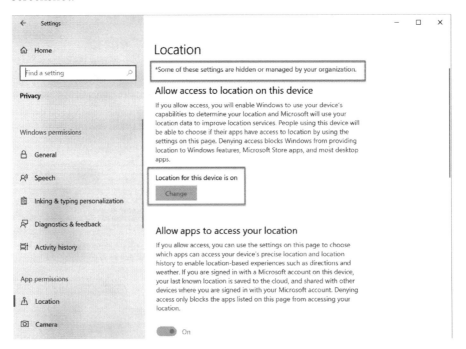

Figure 16.42 – Location service is on

5. Inside the MEM admin center, you can go to **Home | Devices | Windows**, select the device you want to locate, and click the **Locate device** action, as illustrated in the following screenshot:

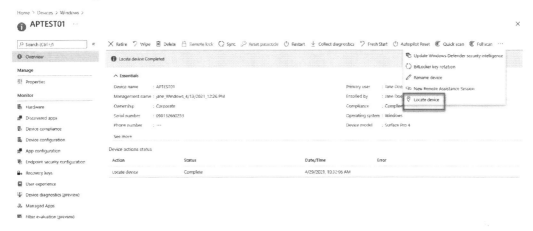

Figure 16.43 – Locate device

6. When the device is located, the device location is shown on a map, as illustrated in the following screenshot:

Figure 16.44 – Map with the device

Troubleshooting Microsoft Edge

Microsoft has released a new Chromium-based version of Microsoft Edge. This new version provides best-in-class compatibility with extensions and websites. This also means that there are new ways to perform troubleshooting and new policies that can manage the Edge browser.

Let's start by taking a look at the policy troubleshooting tool that is built into the browser itself. By entering `Edge://policy/` in the address bar, you can access the **Policies** page, as illustrated in the following screenshot:

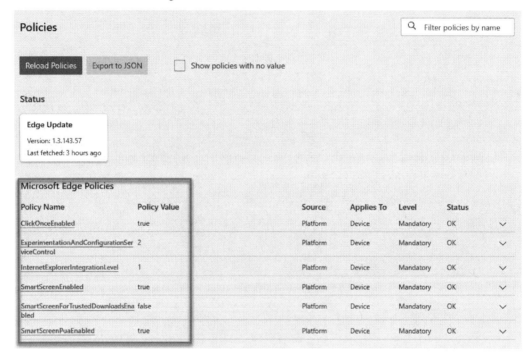

Figure 16.45 – Edge policy

You can see all the policy settings and the policy value of each setting applied to the Edge browser.

To check whether the browser is updated to the latest version, you can enter `edge://settings/help` in the address bar of the Edge browser. This will take you to the following screen:

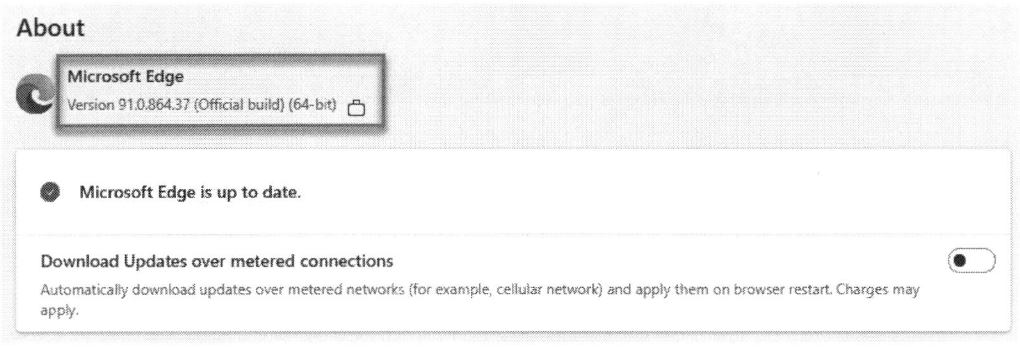

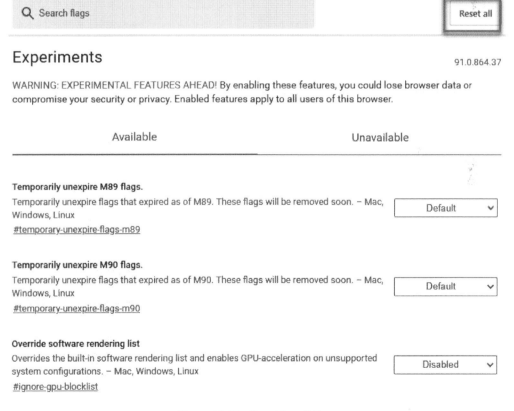

Figure 16.46 – About Edge

To check which flags are configured in the Edge browser, you can enter `edge://flags/` in the address bar of the Edge browser. This will take you to the following screen:

Figure 16.47 – Resetting all flags

You have an option to click **Reset all** to reset all flags from this page.

Summary

In this chapter, you've learned about most of the deployment errors that could occur during the configuration of MEM.

The knowledge you gain after reading this chapter will help you to troubleshoot some common errors while kicking the tires and will enable you to become the expert that you need and want to be in order to maintain production workloads in your business!

In the next chapter, we will learn about troubleshooting Windows 365.

Questions

1. Is Microsoft Support included in your Microsoft Intune subscription?

    a) Yes

    b) No

2. Does Windows Location Services need to be enabled on Windows to work from Microsoft Intune?

    a) Yes

    b) No

Answers

1. (A)

2. (A)

Further reading

In case you want to learn more after reading this chapter, please use one of the following free online resources:

*   *Troubleshoot app installation issues*—Intune | *Microsoft Docs*: `https://docs.microsoft.com/en-us/troubleshoot/mem/intune/troubleshoot-app-install#:~:text=Intune%20provides%20app%20troubleshooting%20details%20based%20on%20the,Select%20user%20to%20select%20a%20user%20to%20troubleshoot`

*   *Troubleshooting packaging, deployment, and query of Windows apps*—Win32 apps | *Microsoft Docs*: `https://docs.microsoft.com/en-us/windows/win32/appxpkg/troubleshooting`

17

Troubleshooting Windows 365

In this chapter, you will learn about the methods to request help when you run into issues configuring your Windows 365 environment and resolve them either yourself or with a little bit of help from Microsoft Support.

Supporting a service is very important, even though most of the components are simplified and managed by Microsoft. A new service is always something you have to learn about first by running into issues. In this chapter, we hope to ramp up your baseline knowledge with different troubleshooting example scenarios.

In this chapter, we'll go through the following topics:

- Troubleshooting yourself and Microsoft Support
- Common issues and fixes
- Windows 365 provisioning errors

Troubleshooting yourself and Microsoft Support

The following sections will cover how you, as an **information technology** (IT) department, can best provide support for your users, as well as how to request support from Microsoft. It's easy to request support via the **Microsoft Endpoint Manager** (MEM) admin center portal via **Troubleshooting + support**.

You can find a rundown of the different support ticket topics here to get the right support engineer assigned to your case:

- **Intune**

  - Managing devices with Intune

  - Endpoint analytics for Intune devices

- **Configuration Manager**

  - Desktop Analytics

  - Endpoint analytics for Configuration Manager devices

  - Tenant attach for Configuration Manager devices

- **Co-management**

  - Co-management workloads with either Intune or Configuration Manager as the management authority

- **Cloud PC**

  - A new way of experiencing Windows, on any device

You can see an overview of **Troubleshooting + support** in the following screenshot:

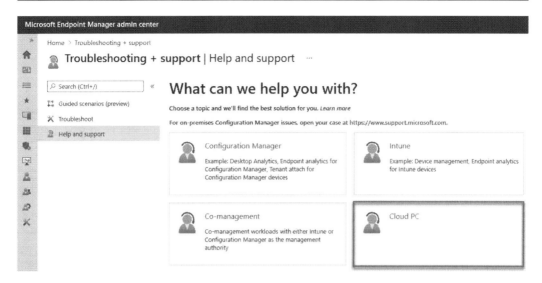

Figure 17.1 – Troubleshooting + support

Under **Help and support**, you select the **Cloud PC** option to create helpdesk tickets.

After that, you enter a quick summary of the problem you have. There is a chance that a resolution will be provided based on your input.

If not, click on **Use search to describe your issue and contact support**, as illustrated in the following screenshot:

 Use search to describe your issue and contact support
Open a service request and get help from a support agent.

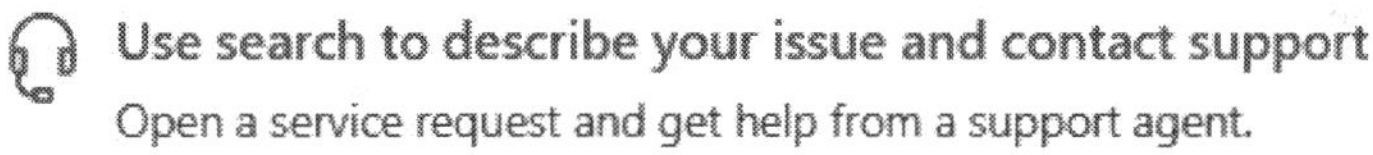

Figure 17.2 – Contact support

Make sure to *include as much technical information as possible* regarding the error to avoid a request for more information from a Microsoft helpdesk employee. You can see an overview of the **Contact support** form in the following screenshot:

Figure 17.3 – Contact support form

Next, we will look at some common issues and how to fix them.

Common issues and fixes

In the next sections, we'll explain the most common troubleshooting scenarios and fixes for Windows 365 Enterprise.

Domain-name resolution

A very common error that happens is customers configure their Azure environment, create an Azure **virtual network** (**VNet**), but forget about changing the **DNS servers** setting on the VNet to their own domain server.

Always make sure to change your **Domain Name System** (**DNS**) server to **Custom** and enter the **Internet Protocol** (**IP**) address of your own DNS service environment that can resolve your **Active Directory Domain Services** (**AD DS**) domain.

The enrollment of your cloud PCs will fail. The good thing is that our Watchdog service, explained earlier in *Chapter 3, Introducing Windows 365*, will notify you about it as well.

The **DNS servers** setting is shown in the following screenshot:

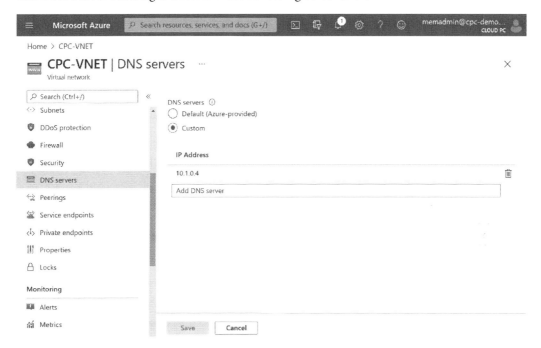

Figure 17.4 – DNS servers

Let's continue with the networking segment of troubleshooting and talk more about the different service **Uniform Resource Locators** (**URLs**) we have to check and whitelist for traffic.

Service URL firewall traffic

Some customers prefer to block all outbound traffic unless it's verified. If that's the case in your organization, you must ensure that all the following URLs and ports are allowed to be used. If that's not the case, the deployment will return an error.

Traffic to both MEM services—Intune and **Azure Virtual Desktop** (**AVD**)—should be allowed in your firewall.

You can perform `nslookup - psping` on the URLs to check whether the connectivity is working or not. You can use port `80/443 TCP` as the outbound port for the following domains:

- `portal.manage.microsoft.com`
- `*.manage.microsoft.com`
- `m.manage.microsoft.com`
- `login.microsoftonline.com`
- `*.officeconfig.msocdn.com`
- `config.office.com`
- `graph.windows.net`
- `enterpriseregistration.windows.net`
- `sts.manage.microsoft.com`
- `Manage.microsoft.com`
- `i.manage.microsoft.com`
- `r.manage.microsoft.com`
- `a.manage.microsoft.com`
- `p.manage.microsoft.com`
- `EnterpriseEnrollment.manage.microsoft.com`
- `EnterpriseEnrollment-s.manage.microsoft.com`

Find all the designated URLs and ports to whitelist for AVD on top of the MEM URLs mentioned in the previous list, as follows:

Address	Outbound Transmission Control Protocol (TCP) port	Purpose
`*.wvd.microsoft.com`	443	Service traffic
`gcs.prod.monitoring.core.windows.net`	443	Agent traffic
`production.diagnostics.monitoring.core.windows.net`	443	Agent traffic
`*xt.blob.core.windows.net`	443	Agent traffic
`*eh.servicebus.windows.net`	443	Agent traffic
`*xt.table.core.windows.net`	443	Agent traffic
`catalogartifact.azureedge.net`	443	Azure Marketplace
`kms.core.windows.net`	1688	Windows activation
`mrsglobalsteus2prod.blob.core.windows.net`	443	Agent and side-by-side (SXS) stack updates
`wvdportalstorageblob.blob.core.windows.net`	443	Azure portal support
`169.254.169.254`	80	Azure Instance Metadata Service (IMDS) endpoint
`168.63.129.16`	80	Session host health monitoring

`cpcsacnrysa1prodprna02.blob.core.windows.net`
 	
`cpcsacnrysa1prodprap01.blob.core.windows.net`
 	
`cpcsacnrysa1prodprau01.blob.core.windows.net`
 	
`cpcsacnrysa1prodpreu01.blob.core.windows.net`
 	
`cpcsacnrysa1prodpreu02.blob.core.windows.net`
 	
`cpcsacnrysa1prodprna01.blob.core.windows.net`
		Cloud PC scaling units

Let's now jump into the most common errors that occur on Windows 365—provisioning the processes of cloud PCs.

Windows 365 provisioning errors

In the following section, you will learn more about all the different errors within the Windows 365 provisioning process as part of our Watchdog network configuration service.

Domain join failed

Windows 365 attempts to join the cloud PC to your on-premises AD domain. This step failure can be caused by many factors that are under the control of your organization, but you can troubleshoot this as follows:

- Please ensure the AD domain, **organizational unit** (**OU**), and credentials in the associated **on-premises network connection** (**OPNC**) are correct.

- Please ensure the domain-join user has sufficient permissions to perform the domain join.

- Please ensure the VNet and subnet can reach a domain controller correctly.

`JsonADDomainExtension` is the Azure function used to perform this domain join. Please ensure everything required for this to be successful is in place.

Resolution: Attach an Azure **virtual machine** (**VM**) to the configured VNet and perform a domain join using the credentials provided.

Hybrid Azure AD Join failed

Windows 365 does not perform any **Hybrid Azure AD Join** (**HAADJ**) functions on behalf of the customer. HAADJ must be configured and healthy as a prerequisite for a cloud PC.

If provisioning fails due to HAADJ, it's likely due to an insufficient sync period configured in your AD Connect synchronization service. Please ensure Microsoft Azure AD Connect is configured to sync the AD computer objects every 30 minutes and no less than every 60 minutes. This step will time out if the Azure AD object does not appear within 90 minutes.

Another factor to consider is your on-premises AD replication time. Ensure the domain controller being used for Windows 365 will be replicated fast enough to make it into Azure AD within this timeout window.

Resolution: Check to see that the AD object appears in the correct OU and that it's successfully synced to Azure AD before provisioning times out.

The SCP record is missing

You might need to modify your hybrid Azure AD configuration to successfully provision cloud PCs. Azure AD Connect synchronizes computer objects, and the computer knows which Azure AD domain to register with by looking for a **service connection point (SCP)** object in AD. You can find these in the **ADSI Edit** tool, under **CN=Configuration | CN=Services | CN=Device Registration Configuration**. You will see a **globally unique identifier (GUID)** and, in that record, a multi-string value with your Azure AD tenant name and GUID, as illustrated in the following screenshot:

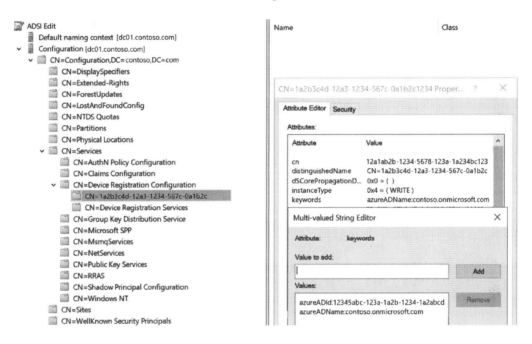

Figure 17.5 – ADSI Edit

If they're missing, you can create them with Azure AD Connect during the hybrid configuration process (`https://docs.microsoft.com/azure/active-directory/devices/hybrid-azuread-join-managed-domains`), as illustrated in the following screenshot:

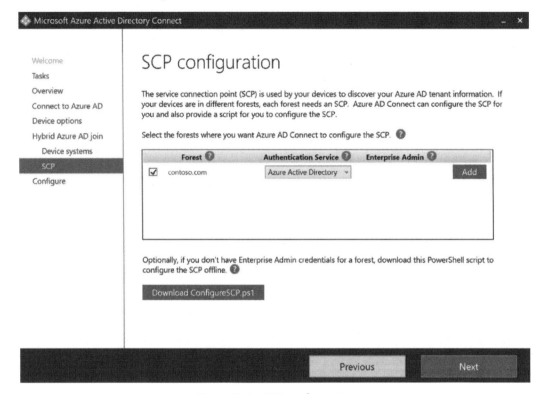

Figure 17.6 – SCP configuration

There may be scenarios where you only want specific computers from an individual OU to perform a HAADJ. To do this, skip the SCP record creation, and instead create a custom **Group Policy Object** (**GPO**) and link it to the OU your cloud PC is in (`https://docs.microsoft.com/azure/active-directory-domain-services/manage-group-policy#create-a-custom-group-policy-object`). In the GPO, you need to create two registry keys with the value names TenantId and TenantName, as shown in the following example:

Figure 17.7 – GPO Policy Management Editor

The OU that you added your cloud PCs to isn't in the scope of your Azure AD Connect synchronization.

If you created a new OU, then it's likely not included, and you'll need to go back into Azure AD Connect and include it in the synchronization rules, as illustrated in the following screenshot:

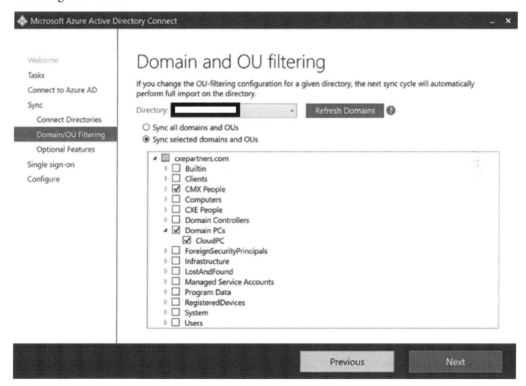

Figure 17.8 – Azure AD Connect domain filtering

Azure AD synchronization and replication cause delays

The cloud PC provisioning process times out after 90 minutes and your environment might be configured to introduce unwanted delays. Let's discuss two scenarios where this occurs: synchronization and replication.

Azure AD synchronization interval

The default Azure AD Connect sync interval is every 30 minutes. The time it takes to complete the synchronization process depends on the number of objects Azure AD Connect is processing.

To prevent your cloud PCs from timing out, you need to make sure that the sync interval and the sync time is less than 90 minutes. First, confirm that your Azure AD Connect sync service is running and that its interval hasn't been extended, for example, to every 2 hours. For instructions, see Azure AD Connect sync: `https://docs.microsoft.com/azure/active-directory/hybrid/how-to-connect-sync-feature-scheduler`. Next, if you are synchronizing a lot of objects, review this document to learn how to optimize your environment: `https://docs.microsoft.com/azure/active-directory/hybrid/plan-connect-performance-factors`.

AD DS inter-site replication

Consider this AD DS topology. We have a domain controller at one site running Azure AD Connect, and a domain controller at a different site that the cloud PC provisioning service uses to create computer objects, as illustrated in the following screenshot:

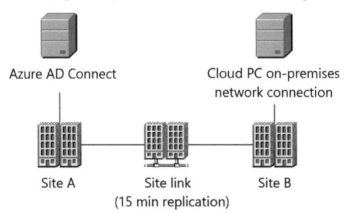

Figure 17.9 – Azure AD Connect topology

We previously explained that the Azure AD Connect sync interval and synchronization time need to complete before cloud PC provisioning times out (90 minutes). This scenario adds another time to consider: the inter-site replication time for the domain. The default for this is 15 minutes, which, if added to the total possible time for computer objects to appear in AD DS and then in Azure AD, creates a new total time of 1 hour, as illustrated in the following diagram:

Figure 17.10 – Azure AD sync cycle

This is the theoretical maximum time and is not applicable to every organization; however, we have seen examples of long inter-site replication times causing timeout issues. The takeaway is that if you have long-running sync times due to size and complexity, try to minimize any other possible delays. With modern connectivity, there isn't often a reason to limit inter-site sync intervals, so you might want to consider setting replication to the default 15 minutes.

Thanks and credits go to Steven DeQuincey, Field PM of Microsoft 365 for Partners, for contributing to this section.

Intune enrollment failed

Windows 365 performs a device-based **Mobile Device Management** (**MDM**) enrollment into Intune. This should be very reliable.

If Intune enrollment is failing, please ensure all of the required Intune endpoints are available on the VNet of your cloud PCs. Also ensure there are no MDM enrollment restrictions on the tenant, and that the Intune tenant is active and healthy.

Resolution: Attempt an Intune enrollment using a test device or VM.

Not enough IP addresses available

When providing a subnet to the OPNC, ensure there are more than sufficient IP addresses.

Every cloud PC provisioning process uses one of the IP addresses provided in the range.

If provisioning fails, it will be retried a total of three times. Each time, a new **virtual network interface card** (**vNIC**) and IP address will be allocated. These IP addresses will be released in a matter of hours, but this can cause issues if the address space is too narrow.

Resolution: Check the VNet for available IP addresses and ensure there are more than enough IPs available for the retry process to succeed.

Provisioning policy not found

While provisioning was in progress, someone deleted the provisioning policy.

Resolution: Ensure the provisioning policy is available and assigned to the correct user group.

User not found

While provisioning was in progress, someone deleted the associated user.

Resolution: Ensure the assigned user account is valid.

License not found

While provisioning was in progress, someone removed the user's Windows 365 license.

Resolution: Ensure the user has a valid Windows 365 license assigned to their account.

Request disallowed by policy

Windows 365 uses the customer-provided VNet to perform vNIC ingestion from the cloud PC VM into the customer's VNet. An enterprise will sometimes implement an Azure policy to restrict certain Azure objects from being created.

Resolution: View **Policy** in the Azure portal and look for any policy events that would stop the Windows 365 service from provisioning the cloud PC.

OPNC isn't healthy

Cloud PC provisioning will be blocked if the associated OPNC is not healthy.

The OPNC will refresh every 6 hours. If the OPNC refresh fails while provisioning is ongoing, it will fail the complete provisioning process.

Resolution: Ensure the OPNC is healthy and retry the provisioning.

Web Proxy Auto-Discovery (WPAD) problems

The cloud PC service uses the AVD agent to connect to the broker services of the virtualization control plane. When you use a proxy via WPAD via DNS, you could run into problems such as the machine account not being allowed to connect to the service URLs of both AVD and MEM.

Resolution: Allow the machine account or IP addresses in your network to connect over the internet to the list of service URLs. As an alternative, you could remove the proxy settings so that they are no longer applied to cloud PCs and use a direct route to the internet (preferred).

Incorrect username and password or permissions to join domain

Windows 365 Enterprise requires a domain environment to join cloud PCs to your AD domain.

Resolution: The AD service account created for this and configured in the OPNC needs to have the following permissions to do this:

1. **Create computer objects in the OU** (join the computer to the domain).
2. **Delete computer objects in the OU** (needed to deprovision the cloud PC to remove the computer account from AD).
3. Permissions to enumerate user objects so that they can be found, to be added to the local `Remote Desktop Users` group when provisioning.

The other problem could be that you just entered in the wrong credentials!

Unable to reach the DSC files

Being unable to reach the **Desired State Configuration** (DSC) files during provisioning causes a failure, showing the following message:

Figure 17.11 – Failure message

Resolution: Ensure the firewall access is correctly configured to allow DSC endpoints across the following:

- `prod.warmpath.msftcloudes.com`

- `cpcsacnrysa1prodprna01.blob.core.windows.net` (North America)

- `cpcsacnrysa1prodprna02.blob.core.windows.net` (North America)

- `cpcsacnrysa1prodprap01.blob.core.windows.net` (Asia Pacific)

- `cpcsacnrysa1prodprau01.blob.core.windows.net` (Australia)

- `cpcsacnrysa1prodpreu01.blob.core.windows.net` (EU)

- `cpcsacnrysa1prodpreu02.blob.core.windows.net` (EU)

- `mrsglobalsteus2prod.blob.core.windows.net`

- `catalogartifact.azureedge.net`

- `kms.core.windows.net`

To check if this is a network connection URL access issue, you can try the following actions:

1. Perform a `nslookup` operation on the Azure container for your region to check you can resolve with your organization's DNS servers, as illustrated in the following screenshot:

```
C:\WINDOWS\system32>nslookup cpcsacnrysa1prodpreu01.blob.core.windows.net
Server:  UnKnown
Address:  172.16.0.1

Non-authoritative answer:
Name:    blob.dub07prdstr05a.store.core.windows.net
Address:  52.239.138.100
Aliases:  cpcsacnrysa1prodpreu01.blob.core.windows.net
```

Figure 17.12 – nslookup on Azure container

2. If DNS resolution is successful, then use `PsPing` to check whether you can establish a connection (you cannot establish this via a browser as you will be unable to authenticate), as illustrated in the following screenshot:

```
C:\tools>psping -n 4 20.150.42.4:443

PsPing v2.10 - PsPing - ping, latency, bandwidth measurement utility
Copyright (C) 2012-2016 Mark Russinovich
Sysinternals - www.sysinternals.com

TCP connect to 20.150.42.4:443:
5 iterations (warmup 1) ping test:
Connecting to 20.150.42.4:443 (warmup): from 172.16.0.9:50429: 28.31ms
Connecting to 20.150.42.4:443: from 172.16.0.9:50430: 26.59ms
Connecting to 20.150.42.4:443: from 172.16.0.9:50431: 30.28ms
Connecting to 20.150.42.4:443: from 172.16.0.9:50432: 26.15ms
Connecting to 20.150.42.4:443: from 172.16.0.9:50433: 29.94ms

TCP connect statistics for 20.150.42.4:443:
  Sent = 4, Received = 4, Lost = 0 (0% loss),
  Minimum = 26.15ms, Maximum = 30.28ms, Average = 28.24ms
```

Figure 17.13 – PsPing to check connection

Cloud PC – device-based filtering

You could run into scenarios where you already have a configured MEM tenant to manage your physical endpoints. Existing policies, application delivery rules, or other configuration items could be filtered to **All Devices** in the Windows 365 blade of the MEM admin center console. This could cause conflict as there might be cases where the setting should only apply to your physical environment.

All cloud PC devices have a specific model name (contains `Cloud PC`) and an enrollment profile name (equals the cloud PC provisioning profile) that can be used to filter them from an **All Devices** assignment.

Users are getting the error "Your access to this Cloud PC ends in 5 days. Back up your files immediately"

When you see the preceding error in the Windows 365 web portal, it means that the IT administrator removed the Windows 365 license from your user account. The cloud PC isn't deleted directly after that but moves into a grace period of 7 days.

To solve this problem, the IT administrator has to re-assign the license to avoid potential data loss for the end user, as illustrated in the following screenshot:

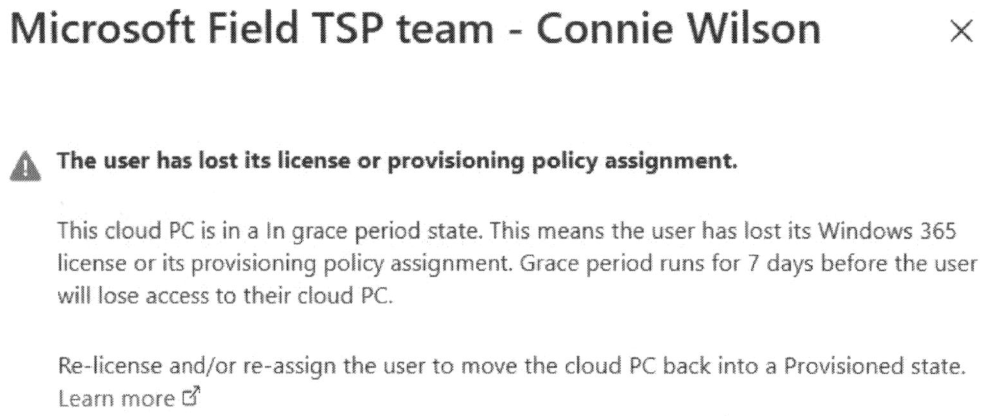

Microsoft Field TSP team - Connie Wilson   ✕

 The user has lost its license or provisioning policy assignment.

This cloud PC is in a In grace period state. This means the user has lost its Windows 365 license or its provisioning policy assignment. Grace period runs for 7 days before the user will lose access to their cloud PC.

Re-license and/or re-assign the user to move the cloud PC back into a Provisioned state. Learn more ⍐

Figure 17.14 – Lost license error

You can find a screenshot of how this error is presented to the end user here:

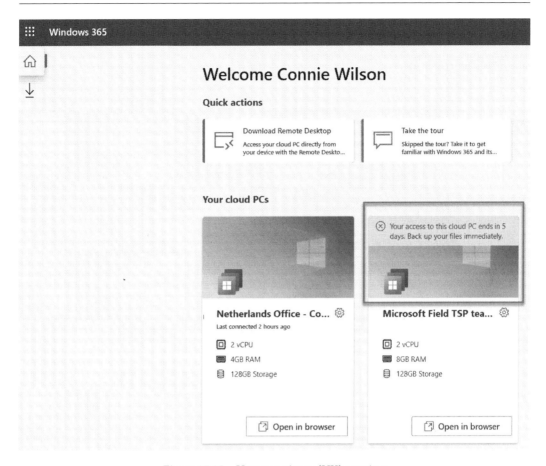

Figure 17.15 – User experience (UX) monitor

When you are experiencing user performance issues within your cloud PC session, you could use the **Experience monitor** tool within the Remote Desktop client. The tool shows valuable information about the connection round-trip time, latency, protocol usage, and bandwidth usage.

You can find the tool via the Remote Desktop client. While you have a session active in the top bar, right-click on the bar and choose **Experience monitor**, as illustrated in the following screenshot:

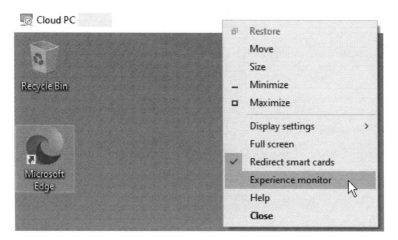

Figure 17.16 – Experience monitor

Click on **See details**, as illustrated in the following screenshot:

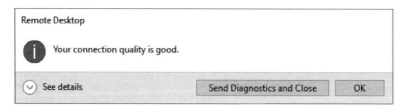

Figure 17.17 – See details

The following screen shows all the relevant information about the active connection. It also shows the gateway being used for the service:

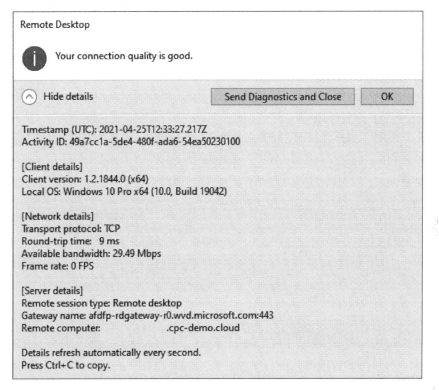

Figure 17.18 – Diagnostics

You can send diagnostics to Microsoft directly from here too, to attach to your support ticket for troubleshooting purposes.

Make sure to align with the requirements for the network bandwidth for your connection, as listed in the Remote Desktop connection requirements table in *Chapter 4, Deploying Windows 365*.

You've now learned a bunch about the most common errors as well as the tools you can use to analyze and track the UX. Most likely, Endpoint Analytics will help and proactively warn you of errors in your environment; however, it's always good to know what you can do to solve problems yourself!

Summary

In this chapter, you've learned about most of the deployment errors that can occur during the enrollment of Windows 365/cloud PCs.

The knowledge you have after reading this chapter will help you resolve any errors while kicking the tires of your new service! In the next chapter, you will find numerous experts from the community, from whom you can gain more knowledge about the subject.

Questions

1. How does it feel to be a Windows 365/cloud PC troubleshooting rockstar?

    A. Feels amazing.

    B. **The day I read this book changed my life!**

    C. Good!

    D. Hold on, let me grab a beer first.

Further reading

If you want to learn more about troubleshooting Windows 365 after reading this chapter, please go to the Microsoft Docs public troubleshooting page to find more information, including the following links:

- Windows 365 troubleshooting documentation: `https://docs.microsoft.com/en-us/windows-365/troubleshooting`

- Windows 365 Tech Community for help from others: `https://techcommunity.microsoft.com/t5/windows-365/bd-p/Windows365Discussions`

18
Community Help

Join the new W365 Community!

Join the new Windows 365 Tech Community and the new MVP-driven W365 Community on Twitter at @W365Community and gather with others to learn more about Windows 365 and Microsoft Endpoint Manager!

Bookmark www.w365community.com in your list of websites!

Microsoft Tech Community and MS Learn

Join our Microsoft Tech Community platform as well today. It includes information about new releases as well as technical information about fixing issues and implementing new features:

Tech Community	Website
Windows 365 Tech Community	`aka.ms/W365TC`
W365 Twitter Community	`@W365community`
Intune Customer Success	`techcommunity.microsoft.com/t5/intune-customer-success/bg-p/IntuneCustomerSuccess`
Microsoft Endpoint Manager Blog	`https://techcommunity.microsoft.com/t5/microsoft-endpoint-manager-blog/bg-p/MicrosoftEndpointManagerBlog`
Microsoft Intune	`https://techcommunity.microsoft.com/t5/microsoft-intune/bd-p/Microsoft-Intune`
Defender for Endpoint	`techcommunity.microsoft.com/t5/microsoft-defender-for-endpoint/bg-p/MicrosoftDefenderATPBlog`
Windows	`community.windows.com`
Windows 365	`https://techcommunity.microsoft.com/t5/windows-365/bd-p/Windows365Discussions`
Windows IT Pro	`techcommunity.microsoft.com/t5/windows-it-pro-blog/bg-p/Windows10Blog`
Microsoft Learn	`learn.microsoft.com`

Other community blogs, Microsoft MVPs, and more...

You can find all kinds of people who contribute to the Microsoft Endpoint Manager, Windows 365, and Azure Virtual Desktop-Enterprise Mobility communities. Some are Microsoft MVPs, while others are working/have worked for Microsoft – and all are great community ambassadors! In this way, you'll have everything in one place, just in case.

> **CAUTION!**
>
> If you go through the following list, your mind will be blown by all the top-notch and free information available. You've been warned!

Name	Website or social channel
Intune Graph Samples	`github.com/microsoftgraph/powershell-intune-samples`
Scott Duffey	`www.learningmem.com`
MSEndpointMgr	`www.msendpointmgr.com`
Ben Whitmore	`www.byteben.com`
Michael Niehaus	`www.oofhours.com`
Aaron Parker	`www.stealthpuppy.com`
Adam Gross	`intune.training`
Mayunk Jain	`www.twitter.com/mayunkj`
Steven Hosking/Ben Reader	`intune.training`
Niall Brady	`www.windows-noob.com`
Sandy Zeng	`www.sandyzeng.com`
Donna Ryan	`www.TheNotoriousDRR.com`
Gerry Hampson	`www.gerryhampsoncm.blogspot.ie`
Panu Saukko	`www.twitter.com/panusaukko`
Peter van der Woude	`www.petervanderwoude.nl`
Robin Hobo	`www.robinhobo.com`
Ronny de Jong	`ronnydejong.com/`
Thijs Lecomte	`www.365bythijs.be`
Thomas Kurth	`www.wpninjas.ch`
Tim de Keukelaere	`dekeukelaere.com/`
Tim Hermie	`www.cloud-boy.be`
Kim Oppalfens/Tom Degreef	`www.oscc.be`
Simon Binder	`www.kneedeepintech.com`
Bryan Dam	`www.damgoodadmin.com`
Ed Baker	`www.ed-baker.com`

Mirko Colemberg	`blog.colemberg.ch`
Peter Daalmans	`www.peterdaalmans.com`
Peter Klapwijk	`www.inthecloud247.com`
Anoop Chandran	`www.howtomanagedevices.com`
Ronni Pedersen	`www.ronnipedersen.com`
Oliver Kieselbach	`www.oliverkieselbach.com`
Martin Bengtson	`www.imab.dk`
James Kindon	`www.jkindon.com`
Jörgen Nilsson	`https://ccmexec.com/`
Freek Berson	`www.themicrosoftplatform.net`
Tim Mangan	`www.tmurgent.com/TmBlog`
Pieter Wigleven	`aka.ms/pieter/windows`
Stefan Georgiev	`www.twitter.com/stg3orgi`
Dean Cefola	`www.youtube.com/AzureAcademy`
Neil McLoughlin	`www.virtualmanc.co.uk`
Bas van Kaam	`www.basvankaam.com`
Christiaan Brinkhoff	`www.christiaanbrinkhoff.com`
Per Larsen	`www.osddeployment.dk`
Marcel Meurer	`blog.itprocloud.de`

Summary

This was the final chapter of the book, where we saw all the mind-blowing social media channels where you can find some great contributors to the tech community. We hope all the knowledge contained in this book was useful for you and thank you for completing this journey with us.

Packt.com

Subscribe to our online digital library for full access to over 7,000 books and videos, as well as industry leading tools to help you plan your personal development and advance your career. For more information, please visit our website.

Why subscribe?

- Spend less time learning and more time coding with practical eBooks and Videos from over 4,000 industry professionals

- Improve your learning with Skill Plans built especially for you

- Get a free eBook or video every month

- Fully searchable for easy access to vital information

- Copy and paste, print, and bookmark content

Did you know that Packt offers eBook versions of every book published, with PDF and ePub files available? You can upgrade to the eBook version at packt.com and as a print book customer, you are entitled to a discount on the eBook copy. Get in touch with us at customercare@packtpub.com for more details.

At www.packt.com, you can also read a collection of free technical articles, sign up for a range of free newsletters, and receive exclusive discounts and offers on Packt books and eBooks.

Other Books You May Enjoy

If you enjoyed this book, you may be interested in these other books by Packt:

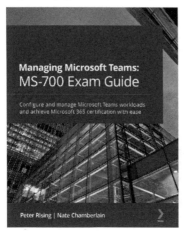

Managing Microsoft Teams: MS-700 Exam Guide

Peter Rising, Nate Chamberlain

ISBN: 9781801071000

- Explore Security Compliance configuration options for Teams features
- Manage meetings, calls, and chat features within Microsoft Teams
- Find out how to manage phone numbers, systems, and settings in Teams
- Manage individual team settings, membership, and guest access
- Create policies for Microsoft Teams apps and features
- Deploy access reviews and dynamic team membership

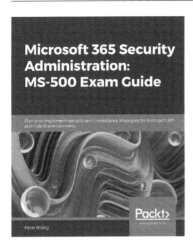

Microsoft 365 Security Administration: MS-500 Exam Guide

Peter Rising

ISBN: 9781838983123

- Get up to speed with implementing and managing identity and access

- Understand how to employ and manage threat protection

- Get to grips with managing governance and compliance features in Microsoft 365

- Explore best practices for effective configuration and deployment

- Implement and manage information protection

- Prepare to pass the Microsoft exam and achieve certification with the help of self-assessment questions and a mock exam

Packt is searching for authors like you

If you're interested in becoming an author for Packt, please visit `authors.packtpub.com` and apply today. We have worked with thousands of developers and tech professionals, just like you, to help them share their insight with the global tech community. You can make a general application, apply for a specific hot topic that we are recruiting an author for, or submit your own idea.

Share Your Thoughts

Now you've finished *Mastering Microsoft Endpoint Manager*, we'd love to hear your thoughts! Scan the QR code below to go straight to the Amazon review page for this book and share your feedback or leave a review on the site that you purchased it from.

`https://packt.link/r/1801078998`

Your review is important to us and the tech community and will help us make sure we're delivering excellent quality content.

Index

Y

Z